Great Deba

Gender and Law

Palgrave Great Debates in Law

Series Editor
Jonathan Herring, Professor of Law, University of Oxford

Company Law
Lorraine Talbot

Contract Law
Jonathan Morgan

Criminal Law
Jonathan Herring

Employment Law
Simon Honeyball

Equity and Trusts
Alastair Hudson

Family Law
Jonathan Herring, Rebecca Probert & Stephen Gilmore

Gender and Law
Rosemary Auchmuty (ed.)

Jurisprudence
Nicholas J McBride & Sandy Steel

Medical Law and Ethics
Imogen Goold & Jonathan Herring

Land Law
David Cowan, Lorna Fox O'Mahony & Neil Cobb

The European Convention on Human Rights
Fiona de Londras & Kanstantsin Dzehtsiarou

Palgrave Great Debates in Law

Great Debates in Gender and Law

Rosemary Auchmuty (Ed)
Professor of Law
School of Law, University of Reading

 macmillan education  palgrave

First published 2018 by
PALGRAVE

Palgrave in the UK is an imprint of Macmillan Publishers Limited, registered in England, company number 785998, of 4 Crinan Street, London N1 9XW.

Palgrave® and Macmillan® are registered trademarks in the United States, the United Kingdom, Europe and other countries.

ISBN 978–1–137–61099–7

A catalogue record for this book is available from the British Library.

A catalog record for this book is available from the Library of Congress.

CONTENTS

Introduction (Rosemary Auchmuty)   xi

1   Contract Law (Máiréad Enright)   1
    Debate 1: Is 'freedom of contract' really freedom?   1
    Debate 2: Can relational contract theory save freedom of contract? 8
    Conclusion   12
    Further Reading   12

2   Tort Law (Kirsty Horsey and Erika Rackley)   13
    *Debate 1: Should tort law provide a bespoke remedy for
    victims of image-based sexual abuse?*   14
    The Relationship Between Tort and Criminal Law   15
    Current Tort Law Remedies for Image-Based Sexual Abuse   16
        Privacy   16
        The Protection from Harassment Act 1997   17
    A Bespoke Tort of Image-Based Sexual Abuse   18
    *Debate 2: Should victim-survivors of domestic abuse use tort law to
    hold police to account where they have failed to prevent third parties
    from committing abuse?*   19
    Domestic Abuse, Sexual Violence and Gender   20
    The Role of Negligence   21
    Countering the Policy Arguments   23
    Conclusion   24
    Further Reading   24

3   Public Law (Harriet Samuels)   25
    Debate 1: Is Parliament truly representative, and should it be?   25
    Debate 2: Does public interest litigation work for women?   31
    Conclusion   35
    Further Reading   35

4   Criminal Law (Caroline Derry)   37
    Debate 1: Is consent in sexual offences adequately defined?   37
    Is the Definition Adequate?   38
    Advantages of the Definition   38
    Criticisms of the Definition   40
    *Debate 2: Should there be a specific criminal offence of
    forced marriage?*   42
    The Law   43
    Why the Offence was Created and Welcomed   44
    Why the Offence was Opposed   45
    Conclusion   47
    Further Reading   48

5   Land Law (Ambreena Manji)   49
    *Debate 1: In co-ownership cases, why have the courts had to look
    for common intention?*   51
    *Debate 2: Whose interests are given priority in undue
    influence cases?*   55
    Conclusion   56
    Further Reading   57

6   Equity and Trusts (Nick Piška)   59
    Debate 1: Is equity a gendered jurisprudence?   60
    The Figuration of Equity as Female   60
    Equity and the Ethic of Care   62
    *Debate 2: Do equitable doctrines and remedies contribute to
    equality or entrench gendered norms?*   64
    Presumption of Advancement   64
    Rescission   67
    Conclusion   70
    Further Reading   70

7   EU Law (Alina Tryfonidou)   71
    Debate 1: Should discrimination against pregnant women be
    considered direct discrimination on the ground of sex?   72
    Arguments Against Considering Pregnancy Discrimination as
    Direct Discrimination on the Ground of Sex   73
    Arguments in Favour of Considering Pregnancy Discrimination
    as Direct Discrimination on the Ground of Sex   75
    Debate 2: Is discrimination on the ground of sexual
    orientation also discrimination on the ground of sex?   76
    Arguments Against Considering Discrimination on the Ground
    of Sexual Orientation as Discrimination on the Ground of Sex   78
    Arguments in Favour of Considering Discrimination on the Ground
    of Sexual Orientation as Discrimination on the Ground of Sex   79
    Conclusion   81
    Further Reading   81

8   International Law and Human Rights (Nora Honkala)   83
    Debate 1: Is international society gendered?   84
    Gender and the Institutional Character of International Society 84
    Feminist Engagements with the Normative Character of
    International Law   87
    Debate 2: Can international human rights tackle
    gender inequality?   89
    Challenges to Rights   89
    Possibilities of Rights   92
    Conclusion   94
    Further Reading   94

9   Family Law (Alison Diduck and Felicity Kaganas)   95
    Debate 1: Should formal equality govern money and asset division
    on divorce?   96
    Debate 2: Should childcare be shared equally after separation
    or divorce?   102
    Welfare   103
    The Law   104
    Recent Changes   107
    Conclusion   108
    Further Reading   108

10 Employment/Labour Law (Rachel Horton)   109

Debate 1: Are 'gender-neutral' or 'gender-specific' workplace rights, or some combination of the two, the best approach to achieving gender equality in relation to the challenges presented by the competing demands of paid work and unpaid care?   **110**

Gender-Specific Rights   111

Gender-Neutral Rights   111

Issues   112

Debate 2: Should positive action be permitted or required in the workplace and, if so, to what extent?   **115**

Law and Policy   116

Issues   117

Conclusion   119

Further Reading   120

11 Health Law, Medicine and Ethics (Marie Fox and Jaime Lindsey) 121

Debate 1: Are women more likely to have their healthcare decisions overruled?   **121**

The Importance of Consent   122

Capacity to Consent   123

Informed Consent   125

Debate 2: Should abortion be decriminalised?   **126**

The Legal Framework   127

The Case for Decriminalisation   128

The Case of Northern Ireland   130

Conclusion   132

Further Reading   132

12 Company Law and Corporate Governance (Sally Wheeler)   133

Debate 1: Is shareholder value a form of gendered governance?   **135**

The Role of Gender in Shareholder Value   138

Debate 2: Boardroom participation – good for business, bad for equality?   **143**

The Diversity Argument for Female Participation   145

Social Justice Arguments for Female Participation   146

Conclusion   147

Further Reading   148

13 Intellectual Property Law (Catherine Easton)   149
      Debate 1: Do we need more flexible patents?   150
      Debate 2: Does copyright law protect women's creativity equally? 155
      Conclusion   159
      Further Reading   160

14 Jurisprudence/Legal Theory (Joanne Conaghan)   161
      Debate 1: Is (the concept of) law gendered?   162
      Debate 2: Is there (always) a right answer to legal disputes?   168
      Further Reading   172

15 Legal History (Rosemary Auchmuty)   173
      Debate 1: Are women persons?   173
      Chorlton v Lings (1868)   174
      Viscountess Rhondda's Claim (1923)   176
      Debate 2: What is legal history?   178
      Conclusion   182
      Further Reading   183

16 Law and Literature/Literary Jurisprudence
      (Melanie L. Williams)   185
      Debate 1: How is sexual violence failed by culture and law?   187
      Rape, Fact and Fiction   191
      Debate 2: Who are law's persons?   193
      Feminist Science Fiction and the Flight from Hegemony   194
      Conclusion   196
      Further Reading   197

17 Sexuality (Rosemary Auchmuty)   199
      Debate 1: Is same-sex marriage a good thing?   200
      Arguments in Favour of Same-Sex Marriage   201
      Arguments Against Same-Sex Marriage   203
      Can Marriage be Transformed?   205
      Debate 2: Can we speak of LGBT rights and an LGBT community?   206

In Support of 'LGBT' 207
Against 'LGBT' 207
Practical Objections to 'LGBT' 209
Conclusion 210
Further Reading 210

18 Legal Professions (Lisa Webley) 211
Debate 1: How effective are the strategies adopted to counter gender inequality in the professions? 212
First-Wave Initiatives 213
Second-Wave Initiatives 214
Third-Wave Initiatives 215
Discussion 216
Debate 2: Does having more women lawyers make a difference? 217
Three Different Cases for Why Women Lawyers Make a Difference 218
Discussion 220
Conclusion 221
Further Reading 221

Index 223

INTRODUCTION

Rosemary Auchmuty

Great Debates in Gender and Law is a book with several intended audiences. First, it is aimed at students and lecturers on undergraduate and postgraduate gender and law modules or modules with similar titles. These are increasingly popular options on LLB and LLM programmes in the UK, and this book offers a survey of a range of fields familiar to law students because they are presented from the point of view of the subject area (e.g. criminal law) rather than the topic (e.g. prostitution).

Second, the book is intended for *all* LLB and LLM students studying English law, who may use it to accompany their studies from their first to their final year, and as a resource for their teachers. Thus, while studying contract or public law in their first year, students can turn to this book for gender debates that may be given little attention in the mainstream syllabus, yet are important to it. The book is premised on the belief that, for too long now, law teaching has proceeded on the basis that there *are* no gender perspectives in most of the curriculum – too often, if you want to 'do gender', you will be advised to take family law as an option – and teachers who would like to raise gendered concerns are not encouraged by most available textbooks.[1] The authors of *Great Debates in Gender and Law* would like *all* law students to emerge from university recognising the importance of gender in everything they study, seeing it not as an optional add-on for a few people who are interested 'in that kind of thing' but integral to law-making and the legal process, as well as their own lives.

Third, and more ambitiously, *Great Debates in Gender and Law* aims to provide a resource for *all* people who are interested in this subject, from prospective law students and students in other disciplines to legal scholars from outside England and Wales, as well as scholars from other disciplines and independent researchers of all kinds.

---

[1] Though there are important exceptions to this, for example Celia Wells and Oliver Quick, *Lacey, Wells and Quick Reconstructing Criminal Law* (Cambridge University Press), and Kirsty Horsey and Erika Rackley, *Tort Law* (Oxford University Press).

STRUCTURE

The book starts with chapters on all seven of the current core 'foundation' subjects of the LLB (contract, tort, public law, criminal law, land law, equity and trusts, and EU law). Lecturers may set tutorial or coursework questions on these less obvious areas to encourage students' research skills, or students may be able to choose their own area to pursue: these chapters will give guidance and inspiration. The chapters on the foundation subjects are followed by chapters on a range of options commonly studied on LLB and LLM programmes. Again, these may be used by students and lecturers to enhance the syllabus on those modules and to inspire new areas of enquiry, perhaps for a longer project or dissertation. Finally, a chapter on sexuality and one on the legal profession may not relate to discrete law options but are integral to a gender and law module and to legal studies generally, and may be useful for other modules such as legal method/systems.

Because of this focus – that is, identifying gender issues in traditional legal subject areas rather than analysing gender as a category in legal scholarship – you will not find a separate chapter on 'feminist theories of law', normally an essential part of a gender and law course. While the chapter on jurisprudence/legal theory offers a couple of debates in the area, intended for students on jurisprudence or legal theory modules where gender is regrettably often absent, theory underpins every chapter in this book. Many chapters draw attention to the limitations of currently fashionable liberal theories of equality, rights, autonomy and choice. Elsewhere, with 20 different authors, each with her or his own preferred perspectives, the reader will meet a range of treatments and approaches. No attempt has been made to present a consistent feminist voice – this is a book about debates, after all – because each author is writing from within the conventions of her or his substantive law subject as well as her or his own perspective on gender. No attempt, moreover, has been made to be impartial in the presentation of debates. Sometimes there may be merits on both sides, or differences of opinion among feminists, but sometimes there is really no defence to an argument, say, that gender is irrelevant to a particular subject area. The book focuses on England and Wales but readers should note that some of the law discussed applies across the whole UK and some does not, since different provisions, and often different debates, exist in Northern Ireland and/or Scotland.

THE AUTHORS

Unlike the other volumes in the *Great Debates* series, no fewer than 20 people have participated in the creation of this book. This kind of collaboration is characteristic of feminist practice, and proceeds from the understanding that shared knowledge and critique produce the best form of scholarship. We are all teachers of our substantive legal areas as well as experienced researchers in gender issues. These days it is hardly worth listing details of our academic posts and achievements; they will be out of date by the time you read this. Better just to Google our names, a process that will also lead you to more of our research on gender and law to follow up if you are interested.

WHAT DO WE MEAN BY 'GENDER'?

The use of 'gender' in the sense employed in this book is relatively recent. People used to speak of 'sex' (as in the Sex Discrimination Act 1975) to refer to the categories of men and women, but an important second-wave feminist insight was that, while biology may be more or less immutable,[2] the ways that men and women are constructed are not.[3] From this came a distinction between biological *sex* and social *gender*. One might be born into one sex, but one's gender was wholly a product of one's place and time; people were 'socialised' into gender roles, which were mapped on to sexed bodies so that male and masculine, and female and feminine, came to seem inseparable. Though the prescribed roles differed from place to place and time to time, they almost always involved the subordination of women. It became clear that, if the sexes were ever to attain equality, then it was gender that we must tackle.

But gender is also a *relationship*, and it is in this sense that the word is used in this book. It is the relationship between men and women which, throughout Western history, has been one not simply of inequality but of power – with men in the dominant position and women subordinate.[4]

Gender as a category of study emerged as a result of feminist struggles against this subordination. Without the women's movements, which challenged men's material and ideological power, there would have been no interest in gender, for one of the most effective ways men have maintained control over women across the centuries has been by treating the masculine perspective as universal and by overlooking women's situation. Thus, English statutes used the pronoun 'he' to stand for both sexes and any differential impact of laws or the legal processes on men and women was ignored. That is why you so rarely come across any reference to gender issues in your law textbooks (with the exception of those rare examples written by feminists), even though half of law's subjects are women and are so often treated differently and affected differently by supposedly gender-neutral laws. Only when law is forced to confront gender difference (as, for example, in dealing with rape or motherhood), do we see legal intervention, and then it is often intrusive and prescriptive of 'appropriate' forms of behaviour in ways that are also problematic for women.[5]

---

[2] I say 'may be' because even this is disputed; see Chapter 17, 'Sexuality', in this book.

[3] Ann Oakley, *Subject Women* (Martin Robertson, 1981).

[4] John Stuart Mill, *The Subjection of Women* (Longmans, 1869).

[5] Rosemary Hunter, 'The gendered "socio" of socio-legal studies' in Dermot Feenan (ed.), *Exploring the 'Socio' of Socio-Legal Studies* (Palgrave, 2013).

We see this when we compare, for example, the chapters 'Criminal Law' and 'Health Law, Medicine and Ethics', where women's differential treatment in law is very evident, with those on legal history and international law and human rights, where gender has largely been ignored. In areas like the former, there are well-developed debates about the impact of gender on many different issues (consent, for example, is a recurrent theme in 'Criminal Law', 'Tort Law' and 'Health Law, Medicine and Ethics'). In areas like the latter, the debate may well be about whether gender has any relevance to the subject at all. We need to settle that first before we can proceed to further debates.

Feminists long ago named the 'public/private' divide as being particularly significant in determining how men and women are treated in law, with men being identified with the public sphere and women with the private. Law's traditional reluctance to intervene in the private sphere allows some of the worst gendered oppression to go unchecked and seriously limits women's freedom, autonomy and choice. The very principles of contract and company law/corporate governance are premised on the public-sphere model associated with men that presupposes unlimited autonomy and choice. In spite of public perceptions, this philosophy has increasingly pervaded family law, too. In land law, the primacy of the market in conveyancing situations is particularly stark, notwithstanding equity's interventions purporting to assist the vulnerable parties to transactions. The chapters 'Land Law' and 'Equity and Trusts' challenge this construction of equity as champion and protector of women. Other themes that cut across several chapters include the role of law in reinforcing gender roles and stereotypes; the role of feminist activism in achieving legal reform; and the limits of legal reform itself.

These common and overlapping themes demonstrate that law in real life is not divided into neat parcels of subject matter. Domestic violence, for example, is a part of family law and criminal law, but also impacts on land law and tort law; while the 'Law and Literature/Literary Jurisprudence' chapter demonstrates that there are still other ways of conceptualising this harm. The currently popular idea of 'diversity' is an issue for public law, company law and corporate governance, employment law, and the legal professions. How legal rules and structures are developed to marginalise women's contribution, and indeed whether women do indeed make a different contribution from men (and, if so, how), are important considerations in 'Intellectual Property Law', 'Company Law and Corporate Governance', 'Legal Professions', and other chapters.

Because the gender bias of law (and all social institutions) was first exposed by feminists, we call scholarship related to gender 'feminist scholarship'. There was a time when this seemed threatening to many scholars because it challenged received knowledge and traditional power structures. Today, when the inequalities in those power structures are well recognised (even by the judiciary), feminist scholarship has become a neutral term referring to a specialist field – the study of gender – not just the study of women, but of the relation of women to men, in which the role of men is at least as important as that of women.

Feminism is also, of course, a political movement, one motivated by the very idea and injustice of gender inequalities. There are many different kinds of feminism, and many different viewpoints, but one goal is shared by all: the elimination of all unnecessary distinctions in society based on gender, and the enlargement of the roles and ways of being available to women and men, so that one day in the future one's gender, and also one's race or sexuality, will become irrelevant.

FURTHER READING

Joanne Conaghan, *Law and Gender* (Oxford University Press, 2013).

Rosemary Hunter, Clare McGlynn and Erika Rackley (eds), *Feminist Judgments: From Theory to Practice* (Hart Publishing, 2010).

Clare McGlynn, *The Woman Lawyer: Making the Difference* (Butterworths, 1998).

Carol Smart, *Feminism and the Power of Law* (Routledge, 1989).

CHAPTER 1

Contract Law

Máiréad Enright

Contracts project our intentions outwards, prolonging our autonomy into an uncertain future.[1] They allow people to create new legal structures; to 'make arrangements for themselves, and so to change their respective rights and duties'.[2] Law promises to support that creative agency; women often distrust that promise. The first debate here introduces critiques of freedom of contract which are concerned with gender and power. The second explores efforts to address those critiques through relational contract theory. For reasons of space, I focus here on the common law rather than statute, and on commercial contracting rather than consumer law.

Debate 1
Is 'freedom of contract' really freedom?

Berlant uses the phrase 'cruel optimism'[3] to describe things we desire and hope for even though they are obstacles to our flourishing. 'Freedom of contract' exemplifies cruel optimism. The cases you read during your studies involve people who bargain for things – dream homes,[4] beautiful objects,[5] financial security,[6] or maybe even chances of fame[7] – that speak to their identity and goals. Marx wrote of contractual exchange that 'what seems to throb there is

---

[1] Marieke De Goede, *Virtue, Fortune, And Faith: A Genealogy of Finance* (University of Minnesota Press, 2005); Hannah Arendt, *The Human Condition: Second Edition* (University of Chicago Press, 2013) p. 238.

[2] Arthur Ripstein, *Force and Freedom* (Harvard University Press, 2010) p. 107.

[3] Lauren Berlant, *Cruel Optimism* (Duke University Press, 2011).

[4] *Farley v Skinner* [2001] UKHL 49; Ronnie Cohen and Shannon O'Byrne, 'Burning down the house: Law, emotion and the subprime mortgage crisis' (2011) *Real Property, Trust and Estate Law Journal* 677.

[5] *Leaf v International Galleries* [1950] 2 KB 86.

[6] *Beswick v Beswick* [1967] UKHL 2.

[7] *Chaplin v Hicks* [1911] 2KB 786.

my own heartbeat'.[8] However, contractual freedom is a thin equality of opportunity, in limited circumstances, to participate in certain capitalist projects. 'Classical'[9] contract law emerged alongside capitalism, as markets became objects of specialist knowledge and regulation. Contract law supposedly mirrors the market, responding to bargains rather than shaping them. 'Freedom of contract' promises that states make no detailed public plan for market transactions. Nineteenth-century laissez-faire economists maintained that, left to their own devices, individuals would voluntarily exchange scarce resources with one another, allowing them to gravitate to their most efficient uses.[10] Law, accordingly, insists that, although the state stands ready to resolve disputes,[11] intervention is exceptional and only takes place at the end of the contract's life. Then law defers to our intentions.[12] Thus, contract is 'private' rather than 'public' law, produced by autonomous individuals rather than by government fiat.

We should be suspicious of easy distinctions between (public) governmental regulation and (private) self-regulation. Law actively constructs opportunities for judicial intervention in contractual disputes: those are neither obvious nor neutral.[13] For example, the promise of judicial deference to parties' intentions is misleading. One of the first lessons you learn is that subjective intentions do not matter to contract doctrine: only the outward 'objective' appearance of agreement counts.[14] As Radin writes, law idealises the bargaining process as an occasion for detailed communication and clear expression of voluntary consent to each contractual term. But law does not actually require any such communication. It is enough for contract terms to bind us that we assent to them, for example by signature.[15] The law on incorporation of terms means that we need not always have specific knowledge of each element of our obligations. Informed consent is not always required: it is enough that we have 'reasonable notice' of the contract's terms (whether or not we fulfil the corresponding duty to read them).[16] Thus, passivity, not shared creativity, is often contract's hallmark.[17]

---

[8] Karl Marx, *Capital, Volume 1* (Penguin, 1990) p. cxxiv.

[9] On the relevance of classical contract law to modern contract, see John Wightman, *Contract: A Critical Commentary* (Pluto Press, 1996) pp. 48–51; Danielle Kie Hart, 'Contract law now – reality meets legal fictions' (2011) 41 *University of Baltimore Law Review* 1. For an alternative history of nineteenth-century contract law, see Anat Rosenberg, 'Classical contract law, past and present', https://works.bepress.com/anat_rosenberg/2/, accessed 9 March 2017.

[10] See further, Alice Belcher, 'A feminist perspective on contract theories from law and economics' (2000) 8 *Feminist Legal Studies* 29.

[11] On the contract enforcement and violence, see Walter Benjamin and Peter Demetz, *Reflections: Essays, Aphorisms, Autobiographical Writing* (Schocken Books, 1986) p. 288.

[12] P.S. Atiyah, *The Rise and Fall of Freedom of Contract* (Clarendon Press, 1985) p. 404.

[13] Martha Minow, *Making All the Difference: Inclusion, Exclusion, and American Law* (Cornell University Press, 1990) p. 280.

[14] *Carlill v Carbolic Smokeball Co.* [1892] 1 QB 256.

[15] *L'Estrange v Graucob* [1934] 2 KB 394.

[16] Margaret Jane Radin, *Boilerplate: The Fine Print, Vanishing Rights, and the Rule of Law* (Princeton University Press, 2013). *Parker v South Eastern Railway* (1877) 2 CPD 416.

[17] Patricia J. Williams, *The Alchemy of Race and Rights* (Harvard University Press, 1991) p. 224.

Nevertheless, courts treat contracts *as if* they embodied freely choosing subjects' active intentions. This fiction[18] has a pragmatic technical function: it allows courts, by formalistically reasoning through contractual disputes, to bypass the lived difficulties of contracting. Thus, it eliminates a source of market uncertainty: if we know that the vagaries of human intention have limited impact on judicial decision-making, we feel more confident about entering into complex contracts. This minimalist approach makes some transactions more secure and more readily calculable. It also performs a political function.[19] It allows courts to bypass detailed engagement with the conditions in which contractual intention is formed, producing rules that are 'singular, daunting, rigid and cocksure'.[20] Leaving messy reality behind, law can turn to idealised narratives of contractual freedom. The idea of 'objectivity', so often repeated in your contract course, suggests rigour and certainty, but also responsiveness to shared market rationality. That rationality, however, may not be shared by all market actors:[21] the preferred practices of some are made the universal rule in order to discipline others. This is where gender inequality comes in.

Ideal contractual subjects are strong, independent, self-possessed and productive. They are autonomous beings who possess and trade in concrete legal rights.[22] This ideal is rooted in a particular theory of equality. Classical contract theorists were influenced by liberal political thinkers who argued that men should be owners of their own labour and property, and trade them freely with others. Contract was often contrasted with status:[23] freedom to contract implies equal capacity to bargain in the market, unshackled from traditional authority. This vision of universal equality seems admirable, but some subjects will have to work harder than others to claim that equality.[24] Recall nineteenth-century feminist struggles for married women's right to form property and employment contracts. As Pateman writes, the originary contract between men and women was the sexual contract, under which married women supposedly willingly subordinated themselves to their husbands.[25] Women were not

---

[18] Annelise Riles, *Collateral Knowledge: Legal Reasoning in the Global Financial Markets* (University of Chicago Press, 2011) p. 24.

[19] Ibid. p. 176.

[20] Mary Joe Frug, 'Rescuing impossibility doctrine: A postmodern feminist analysis of contract law' (1992) 140 *University of Pennsylvania Law Review* 1029, 1035.

[21] Patricia J. Williams, 'Metro Broadcasting, Inc. v. FCC: Regrouping in singular times' (1990) 104 *Harvard Law Review* 525, 534.

[22] Angela Mitropoulos, *Contract and Contagion: From Biopolitics to Oikonomia* (Minor Compositions, 2012) p. 176.

[23] Minow (n. 13) pp. 121–122.

[24] Ibid. p. 151.

[25] Carole Pateman, *The Sexual Contract* (John Wiley & Sons, 2014); Colin Dayan, *The Law Is a White Dog – How Legal Rituals Make and Unmake Persons* (Princeton University Press, 2013) p. 149.

fully in possession of themselves,[26] but were rather objects to be exchanged between men.[27]

Contract law now formally includes a wider range of subjects, including women, but substantive inclusion is another matter. We have said that contract rarely enquires into the forces that produce our thoughts, plans or desires: it flattens and generalises experience. If contract law presumes some equality between market actors, it is 'equal measure'[28] with idealised commercial men. Contract makes persons equivalent to one another in an abstract sense, apportioning and rationalising inequality rather than transcending it.[29] This is problematic because structural inequalities of class, race or gender often mean that we will not be able to contract for ideal opportunities. We contract for compromise because nothing better is available,[30] and we find that our contracts are more expensive to perform. If you are from the UK you could consider, for example, how issues of inequality interact with your own student loan contract. Of course you all formed the same online contract on the same terms: you were formally equal. But behind the mask of formal equality lie deep issues of class and gender. Most of you would have preferred not to take out a loan at all, but that option is no longer available, except perhaps for those with wealthy parents. Those of you raised in a single-parent household are less likely to enjoy that wealth, especially if it is female-headed. You may have had to borrow more, in fact; since maintenance grants were abolished, many of you will be borrowing (as well as working) to fund living costs, in addition to the debt you have taken on to pay fees. The contract also costs more to perform if you earn less: you are in debt for longer, and you pay back more in total.[31] Women, as you will know, are still likely to earn less than men and to suffer earning penalties for fulfilling caring responsibilities, so they are more likely to be affected by this inequality.[32] Meanwhile, others do very well out of the market in student loans, particularly private investors who have benefited from sales from the

---

[26] We could make similar points about enslaved people: Diane J. Klein, 'Paying Eliza: Comity, contracts, and critical race theory – 19th century choice of law doctrine and the validation of antebellum contracts for the purchase and sale of human beings' (2006) 20 *National Black Law Journal* 1; Amy Dru Stanley, *From Bondage to Contract: Wage Labor, Marriage, and the Market in the Age of Slave Emancipation* (Cambridge University Press, 1998); Sora Han, 'Slavery as contract: Betty's case and the question of freedom' (2015) 27 *Law & Literature* 395.

[27] Luce Irigaray, *This Sex Which Is Not One* (Cornell University Press, 1985) p. 173. See similarly Saskia Lettmaier, *Broken Engagements: The Action for Breach of Promise of Marriage and the Feminine Ideal, 1800–1940* (Oxford University Press, 2010).

[28] Drucilla Cornell, *Beyond Accommodation: Ethical Feminism, Deconstruction, and the Law* (Rowman & Littlefield, 1999) p. 114.

[29] Mitropoulos (n. 22) p. 25.

[30] Fleur Johns, *Non-Legality in International Law: Unruly Law* (Cambridge University Press, 2013) p. 118.

[31] See further http://blogs.lse.ac.uk/politicsandpolicy/student-debt-and-the-next-generation-of-british-public-sector-professionals/, accessed 17 January 2018.

[32] https://www.fawcettsociety.org.uk/policy-research/the-gender-pay-gap/, accessed 17 January 2018.

student loan book.[33] Insofar as law ignores the effects of economic inequality on contractual freedom then, as Williams says, it 'reduces life to fairytale'.[34]

Of course, law reassures us that unjust contracts will not be enforced. The fiction of contractual intention only temporarily forecloses enquiry[35] into the circumstances of the contract's formation. Wronged parties can always demand law's attention. However, courts administer corrective justice:[36] redressing wrongs done by one to the other rather than addressing contracts' substantive fairness, or their tendency to facilitate unequal accumulation of resources.[37] The courts' role is to uphold relations of commodification based on the parties' subjective valuation of the thing bought or sold. It is rarely law's concern if a commercial contract is one-sided, or an individual sells at apparent gross undervalue. There is no general principle that allows a contract to be set aside merely because it is unfair, without some additional evidence of morally reprehensible conduct.[38] The law on damages, based primarily in expectation loss, restores to me only what I had bargained for, rather than a fair price for my lost goods or wasted services. Thus, contractual freedom is not a substantive right to transform one's position by entering into emancipatory legal relations.[39] In many cases, contractual freedom means making the best of a precarious bargaining position.

You might have learned that, although contract law is not concerned with substantive unfairness, it carefully polices procedural unfairness: where some defect in the contract's formation taints one party's consent to the bargain. Duress, for example, only allows a contract to be set aside where one party's consent is produced by the other's serious and illegitimate threat. Coercion must be traceable to some act of the aggressor. The victim must show that they had no reasonable alternative but to accept the contract. Gan argues that these requirements exclude consideration of pre-existing inequality of bargaining power as between the parties.[40] They trivialise domination and legitimise subtle exploitation of economic inferiority. Even very harsh or discriminatory bargains can be enforced. Duress solidifies contract's commitment to preserve 'the rough and tumble of the normal pressures of commercial bargaining'.[41] It asks each party to look after their own interests without requiring concessions from the other. There is no independent doctrine of inequality of bargaining

---

[33] Andrew McGettigan, 'Cash Today', https://www.lrb.co.uk/v37/n05/andrew-mcgettigan/cash-today, accessed 17 January 2018.

[34] Williams, *The Alchemy of Race and Rights* (n. 17) p. 224.

[35] Riles (n. 18) p. 167.

[36] See Ernest J. Weinrib, *The Idea of Private Law* (Oxford University Press, 2012).

[37] Partha Chatterjee, *Empire and Nation: Selected Essays* (Columbia University Press, 2010) p. 255.

[38] *Portman Building Soc v Dusangh* [2000] 2 All ER (Comm 221).

[39] Williams, 'Metro Broadcasting, Inc. v. FCC' (n. 21).

[40] Orit Gan, 'Contractual duress and relations of power', https://papers.ssrn.com/sol3/papers.cfm?abstract_id=2134630, accessed 9 March 2017.

[41] *Atlas Express v Kafko* [1989] QB 833, 839.

power.[42] Moreover, the few doctrines allowing courts to address contractual injustice, or excuse non-performance, are made piecemeal and remain on law's margins.[43] (The concepts of undue influence and unconscionable bargain, for example, come from Equity.) Ordinary bargains may contain elements that are freely chosen, and others that are less so.[44] However, as Mulcahy argues, law exceptionalises failure to meet the standards of the robust contracting agent. Those who call on law for protection are imagined as presumptively deficient victims.[45] In this way, law suggests that most bargains are freely chosen rather than coerced.[46]

So far, we have talked about contractual freedom in terms of power and potential. But contract is also marked by hazard and uncertainty. Johns' work on the lived experience of transnational corporate deals presents parties less as powerful and assured than as inhabiting 'fraught' processes of deal-making on a 'hazard-riddled' landscape suffused with risk which is at once 'invigorating', 'bountiful', 'life-giving' and a constant reminder of the deal's fragility.[47] Mitropoulos suggests that contract is about 'proliferation of limits'[48] at risky 'frontiers'.[49] Early capitalism identified risk-taking as essential to accumulating wealth. As national and international commercial markets expanded under industrialisation and colonisation,[50] market actors had to master new profitable risks. They had to be willing to trade in markets for untested products, deal with unknown partners in faraway jurisdictions, and form executory contracts which might not reap financial rewards for years.[51] Law had to stabilise these new behaviours by generating 'an injunction to perform'[52] contracts, disciplining unruly responses to market risk.

Contract law cannot eliminate all market risks, but it can make us responsible for managing them. The rules governing the end of the contractual relationship make clear that we must weather risk; even if keeping our contractual

---

[42] *National Westminster Bank v Morgan* [1985] AC 686.

[43] Grant Gilmore, *The Death of Contract* (Ohio State University Press, 1977) pp. 52–53.

[44] Gillian K. Hadfield, 'An expressive theory of contract: From feminist dilemmas to a reconceptualization of rational choice in contract law' (1998) 146 *University of Pennsylvania Law Review* 1235, 1238.

[45] Linda Mulcahy and Sally Wheeler, *Feminist Perspectives on Contract Law* (Routledge, 2005) p. 11.

[46] Gan (n. 40) pp. 192–193; Alan Thomson, 'The law of contract' (1992) in Ian Grigg-Spall and Paddy Ireland (eds), *The Critical Lawyers' Handbook*, vol. 1: http://nclg.org.uk/wp-content/uploads/2011/10/The_Critical_Lawyers_Handbook_Volume_1.pdf, accessed 17 January 2018.

[47] Fleur Johns, 'Performing power: The deal, corporate rule, and the constitution of global legal order' (2007) 34 *Journal of Law and Society* 116, 125.

[48] Mitropoulos (n. 22) p. 18.

[49] Ibid. p. 45.

[50] Ibid. p. 19.

[51] Anthony T. Kronman, 'Contract law and the state of nature' (1985) *Journal of Law, Economics, & Organization* 5.

[52] Mitropoulos (n. 22) p. 40.

obligations entails hardship, inconvenience or significant financial loss,[53] we cannot lightly escape it. There are high thresholds for termination of a contract[54] or for frustration.[55] We must mitigate our losses. The courts will not save us from so-called 'bad bargains'.[56] This position is purportedly justified because we are understood to have the opportunity, at the point of contract formation, to exercise foresight; to calculate how risks might materialise in future[57] and to use express terms to allocate them between ourselves. To this end, law expects us to articulate our intentions clearly in advance.[58] In consequence, courts respect formal contractual documents, and are reluctant to alter or supplement a contract's express terms. Courts will construe an existing contract to determine responsibility for the consequences of non-performance, but will not 'make' a new contract for the parties after the event.[59] Thus, for example, the courts' acknowledged power to imply a term into a contract will only be exercised where it is 'necessary' to do so.[60]

The courts' expectations of contractual planning may be unrealistic. For example, Gelpern and Gulati's work on 'boilerplate' clauses shows that sometimes even sophisticated contract drafters behave irrationally. Standard form contracts and standardised clauses[61] (boilerplate) are highly efficient tools because they reduce the costs associated with making and negotiating new contracts. Terms need not be coined from scratch: drafters can use terms already accepted within the industry and, perhaps, that have been tested in the courts.[62] However, Gelpern and Gulati suggest drafters also include boilerplate in contract documents 'because they feel better for *saying it*, even where they know full well that the term will *do* little or nothing to advance their cause'.[63] Unthinking recycling, arrangement and accumulation of talismanic phrases of proven weight do not reflect thoughtful, rational agency. Instead, these phrases may symbolise desire for impossible reassurance.[64] These observations resonate

---

[53] *Davis Contractors v Fareham UDC* [1956] AC 696.
[54] *Decro-Wall Ltd v Practitioners in Marketing* [1971] 1 WLR 361.
[55] *Gold Group Properties v BDW* [2010] EWHC 323.
[56] *Arnold v Britton* [2015] UKSC 36.
[57] Pat O'Malley, 'Uncertain subjects: Risks, liberalism and contract' (2000) 29 *Economy and Society* 460; Beverly Brown, 'Contracting out/contracting in: Some feminist considerations' in Anne Bottomley (ed.), *Feminist Perspectives on the Foundational Subjects of Law* (Cavendish, 1996) pp. 5, 10.
[58] Johns (n. 30) p. 117.
[59] *Hilas v Arcos* (1932) 147 LT 503.
[60] *AG of Belize v Belize Telecom* [2009] UKPC 10.
[61] See Anna Gelpern and Mitu Gulati, 'How CACs became boilerplate: Governments in 'market-based' [2010] change' in B. Herman, J.A. Ocampo and S. Spiegel (eds), *Overcoming Developing Country Debt Crises* (Oxford University Press, 2010).
[62] Riles (n. 18) p. 58.
[63] Anna Gelpern and Mitu Gulati, 'Feel-good formalism' (2009) 35 *Queen's Law Journal* 97.
[64] Anna Gelpern and Mitu Gulati, 'Public symbol in private contract: A case study' (2006) 84 *Washington University Law Review* 1627.

with feminist work on bargaining and vulnerability. Berlant describes contracting as a process which attempts

> to induce through an improvised relation with a semi-stranger an attachment that might become a solidarity that could produce more and better traction in the world.[65]

On Berlant's reading, none of us, in contracting, occupies the powerful 'self-authoring' position assumed by law. We may care deeply about a particular contract, but we must acknowledge that it is fragile: improvised, impulsive, indirect, speculative, and ultimately dependent on others' responses.

Debate 2
Can relational contract theory save freedom of contract?

Some theorists turn to relational contract theory in order to reimagine freedom of contract. Contract's autonomous, rational subjects are disembedded from wider relationships. Early capitalism presented traditional communal standards of contractual fairness[66] as incompatible with new forms of exchange between individuals who were not connected by ties of kinship, neighbourliness or even nation.[67] As part of colonialism's civilising mission,[68] it was similarly necessary to overcome cultural market ethics, and impose contractual discipline. Classical contract recoded social and religious obligations in line with modern economic logic.[69] By stripping away relational particularity, contract made everything interchangeable with money.[70] Contract imagines us as separated not only from community but from one another. We are atomistic, unattached, bargaining at arm's length, each pursuing our own projects in a series of discrete, bipolar transactions. Parties ideally do not owe one another duties unless they consented to them; they are sovereign within the contract. This is one reason for the doctrine of privity.[71] It also explains why the traditional rules on contract formation – such as those on 'the battle of the forms' – still emphasise the need to find a precise moment of agreement.[72] This approach obscures

---

[65] Berlant (n. 3) p. 161.
[66] Wim Decock, *Theologians and Contract Law: The Moral Transformation of the Ius Commune (ca. 1500–1650)* (Martinus Nijhoff Publishers, 2013) p. 16.
[67] Peter Gabel and Jay Feinman, 'Contract law as ideology' in David Kairys (ed.), *The Politics of Law: A Progressive Critique* (Basic Books, 3rd edn, 1998) p. 172.
[68] Karl Polanyi, *The Great Transformation: The Political and Economic Origins of Our Time* (Beacon Press, 2001) p. 171.
[69] Ritu Birla, 'Law as economy: Convention, corporation, currency' (2011) 1 *University of California Irvine Law Review* 1015, 1019.
[70] Ian R. Macneil, 'Contracts: Adjustment of long-term economic relations under classical, neoclassical, and relational contract law' (1977) 72 *Northwestern University Law Review* 854.
[71] *Beswick v Beswick* [1968] AC 58.
[72] Macneil (n. 70). See, e.g., *Tekdata Interconnections Ltd. v Amphenol Ltd.* [2009] EWCA Civ. 1209 [21].

the understanding that agreement may often crystallise only gradually, as the contract is performed.[73] As Tidwell and Linzer write, some obligations may be tacit and unspoken; they 'arise as mysteriously and frequently as dust ... float through the central air ducts, the loud speaker, the light fixtures'.[74]

The distinction between contract and more protective forms of relationship is sharpest in its treatment of family bargains. Law assumes that these are made without intention to create legal relations.[75] Here, law relies again on a capitalist distinction between public and private;[76] between the male-dominated realm of market exchange, and the domestic sphere, where women's primary duties lay.[77] It survives in the presumption against enforcement of domestic agreements, the tentative acceptance of surrogacy contracts, the history of reluctance to enforce marital agreements,[78] and the refusal to enforce contracts for sexual services[79] as a matter of public policy. Contract's presumptive split between commercial and domestic bargains devalues social reproduction: the intimate labour of care for workers and their children which enables much market activity.[80] Split responsibility produces split governing norms. Unger argues that within families, trust rather than formal entitlement governs our relations to one another.[81] The domestic (however flawed) makes the market tolerable.[82] By excluding family from its sphere of concern, contract solidifies a vision of contractual freedom stripped both of the burdens of domestic power and of family-like expectations of selflessness. At the same time, contract law struggles to regulate anything but hard-nosed commercial bargains, or to provide damages that recognise our emotional investment in important transactions.[83]

Relational contract theory suggests that we can reintroduce family-like values to the contractual sphere, by recalibrating our understanding of market behaviour. J.K. Gibson-Graham wrote against 'economic atomism', which conceives of markets as 'cold' places where 'antipolitical, asocial, individual, disembedded,

---

[73] Gan (n. 40) p. 23.

[74] Patricia A. Tidwell and Peter Linzer, 'The flesh-colored band aid – contracts, feminism, dialogue, and norms' (1991) 28 *Houston Law Review* 791, 806.

[75] *Balfour v Balfour* [1919] 2 KB 571.

[76] Nicholas Rose, 'Beyond the public/private division: Law' (1987) 14 *Power and the Family* 68. See further Jill Elaine Hasday, 'Intimacy and economic exchange' (2005) *Harvard Law Review* 491.

[77] Debora L. Threedy, 'Feminists & (and) contract doctrine' (1998) 32 *Indiana Law Review* 1247, 1251. See similarly the cases on wifely duties and consideration, e.g. *Ward v Byham* [1956] 1 WLR 496; *Williams v Williams* [1957] 1 WLR 14.

[78] *Radmacher v Granatino* [2010] UKSC 42.

[79] *Pearce v Brookes* (1866) LR 1 Ex 213.

[80] See Silvia Federici, '4. Wages Against Housework', http://www.commoner.org.uk/wp-content/uploads/2012/02/04-federici.pdf, accessed 9 March 2017.

[81] Roberto Mangabeira Unger, 'The critical legal studies movement' (1983) 96 *Harvard Law Review* 561, 623.

[82] For critique of this position see Susan Moller Okin, *Justice, Gender, and the Family* (Basic Books, 1989) pp. 120–124.

[83] Hillary L Berk, 'The legalization of emotion: Managing risk by managing feelings in contracts for surrogate labor' (2015) 49 *Law & Society Review* 143, 146–147.

rational, efficient, short-term, calculable, incontestable'[84] bargains are formed. Instead, they argued, market actors' projects are often dependent on and inseparable from one another. Relational contract theory similarly understands contractual rights as 'entangled, not delineated'.[85] It casts each contract as a node in a network of cross-cutting relationships. Contract always implies contact; a drawing together of subjects and projects.[86] Contact is rarely a discrete 'alienated moment of mutual exploitation'.[87] As Macneil shows, contracts dwell amid ongoing long-term business relationships.[88] Parties value and seek to preserve these relationships. Macaulay found that businessmen often deliberately depart from contract law's expectations. They fail to plan contracts in detail at the point of formation, instead renegotiating necessary terms as the need arises.[89] Yet deals do not collapse for want of compliance with traditional models of contracting. Rather, undergirding relationships stabilise contracts: contractual norms evolve in tune with parties' friendships.[90] In cases of conflict, parties are more likely to seek to repair a failing contract than to have resort to the courts.[91] In this sense, relational contract theory also teaches that commercial contracting shares much with domestic exchange.[92] Solidarity, reciprocity, trust and even dependency are characteristics of ordinary market behaviour.[93] These ameliorate otherwise irrational behaviour, and may drive towards deeper bargaining fairness; for example, one party may forego their more selfish interests, for the long-term benefit of the relationship.[94] For Williams, contract law is about the 'making strange, putting at a distance' which makes alienation and sale possible.[95] Relational contract theory recovers proximity and familiarity in contracting.[96]

Whatever we can say about how business works in practice, as a general matter contract law is inhospitable to relational expectations. There is no broad duty

---

[84] J.K. Gibson-Graham, *A Postcapitalist Politics* (University of Minnesota Press, 2006) p. 83. J.K. Gibson-Graham is a joint pseudonym adopted by two women, Julie Graham and Katherine Gibson, who wrote together.

[85] Riles (n. 18) p. 165.

[86] Mitropoulos (n. 22) p. 14.

[87] Robert W Gordon, 'Macaulay, Macneil, and the discovery of solidarity and power in contract law, private governance and continuing relationships' (1985) *Wisconsin Law Review* 565, 569.

[88] Macneil (n. 70).

[89] Discussed in John Wightman, 'Intimate relationships, relational contract theory, and the reach of contract' (2000) 8 *Feminist Legal Studies* 93, 103.

[90] Carl F. Stychin, 'De-meaning of contract' (2007) *Sexuality and the Law* 73, 80.

[91] See, for example, Stewart Macaulay, 'Organic transactions: Contract, Frank Lloyd Wright and the Johnson Building' (1996) *Wisconsin Law Review* 75.

[92] Mulcahy and Wheeler (n. 45) p. 12. Lisa Bernstein, 'Beyond relational contracts: Social capital and network governance in procurement contracts' (2015) *Journal of Legal Analysis* 561.

[93] See, for example, Robin West, 'Economic man and literary woman: One contrast' (1987) 39 *Mercer Law Review* 867.

[94] Stychin (n. 90) 83.

[95] Patricia J. Williams, 'Keynote address, National Conference on racism 2000', https://www. sahrc.org.za/home/21/files/Reports/national_conference_on%20racism%20report%202001. pdf, accessed 19 March 2017.

[96] Mulcahy and Wheeler (n. 45) p. 10.

of disclosure in contract law, for example; parties are free to keep material facts to themselves.[97] Courts have also been hostile to attempts to introduce duties to bargain, or perform, contracts in good faith, unless the parties have directly bargained for them.[98] That said, although they will not impose broad duties,[99] the courts are often responsive to market practices, and to the reasonable expectations of the individual parties. For instance, in interpreting a contract, the courts will often supplement the written document with conclusions drawn from the context of the bargain;[100] they will attempt to enforce the 'real' rather than the 'paper' deal between the parties.

We should remember that relationality is not innocent of power: informal solidarity and unwritten custom are compatible with capitalist hierarchy.[101] Williams tells a story in which she contrasts her insistence on a 'detailed negotiated finely printed lease' with her White male colleague's preference for a verbal agreement concluded on a handshake and backed by a cash deposit. She locates her caution in her childhood experience of landlords who breached Black tenants' informal leases.[102] Some of us flourish under regimes of relationality which exploit and unsettle others. *Baird v M&S* is a well-known example of this problem; the smaller company adopted a series of risky business practices in order to fulfil the interests of its larger, stronger, partner.[103] Another pressing example is that of government outsourcing of state service provision to corporations such as Serco, Atos and G4S. Although these companies' breaches of contract are well-documented,[104] the contracts' relational characteristics diminish the costs of failure, and these companies continue to flourish. The state repeatedly enters into long-term contracts with the same companies over time. These contracts build deeply interconnected relationships of dependence; service provision is eventually moulded to suit these companies' interests and working methods. Staff move from the civil service to the companies and back again. In classic relational style, the contracts' terms are flexible and rarely litigated. Even when serious breach is penalised with refusal to renew one kind of contract, these firms or their subsidiaries can successfully

---

[97] *Keates v Cadogan* (1851) 10 CB 591.

[98] *Walford v Miles* [1992] 2 AC 128; *Interfoto Picture Library v Stiletto* [1989] QB 433; *Compass Group v Mid Essex* [2013] EWCA Civ 200. Contrast *Blackpool v Fylde Aeroclub* [1990] EWCA Civ 13; *Yam Seng v International Trade* [2013] EWHC 111.

[99] For examples of what a relational law of contract would look like see Melvin Eisenberg, 'Why there is no law of relational contracts' (1999) *Northwestern University Law Review* 805, 815.

[100] *Investors Compensation Scheme v West Bromwich* [1997] UKHL 28.

[101] See further, Stychin (n. 90) p. 83.

[102] Williams, *The Alchemy of Race and Rights* (n. 17) p. 146.

[103] Linda Mulcahy and Cathy Andrews, 'Baird textile holdings v Marks and Spencer plc' in Rosemary Hunter, Clare McGlynn and Erika Rackley (eds), *Feminist Judgments: From Theory to Practice* (Hart Publishing Ltd, 2010) pp. 189–204.

[104] 'Kristen Rundle – Legality in the Contracting Out State: Cues from the Case of Jimmy Mubenga', http://backdoorbroadcasting.net/2013/01/kristen-rundle-legality-in-the-contracting-out-state-cues-from-the-case-of-jimmy-mubenga/, accessed 21 March 2017; Steven Hirschler, 'Beyond the camp: The biopolitics of asylum seeker housing under the UK' (2013) 45 *Modern Law Review* 179.

compete for others. Relationality keeps these companies in the market for public services, at a significant cost to the vulnerable people (young prisoners, asylum seekers, jobseekers) whose lives are governed by these contracts. In this context, there are arguments for returning to a perhaps more formalistic approach to contract; detailing companies' obligations to re-orientate these contracts towards human rights protection, and enforcing the contracts properly. But it is also clear that a new vision of relationality is required which re-examines, not only government's dealings with these companies, but the underpinning norms of the market they have created.[105]

CONCLUSION

Even the more traditional textbooks you have read will criticise the artificiality of the contract law course. For example, it (i) focuses on traditional business rather than consumer contracts, (ii) marginalises specialist areas of contract such as employment law, public procurement or new familial and reproductive contracts and so suggests a unity of rules and purpose that no longer exists, (iii) talks primarily about common law doctrine rather than statute, and often marginalises Equity. The contract law syllabus cannot tell you very much about commercial practice. Instead it performs a different function. It is a core undergraduate, and often first-year module. It provides a space where you encounter detailed authoritative messages about ownership, reason and autonomy which you carry with you into new areas of study. This chapter demonstrates tools for disrupting those messages. The first debate upsets standard narratives of 'free' contracting behaviour and the unattainable expectations they uphold. The second returns us to questions of relationality as a supplement to contract doctrine, not as a means to eliminate our worries about contract law's sharp edges but as a call to contractual responsibility and to deep questioning of prevailing market norms.

FURTHER READING

John N. Adams and Roger Brownsword, 'The ideologies of contract' (1987) 7 *Legal Studies* 205.

Duncan Kennedy, 'Form and substance in private law adjudication' (1976) 89 *Harvard Law Review* 1685.

Linda Mulcahy and Cathy Andrews, 'Baird textile holdings v Marks and Spencer plc' in Rosemary Hunter, Clare McGlynn and Erika Rackley (eds), *Feminist Judgments: From Theory to Practice* (Hart Publishing Ltd, 2010) pp. 189–204.

Linda Mulcahy and Sally Wheeler, *Feminist Perspectives on Contract Law* (Routledge, 2005).

Carey Young, *Subject to Contract* (JP Ringier, 2013).

---

[105] For an overview of issues see Jody Freeman and Martha Minow, *Government by Contract: Outsourcing and American Democracy* (Harvard University Press, 2009).

CHAPTER 2

Tort Law

Kirsty Horsey and Erika Rackley

The relationship between tort law and gender is longstanding. Feminist legal scholars have long sought to expose gendered assumptions behind key concepts of tort law (such as reasonableness, autonomy, personhood), the gendered nature of specific harms (for example, sexual harassment, 'nervous shock', reproductive harms) and/or the gendering effects of tort law itself (in the assessment of damages, for example, or its failure to respond to 'relational harms').[1] At other times, the overlapping nature of criminal law and tort has been harnessed to argue for recourse to tort in order to expose failings in the criminal justice system and to provide victim-survivors,[2] particularly in the context of sexual and domestic abuse, with effective redress.[3]

This chapter considers two such debates. The first asks whether tort might provide an avenue for redress for victim-survivors of image-based sexual abuse, including so-called revenge porn and, if so, the form this might take. The second considers whether victim-survivors of domestic abuse should be able to utilise tort not against their abuser but against the police, where their faults have failed to prevent abuse from occurring. In both debates, an overarching question is whether tort should plug the gaps left by criminal, public and/or human rights law responses.

---

[1] See, e.g., Joanne Conaghan, 'Tort law and feminist critique' (2003) *Current Legal Problems* 175 and references therein.

[2] We use the term victim-survivor in this chapter to highlight the continuous connected position between being a victim and survivor. However, we know that, sadly, not all women who are raped or who have experienced domestic abuse survive.

[3] Joanne Conaghan, 'Challenging and redressing police failures in the context of rape investigations: The Civil Liability Route' (2015) 5 *feminists@law*; Nikki Godden-Rasul, 'Retribution, redress, and the harms of rape: The role of tort law' in Nicola Henry, Anastasia Powell and Asher Flynn (eds), *Rape Justice: Beyond the Realm of Law* (Palgrave Macmillan, 2015) pp. 112–126.

Debate 1

Should tort law provide a bespoke remedy for victims of image-based sexual abuse?

Jennifer Lawrence, John Schindler, Holly Jacobs, Tulisa Contostavlos and Emma Watson have something in common. They are victim-survivors, or threatened victims, of image-based sexual abuse.[4] There are others. They are not famous. You're unlikely to know their names. But you could easily find them out. If you did, chances are you would see them posted alongside private, sexual images – images that may or may not have been taken and/or shared consensually with a partner. But, either way, images that the person depicted never expected *you*, and people like you – strangers – or friends and family, to see. Images that quickly go viral, travelling around the world by text, email, and on dedicated 'revenge' and regular pornography websites. The impact on the victim-survivor can be devastating: unemployment, loss of job opportunities, family and relationship breakdown, death and rape threats, physical and mental health difficulties, even suicide.

Of course, abuse and harassment of women are not new. Nor is the taking/ distribution of private sexual images, with or without the party's consent, or for sexual or non-sexual purposes. Neither are we simply concerned here with so-called revenge porn. Rather, it is about a range or 'continuum' of gendered, sexualised forms of abuse of women (and it is mostly women)[5] involving non-consensual taking and/or distributing of private sexual images.[6] It is about (but not limited to) – to use Clare McGlynn et al.'s examples – upskirting, voyeurism, sexualised photoshopping, sexual exhortation, and recordings of sexual assault and rape, as well as theft or hacking of non-/consensually taken sexual images.

While campaigns for criminal laws aimed at those who take and post private sexual images continue to gather momentum worldwide,[7] less attention has been paid to the role tort law might play in this context.[8] Could, say, the

---

[4] Clare McGlynn and Erika Rackley, 'Not "revenge porn" but abuse: Let's call it image-based sexual abuse', *Everyday Victim Blaming*, 9 March 2016; Clare McGlynn and Erika Rackley, 'Image-based sexual abuse' (2017) 37 *Oxford Journal of Legal Studies* 1.

[5] Figures show that women made 75 per cent of 1,800 calls to the UK's Revenge Porn Helpline over a six-month period: Government Equalities Office Press Release, 'Hundreds of victim-survivors of revenge porn seek support from helpline', 20 August 2015.

[6] Clare McGlynn, Erika Rackley and Ruth Houghton, '"Beyond revenge porn": The continuum of image-based sexual abuse' (2017) 25(1) *Feminist Legal Studies* 25.

[7] In England and Wales the criminal offence of 'disclosing private sexual photographs or films with intent to cause distress' reached the statute book in February 2015 (Criminal Justice and Courts Act 2015 ss 33–35). Clare McGlynn and Erika Rackley, 'The new law against "revenge porn" is welcome, but no guarantee of success' *The Conversation*, 15 February 2015.

[8] Although see McGlynn and Rackley, 'Image-based sexual abuse' (n. 4); 'Written submission from Professor Clare McGlynn (Durham University) and Professor Erika Rackley (University of Birmingham). Justice Committee: Abusive Behaviour and Sexual Harm (Scotland) Bill' (5 November 2015) and (in the US) Danielle Keats Citron, *Hate Crimes in Cyber Space* (Harvard University Press, 2014); Derek E. Bambauer, 'Exposed' (2013–2014) *Minnesota Law Review* 2025.

torts of privacy and harassment be harnessed to protect women's interests and provide a remedy? Or do we need a bespoke tort of image-based sexual abuse?

The Relationship Between Tort and Criminal Law

Should tort play a role at all? Isn't responding to the harm of image-based sexual abuse more appropriately a matter for the criminal law?

We might think that the harms of image-based sexual abuse are so obvious as to warrant society taking a stand with the full force of the criminal law, and that anything that distracts from this – including a private right of individuals affected by image-based sexual abuse being able to hold the perpetrator to account – risks 'downgrading' the issue. Certainly there should be no expectation that victim-survivors take on the further burden of bringing a claim – not least given, in this post-Legal Aid era, the financial costs of doing so. Many perpetrators may well be to all intents and purposes 'judgment proof', having neither the means nor the inclination to respond appropriately to a judgment against them.[9] And, while damages awards may go some way to paying the bills (e.g. for victim-survivors who lose their jobs or incur medical and/or other expenses), they do not remove the images from the web. This is particularly problematic where the images are hosted outside the court's jurisdiction. Nor do they prevent the reposting of the image elsewhere, with the result that claimants can find themselves caught in a particularly pernicious and extended version of the 1970s fairground game 'Whack-A-Mole' as they seek to prevent images from reappearing. However, while it may be true, as Danielle Keats Citron and Mary Anne Franks have argued in the US context, that tort law has a more limited bite than criminal law,[10] it can – and arguably should – still show its teeth.

In the early days of the common law, the remedies provided by what we now call 'crime' and 'tort' were seen as 'equally valid' options.[11] Unlike the criminal law, tort law puts the victim-survivor/claimant – or, at least, those who can afford to bring a claim – back in control. It is the victim-survivor who brings the action, not the Crown Prosecution Service or police. In the context of image-based sexual abuse, where the non-consensual nature of the harms perpetrated has taken control away from the victim-survivor, this is particularly important. So too, against a backdrop of continuing 'victim blaming',[12] is the ability to bring a claim in tort without having to first persuade others, most obviously the police, of the seriousness of the harm and/or strength of the victim-survivor's case. Further, the pre-emptive use of injunctions and non-disclosure orders might not only stem the tide once an image is published, but also (at least sometimes) prevent its circulation in the first place.

---

[9] Danielle Keats Citron and Mary Anne Franks, 'Criminalizing revenge porn' (2014) 49 *Wake Forest Law Review* 358.

[10] Ibid.

[11] Matthew Dyson, 'The timing of tortious and criminal actions for the same wrong' (2012) 70 *Cambridge Law Journal* 89.

[12] For example, Australian federal police assistant commissioner, Shane Connelly: Australian Associated Press, '"Grow up" and stop taking naked photos of yourself, police tell revenge porn inquiry', *The Guardian*, 18 February 2016.

CURRENT TORT LAW REMEDIES FOR IMAGE-BASED SEXUAL ABUSE

How far does tort law already provide a remedy for victims of image-based sexual abuse? In this section we look at two options: privacy and harassment.[13]

Privacy

It is well established that, in accordance with Article 8 of the European Convention on Human Rights, an individual has a 'reasonable expectation of privacy' in relation to information relating to their private consensual sexual activities:

> people's sex lives are to be regarded as especially their own business – provided at least that the participants are genuinely consenting adults and there is no question of exploiting the young or vulnerable.[14]

There is also a longstanding recognition that photographs are 'more intrusive' than verbal or written descriptions:[15]

> The objection to the publication of unauthorised photographs taken on a private occasion is not simply that the images that they disclose convey secret information, or impressions that are unflattering. It is that they disclose information that is private. The offence is caused because what the claimant could reasonably expect would remain private has been made public. The intrusion into the private domain is, of itself, objectionable.[16]

The courts have also recognised privacy claims in relation to private information, including information about sexual relationships, shared in the course of a friendship or relationship,[17] as well as in relation to images and footage of 'sexual activities' obtained via CCTV.[18] In *Contostavlos v Mendahun,* singer and former X Factor judge, Tulisa Contostavlos, obtained an interim non-disclosure order preventing the further dissemination of a 'sex video' by her former boyfriend, Justin Edwards.[19] The video had been placed for a short time on a website charging £3.90 to download it during which time it received over 50,000 views.[20] While celebrities are perhaps more lucrative quarry,[21] they are

---

[13] Other options include the tort in *Wilkinson v Downton* and defamation. Other civil law actions include those in data protection and for copyright infringement.

[14] Eady J in *Mosley v News Group Newspapers* [2008] EWHC 1777 (QB) at para. 100.

[15] Tugendhat J in *Contostavlos v Mendahun* [2012] EWHC 850 at para. 25.

[16] *Douglas v Hello!* [2005] EWCA Civ 596 at para. 107.

[17] *McKennitt v Ash* [2006] EWCA Civ 1714.

[18] *Jagger v Darling* [2005] EWHC 683 (Ch).

[19] *Contostavlos v Mendahun* [2012] EWHC 850 (QB).

[20] Almost four months after the video was first posted online, Edwards admitted responsibility for publication of the sex tape and undertook, in a statement in open court, not to do it again.

[21] They are also, of course, in a better position to utilise the civil law in response.

not the only targets. In *ABK v KDT & FGH* the claimant had been having an affair, which she had ended, with the second defendant. The first defendant, with whom the second defendant was also in a relationship, emailed three 'sexual' photos (sent to the first defendant by the claimant during their affair) to the claimant's husband, to two of her friends, and to a friend of her husband, with a message threatening to inflict on the claimant 'enough pain and humiliation matching my own during your love affair'.[22] The claimant was granted an interim non-disclosure order to protect her right to confidentiality and privacy.

The Protection from Harassment Act 1997

Individuals are not expected to tolerate behaviour which the defendant knows, or ought to have known, amounts to harassment – that is, acts which cross the line from 'unattractive and unreasonable' to 'oppressive and unacceptable',[23] which occur on two or more occasions, and which cause the individual alarm or distress.[24]

Incidents of image-based sexual abuse might be thought to be archetypal examples of harassing behaviour, and certainly the courts have been willing to adopt novel strategies and approaches to provide a response. In *AMP v Persons Unknown* the claimant (a university student) sought to prevent the transmission, storage and indexing of a number of explicit sexual photos which she had taken to send to her boyfriend and which had been uploaded from a stolen or lost mobile phone, together with a link to her Facebook profile.[25] Although the images were promptly removed from the original site, they continued to be shared via peer-to-peer technology. The difficulty for the claimant was that the identification of individual defendants who had downloaded the pictures – or might in the future – would be both time-consuming and costly. This would not only cause delay (where there was a need to move quickly in order to prevent further distribution) but was also likely, through increased publicity, to draw further attention to the images, leading to further breaches of the claimant's confidentiality. Ramsey J held that there was an arguable case that the actions of the so-called 'seeders' amounted to harassment and a breach of the claimant's privacy rights, and granted an interim injunction against 'persons unknown', the effect of which meant that any further distribution of the images would automatically be an offence.

---

[22] *ABK v KDT & FGH* [2013] EWHC 1192 (QB) at para. 4.

[23] Lord Nicholls in *Majrowski v Guy's and St Thomas' NHS Trust* [2006] UKHL 34 at para. 30.

[24] Protection from Harassment Act 1997 s. 1. Following *Law Society v Kordowski* [2011] EWHC 3185 a single publication will amount to a 'course of conduct' (defined in the Act as on two or more occasions (s. 7(3)) where the defendant does so 'in the knowledge that such publications will inevitably come to [the claimant's] attention on more than one occasion and on each occasion cause them alarm and distress constitutes harassment' (at para. 61). The same is true for invasions of privacy (see, e.g., *Contostavlos* at para. 25).

[25] *AMP v Persons Unknown* [2011] EWHC 3454 (TCC).

A BESPOKE TORT OF IMAGE-BASED SEXUAL ABUSE

It is clear that various tort law actions have been – and could be – utilised to provide victim-survivors of image-based sexual abuse with redress.[26] So do we need a bespoke tort?

What is also clear is that, in practice, tort law's responses have been somewhat uneven. Victim-survivors often find it hard to find a lawyer with the necessary expertise and inclination to navigate the many and varied legal avenues. Few cases fit neatly within the confines of a particular claim, and those that do require the harm to be reframed as 'distress' rather than anger or non-consent. Cases of image-based sexual abuse typically involve a 'perfect storm' of time and cost: fast-moving technological innovations, novel applications of particular and often contested facts to pre-internet common law actions, multiple potential causes of action, and a large number of often unknown and cross-jurisdictional defendants, as well as complex technological and legal arguments. The result is that, even in relation to more straightforward actions, the cost of bringing a claim is prohibitively expensive for most victim-survivors.[27]

A bespoke tort of image-based sexual abuse would go a long way to addressing some of these difficulties. It would provide victim-survivors of image-based sexual abuse with a cost-effective, flexible and – most importantly – accessible avenue of redress. But what form might such a tort take? McGlynn and Rackley suggest that a tort of image-based sexual abuse should include the following features:[28]

1. A broad definition of image-based sexual abuse in order to ensure its application to current (and future) ways in which private sexual images are non-consensually taken and/or distributed.
2. A focus on consent (or lack thereof) and on the defendant's actions, rather than on the defendant's motivations for, or the victim-survivor's reaction to, the abuse.
3. An automatic guarantee of victim-survivors' anonymity.

---

[26] As this collection went to press, two important cases involving the use of civil law in this context were reported. The first involved a claim against Facebook for misuse of private information, negligence and a breach of data protection laws after a naked photo of a teenager from Northen Ireland was posted on a so-called 'shame page'. In the second, Chrissy Chambers (a singer and video blogger) sued her former boyfriend for harassment, breach of confidence and misuse of private information after he secretly recorded them having sex and posted the recording on a pornographic website. Both cases were settled out of court, and so offer little by way of clarity as to the likely success of the various actions. However, what they do is put both the hosters and perpetrators of image-based sexual abuse on notice: the civil law has teeth in this context and – if it bites – you will be liable for substantial damages. (See further Alan Reid, 'Landmark revenge porn cases are a stark warning for perpetrators and social networks', *The Conversation*, 17 January 2018.)

[27] This is true even for some celebrities. Chrissy Chambers turned to crowd-funding to raise the £22,000 needed to finance her suit against her former boyfriend (Agency, 'You Tube star Chrissy Chambers launches crowd-funding bid to bring revenge porn case against ex', *The Telegraph*, 28 February 2016). Read more about Chambers' landmark case in Jenny Kleeman, 'The YouTube star who fought back against revenge porn – and won', *The Guardian*, 18 January 2018.

[28] McGlynn and Rackley, 'Image-based sexual abuse', n. 4.

4. The ability, subject to appropriate defences, to bring a claim against all those who have engaged or may engage in or facilitate image-based sexual abuse. This would include those who originally take and/or post the private sexual image, as well as those who 'simply' forward it or provide forums for disseminating, or allow forums for which they are responsible to 'host', the image/s.

5. A range of proactive and reactive relief preventing (where possible) the initial and subsequent distribution of the image/s and also financial compensation.

6. Mirroring the Protection from Harassment Act 1997, the civil claim should be underpinned by a criminal offence.

Of course such a tort is unlikely to be a panacea for all the difficulties faced by victim-survivors of image-based sexual abuse. Nor is it likely to be able to do much to stem the tide of harassment and abuse that is widespread in society. But combined with effective criminal laws and targeted educative strategies, it could go some way to ensuring women's right to privacy, dignity and sexual expression in both physical and digital spaces.

Debate 2

Should victim-survivors of domestic abuse use tort law to hold police to account where they have failed to prevent third parties from committing abuse?

Unlike the previous debate, where debate arises when looking for a solution to the problem of ill-fitting and complicated pockets of liability within which tort claims may be brought, a clear avenue of redress already exists for actions against the police by victims of domestic abuse.[29] The tort of negligence could clearly allow individuals to hold the police to account for serious investigative failures which allow domestic abuse (including rape and murder) to occur.[30] The problem is that the police only owe a general public duty; they owe no

---

[29] This debate would also apply to other harms, including rape, where the police fail victim-survivors by negligently conducted investigations. See, e.g., the appeal by the Metropolitan Police against findings that they violated the human rights of victims of serial rapist John Worboys by their investigational negligence (*Commissioner of Police of the Metropolis v DSD and another* UKSC 2015/0166) heard by the UKSC in March 2017. At the time of writing, no decision had been published, though there was much discussion about the decision of the Parole Board to release Worboys on licence after serving 10 years of his 'indeterminate sentence for public protection', and a judicial review of the decision had been launched by the Mayor of London as well as the initiation of proceedings by two (of more than 100 suspected) of his victims: 'DSD' and 'NBV' from the human rights claim (see BBC News, 'Sadiq Khan launches John Worboys judicial review bid', 25 January 2018; Centre for Women's Justice Press Release, 'Judicial Review on behalf of two victims of John Worboys issued in High Court today', 25 January 2018). On the Court of Appeal decision see Joanne Conaghan, 'Investigating rape: Human rights and police accountability' (2017) 37(1) *Legal Studies* 54.

[30] See the Canadian case *Doe v Metropolitan Toronto (Municipality) Commissioners of Police* [1998] 160 DLR (4th) 289 (SC (Ont)).

duty of care (in respect of investigative functions) to individuals harmed by their actions or inactions in respect of these crimes. Should they?

DOMESTIC ABUSE, SEXUAL VIOLENCE AND GENDER

Domestic abuse is a gendered issue, both in the manner and form in which it is practised and also, most obviously (not to downplay experiences of male victim-survivors), because victim-survivors of domestic abuse are predominantly women.[31] Moreover, it is a widespread – and increasing – problem, making up 11.1 per cent of all recorded crimes (excluding fraud) in England and Wales in the 12 months up to 30 June 2016.[32] Police failures regarding domestic abuse have been excruciatingly, embarrassingly highlighted.[33] Indeed, one headline of Her Majesty's Inspectorate of Constabularies' (HMIC's) 2014 Report revealed that '[d]omestic abuse is a priority on paper but, in the majority of forces, not in practice'.[34]

Domestic violence is a primary public policy focus of the current government, led by the Prime Minister who has promised to directly oversee a 'major programme of work' leading to new legislation.[35] In Downing Street's

---

[31] 1.8 million people aged 16–59 reported, to the Crime Survey for England and Wales, experiencing domestic violence and/or abuse during the year ending March 2016 (Office of National Statistics, 'Domestic abuse in England and Wales: Year ending March 2016', 8 December 2016). Of these '[w]omen were more likely to say they have experienced domestic abuse than men, with an estimated 1.2 million female victims compared to 651,000 male victims' (p. 4).

[32] Her Majesty's Inspectorate of Constabularies, *PEEL: Police Effectiveness 2016: A National Overview*, 2 March 2017, p. 7.

[33] HMIC's 2017 Report (ibid.) considered the effectiveness of policing in the UK and noted the 'HMIC has discovered an increasing number of unwelcome practices in some forces which, too often, have the effect of artificially suppressing the demand for the police to take prompt and effective action … too often emergency calls are reclassified as less urgent when there is a shortage of officers to respond and, on occasions, decisions are taken to reclassify high-risk victims of domestic violence to medium risk' (p. 4).

[34] HMIC, *Everyone's Business: Improving the Police Response to Domestic Abuse* (2014).

[35] 10 Downing Street, 'Prime Minister's plans to transform the way we tackle domestic violence and abuse', 17 February 2017. In June 2017, in the lead up to the General Election, Theresa May announced that a Tory Government would introduce a new Domestic Violence and Abuse Bill (containing among other things a statutory definition of domestic violence), and would review cuts on front-line services ('Tories pledge new law over domestic violence directed at children', *The Guardian*, 28 May 2017). Of course, any solution is dependent on funding, not only for refuges and shelters but also to allow victim-survivors to enforce their rights through an effective system of Legal Aid. It remains to be seen whether May's programme of work will (re)address this and, as of going to press, no Bill had been laid, though various consultations and debates were continuing. See, e.g., Ministry of Housing, Communities and Local Government Press Release, 'New guidance to ensure victims of domestic abuse can access safe social housing', 30 October 2017. For critiques of the Tory role in the cuts already seen, see Sarah Champion, 'Whatever she says, Theresa May has failed victims of domestic violence', *The Guardian*, 8 September 2016, and Sarah Jane Ewart, 'The round up: Election coverage, domestic violence and free movement', UK Human Rights Blog, 4 June 2017, https://ukhumanrightsblog.com/2017/06/04/the-round-up-election-coverage-domestic-violence-and-free-movement/, accessed 26 January 2018.

February 2017 press release, Theresa May called differing responses across the country 'unacceptable', referring to 'victims … often [being] let down by the legal system':

> Like the Modern Slavery Act, the Prime Minister believes that the measures that come out of this work will raise public awareness of the problem – as well as encourage victims to report their abusers and see them brought to justice.[36]

All victim-survivors of domestic abuse deserve better protection by the police than is currently given. Domestic abuse is clearly criminal, and its perpetrators should be dealt with by the criminal law. But, it is widely known, particularly among feminist lawyers or others dealing with social, legal and political issues to do with gender, that there are many failures in the criminal system – starting with under-reporting of crimes and ending with high attrition/low conviction rates. Of course civil liability cannot address this alone but, as part of a full package of measures attacking the problem from all directions, it offers an important avenue of redress.

The Role of Negligence

Tort law is about *righting* wrongs. Criminal convictions against the perpetrator of the abuse don't necessarily do this – they don't always bring 'closure'. Nor does an internal Independent Office for Police Conduct (IOPC) investigation into the police officers' conduct: a few days' suspended pay does not right a wrong.[37] Recognising duties of care would provide victim-survivors with a route to individualised justice (not only compensation, but vindication, apology etc). Without this police behaviour cannot be fully or openly scrutinised.[38] Without a full trial, we cannot know whether actions fell below the standard of care expected in the circumstances. Moreover, tort has a preventative/deterrent function, meaning that following the close scrutiny of a trial, police officers, or indeed whole forces, may learn from mistakes made. So why are the courts reluctant to impose a duty of care?

The most recent case to have considered tort's potential in this respect is *Michael v Chief Constable of South Wales Police*,[39] in which the young children and parents of a woman killed by her ex-boyfriend, Cyron Williams,

---

[36] 10 Downing Street, ibid.

[37] Especially because it just *keeps* happening: Josh Halliday, 'Alice Ruggles murder: IPCC to investigate after victim felt "palmed off"', *The Guardian*, 12 October 2017. The IPOC was formerly (until January 2018) the Independent Police Complaints Commission (IPCC).

[38] A simple trawl of the IOPC/IPCC's web pages tells us just how bad some of the police's responses to domestic abuse are – and how often this occurs – prompting the IPCC itself to call for *national* improvement (IPCC, 'IPCC calls for improvements in how police forces treat complainants', 26 September 2017; IOPC, 'National recommendation accepted following investigation into police contact with murder victim Katrina O'Hara', 8 January 2018).

[39] *Michael v Chief Constable of South Wales Police* [2015] UKSC 2, hereafter *Michael*.

sued the police in negligence. Joanna Michael called the police in fear of attack from Williams, who had been in her house, threatening her, had bitten her and had left – taking her current boyfriend with him – saying he would return to kill her. Due to failures in the police's call-handling procedures, her call was graded as of lower priority than it should have been. She called the police again, screamed, then the line cut out. By the time the police arrived she was dead from multiple stab wounds. Yet – astonishingly (at least to those unfamiliar with the history of this area of tort law) – the Supreme Court, albeit with two strong dissents, found that the police owed her no duty of care.[40]

For those familiar with the history, the decision was less surprising but no less disappointing. One problem is that duties of care do not usually arise when harms result from a defendant's omissions, nor in respect of a third party's actions.[41] Couple these with a public authority defendant, such as the police, and public policy arguments *against* the imposition of liability have traditionally weighed heavily against claimants: public law is the right place to hold public bodies to account; authorities' duties are to the public at large, not individuals; authorities are paid for out of the public purse; imposing liability would result in 'defensive practices'; internal investigations can focus on and rectify the failures of particular officers and improve practices etc.[42]

Of course, this would be less problematic if victim-survivors could rely on human rights arguments instead of tort. After all, doesn't the Human Rights Act 1998 (HRA) allow us to hold agents of the state – including the police – accountable for unjustifiably taking life, failing to protect life from serious threat, or allowing people to be subjected to inhuman or degrading treatment?[43] Inroads in respect of claims of this type against the police have already been made in relation to both the right to life and freedom from inhuman or degrading treatment.[44] But Lord Toulson, giving the majority judgment in *Michael*, was clear that, despite wider policy arguments regarding domestic violence/ abuse, a potential human rights claim should not lead to a corresponding

---

[40] The human rights claim fared better – the Court unanimously refused to strike it out. Police forces, heavily criticised by the IOPC/IPCC, now seem to be settling similar claims: see, e.g., Diane Taylor, 'Police apologise to dead woman's kin after failure to respond to 999 call' *The Guardian*, 5 January 2017 (over £20,000 compensation paid).

[41] Other than where exceptions can be found on the basis of proximity of relationship based on authority, control or assumed responsibility, including when the defendant is the police (see, e.g., *Chief Constable of Northumbria v Costello* [1998] EWCA Civ 3536; *Swinney v Chief Constable of Northumbria Police* [1996] EWCA Civ 1322; *Waters v Commissioner of Police for the Metropolis* [2000] UKHL 50).

[42] *Hill v Chief Constable of West Yorkshire* [1989] AC 53 (especially Lord Keith, at 63).

[43] These rights being derived from Articles 2 and 3 of the European Convention on Human Rights, respectively.

[44] See, e.g. (re Article 2), *Van Colle v Chief Constable of Hertfordshire* [2008] UKHL 50, *Sarjantson v Chief Constable of Humberside Police* [2013] EWCA Civ 1252, and *Michael*. In *Commissioner of the Police for the Metropolis v DSD and another* [2015] EWCA Civ 646, the Court of Appeal found that police have a positive duty under Article 3 ECHR to properly investigate into alleged ill-treatment (here rape), even by private individuals.

duty of care in negligence. Indeed, quite the opposite. There is no corresponding civil liability *because* the HRA supposedly fills the gaps.[45]

COUNTERING THE POLICY ARGUMENTS

It is, of course, equally arguable – on policy grounds – that where the police have actual or constructive knowledge of a particular victim's situation they *should* owe a duty of care to individuals whom they fail to protect.[46] First, victim-survivors of domestic abuse, like those of image-based sexual abuse, ought to be able to harness the power of civil law to take control, and seek redress from those they rely on and who let them down. The difference here is that the police are not the perpetrators, but merely a vehicle through which abuse by a third party has been allowed to occur or continue. Second, the societal harm of domestic abuse must be tackled by all means possible. This outweighs concerns about 'defensive policing' or that potential liability would divert resources better spent elsewhere.[47] In fact, if 'defensive policing' led to increased efficiency – and in turn saved just one future victim from harm (and hopefully many more) – that would be no bad thing.

In the same vein the much-feared 'floodgates' of multiple claims might be controlled through a varied *standard* of care. Thus, while when the police have knowledge of a person at risk of domestic abuse a duty would be owed (with the concomitant changes in attitude and behaviour this ought to bring about), to establish *liability* claimants would need to show that the actions of the police were *so* careless in nature that they fell below the standard expected.

Indeed, none of the usually stated policy considerations used to justify denying a duty should outweigh a victim-survivor's ability to seek individual redress, in the context of police failure *by their own negligence* to prevent domestic abuse. Feminist legal scholars have long argued that hidden among the common law rules – and their apparent neutrality – are examples of tort law's failure to recognise certain harms.[48] When police failures result in certain groups of claimants finding it hard or impossible to succeed (despite evident gross negligence), because of the very nature of the harm suffered, it is time to seriously interrogate the judges' reasoning.

---

[45] At paras 125–128. Lord Hoffmann was of the same view in relation to invasions of privacy – the HRA would 'fill the gaps' left by the common law (*Wainwright v Home Office* [2003] UKHL 53) – yet this has proved not to be the case.

[46] See *Smith v Chief Constable of Sussex Police* [2008] UKHL 50 – where it was the investigating officers' own failures that led to the lack of knowledge, such as in not filing reports that could be linked to previous events.

[47] On the rejection of the defensive policing and resource diversion arguments, see Stelios Tofaris and Sandy Steel, 'Negligence liability for omissions and the police' (2016) 75(1) *Cambridge Law Journal* 128, 134–136.

[48] See, e.g., Joanne Conaghan, 'Law, harm and redress: A feminist perspective' (2002) 22(3) *Legal Studies* 319.

Nor it is enough to rely on the HRA to fill the gaps. Though it has opened some avenues into police accountability, it does not do enough. Rather, we think that a common law duty should operate alongside the HRA duties in respect of the police, where the required level of proximity is established. Here we are in agreement with Lady Hale's reasoning (in dissent) in *Michael*:

> It is difficult indeed to see how recognising the possibility of such claims could make the task of policing any more difficult than it already is. It might conceivably, however, lead to some much-needed improvements in their response to threats of serious domestic abuse.[49]

CONCLUSION

While there is some evidence of the adaptability of tort law to gendered harms, the continued absence, inaccessibility or denial of effective civil remedies is deeply problematic. On an individual level it leaves serious wrongs *un*righted. On a societal level, it gives credence to those who view the harms of domestic and sexual abuse as lesser, private, unknown, unreachable. Without doubt tort law could – and should – be utilised to provide victim-survivors of image-based sexual abuse and domestic abuse (as well as other forms of sexual violence and abuse) with a fruitful avenue for redress. All we need now are some imaginative tort lawyers to make it happen.

Postscript Twice in this chapter we refer to the Court of Appeal decision in *Commissioner of Police of the Metropolis v DSD and another* [2015] EWCA Civ 646 and its further appeal to the Supreme Court (at footnotes 29 and 44). On 21 February 2018, while we were editing the proofs, the Supreme Court refused the Metropolitan Police's appeal. Thus, the police *do* have a human rights duty to victims of behaviour (even that of a third party) covered by Article 3. In relation to this chapter, this means that victim-survivors of rape – and potentially those of domestic abuse – who are failed by incompetent policing may be able to hold the police to account. Nevertheless, as we argue, the human rights duty should run alongside a common law duty of care.

FURTHER READING

Kirsty Horsey, 'Trust in the police? Police negligence, invisible immunity and disadvantaged claimants' in Janice Richardson and Erika Rackley (eds), *Feminist Perspectives on Tort Law* (Routledge, 2013) pp. 80–106.

Clare McGlynn and Erika Rackley, 'Image-based sexual abuse' (2017) 37 *Oxford Journal of Legal Studies* 1.

Janice Richardson, 'If I cannot have her everybody can: Sexual disclosure and privacy law' in Janice Richardson and Erika Rackley (eds), *Feminist Perspectives on Tort Law* (Routledge, 2013) pp. 145–162.

Stelios Tofaris and Sandy Steel, 'Negligence liability for omissions and the police' (2016) 75(1) *Cambridge Law Journal* 128.

---

[49] at para. 198.

CHAPTER 3

Public Law

Harriet Samuels

Constitutional and administrative law has been a remarkably closed world to feminist critique and very few of the traditional textbooks consider issues of equality and non-discrimination. Perhaps this is not surprising given that the leading scholar on the British constitution, A.V. Dicey – whose work still dominates most public law syllabuses – was actively against female suffrage![1] In public law textbooks, women's struggles for the vote and for equal representation in key institutions are rarely considered worthy of mention.

Today, however, there exists an evolving scholarship on feminism and public law that engages with the key areas of constitutional, administrative and human rights laws. This is partly in recognition of the fact that constitutional law, and public law in general, provide a framework for much of the legal system, and that, if feminists are to transform law, they must consider the means by which the constitution shapes the law.[2] The United Kingdom has no written constitution and this has meant that constitutional values such as equality are not explicitly written down in one foundational document. Feminists should question whether a written constitution or a future British Bill of Rights might be an opportunity to press for more effective guarantees of equality. Public law raises questions of institutional legitimacy, participation, rights and responsibilities, and for too long feminist critiques have been absent. This chapter gives two examples of where feminists offer a different perspective on equality: judicial review and human rights.

Debate 1
Is Parliament truly representative, and should it be?

The composition of Parliament (the House of Commons and the House of Lords) is one of the subjects studied in depth in constitutional law. One area

---

[1] A.V. Dicey, *Letters to a Friend on Votes for Women* (Murray, 1909).
[2] Susan Millns and Noel Whitty (eds), *Feminist Perspectives on Public Law* (Cavendish, 1999) and Beverley Baines, Daphne Barak-Erez and Tsvi Kahana (eds), *Feminist Constitutionalism: Global Perspectives* (Cambridge University Press, 2012).

neglected by constitutional scholars is its representativeness. Women have been able to stand for election in the House of Commons since 1918 but, despite constituting 50.8 per cent of the population, women made up only 32 per cent of members of Parliament (MPs) returned to the House of Commons after the 2017 election. This figure is regarded as a historic high. Only 26 per cent of the members of the appointed House of Lords are women, while the numbers of women in the devolved legislatures are as follows: 35 per cent of members of the Scottish Parliament, 42 per cent of the Welsh Assembly and 30 per cent of the Northern Ireland Assembly. Clearly, then, women are under-represented in all our legislative institutions. The discussion here will focus on the national democratically elected House of Commons.

Members of the House of Commons are currently elected for five-year terms using the first-past-the-post electoral system whereby the country is divided into 650 constituencies, each returning a single MP.[3] This is different from the various kinds of proportional representation practised in other countries and in the devolved legislatures. Most MPs are members of political parties, first chosen as candidates by their local constituency by various methods, depending on the political party. They have then to go on to win their seat in an election against candidates from other political parties. The importance of political parties in choosing candidates in the UK system has meant there has been a focus on ensuring that they encourage the selection of women. It is only if women are chosen as candidates by political parties that they can be elected as MPs.

Internationally the under-representation of women has been recognised as a problem and various methods have been adopted to address it.[4] Constitutional quotas provide that a certain number of seats in the legislature must be reserved for women and that the electoral system is engineered to provide this outcome.[5] Alternatively, legislative quotas can be used that require all political parties to put forward a set number of candidates for election. For example, it might be mandated that 25–50 per cent of candidates must be women. The quotas are implemented by legislation, and the exact mechanism will depend on the political system. Party quotas are similar to legislative quotas in that they rely on political parties to field a set number of female candidates for election. However, unlike legislative quotas, individual political parties adopt them voluntarily.[6] These methods are forms of positive discrimination which means that an under-represented or minority group is favoured in, for example, education or employment, to make up for past discrimination. This is different from

---

[3] Parliamentary Constituencies Act 1986. But see the Parliamentary Voting System and Constituency Act 2011.

[4] See UN Women, *Facts and Figures: Leadership and Political Participation, Women in Parliaments*, www.unwomen.org/en/what-we-do/leadership-and-political-participation/facts-and-figures, accessed 28 February 2017.

[5] Mona Lena Krook, *Quotas for Women in Politics* (Oxford University Press, 2009).

[6] Susan Franceschet, Drude Dahlerup, Mona Lena Krook and Jennifer M. Piscopo (eds), *The Impact of Gender Quotas* (Oxford University Press, 2012) p. 5.

positive action where a minority or under-represented group might be targeted for inclusion by special training or advertising for a position, but it is not permitted to favour a member of an under-represented group over anyone else when conferring a benefit such as a job or university place.

Most political parties in the UK have made some effort to increase the proportion of women candidates by adopting voluntary measures such as mentoring and training. However, the Labour Party has made the most far-reaching attempt to address gender inequality by its use of all-women shortlists (AWS). The Labour Party adopted this policy for various reasons, including the disappointment that few women MPs (14 per cent of all Labour MPs) were elected in the 1992 general election won by the Conservatives, the example of the adoption of quotas in other countries and the hope that fielding more women candidates would persuade women to vote Labour in the 1997 general election.[7]

AWS requires a constituency selecting a candidate to stand at the next general election to consider *only* women for the position. The women are interviewed by the local party and go through the arduous selection process, and one woman is chosen from the list to be the candidate. The Labour Party applied this policy to half of the *winnable* seats it was going to contest in 1997. This was important because in the past women had often been chosen for seats where the Labour Party had little chance of winning, and so even if there was an increase in the number of women candidates it was unlikely to affect the gender ratio in Parliament. The implementation of AWS was discontinued in 1996 when there was a successful challenge to the policy on the grounds that it violated the Sex Discrimination Act 1975.[8] Nevertheless, as a result of the policy a substantial number of constituencies had already chosen women candidates to contest the 1997 general election. Consequently, there were a record number of women MPs elected in 1997 when Labour was returned to government with a landslide victory. The number of Labour women MPs almost trebled from 37 to 101.[9] AWS were not used by Labour in the 2001 election and the number of women MPs decreased slightly. This provided the impetus for the enactment of the Sex Discrimination (Election Candidates) Act 2002, which exempted the selection of candidates by political parties from the Sex Discrimination Act 1975.[10] In effect, this permitted, but did not compel, political parties to positively discriminate in favour of women when they selected candidates allowing mechanisms such as AWS. This legislation was due to expire in 2015, as unusually it has a 'sunset' clause. However, as equal representation had not been achieved by 2015 the provision will now remain in force until 2030.[11]

---

[7] Judith Squires, 'Quotas for women: Fair representation?' (1996) 49 *Parliamentary Affairs* 708.

[8] *Jepson and Dyas Elliott v The Labour Party and Others* [1996] IRLR 166.

[9] Maria Eagle and Joni Lovenduski, *High Time or High Tide for Labour Women* (London: Fabian Society, 1998) p. 4.

[10] These provisions are now in the Equality Act s. 104.

[11] Equality Act s. 105.

Other political parties have taken steps to improve gender diversity. These steps have been voluntary and stopped short of quotas. However, it has been reported that the Liberal Democrats and the Scottish National Party (SNP) have amended their procedures to allow the use of AWS.[12] The Conservative Party has rejected using AWS but adopted various other measures – for example, it has undertaken a mentoring and training programme run by the Conservative Women's Organisation and Women 2 Win. The number of women Conservative MPs increased from 48 in 2010 to 64 in 2015. This increase from 15 to 19 per cent represented a significant advance for the Conservative Party.[13] By using AWS the Labour Party has ensured that 43 per cent of its MPs are women but this falls short of its ambition to achieve 50 per cent.[14] A report of the House of Commons Women and Equalities Committee noted the effectiveness of AWS:

> The evidence demonstrates that the use of all-women shortlists has been very effective in increasing the number of women MPs. We support the continued use of all-women shortlists by political parties, and welcome the decision taken by the SNP and the Liberal Democrats to join the Labour Party in using them as part of their processes for selecting parliamentary candidates.[15]

Given this evidence, should all political parties be compelled to use AWS, and what are the arguments for and against requiring political parties to adopt AWS?

A central reason for improving the gender balance in Parliament is the injustice done to women by their exclusion from the most crucial political forum in the United Kingdom.[16] The argument is that it is simply unfair that men should dominate Parliament. As Phillips states, this 'presents gender parity as a straightforward matter of justice: that it is patently and grotesquely unfair for men to monopolise representation'.[17] A second reason targets diversity and suggests that women will bring their own perspectives and way of working to Parliament, and that this might change the nature of politics; for example, women might be more consensual and less confrontational in their approach.[18] This is reinforced by research that indicates that women may see themselves as engaging in a different style of politics even though this is outwardly hard to measure.[19] It may also be necessary to examine whether there

---

[12] House of Commons Women and Equalities Committee on *Women in the House of Commons after the 2020 Election*, January 2017, HC 360, para. 61.
[13] Fawcett Society, 'Women in the 2015 General Election', www.fawcettsociety.org.uk/Blog/women-2015-general-election, accessed 8 December 2017.
[14] Ibid.
[15] House of Commons Women and Equalities Committee (n. 12) para. 99.
[16] Squires (n. 7).
[17] Anne Phillips, *The Politics of Presence* (Oxford University Press, 1998) p. 63.
[18] Squires (n. 7).
[19] Sarah Childs, 'A feminised style of politics? Women MPs in the House of Commons' (2004) *BJIP* 14. See also Stephanie Jones, Nickie Charles, Charlotte Aull Davies, 'Transforming masculinist political cultures?' (2009) 2 *Sociological Research Online*, www.socresonline.org.uk/14/2/1.html, accessed 30 November 2017.

are institutional barriers to tackle if a feminised politics is going to material-ise. Childs, for example, found that many of the Labour women MPs who were elected for the first time in 1997 thought that the traditions and func-tions of the House of Commons made it hard for women to practise a more collaborative politics.[20] So it is not enough for women to be present; it is also important to tackle these cultural and institutional obstacles if change is to be transformative. The third argument is that women are needed to act as role models to break the mould of male politics, and shatter the idea that politi-cians are male. So women's presence is partly symbolic in demonstrating that women can be successful MPs. This can provide momentum and encourage other women to enter politics. The fourth argument centres on representa-tiveness and democracy. It is claimed that men cannot adequately represent women as they have different interests and life experiences. If Parliament is to represent the society around it and take account of different interests then women need to be present. Otherwise, issues such as domestic violence, rape and childcare will be viewed from a male point of view or may not be on the political agenda at all.

Many of the objections to quotas, especially compulsory quotas, are rooted in arguments against reverse or positive discrimination. Positive discrimination is recognised as an effective means to allow minority and under-represented groups to achieve substantive equality, but many people are hostile to such methods because they discriminate against those who do not belong to the under-represented group and are seen as violating the principle of meritocracy, whereby the best-qualified or best-suited individual should succeed. These arguments are usually made in relation to employment and education, but can also be applied to the quotas debate. However, the points made about the nature of representation are particular to the discussion about elected representatives.

Those who object to quotas for the election of women MPs often state that they are patronising and undermine the principle of equality. They worry that women may be seen as having special privileges rather than having attained their seat in Parliament on their own merits. For example, the Labour MPs newly elected in 1997 were often referred to as Blair's Babes, implying that they were dependent on the leader Tony Blair for their position, and were not good enough to get elected without special help. Other objections are that AWS can lead to a backlash against women – as happened, for instance, with the case brought by other potential male Labour candidates – and that it takes autonomy away from local political parties.[21] However, these arguments ignore the institutional barriers that women face that make it difficult for them to be selected. Women may be reluctant to put themselves forward because they view Parliament and its working style as masculine – as suggested by the hours that MPs work and the frequent need to travel long distances or live away from home for most of the week, making it hard to balance work and family life.

[20] Childs (ibid. 14).
[21] Eagle and Lovenduski (n. 9).

Women may also face prejudice and sexual harassment and be subject to sexist abuse on social media. The murder of MP Jo Cox in 2016 is a reminder that violence against women representatives can occur in the UK.[22]

In response to the arguments about merit, Murray observes:

> No-one likes to be called a 'quota woman'. Everyone wants to say they made it on their own. But it's gender inequality and discrimination that are the problem, not quotas. It's even more patronising to exclude women and then blame them for their own exclusion. At least quotas give women the chance to prove that they should have been there all along.[23]

Other arguments against AWS require us to look more closely at what we mean by the idea of representation. When MPs are elected they are often expected to represent the people in a geographically defined area – their constituency – and also their political party. It is often said that MPs are not delegates of their constituents but have to follow their own notion of what is in the nation's interest.[24] These principles also apply to women MPs, but are they also required to represent women's interests? This is problematic as it might lead to women MPs becoming pigeon-holed, and only being concerned with so-called soft issues. This might prevent them from achieving in areas such as finance and foreign affairs. The expectations about women having to push a female agenda can also be criticised for being essentialist (that is, assuming that women always have common interests). The reality is that women from different social backgrounds and ethnicities may have needs that cannot be represented by any one woman. In addition, it has also been argued that there are many different groups who are insufficiently represented; for example, there are disparities in terms of ethnicity, religion and age. Why should women be singled out for special treatment? One response might be to point out that the partial success of the measures to increase female representation has drawn attention to the under-representation of black, Asian and minority ethnic (BAME) communities. The Speaker's Conference, for example, recommended amendment of the law to permit all-black shortlists.[25] It may be that the use of AWS and increased representation for women will energise those calling for greater ethnic diversity.

In sum, despite the many doubts about the use of quotas, there is a consensus that the under-representation of women in the House of Commons is

[22] House of Commons Women and Equalities Committee (n. 12) p. 3.

[23] Rainbow Murray, 'The Great Quotas Debate', https://www.fawcettsociety.org.uk/Blog/great-quotas-debate, accessed 8 December 2017.

[24] For a discussion of notions of representation, see Squires (n. 7) and Phillips (n. 17).

[25] House of Commons, *Speaker's Conference on Parliamentary Representation*, HC 2391-1, 11 January 2010, para. 149. For a discussion of some of these issues and an account of the Labour Party's effort to increase the number of BAME MPs, see Mona Lena Krook and Mary K. Nugent, 'Intersectional institutions: Representing women and ethnic minorities in the Labour Party' (2016) 22 *Party Politics* 620.

a problem. For some the problem is so serious that it requires firm action such as AWS. Others recognise the need for change but prefer to proceed slowly using positive action such as mentoring and training so that more women come forward and want to be candidates.

Debate 2

Does public interest litigation work for women?

Public interest litigation is where an individual case is brought not just to settle the dispute between the parties, but to challenge a policy or decision that has wider public interest implications. Some feminists would argue that using the law in this way is risky because judges may be hostile and set unhelpful precedents, it is expensive to bring cases and it would be better for feminists to focus their energies on achieving change through political lobbying and pressure.[26] There are also those public law theorists who argue that this type of litigation politicises the law and risks undermining law's impartiality.[27]

The courts have developed the principles of administrative law in cases brought against public authorities, usually by judicial review. These include the basic principles of administrative fairness such as, for instance, that administrators must abide by the rules of natural justice by listening to both sides in a dispute and act without bias,[28] that discretionary powers in a statute must not be exercised unreasonably, and that the decision maker must act consistently with the statutory purpose as well as taking into account only the relevant factors and excluding from her mind any irrelevant matters.[29] Feminists have pointed out that judges have adopted traditional views of women's functions and have failed to develop the common law to include substantive principles of equality. The values they adopt often determine how they interpret the law and whether they are willing to uphold a decision or to intervene and hold a decision to be unlawful.[30] One instance of this is the historic case of *Roberts v Hopwood* where Poplar Borough Council exercised its discretion to pay such wages 'as it thought fit' to provide its workers with a minimum wage and equal pay to men and women.[31] The House of Lords held that the council

---

[26] For a critique of the use of public interest law generally as a form of progressive politics, see Wendy Brown and Janet Halley (eds), *Left Legalism/Left Critique* (Duke University Press, 2002).

[27] For a discussion of this issue see Carol Harlow and Richard Rawlings, *Pressure through Law* (Routledge, 1992). For a discussion on the law and politics debate see Martin Loughlin, *The Idea of Public Law* (Oxford University Press, 2003).

[28] *Ridge v Baldwin* [1964] AC 40.

[29] *Padfield v Minister for Agriculture, Fisheries and Food* [1968] AC 997.

[30] Mary Jane Mossman, 'Feminism and legal method: The difference it makes' (1987) *Wisconsin Women's Law Journal* 147.

[31] *Roberts v Hopwood* [1925] AC 578. See s. 62 of the Metropolis Management Act of 1855.

had abused its powers by not paying the market rate. Lord Atkinson famously stated that the council had acted unlawfully by:

> allowing themselves to be guided … by some eccentric principles of socialistic philanthropy, or by a feminist ambition to secure the equality of the sexes in the matter of wages in the world of labour.[32]

Judges displayed similar attitudes towards women in a series of challenges by women teachers to the marriage bar in the 1920s. The courts in *Short v Poole Corporation*, for instance, upheld local authorities' use of their statutory discretion to appoint and remove teachers and to dismiss married teachers 'as they thought fit'.[33] The court accepted, as reasonable and relevant, the local authority's view that married women could not be effective teachers as their primary duty was to their family, and that married women could depend on their husband financially.

While these cases would be decided differently today, owing to hard-won equality and non-discrimination reforms, they alert us to the means by which judges can use their own values in public law cases and allow so-called 'common sense' ideas to develop, which actually represent their own or society's prejudices. They also make us aware of the flexibility of the law, and for some feminists this opens up the possibility of using feminist legal methods to achieve outcomes that are more favourable to women.[34] There are occasions when feminists have used these administrative law principles to good effect. One recent example was Rights of Women's judicial review challenge to the Ministry of Justice's regulations made under the Legal Aid, Sentencing and Punishment of Offenders Act 2012 (LASPO).[35] LASPO, in accordance with the government's austerity agenda, severely restricted the availability of Legal Aid but made an exception for victims of domestic violence seeking protection orders or for family law proceedings. The regulations provided that, as well as the typical merits-based and financial criteria, there must be documentary evidence of domestic violence within the last 24 months before the application. This disadvantaged women who had not reported the domestic violence or where the perpetrator had been in prison. Here the court used common law principles to hold that the regulations frustrated the purpose of the legislation, which was to provide Legal Aid for women who had suffered from domestic violence, and were therefore ultra vires.

Feminist engagement in judicial review has had varying results. Historically, administrative law has not tackled the issue of discrimination and has failed to develop principles of equality, forcing legislation to fill this gap. The introduction

---

[32] Ibid. 594.

[33] 1926 ch. 66. See Education Act 1921, sections 17 and 148.

[34] See for example Katharine Bartlett, 'Feminist legal methods' (1990) *Harvard Law Review* 829 and Rosemary Hunter, 'Can feminist judges make a difference?' (2008) *International Journal of the Legal Profession* 7.

[35] *R (Rights of Women) v The Lord Chancellor* [2016] EWCA Civ 91.

of the statutory equalities duties now consolidated in section 149 Equality Act 2010 requires public authorities to pay 'due regard' to the need to eliminate discrimination, advance equality of opportunity and foster good relations within and between those in protected categories. It applies to all of the protected categories listed in section 149 (7), which include age, disability, gender reassignment, pregnancy and maternity, race, religion or belief, sex and sexual orientation.[36] While this is a welcome attempt to mainstream equality issues into the work of public authorities, the most controversial legislation, and the one focused on here, is the Human Rights Act 1998 (HRA). This raises the issue of the utility of rights-based litigation to progress gender justice and has been the subject of much feminist discussion.

Some feminists see rights as problematic because they are balanced against other rights and interests and women's rights often lose out.[37] This is exemplified by the judgment in *R v A (no. 2)*, one of the early HRA cases. The House of Lords used the strong interpretive provisions in section 3 (1) of the HRA that require it, so far as possible, to read and give effect to legislation consistently with Convention rights, to effectively neutralise the rape shield laws on the grounds that they deprived the defendant of a fair trial contrary to Article 6.[38] Other feminists are more optimistic about the use of the HRA seeing the strategic value of rights.[39] They point to the recognition by the European Court of Human Rights that rape can be a form of torture or inhuman and degrading treatment under Article 3 and that the state has been held to be liable for failure to deal effectively with forms of gender-based violence such as domestic violence.[40]

The dilemmas of relying on human rights has been exposed by recent attempts to use the HRA 1998 to judicially review the government's austerity policy and the cuts in welfare benefits. Article 14 of the European Convention on Human Rights, which provides for freedom from discrimination, has been deployed to argue that two of the government's most contested policies in relation to the benefits cap and the bedroom tax discriminate against women. Article 14 is not a freestanding equality clause, and is more limited as it has to be used in conjunction with another article in the Convention. This is because it provides for non-discrimination in the enjoyment of the rights and freedoms in the Convention. The European Court of Human Rights has been slow to develop Article 14, although in recent years the case law shows a strengthening of the

[36] See generally Sandra Fredman, 'The public sector equality duty' (2011) *Industrial Law Journal* 405.
[37] Aileen McColgan, *Women Under the Law: The False Promise of Human Rights* (Longman, 2000).
[38] [2002] 1 AC 45.
[39] Stephanie Palmer, 'Feminism and the promise of human rights: Possibilities and paradoxes' in Susan James and Stephanie Palmer (eds), *Visible Women: Essays on Feminist Legal Theory and Political Philosophy* (Hart, 2002) pp. 91–111.
[40] Ibid. See also Ronagh McQuigg, 'Domestic violence as a human rights issue: Rumor v Italy' (2015) *European Journal of International Law* 1009 and Joanne Conaghan, 'Extending the reach of human rights to encompass victims of rape: *M.C. v. Bulgaria*' (2005) *Feminist Legal Studies* 155. See further *Commissioner of Police of the Metropolis v DSD & Another* [2018] UKSC 11.

right.[41] While the UK courts have recognised the importance of the principles of equality introduced by Article 14 they have been reluctant to apply it vigorously. This is often because the decisions involve social and economic rights where the courts are reticent to intervene. The courts will only hold such provisions in conflict with Article 14 where the government policy was 'manifestly without reasonable foundation',[42] a stricter test than in other types of human rights cases.

The benefits cap limits the amount that a family can receive in welfare payments and has a disproportionate impact on single parents who are largely women. The Supreme Court declined in its decision in *R (on the application of SG and others) v Secretary of State for Work and Pensions* to find that this was a breach of Article 14.[43] The majority accepted the government's argument that the indirect sex discrimination was justified on the grounds that it was intended to reduce public expenditure and to safeguard the economic well-being of the country. Similarly, in *R (A) v Secretary of State for Work and Pensions* a claimant who had suffered gender-based violence failed in a challenge to the government's bedroom tax,[44] according to which residents of social housing had to pay an increased rent if they occupied a property with more bedrooms than deemed to be necessary by the housing regulations. The claimant was part of a sanctuary scheme whereby her home was specially adapted in the event of her being violently attacked by an ex-partner. She argued that she should not be compelled to move because of the bedroom tax and that an exception should be made for sanctuary schemes in the housing regulations. The majority of the Supreme Court disagreed, holding that the tax was not discriminatory because it was not manifestly without reasonable foundation to deal with cases by a general provision rather than on an individual basis.

It is interesting that in both the bedroom tax and benefit cap cases Lady Hale, the only woman then sitting in the Supreme Court, dissented. Unlike the majority in the bedroom tax case, she held that the government had a positive duty to protect women against gender-based violence and that there should have been an exception to this effect in the housing regulations.[45] Similarly, in relation to the benefit cap Lady Hale stressed that, although social and economic policy was a matter for government, the courts had a constitutional responsibility to scrutinise decisions to ensure there was no unjustified sex discrimination.[46] She found that the way that the benefit cap had been

---

[41] Sandra Fredman, 'Emerging from the shadows: Substantive equality and Article 14 of the European Convention on Human Rights' (2016) 16 *Human Rights Law Review* 273.

[42] *Humphreys v The Commissioners for Her Majesty's Revenue and Customs* [2012] UKSC 18.

[43] [2015] UKSC 16. Hereafter the *Benefits Cap* case.

[44] The *R (A) v Secretary of State for Work and Pensions* case was joined with several other cases that relied on disability discrimination. See *R (MA and others) v Secretary of State for Work and Pensions and R (Rutherford and others) v Secretary of State for Work and Pensions.* The court gave one judgment reported at [2016] UKSC 58. Some of these cases were successful. Hereafter referred to as the *Bedroom Tax* cases.

[45] The *Bedroom Tax* cases n. 44, at paras 72–78.

[46] The *Benefits Cap* case n. 43, at para. 160.

implemented was not a proportionate means of achieving the government's aim of saving money.

These human rights cases may have had disappointing results for the claimants, and for some feminists demonstrate the futility of human rights. But it is also argued that Lady Hale's dissenting judgments show that there are alternative interpretations of the law and that in time these may be adopted by other judges. Rather than giving up on rights, it may be argued that feminists should be instrumental in using them to expose the gendered nature of government policy and reconstructing and adapting rights so that they can be used to promote equality and challenge discrimination.

CONCLUSION

Feminist contributions to public law have the potential to force a rethink of issues of participation and diversity that tend to be sidelined by more traditional public law concerns. The representation of women and minorities matters and deserves to be treated as a mainstream topic by constitutional law scholarship. Similarly, the common law principles of judicial review need to be firmly scrutinised and their gendered assumptions exposed where necessary. The debate on the HRA and how rights might be used to progress gender justice will be enriched by greater feminist analysis. The examination of the two debates in this chapter has shown that feminist methods can enhance constitutional discussion on rights, the law/politics boundary and political representation.

FURTHER READING

Beverley Baines, Daphne Barak-Erez and Tsvi Kahana (eds), *Feminist Constitutionalism: Global Perspectives* (Cambridge University Press, 2012).

Mona Lena Krook, *Quotas for Women in Politics* (Oxford University Press, 2009).

Susan Millns and Noel Whitty (eds), *Feminist Perspectives on Public Law* (Cavendish, 1999).

CHAPTER 4

Criminal Law

Caroline Derry

All law aims to regulate our behaviour and conduct towards each other, but the criminal law has a uniquely coercive role. It defines behaviour that is not allowed; if a person breaches its rules, then they may be subjected to punishment including permanent loss of liberty. Given such serious consequences, behaviour ought not to be criminalised without strong justification, but there is no consensus on what does justify making something a crime. For example, the liberal harm principle asserts that state power should only be exercised against the individual 'to prevent harm to others', not to enforce notions of morality.[1] By contrast, Lord Devlin argued that the purpose of criminal law is precisely to protect a shared morality which binds the community together.[2] In practice, the criminal law is based on a mixture of both approaches: inevitably, it reflects and reinforces social norms.

The criminal law is, on its face, largely gender-neutral. (There are exceptions: for example, one must have a penis to commit rape as a principal, and must give birth in order to commit infanticide.) However, its practical impact is often highly dependent upon the genders of the parties: in a profoundly gendered society, the criminal law cannot escape gendered assumptions and controversies. We will consider two very different debates which show the extent to which gender is an issue in criminal law. Both focus on areas where the law has been reformed in response to feminist criticisms, but the controversy has not gone away.

Debate 1

Is consent in sexual offences adequately defined?

Section 74 of the Sexual Offences Act 2003 defines consent as where a person 'agrees by choice, and has the freedom and capacity to make that choice'. Thus, legal consent requires not only factual consent (the complainant 'agrees'), but

---

[1] John Stuart Mill, *On Liberty* (Wordsworth Classics, 1996) p. 13.
[2] Patrick Devlin, *The Enforcement of Morals* (Oxford University Press, 1965).

also that the agreement is 'by choice', which needs 'freedom and capacity'.[3] There is no further definition of these terms, although section 75 sets out a list of situations in which the law presumes that there is no consent unless the defendant can show otherwise. These include, among others, circumstances where violence was used or threatened, or where the defendant was asleep or unconscious, or had without her consent taken a substance capable of stupefying or overpowering her. Section 76 creates two irrebuttable presumptions, which apply where the defendant intentionally deceived the complainant about the nature or purpose of the act, or intentionally impersonated a person known personally to her. In these situations, there is legally no consent; the defendant cannot rebut the presumption.[4]

IS THE DEFINITION ADEQUATE?

The overwhelming majority of sexual offences are committed by men[5] and the overwhelming majority of complainants are women.[6] Further, before 2003, criminal law on sexual offences was highly gender-specific. For example, indecent assault on a female and indecent assault on a male were separate offences with different sentences. Until section 142 Criminal Justice and Public Order Act 1994 amended the definition, only women could be victims of rape. Until 1967 all sexual contact between men, with or without consent, was illegal; full legal equality was only achieved under the 2003 Act. Thus, until relatively recently, lack of consent did not have to be proved where both accused and complainant were male. As a result, the law on consent has largely developed in the context of offences committed by males against female victims. Consequently, myths and stereotypes about male and female behaviour became embedded in the law. The definition of consent in the 2003 Act attempts to move away from these, but how far has it been successful? We will test this by focusing on one controversial situation, the criminal courts' approach to drunken consent.

ADVANTAGES OF THE DEFINITION

Before 2003, there was no statutory definition of consent for sexual offences. Instead, a definition was found in cases such as *Olugboja* [1982] QB 323, in which Dunn LJ asserted that consent included 'reluctant acquiescence' and that

---

[3] For contrasting legal approaches to consent, see 'Health Law, Medical Law and Ethics' (Chapter 11) and 'Law and Literature/Literary Jurisprudence' (Chapter 16).

[4] On fraudulent consent, see Jonathan Herring, *Great Debates in Criminal Law* (Palgrave, 3rd edn, 2015) Chapter 5.

[5] In 2011, 98.2 per cent of defendants in sexual offences cases were males (Ministry of Justice, Home Office and the Office for National Statistics, *An Overview of Sexual Offending in England and Wales*, 10 January 2013, pp. 32–33).

[6] In 2011, 14,767 rapes of a female were reported to police, and 1,274 rapes of a male. 19,780 sexual assaults on a female were reported, and 2,273 on a male (*Overview of Sexual Offending* (n. 5) p. 20).

'every consent involves a submission, but it by no means follows that a mere submission involves consent'.[7] Although this was an improvement on earlier definitions requiring 'force, fear or fraud',[8] the *Olugboja* formulation was problematic. Its model of men seeking sex and women submitting to it assumed that men are sexually active and dominant, while women are sexually passive and submissive; that both are heterosexual; and that sex is something men choose and women are persuaded to accept. Not only is that a highly inaccurate description of human sexuality, but it does not recognise the possibility of women being equal, active partners.

The new emphasis upon consent as a positive act, 'agreement by choice', is a significant improvement. The terms used also allow more flexibility to courts, which Sjölin suggests they value because '[s]exual relations are an area of infinite variety and choice in the modern age'.[9]

One circumstance where the definition has come under scrutiny is where the complainant was drunk at the time of the sexual act. Can a seriously intoxicated person have 'capacity' to 'agree by choice'? We know that they cannot if they are actually unconscious, or if the intoxicants were administered without their consent, since these situations give rise to a rebuttable presumption;[10] but at what point does their intoxication remove their ability to give legal consent? The courts are being asked to balance competing concerns: on the one hand, an intoxicated person may be unable to make any decision or any rational one, and may be vulnerable because of their condition. On the other, autonomy includes the ability to choose to have drunken sex, and would be undermined by paternalistic rules which go too far in limiting the legal ability to consent.

The Court of Appeal aimed for a pragmatic response to this situation in *Bree* [2007] EWCA Crim 804. The accused and complainant had been drinking heavily together before going to her flat, where she was repeatedly sick in the shower and the accused looked after her. At some later point, by her account, she woke up on her bed to find the accused having sex with her; she did not consent, although her memory of the night was 'patchy'. The accused claimed that she was lucid enough to consent, and had done so. In his summing up, the judge gave the statutory definition of consent but did not offer any guidance on the effect of self-induced intoxication. The Court of Appeal confirmed that '"capacity" is integral to the concept of "choice", and therefore to "consent"': if the complainant had not had capacity to consent then this would be rape (subject to the defendant's mens rea).[11] However, if she had capacity and chose – albeit drunkenly – to consent then that would not be rape. *Bree* was emphatic that section 74 'provides a clear definition of "consent" for the

---

[7] At pp. 331–332.
[8] See, for example, Lord Hailsham in *DPP v Morgan* [1976] AC 182 at 210.
[9] Catarina Sjölin, 'Ten years on: Consent under the Sexual Offences Act 2003' (2015) *Journal of Criminal Law* 20, 27.
[10] Section 75(2)(d) and (f).
[11] *Bree* [2007] EWCA Crim 804, para. 23.

purposes of the law of rape and, by defining it with reference to "capacity to make that choice", sufficiently addresses the issue of consent in the context of voluntary consumption of alcohol by the complainant'.[12]

CRITICISMS OF THE DEFINITION

Not all critics agree that section 74 offers a sufficient and appropriate definition of consent. The first problem is that key terms including 'choice', 'freedom' and 'capacity' are not defined by the statute. For example, we never have absolute freedom, so what level of free choice is required here? Capacity poses similar issues: for example, intoxication has a whole spectrum of effects, so at what point does the complainant lose the capacity to consent? It is hard to disagree with Ashworth and Temkin that '"freedom" and "choice" are ideas which raise philosophical issues of such complexity as to be ill-suited to the needs of criminal justice'.[13]

Despite these difficulties, the courts have been reluctant to expand upon the meaning of these terms. Indeed, Sjölin suggests that, in order to preserve flexibility, the courts have narrowed the application of the presumptions in sections 75 and 76, increasing reliance on section 74 even as they fail to offer juries much guidance on how to apply it.[14] In the context of intoxication and consent, section 75 applies to involuntary intoxication; but for voluntary intoxication we have only the section 74 definition. There has been little further clarification: in *Bree*, the Court of Appeal did say that the jury should be given assistance with the meaning of 'capacity', but offered scant guidance beyond saying that it will depend upon the facts of the case, and that 'capacity to consent may evaporate well before a complainant becomes unconscious'. Exactly when 'depends on the actual state of mind of the individuals involved on the particular occasion'.[15] Following *Bree*, the trial judge in *Kamki* gave a direction inviting the jury to use 'common sense', which the Court of Appeal approved.[16]

A second, related problem is that the breadth of the definition allows for a lot of variation in interpretation. One consequence is that the courts may take a more conservative view than Parliament intended, rather than fully discarding *Olugboja*'s gendered and problematic formulation of consent in terms of acquiescence or submission. Indeed, in *Bree*, Judge P echoed the judgment in *Olugboja* by stating that consent 'extends from passionate enthusiasm to

[12] Ibid. para. 36.

[13] Andrew Ashworth and Jennifer Temkin, 'The Sexual Offences Act 2003 (1): Rape, sexual assaults and the problems of consent' (2004) *Criminal Law Review* 336.

[14] Sjölin, 'Ten years on' (n. 9) 27.

[15] *Bree* (n. 11) para. 34. See further Phil Rumney and Rebecca Fenton, 'Intoxicated consent in rape: *Bree* and juror decision-making' (2008) 71 *Modern Law Review* 279.

[16] *R v Kamki* [2013] EWCA Crim 2335. For the unpredictable consequences of relying on juror 'common sense' about capacity, see Emily Finch and Vanessa E. Munro, 'Breaking boundaries? Sexual consent in the jury room' (2006) 26 *Legal Studies* 303, 314–315.

reluctant or bored acquiescence, and its absence includes quiet submission or surrender as well as determined physical resistance'.[17] *Bree* also drew an analogy between the intoxicated complainant and an intoxicated defendant: a drunken consent is still consent, just as a drunken intention is still intention.[18] However, Wallerstein points out that this analogy is inappropriate. First, consent and intention are not equivalent states of mind: for example, one can consent passively to someone else's actions, while intention relates to one's own actions. Second, the law of intoxication and mens rea is based on the idea of prior fault; but the language of fault is not appropriate to a victim, who did not cause harm to another and did not commit a wrong by getting drunk.[19]

The difficulty here is not in the definition itself so much as its implementation by the criminal justice system. The impact of myths about rape upon all levels of the system is well-documented.[20] As Lacey reminds us,

> in the absence of changes in the prosecution and trial process and in professional ethics designed to limit the impact of the most prejudicial assumptions about women's and gay sexuality, criminal law's scope for advancing progressive sexual values is circumscribed.'[21]

Thus wider cultural attitudes to sexual violence against drunken women will play a role in these cases: for example, that women who choose to get drunk bear responsibility for what happens to them.[22] Such myths too often form part of the 'common sense' *Kamki* invited juries to use. And it is not only the jury who may be affected: police, prosecutors, defence counsel and judges can all be influenced by them.

Finally, is this legal definition of consent, with its close connection to liberal ideas of individual autonomy, fundamentally problematic? First, the emphasis upon consent places too much focus on the complainant's behaviour, extending far beyond the incident itself. Second, decisions are made within a social context where patriarchal power structures create significant imbalances of power. MacKinnon argues that the law 'presents consent as free exercise of

---

[17] *Bree* (n. 11) para. 22.

[18] Ibid. para. 32.

[19] Shlomit Wallerstein, '"A drunken consent is still consent" – or is it? A critical analysis of the law on a drunken consent to sex following Bree' (2009) *Journal of Criminal Law* 318, 323–329.

[20] For example Jennifer Temkin, *Rape and the Legal Process* (Oxford University Press, 2nd edn, 2003); Jennifer Temkin, Jacqueline M. Gray and Jastine Barrett, 'Different functions of rape myth use in court: Findings from a trial observation study' (2016) *Feminist Criminology* 1; Katrin Hohl and Elisabeth Stanko, 'Complaints of rape and the criminal justice system: Fresh evidence on the attrition problem in England and Wales' (2015) 12 *European Journal of Criminology* 324.

[21] Nicola Lacey, 'Beset by boundaries: The Home Office review of sex offences' (2001) *Criminal Law Review* 3, 14.

[22] Emily Finch and Vanessa Munro, 'Juror stereotypes and blame attribution in rape cases involving intoxicants' (2005) 45 *British Journal of Criminology* 25.

sexual choice under conditions of equality of power without exposing the underlying structure of constraint and disparity'.[23] Thus some critics argue that the term 'consent' should not be central to sexual offences definitions at all.[24]

In conclusion, would a clearer definition of consent resolve these problems? It seems unlikely: the law does not operate in isolation, and rape myths and gender stereotypes continue to exert a powerful influence throughout the criminal justice system. Until wider social and cultural perceptions change, a new legal definition alone cannot resolve all the issues around consent in sexual offences cases. It can send a message, though, about what is acceptable behaviour and what is criminal; the complexities of using the criminal law to communicate such messages are considered in the next debate.

Debate 2
Should there be a specific criminal offence of forced marriage?

In 2015, the UK Government's Forced Marriage Unit (FMU) gave advice or support in 1,220 cases involving 67 different countries. Eighty per cent of cases for which it provided support involved female victims of forced marriage.[25] However, the problem is even greater than these figures suggest: the FMU acknowledges that the calls it receives are unlikely to reflect the full scale of abuse.

In English civil law, a marriage must fulfil a number of conditions in order to be valid, including that both parties consent.[26] International law also emphasises consent: Article 16(2) of the Universal Declaration of Human Rights states that '[m]arriage shall be entered into only with the free and full consent of the intending spouses'. Consent is missing in a forced marriage, either because one or both parties have been coerced into marrying, or because one or both parties lacks the capacity to consent. It is this which distinguishes forced marriages from, for example, arranged marriages which have the consent of both parties.

There are a number of remedies available in civil law. Before the marriage takes place, forced marriage protection orders can be made under section 4A of the Family Law Act 1996 (inserted by the Forced Marriage (Civil Protection) Act 2007). These orders can contain various terms, for example prohibiting the marriage itself or preventing the person being taken abroad, and breaching them is a criminal offence. After the parties are married, an application can be made for the marriage to be annulled under section 12(c) of the Matrimonial

[23] Catharine MacKinnon, *Towards a Feminist Theory of the State* (Harvard University Press, 1989) p. 175.

[24] For example, Victor Tadros, 'Rape without consent' (2006) 26 *Oxford Journal of Legal Studies*, 515.

[25] Forced Marriage Unit, *Forced Marriage Unit Statistics 2015*, 8 March 2016, https://www.gov.uk/government/uploads/system/uploads/attachment_data/file/505827/Forced_Marriage_Unit_statistics_2015.pdf, accessed 11 December 2016.

[26] Section 12(c), Matrimonial Causes Act 1973.

Causes Act 1973 if either party did not validly consent to it. A discussion of civil remedies is outside the scope of this chapter, but they have certainly not solved the issue.

There is a significant problem with forced marriage, then; and it is a gendered problem. Statistically, the victims are overwhelmingly female. The cultural context of marriage in most communities where forced marriage occurs also genders its impact. Women's behaviour is placed under particular scrutiny, and forced marriage may be used to control behaviour which is disapproved of including extra-marital sexual activity, a relationship considered undesirable, pursuing education or employment, or actions which threaten family 'honour'. The purpose of the marriage may be for the woman to become carer to a husband with significant disabilities (who is also a victim if he does not, or lacks capacity to, consent), or to the children of an earlier marriage. Women and girls also experience disproportionate consequences: their husband will have significant control over their lives, and they are likely to be expected to bear and raise children within the marriage.

THE LAW

Section 121(1) of the Anti-Social Behaviour, Crime and Policing Act 2014 created a criminal offence of 'forced marriage':

1. A person commits an offence under the law of England and Wales if he or she –
   (a) uses violence, threats or any other form of coercion for the purpose of causing another person to enter into a marriage, and
   (b) believes, or ought reasonably to believe, that the conduct may cause the other person to enter into the marriage without free and full consent.
2. In relation to a victim who lacks capacity to consent to marriage, the offence under subsection (1) is capable of being committed by any conduct carried out for the purpose of causing the victim to enter into a marriage (whether or not the conduct amounts to violence, threats or any other form of coercion).

Thus the offence is committed where the accused coerces someone into marriage, or causes a person who lacks capacity to enter into a marriage,[27] and the accused believes or ought reasonably to believe that the person may not freely consent. The marriage need not be legally binding.[28] The maximum sentence is seven years' imprisonment.

In addition, forced marriage may involve the commission of other crimes ranging from threatening behaviour, threats to kill, aggravated assault, false imprisonment or kidnap as part of the initial coercion, to rape or aggravated assault within the resulting marriage. The presence of these other crimes gives rise to a question: was a specific offence needed or desirable?

---

[27] See the discussion of the Mental Capacity Act 2006 in the 'Health Law, Medicine and Ethics' chapter (Chapter 11).
[28] Section 121(4).

WHY THE OFFENCE WAS CREATED AND WELCOMED

The offence was created in response to arguments that relying on general offences was not enough. First, it better captures the harm done to the victim than an alternative such as assault. While assault involves a single instance of injury, coercion into forced marriage involves more extensive and longer-term harm to the person. Beyond the circumstances leading to the marriage, the marital relationship itself may involve the victim losing autonomy in most or all areas of her life. Second, some forced marriages might be difficult to prosecute at all without the specific offence, particularly where the coercion is primarily emotional and psychological, sometimes over long periods of time.[29] In these cases, it may be difficult to identify an alternative criminal offence.

In addition, by having a specific offence the criminal law is giving a clear message that forced marriages are wrong. It may therefore be a deterrent to those considering forcing others into marriage: the potential shame of conviction might outweigh their motivations for coercing the victim. The offence can also serve an educational role, by clearly communicating what is not permissible behaviour.

Civil remedies are vitally important, but they also have some drawbacks which a criminal offence does not share. For example, the person at risk or someone acting on their behalf has to apply for a civil order; and the person who has been forced into a marriage must make the application for its annulment. By contrast, the criminal offence is prosecuted by the state, not the victim. Importantly, since the victim has little control over the criminal process, she may be less vulnerable to family pressure to stop her pursuing the case.[30] Jasvinder Sanghera, a survivor of attempted forced marriage whose charity Karma Nirvana has campaigned for its criminalisation, argued that convictions for forced marriage increase the likelihood of victims reporting to professionals; help to create a culture of accountability; and should not be avoided for fear of offending communities, since victims are entitled to equality under the law.[31] There is some early evidence to support this view: in the three months after the new offence came into force, the number of forced marriage protection orders granted by the civil courts increased significantly.[32]

---

[29] Home Office, *Forced Marriage – A Consultation: Summary of Responses*, June 2012, https://www.gov.uk/government/uploads/system/uploads/attachment_data/file/157837/forced-marriage-response.pdf, accessed 30 January 2018, p. 9, quoting Karma Nirvana.

[30] A similar point is made by Mohammed Mazher Idriss, 'Forced marriages – the need for criminalisation?' (2015) *Criminal Law Review* 694.

[31] Jasvinder Sanghera, 'First forced marriage prosecution: One conviction is good, but there are thousands more cases to work through', *The Independent*, 10 June 2015, http://www.independent.co.uk/voices/comment/first-forced-marriage-prosecution-one-conviction-is-good-but-there-are-thousands-more-cases-to-work-10311912.html, accessed 11 December 2016.

[32] Ruth Gaffney-Rhys, 'Criminalisation of forced marriage: One year on' (2015) *Family Law* 1378.

Why the Offence was Opposed

Given the potential benefits of the offence, why was there opposition to it? One key disadvantage is that if it is seen as a criminal wrong then people may be deterred from reporting their concerns. They must balance their desire to stop the marriage with their reluctance to see family members or friends prosecuted. They must also face giving evidence in a public trial, rather than a private family court hearing.[33] These can be significant factors for victims: despite the coercion they are experiencing, they may not want to see their parents punished,[34] or they may fear ostracism or retaliation if family members are imprisoned. In addition, the practice could be driven further underground, with children being taken abroad at a younger age to be forced into marriage. Meanwhile, the focus of criminal proceedings is upon punishing the accused rather than protecting the victim. She may have no say in whether a prosecution is brought, may face further consequences from her family and community, and will have less chance of reconciliation with her family should she want this.[35]

The offence may also make a different statement to that intended. While it aims to place forced marriage on a footing with other serious offences, does the rarity of prosecutions (discussed below) undermine the idea that forced marriage is taken seriously? The Government itself had previously raised concerns about the effect on victims when charges could not be brought or the accused was found not guilty.[36]

At the same time, does the offence risk appearing to unfairly target minority communities? Fear of insensitivity cannot be a justification for failing to protect victims, but might this offence feel like an attack on certain cultures and result in more defensive responses?[37] Further, does it obscure the fact that this is gendered violence? Rights of Women argued that

> the very use of definitions which explicitly single out violence suffered by BME women, feeds into the 'separateness' and 'othering' of such abuses. ... [T]he more cogent approach would be for the Government to adopt a clear definition of violence against women, encompassing all manifestations of gendered violence.[38]

---

[33] Idriss (n. 30) 694.

[34] Aisha K. Gill and Anicee Van Engeland, 'Criminalization or "multiculturalism without culture"? Comparing British and French approaches to tackling forced marriage' (2014) 36 *Journal of Social Welfare and Family Law* 245.

[35] Aisha K. Gill, *Exploring the Viability of Creating a Specific Offence for Forced Marriage in England and Wales: Report on Findings* (University of Roehampton, 2011) pp. 7–9.

[36] *Forced Marriage: The Government Response to the Eighth Report from the Home Affairs Committee, Session 2010–12 HC 880*, Cm 8151, July 2011, p. 3.

[37] Particularly given prevalent political anti-immigration rhetoric: see Sundari Anitha and Aisha Gill, 'Coercion, consent and the forced marriage debate in the UK' (2009) 17 *Feminist Legal Studies* 165, 174.

[38] Rights of Women, *Response to the Home Office – Foreign and Commonwealth Office Consultation on Criminalisation*, 2012, p. 2.

Anitha and Gill similarly argue that by suggesting this is a cultural problem the debate constructs forced marriage as 'an aberration' which ignores 'the many ways in which all women located within a matrix of structural inequalities can face social expectations, pressure and constraint in matters of marriage.'[39]

Arguably, having this offence but failing to use it effectively is the worst of all worlds. Yet since it came into force there have been very few prosecutions. One difficulty arises from the definition of the offence: a person must use 'violence, threats or any other form of coercion' against someone who possesses the capacity to consent. However, 'coercion' is an imprecise term, especially in the context of family relationships: the precise line between forced and arranged marriage is not always obvious.[40]

The main barriers to prosecution, though, are outside the scope of the criminal law: the failure of authorities to recognise warning signs that someone is at risk of forced marriage, a lack of awareness among possible offenders that their behaviour is unlawful, and the unwillingness of young women to see their families prosecuted. There are also difficulties in gathering sufficient evidence to satisfy the criminal standard of proof beyond reasonable doubt. Rani Bilkhu of Jeena International has argued that '[c]hallenging and changing hearts and minds from voices within communities is the answer, as opposed to shouting from the outside and legislation'.[41]

The first conviction for the offence of forced marriage came in June 2015, at Merthyr Crown Court. The defendant (unnamed for legal reasons) had repeatedly raped the victim before and after the marriage, blackmailed her after secretly filming her in the shower, and forced her to marry him – although he was already married – by threatening to kill her father. In addition to the forced marriage offence, the defendant was convicted of rape, bigamy and voyeurism. He was sentenced to 16 years' imprisonment for rape, with a concurrent sentence of four years for the forced marriage offence. Iwan Jenkins, Head of CPS Wales, said 'We hope that today's sentence sends a strong message that forced marriage will not be tolerated in today's Britain.'[42] Reporting of the case also raised awareness of the issue and the legal remedies available. However, was the offence's significance more than symbolic? It was not the most serious offence for which the defendant was convicted, and his total sentence was considerably in excess of the maximum seven-year sentence for forced marriage.

---

[39] Anitha and Gill, 'Coercion, consent and the forced marriage debate' (n. 37) 166.
[40] *Re SK (Proposed Plaintiff) (An adult by way of her litigation friend)* [2004] EWHC 3202 (Fam); Idriss (n. 30) 697.
[41] Quoted by Yasminara Khan, 'Why are there so few forced marriage prosecutions?', BBC News, 10 June 2015, http://www.bbc.co.uk/news/uk-33073875, accessed 11 December 2016.
[42] Crown Prosecution Service, '34 year old man sentenced to 16 years following UK's first forced marriage conviction', 10 June 2015, http://blog.cps.gov.uk/2015/06/34-year-old-man-sentenced-to-16-years-following-uks-first-forced-marriage-conviction.html, accessed 30 January 2018.

This prosecution was the only one for this specific offence commenced in 2014–2015,[43] although 46 prosecutions were brought that year in relation to forced marriages, with 29 convictions.[44] By April 2016, there had been no further convictions under this offence, although five prosecutions were commenced during the year.[45] A *Guardian* report found that although there had been about 800 civil protection orders granted in England and Wales since 2014, only a minority of police investigations ended in criminal charges: five out of 51 in West Yorkshire and 12 out of 31 in the West Midlands.[46]

The issue is a complex and difficult one; we might provisionally conclude that if properly used, this offence could be an important weapon in the legal and professional armoury against forced marriage. However, it is not the only or most important one. Indeed, if the current pattern of under-use continues, there is a real risk that the offence might prove counter-productive. More fundamentally, does this legislation miss or obscure the role of forced marriage as a form of violence against women? From that perspective, the shortcomings of the particular legislation are symptomatic of a wider problem: the inadequacies of the way the criminal justice system deals with violence against women in all its manifestations.

Conclusion

The criminal law interacts in complex ways with the criminal justice system which gives effect to its provisions, and with wider society. It both affects and is affected by prevalent gender myths, ideologies and stereotypes. Addressing these is a complex undertaking, in which changes to criminal definitions alone are not enough; and even those changes can have unintended consequences. We have seen this in relation to consent in sexual offences and to the creation of an offence of forced marriage, but you can see its effect throughout the criminal law. For example, analyses of gender have been central to critiques of consent as a defence to aggravated assaults; of sexual offences more generally; and of the partial defences to murder. Feminist critiques have been a key influence on the law's recent reforms of the latter two areas. It is not an overstatement to say that the criminal law cannot be properly understood without an understanding of its gendered nature.

---

[43] Jeremy Wright in answer to Naz Shah, 'Forced marriage: Prosecutions: Written question – 36316', House of Commons, 10 May 2016, http://www.parliament.uk/business/publications/written-questions-answers-statements/written-question/Commons/2016-05-03/36316/, accessed 11 December 2016.

[44] Crown Prosecution Service, 'Violence against women and girls crime report 2015–16', CPS, 2016, p. 66.

[45] Ibid. p. 8.

[46] Josh Halliday, 'Boy aged eight among known potential victims of forced marriage in UK', *The Guardian*, 20 April 2016, https://www.theguardian.com/society/2016/apr/20/boy-eight-among-known-potential-victims-forced-marriage-uk, accessed 11 December 2016.

FURTHER READING

Sundari Anitha and Aisha Gill, 'Coercion, consent and the forced marriage debate in the UK' (2009) 17 *Feminist Legal Studies* 165.

Emily Finch and Vanessa Munro, 'Breaking boundaries? Sexual consent in the jury room' (2006) 26 *Legal Studies* 303.

Home Office, *Forced Marriage – A Consultation: Summary of Responses*, Home Office, June 2012, https://www.gov.uk/government/uploads/system/uploads/attachment_data/file/157837/forced-marriage-response.pdf, accessed 30 January 2018.

Shlomit Wallerstein, '"A drunken consent is still consent" – or is it? A critical analysis of the law on a drunken consent to sex following Bree' (2009) *Journal of Criminal Law* 318.

CHAPTER 5

Land Law

Ambreena Manji *

Perhaps more than any other area of the law curriculum, land law is most often presented as gender-neutral, devoid of power, highly technical and fundamentally apolitical. Its students, relying heavily on standard textbooks and rarely encouraged to read anything else on the subject, find it 'mystifying and uncongenial'.[1] Cowan et al. diagnose the reason as follows:

> Perhaps because land law is a foundational subject for the professional bodies in the UK, it is somehow regarded by many as 'bounded' by the needs of the profession; and property law teaching is often geared to imply that the subject exists to underpin conveyancing practice.[2]

In contrast, Cowan et al. write, 'land law lives and breathes in society, and it offers us a powerful "socio-legal object" through which to understand law in society'.[3] Like Cowan et al., my starting point for this chapter is that we can best understand contemporary society through understanding its laws.[4] If we want to do this accurately, we need to think about and seek to understand the assumptions about gender relations that are often at play in legal practice and legal doctrine. These assumptions are often obscured when gender is not explicitly addressed in the mainstream legal curriculum. By insisting that law is studied in its political and economic context, feminist scholarship has opened up gender and law as a subject of enquiry and brought it in from the margins of the LLB curriculum.

In this chapter, I review two key debates surrounding gender and land law and argue that in order to understand law's gendered outcomes we should

---

* I am grateful to Jack Pankhurst for research assistance in preparation for this chapter.

[1] William Twining, 'McAuslan in context: Early days in Dar and Warwick' in Thanos Zartaloudis (ed.), *Land Law and Urban Policy in Context: Essays on the Contributions of Patrick McAuslan* (Birkbeck Law Press, 2016) pp. 35–55.

[2] David Cowan, Lorna Fox O'Mahony and Neil Cobb, *Great Debates in Land Law* (Palgrave Macmillan, 2016) p. 2.

[3] Ibid.

[4] William Twining, *Blackstone's Tower: The English Law School* (Sweet & Maxwell, 1994).

49

investigate legal practices surrounding the family home, one of the most ubiq-
uitous and commonplace dealings in land in society. In land law, feminist
scholarship has made a critical contribution by revealing the gendered assumptions, working and outcomes of laws that are otherwise presented as neutral,
universal and objective. Whether attempting to recover the biographies and
real lives at the heart of leading cases,[5] drawing attention to competing visions
of home or asset/security,[6] understanding the behaviour and impact of commercial lenders,[7] or calling into question the assumptions at play in legal
doctrine,[8] feminist legal scholarship has challenged the sub-discipline of land
law at its core. Drawing on this scholarship, the focus on this chapter is on the
role not just of law but of lawyers in dealing with of two of the most important and salient social and economic problems of contemporary society. The
two debates selected here allow us to examine the role of a range of important social and political institutions: cohabitation, the market, paid and unpaid
work, commercial lenders, and the legal profession.

The first of these is the problem of what should happen to the property,
usually the home, of two people who have been living together (cohabiting)
for a time and are now to separate, but who cannot agree on how to divide
the home or the proceeds of its sale between them. This chapter shows that
the mechanism that is used to address this problem – the implied trust of the
family home – operates against women because it is often they who have borne
the burden of caring for a family, altering their working lives and earning less
than men in order to so. But the law does not recognise their contribution
to childcare and to labour in the home, so women lose out in a very concrete
way because of the gendered assumption that homemaking is naturally their
role. The second common social problem this chapter will consider is the one
in which an applicant for a mortgage in some way influences their partner to
agree to the transaction without informing them fully of the risks involved. The
question of the role the lending bank should play in ensuring a partner – most
often a woman – is protected from 'undue influence' has been raised time and
again. Again, this chapter asks: what is it about the process that means vulnerable parties are not adequately informed and advised?

This chapter therefore has a 'transactions focus' which emphasises the study
not just of gendered legal rules but more widely of gendered legal processes'.[9]
This focus on transactions allows us to see that there is considerable time pressure at the time of conveyance and a range of powerful interests are at play. For

---

[5] See Dawn Watkins, 'Recovering the lost human stories of law: Finding Mrs Burns' (2013) 7
Law and Humanities 68.

[6] See Lorna Fox O'Mahony, *Conceptualising Home* (Hart, 2007).

[7] Rosemary Auchmuty, 'Men behaving badly: An analysis of English undue influence cases'
(2002) 11 *Social and Legal Studies* 257, 271.

[8] Hilary Lim and Anne Bottomley (eds), *Feminist Perspectives on Land Law* (Routledge-
Cavendish, 2007).

[9] Ralph H. Folsom and Neal A. Roberts, 'The Warwick story: Being led down the contextual
path of law' (1979) 30 *Journal of Legal Education* 166.

both debates, I identify the role of what I call the 'tyranny of the transaction'. By this I mean the urgency with which conveyancing transactions take place, or more accurately the urgency with which they are treated. Nothing must delay or postpone them: difficult legal questions about how a couple would like to share the ownership of a home (Debate 1) or whether a wife has fully understood what it means to stand surety for her husband (Debate 2) threaten to delay the legal process, raise costs and ultimately deter powerful economic actors, banks and lawyers from partaking in transactions relating to domestic properties. In a society underpinned by the idea of private home ownership and the centrality of equity secured on the family home to business enterprise, the smooth running of a mortgage and conveyancing market takes priority over all else. Banks and lawyers – and indeed judges – repeatedly warn of the dangers of getting in their way by imposing further legal requirements (to make adequate enquiries, for example) on them. This perspective helps us to see what the two debates explored in this chapter have in common. Often treated separately by standard land law text-books, what unifies the two debates explored here is that they are underpinned by transactions in which the onus has been placed on powerful commercial players – banks in the domestic mortgage market – to take steps which are at odds with their interest in speedily wrapping up a sale. Unsurprisingly, banks have resisted this responsibility or contrived to do as little as possible to meet their legal duties.[10] What we see is that at the heart of conveyancing practice are institutional priorities and imperatives far removed from issues of fairness and equity. This emphasis on speedy transactions is encapsulated in the words of Lord Templeman during a Parliamentary debate: 'No one has great sympathy for lenders or banks … [but] the point is that at the end of the day it is the borrower who pays, unless there is some speedy and efficient method of conveyance.'[11]

Understanding what drives this punitive suggestion that ultimately borrowers will pay for more thoughtful and careful conveyancing practices helps us to see why it has been so difficult to develop mechanisms to protect women against unfairness in relation to the family home. This is in turn important if we are to identify the further public policy changes and law reform that might be needed.

Debate 1

In co-ownership cases, why have the courts had to look for common intention?

What happens when someone who buys a property such as their home in their sole name and so holds the legal title to the land, and then their partner comes to live with them, makes improvements to the home, takes care of children and

---

[10] This is acknowledged by Lord Justice Millett in a paper in which he notes bank's poor practice in advising surety wives. See P.J. Millett, 'Equity's place in the law of commerce' (1998) 114 *Law Quarterly Review* 214, 220.

[11] Lord Templeman in HL Deb 15 December 1982, cited in Cowan et al. (n. 2) p. 206.

perhaps stops work or works part-time in order to do most of the homemaking and enable their partner to work? Can that other person claim a share in the ownership of the property? Remember from the outset that, if they can do so, that share would be in the equitable interest because it is the owner into whose sole name the home has been conveyed who holds the legal title. Also, remember why it is important that the non-owner can establish an equitable interest. This means that although the legal title is in a sole name, the equitable interest is co-owned; that is, a trust of land has come about.[12] Put another way, there is one trustee of land, but in equity there are now two co-owners. However, if this equitable interest has arisen, it has done so informally and so invisibly. This is because the interest has arisen through a resulting or constructive trust and with no formalities involved. Any future purchaser of the property or any bank that might be considering lending money on the security of that property needs to know of the interest's existence, but it may not now be obvious. They are unable to use overreaching to get priority over the equitable owner and so, if they do not discover it, will be bound by their interest.[13]

These days, most homes bought by couples are expressly co-owned;[14] lenders like to make sure that all those with interests in the property are named on the documents of title so that they are not caught out by an interest they were unaware of.[15] But what is often forgotten by students of co-ownership is that it is possible, where the property is not in joint names, for a legal owner to make sure another person has an interest in the land by creating an express trust: they can simply carry out the formalities needed and accompany this with a written declaration as to the size of their share.[16] The co-ownership cases and the considerable problems to which they have given rise have come about because this simple expedient is rarely used. Douglas et al., reporting the findings of a 2007 project on what happens to property when a cohabiting couple split up,[17] observed that conveyancing solicitors rarely pushed couples to specify the shares in which they wished to hold their property, preferring instead that the transaction proceeded without this distraction. Family lawyers who become involved in resolving property disputes at the end of relationships expressed considerable criticism of this approach by conveyancers, feeling that their fellow lawyers in the conveyancing branch of the profession do not do all they should to ensure that couples specify their shares in their home

[12] *Bull v Bull* [1955] 1 QB 234.

[13] Law of Property Act 1925, s. 2.

[14] Philipp Lersch and Sergi Vidal, 'My house or our home? Entry into sole ownership on the breakdown of cohabitation' Demography Society Working Paper No 2015 – 57 (Universitat Pompeu Fabia, Barcelona, 2015).

[15] *Williams & Glyns Bank v Boland* [1981] 1 AC 487.

[16] Law of Property Act 1925, s. 53(1). See *Richards v Wood* [2014] EWCA Civ 327.

[17] Gillian Douglas, Julia Pearce and Hilary Woodward, 'Money, property, cohabitation and separation' in Joanna Miles and Rebecca Probert (eds), *Sharing Lives, Dividing Assets: An Interdisciplinary Study* (Hart, 2009) pp. 139–160.

from the outset. Doing this would prevent subsequent scenarios in which the courts have found themselves having to work out if a non-owning partner does indeed have an equitable interest in the property. But institutional priorities, not attempts to ensure fairness and transparency between two people in a relationship, drive the transaction.

In such situations, where shares are not decided – as happens when transactions are rushed and care is not taken to discuss all the implications of the conveyance with the parties – and then a relationship comes to an end, we have to fall back on the doctrine of constructive trust in order for a claimant, most often a woman who has been cohabiting, to assert an equitable interest as a legal owner. For this to happen, she will need to show that she and her partner shared a 'common intention' that the claimant would have some interest in the land or (if the home is jointly owned) that the intention was not to let 'equity follow the law' (i.e. for the parties to enjoy the *same* interest in the home). This principle has been expounded in a line of cases following *Lloyds Bank v Rosset*,[18] most importantly two key cases in the House of Lords (*Stack v Dowden*)[19] and the Supreme Court (*Jones v Kernott*).[20] If a property dispute arises when cohabitants split up and the conveyance is silent or unclear about the beneficial ownership in the property, or if a joint owner claims to have a larger share than the joint beneficial interest, the applicable rules will be those of trust law.

Feminist research has, however, shown that relying on trusts of the family home has often worked to women's disadvantage. This is because, in the absence of an express agreement, the equitable rules that determine if a constructive trust has arisen almost always require direct financial contributions. It is most often women who have the responsibility of labour in the home and of childcare and who may have left the workforce because of maternity or, even if they continued to work, did so on a part-time basis or earned less than men. This means that they are less likely than men to be able to make direct financial contributions to the property, for example by paying the mortgage instalments. Instead they make a contribution to keeping the household running, provide care labour and reduce their own workforce participation. They make what is essentially an invisible contribution from the point of view of the law, though there have been attempts in the past – notably by Lord Denning – to recognise and reward this labour.[21] These attempts failed because housekeeping and childcare were (and are) not perceived as adding value to a property. A woman's labour in the home may enable a man to work full-time, for example, but the equitable requirement that her financial contribution be direct means

---

[18] [1991] 1 AC 107.
[19] [2007] UKHL 17.
[20] [2011] UKSC 53.
[21] Compare *Gissing v Gissing* [1969] 2 Ch 87 (Court of Appeal) and *Gissing v Gissing* [1971] AC 886 (House of Lords).

that this does not amount to the sort of contribution recognised by the courts. Both *Stack v Dowden* and *Jones v Kernott* are instructive in this regard. Here, unusually, both Ms Dowden and Ms Jones did better than their male partners but it is important to see that this was because they could evidence larger direct financial contributions. This means that these two key cohabitation cases are highly unusual on the facts. Gender inequality in the workplace, in relationships and in the home mean that, in the vast majority of cases, women will not be able to show equal or any direct financial contributions.[22]

Given these drawbacks of implied trusts of the family home, it is clear that the actual practice of lawyers when it comes to advising on and conveyancing the home could avoid women facing these disadvantageous outcomes. Focusing on the legal transaction allows us to recognise that despite the 'judicial warnings given to [...] legal advisers'[23] to ensure couples specify the shares in which they wish to hold their homes, in practice conveyancing lawyers see questions pertaining to this as holding up the transaction and as causing undesirable delays for buyers excitedly wanting to move into their new home. Conveyancing practices that ensure that all homes are jointly owned and that the parties fully understand the legal implications of what they are doing would avoid the unfairness that we have identified above.

Let us remind ourselves that to determine ownership of a home, we must ask what are the legal and the beneficial interests held by a couple in the property. The most conclusive evidence of this is where a document expressly declares who holds both the legal and the equitable interest. It follows that the best way to ensure that a dispute does not arise is for the parties, at the point where the legal estate is being transferred into their names, to specify explicitly in what shares they wish to hold the beneficial estate. This can be done by signing a TR1 form when the property is purchased. However, the primary parties envisaged by this form are actually the vendor and the purchaser – it has the effect of making the transfer valid even if the part of the form asking the couple to specify whether they wish to hold the property as joint tenants or tenants in common is not completed. Another way to describe this is to say the future cohabitants are decentred by the transaction, the most important parties to it being the vendor and the purchaser (one member of the couple).

From this debate we see the importance of studying the part played by lawyers in society, paying close attention to how they go about their work, what they do and do not do, that requires us to go beyond reading legal textbooks. We see that institutional power and market considerations have significant impact on how property is held by cohabiting couples. In *Stack v Dowden* Lady Hale recognised this when she argued for mandatory declarations of trust to become the norm.[24]

---

[22] See 'Employment/Labour Law' (Chapter 10) in this book.

[23] See *Springette v Defoe* [1992] 2 FLR 388, 396.

[24] *Stack v Dowden* (n. 19), para. 52.

Debate 2

Whose interests are given priority in undue influence cases?

When someone purchases a home with a mortgage, the lender (the bank or building society) will ensure that the borrower identifies anyone resident in this way and will get them to sign a document agreeing that the mortgagee's interests come first and can be enforced against both the borrower and the other residents, who are usually family members. If the home is co-owned, the bank will seek to get the signatures of all the legal owners. What happens, however, if a spouse or partner who signed the document later argues that they are not bound by the mortgage because they were improperly induced into agreeing to sign it? The equitable doctrine of undue influence can be invoked by someone in a close relationship with a borrower, where there is a level of trust and intimacy, to argue that they were coerced or forced to sign the agreement and that it should be void for this reason. Might it also be void against a third party such as a lending bank? Here, a wife might want to argue that an agreement giving rights to a bank (for example, to repossess and force a sale if the borrower default on the mortgage) does not bind her if she was pressured into signing it. She wishes to hold on to her home and protect her rights. If it can be shown that the bank knew or should have known that undue influence might have been used to get her to agree to the mortgage, then the transaction would not be enforceable by the bank.

The authority in this area is the House of Lords case of *Royal Bank of Scotland v Etridge*.[25] In this case, eight conjoined cases were brought in which undue influence was alleged. The case laid down clear guidance on how to avoid this problem in the future. Specifically, it set out what a bank needs to do in order to protect its own interests. So, for example, if a spouse or partner signs an agreement to a transaction that does not manifestly advantage them (for example, arguably for a loan for a business run by their husband), the bank should ensure that this person receives independent legal advice about the implications of the deal and only signs after the transaction has been explained to them and the bank has received confirmation from the solicitor that the explanation has been given.[26]

The workings of the doctrine of undue influence and the behaviours of the banks in following the advice set out in *Etridge* – and the impact of both of these on women's position – have been the subject of a significant body of gender and the law scholarship. In her analysis of the undue influence cases, Auchmuty has shown that, although judges evoke the principle that equity should protect the vulnerable in these cases, and so step in when wives are being pressured to stand surety for their husband, this is masking what is really going on. This is that the courts 'still find the need to protect the banks more

---

[25] [2002] 2 AC 773.
[26] See Lord Browne-Wilkinson in *Barclays Bank plc v O'Brien* [1993] 3 WLR 185–199.

compelling.'[27] Auchmuty explores the case law to show that, although the courts purport to be trying to balance the interests of the lenders against those of the surety, in fact '[t]here is no balancing of interests; the bank's interests are almost always prioritized.'[28] This returns us to the notion of the tyranny of the transaction that this chapter introduced above. We see that banks do as little as possible to ensure that the surety is treated fairly and their interests fully explained to them, and we see that the courts are reluctant to step in to make sure that lenders do this. To do so would require us to tolerate slower convey-ancing, more elongated transactions and more careful consideration of fairness in the context of mortgage lending. Feminist scholars, by paying attention to the gendered nature of the transaction and moving beyond the doctrine of undue influence, have shown how little real willingness there is for the law to safeguard the interests of women who stand surety.[29]

But Auchmuty argues that we have to understand the undue influence cases not just in terms of the commercial lenders and their priorities as we have done so far, but also as evidence of the intertwining of patriarchy and capitalism. She writes 'it is not enough ... simply to analyse these cases in terms of reproduc-ing capitalism: they also reproduce patriarchy'.[30] What does she mean by this? Attention to inequality in gender relations allows us to see that wives may be well aware of the risks of particular transactions: that the family home is being used as collateral for a loan for a risky business venture in which they might not have much faith, for example. The contribution of feminist scholarship has been to show how ideas of free will and autonomy do not fully explain what takes place in relation to property. Paying attention to the workings of patriar-chal relations enables us to recognise what else is at stake beyond the banks and their commercial interests. Because of the way that unequal gender relations work in everyday life, women may have all the facts in their possession but still find themselves unable to speak up against a decision even when they are fully aware of what is taking place. Here we see women's subordination working in the interests of both men and lenders.

CONCLUSION

In contrast to mainstream presentations of land law as a subject, both debates presented here strongly suggest that land law teaching needs to take social prob-lems rather than legal rules as its starting point. Understanding the intersection

---

[27] Rosemary Auchmuty, 'Men behaving badly: An analysis of English undue influence cases' (2002) 11 *Social and Legal Studies* 257, 271.

[28] Ibid.

[29] Rosemary Auchmuty has written an alternative feminist judgment to *Royal Bank of Scotland v Etridge (No 2)* to demonstrate that how differently the court, while still following the law, might have decided this case. See the judgment in Rosemary Hunter, Clare McGlynn and Erika Rackley (eds), *Feminist Judgments: From Theory to Practice* (Hart Publishing, 2010) pp. 155–169.

[30] Auchmuty, 'Men behaving badly' (n. 27) 271.

of gender and property relations is fundamental to this effort. As Auchmuty has shown in relation to undue influence, those who are really being protected are banks rather than the surety who in fact stands to lose from the use of their home to access borrowing. These interests are 'always expressed in terms of gender neutral legal rules'[31] and so we risk missing what is really going on if we focus simply on the legal doctrine arising from case law. We need to dig deeper and recognise that behind the judicial language of balance, fairness and efficiency there are assumptions made about women's role in the home and in the workplace and the propriety of their dealings in property. Powerful commercial institutions driven by the pursuit of profit do not have gender equity as a goal. It is only if our land law curricula pays attention to legal practices, institutions, processes and structures over de-contextualised rules and concepts, as pioneering feminist legal scholarship in this sub-field has tried to do, that law students can be introduced to the social and economic complexity of law in the real world, rather than shielded from it. In addition, both debates discussed in this chapter have the realities of the legal profession and its practices at their heart. This institutional approach has the merit of demonstrating that legal practice, and especially the moment of transaction in the case of land law, is as much the locus for unfair and unjust outcomes for women as legal concepts and rules are. Recognising the powerful influence exerted by banks, with the legal profession as their handmaiden, is critical to understanding the persistence of gender inequality raised by the two debates explored here.

Further Reading

Rosemary Auchmuty, 'Men behaving badly: An analysis of English undue influence cases' (2002) 11 *Social and Legal Studies* 257.

Belinda Fehlberg, 'The husband, the bank, the wife and her signature' (1994) 57 *Modern Law Review* 467.

Lorna Fox O'Mahony, *Conceptualising Home* (Hart, 2007).

Hilary Lim and Anne Bottomley (eds), *Feminist Perspectives on Land Law* (Routledge-Cavendish, 2007).

---

[31] Auchmuty, 'Men behaving badly' (n. 27) 272.

CHAPTER 6

Equity and Trusts

Nick Piška

Questions of gender permeate 'Equity & Trusts'. For example, equity's duty of care refers to the prudent *man* of business[1] and the presumptions of resulting trust and advancement differentiate between women's and men's respective intentions in transferring property. But these are treated as historical anomalies, with no real effect (the prudent man of business) or of diminishing relevance and soon to be abolished (the presumption of advancement). To the extent that there is engagement with the gendered aspects of Equity & Trusts, the tendency is to focus on the family home, most notably on implied trusts, undue influence and the liability of sureties.[2] Here the gendered aspect is not considered to be some historical trace but as equity's active intervention – and invention – for the protection of women. This in turn cultivates an image of equity as the protector of women and of equity as a 'feminine jurisprudence'. Unlike other areas of law, equity does not hold it itself out to be neutral, but intervenes to prevent the exploitation of positions of trust and confidence.[3] Equitable doctrines and remedies are seen as creative, flexible and holding the potential for recognising women's experiences and advancing women's equality. However, feminists have also been suspicious of the 'siren call' of equity.[4] For example, they have noted that equitable remedies possibly entrench gendered assumptions about the roles of women and men and that equity's rhetoric does not always match reality, particularly in the context of claims over the family home and the liability of sureties.

---

[1] See Alison Dunn, 'Trusting in the prudent woman of business: Risk, reconciliation and the trustees' standard of care on investment' in Susan Scott-Hunt and Hilary Lim (eds), *Feminist Perspectives on Equity and Trusts* (Routledge, 2001).

[2] See Ambreena Manji, 'Land Law', Chapter 5 in this book.

[3] See Dianne Otto, 'A Barren future? Equity's conscience and women's inequality' (1992) 18 *Melbourne University Law Review* 808; Lisa Sarmas, 'Uncovering issues of sexual violence in equity and trusts law' (1995) 6 *Legal Education Review* 207; Tom Allen, 'Civil liability for sexual exploitation in professional relationships' (1996) 59(1) *Modern Law Review* 56.

[4] Scott-Hunt and Lim (n. 1) p. xxxv.

This chapter explores two debates concerning how the jurisprudence of equity is gendered. 'Jurisprudence of equity' refers to both the law (doctrines and remedies) emanating from the former Court of Chancery (Equity) and the way that law is conceptualised (equity). Modern textbooks tend to draw a sharp distinction between Equity and equity, but it is clear that the general jurisprudence of equity informs the specific jurisprudence of Equity, such that a sharp distinction cannot always be made between equity and Equity. The first debate focuses on the claim that equity is a feminine jurisprudence, that equity is 'female'. The second debate considers whether or not equity contributes to women's equality and analyses the extent to which equitable doctrines and remedies are gendered.

Debate 1

Is equity a gendered jurisprudence?

What does it mean to ask whether equity is a 'gendered jurisprudence'? Feminists have for some time argued that 'law is male'.[5] As Joanne Conaghan has explained, this can mean that law serves the interests of men or that legal reasoning's claims to be neutral and objective conceal gendered assumptions or reflect a 'male' approach to decision-making that overlooks or excludes feminine forms of decision-making. This is further reflected in the symbolic linking of law and masculinity; this is contrasted with femininity, which is instead linked to justice and fairness.

On the face of it, equity reverses the problem. In contrast to the idea of law above, equity is associated with mitigating the rigour of the law where justice requires, counteracting the generality of the law in particular cases, and employing equitable remedies with flexibility, discretion and 'good conscience'.[6] The association of equity with femininity can be understood through the historical figuration and representation of equity as *female*, and the argument that particular modes of thought or decision-making associated with equity are distinctly 'feminine'.

THE FIGURATION OF EQUITY AS FEMALE

Equity has long both personified and figured as female. In his explanation of *epieikeia* in *Rhetoric*, Aristotle refers to the figure of Antigone as representing equity; in ancient Rome, *aequitas* was shown on a coin as a goddess holding the scales of justice and the cornucopia of plenty; and Portia in Shakespeare's *Merchant of Venice* has been claimed as the representative of equity and mercy. Similarly, Chancery Equity is often personified as female. In the *Earl of Oxford's case*, Lord Chancellor Ellesmere stated that law and equity ought to join 'hand in hand in moderating and restraining all Extremities and Hardships',[7]

---

[5] See Joanne Conaghan, Chapter 14, 'Jurisprudence/Legal Theory', in this book.
[6] See, for example, Graham Virgo, *The Principles of Equity & Trusts* (Oxford University Press, 2012) pp. 4–5.
[7] (1615) 1 Reports in Chancery 1, 5; 21 ER 485, 486.

suggesting that justice is the marriage of law and equity. In 1953 Lord Evershed published an article entitled 'Equity is not to be presumed to be past the age of child-bearing',[8] suggesting that equity was a fertile, creative jurisdiction even after the Judicature Act 1873. Lord Denning MR referred to this modern 'maxim' in *Eves v Eves*:[9]

> It often happens that a man and a woman set up house together and have children. They cannot marry because one or other or both are already married. But they intend to marry as soon as they are free to do so. She takes his name. They live as husband and wife. They are known to their neighbours as husband and wife. They get a house; but it is put in his name alone. Then, before they get married, the relationship breaks down. In strict law she has no claim on him whatever. She is not his wife. He is not bound to provide a roof over her head. He can turn her into the street. She is not entitled to any maintenance from him for herself. All she can do is to go to the magistrates and ask for an affiliation order against him on the footing that she is a 'single woman': and get an order for him to pay maintenance for the children. If he does not pay, she may have great difficulty in getting any money out of him, even for the children. Such is the strict law. And a few years ago even equity would not have helped her. But things have altered now. Equity is not past the age of childbearing. One of her latest progeny is a constructive trust of a new model. Lord Diplock brought it into the world and we have nourished it.[10]

This quote brings together the representation of equity as female, as mitigator of the strict law, as still 'fertile', and (therefore) providing protection to women. The phrase, with its connotations, continues to be used to this day.[11]

In *Equity Stirring* Gary Watt criticises the 'stereotype of Female Equity'.[12] He states that 'the stereotype depends on sweeping general assumptions about the natures of "equity" and "female"'.[13] For Watt, the association of femininity and equity is problematic because it works on the assumption that women have the virtues of equity and men do not:

> Powerful men must not be encouraged to think that equity is a virtue that should be left to women to fulfil in a place removed from power, and powerful women must not be encouraged to assume that equity is a virtue which by the mere fact of their gender they have already attained.[14]

---

[8] Raymond Evershed, '"Equity is not to be presumed to be past the age of child-bearing"' (1953) 1 *Sydney Law Review* 1, which itself was quoting remarks said to be made by Harman J, himself paraphrasing Lord Mansfield.

[9] [1975] 1 WLR 1338.

[10] [1975] 1 WLR 1338, 1341.

[11] See Lord Neuberger, 'Has equity had its day?' Hong Kong University Lecture 2010 (12 October 2010); Mark Pawlowski, 'Is equity past the age of childbearing?' (2016) 22 *Trusts & Trustees* 892.

[12] See Gary Watt, *Equity Stirring: The Story of Justice Beyond Law* (Hart, 2009) pp. 179–183.

[13] Ibid. p. 181.

[14] Ibid. pp. 180f.

He goes on to challenge the very stereotype of equity as female through a reading of Dickens's *Bleak House* to show that the most stereotypically masculine character – Mr George – is also the most equitable.[15] Nevertheless, it is Esther Summerson in *Bleak House* who for Watt is the most nuanced personification of equity in English literature, *not* because she is female but because she embodies what he calls 'motive moderation', an emotive concept of equity which unsettles settled positions and settles the unsettled – a stirring and a calming influence respectively. We might query though why equity has been figured so often in its history as female, which brings us to the second reason equity is associated with the feminine.

EQUITY AND THE ETHIC OF CARE

It has been said that equity encompasses a feminine model of decision-making. This seems to be how Alastair Hudson understands the link between equity and the feminine:

> There are people who consider equity to be a 'feminine' way of thinking because it is not obsessed with detailed rules and does not treat law-making as being a sort of car maintenance which operates mechanically but rather involved open-textured, sensitive decision-making which fits the context.[16]

The claim has been associated with the work of Carol Gilligan who argued in *In a Different Voice* that men tend to 'make moral judgments according to an ethic of rights ... and women according to an ethic of care, or desire to avoid pain'.[17] Gilligan's argument, developed through various empirical psychological studies, distinguishes between men, who base their decision-making on abstract rules, and women, who focus on relationships and outcomes for individuals.

It is easy to see how this framework can be mapped on to law and equity. For example, Richard Posner contrasts law, rule and objectivity on the one side and equity, discretion and subjectivity on the other. For Posner, the ethic of care – as an aspect of legal reasoning – is embodied in the common law through equitable principles.[18] For this reason it could be said that equity is a feminine jurisprudence, in that it expresses in law women's modes of decision-making. However, for Posner equity and the ethic of care are not confined to women nor are they distinctly 'feminine'. Likewise Hudson rejects this association of equity with femininity:

---

[15] Ibid. pp. 181f.

[16] Alastair Hudson, *Great Debates in Equity and Trusts* (Palgrave, 2014) p. 235.

[17] See Carol Gilligan, *In a Different Voice: Psychological Theory and Women's Development* (Harvard University Press, 1990), as discussed by Rosemary Auchmuty, 'The fiction of equity' in Scott-Hunt and Lim, n. 1.

[18] See Richard Posner, *Law and Literature* (Harvard University Press, 3rd edn, 2009), Chapter 3.

There is only so far one can get with that sort of nonsense: just imagine a woman with a spanner or a man choosing furniture for his living-room, and these stereo-types collapse. Not all men think alike and not all women think alike.[19]

On the other hand, Rosemary Auchmuty, while acknowledging criticisms of Gilligan's work, argues that, whether or not we consider particular modes of thought or decision-making as 'female' or 'male', women have different inter-ests to men and may perceive moral and legal dilemmas differently in a way which fits the ethic of care.[20]

In this respect, then, Auchmuty and Hudson are in agreement: equity is a 'feminine jurisprudence', if by that we mean an 'ethic of care'. But while Hudson disregards the claim that equity is a 'feminine jurisprudence' on the basis that men can occupy feminine social roles and women masculine ones, he denies that there is any particular gendered mode of thought or experi-ence. Auchmuty, however, accepts that men and women often do approach moral and legal dilemmas differently, and that equity *may* enable such a mode of judgment through its focus on particular facts, through looking to intent rather than form, through its flexible and discretionary jurisprudence. But she also holds that the rhetoric of equity's care is different from its reality, as equita-ble doctrines do not function to speak for women or look after their interests;[21] law generally – including equity – privileges men's experiences and interests and downplays or excludes women's experiences.

Even if we accept that flexibility and discretion are 'feminine', it has been argued that equitable doctrines and remedies are not in fact discretionary or flexible in a way that the common law is not, and also that the underlying prin-ciple of conscience is either legally irrelevant or the dangerous application of subjective moral values of the judge, inappropriate in modern law.[22] Instances of rigid equitable doctrines, principles and remedies and harsh applications thereof (for example, strict liability of fiduciaries to account for profits) are often provided. This is the view of equity commonly held by those advocating the 'fusion' of equity and common law. But, as Lionel Smith has observed, con-science, discretion and flexibility remain important in the 'tradition of equity' as they are often invoked in judgments and many textbooks continue to refer to them as the hallmarks of equity.[23]

By separating the characterisation and functioning of equity from those of law, an idea of law as neutral, objective and rational *by contrast with equity* is made possible. Equity's 'difference' makes possible law's masculinity with the result that, following *Earl of Oxford's case*, complete or true justice becomes

---

[19] Hudson (n. 16) p. 235.

[20] Auchmuty (n. 17) p. 3.

[21] Ibid. p. 25.

[22] See, for example, Sarah Worthington, *Equity* (Clarendon, 2nd edn, 2006) Chapters 1 and 10; Peter Birks, 'Equity in modern law: An exercise in taxonomy' (1996) *University of Western Australia Law Review* 1.

[23] Lionel Smith, 'Fusion and tradition' in Simone Degeling and James Edelman (eds), *Equity in Commercial Law* (Lawbook, 2005).

the combination of law and equity. In short, the claim that equity is feminine may tell us more about how law itself is gendered.

Debate 2

Do equitable doctrines and remedies contribute to equality or entrench gendered norms?

Equity has been seen, by some, as holding potential for protecting women's interests and contributing to women's equality.[24] First, it has been suggested that equity's historical protection of married women's property may indicate an historic contribution of equity to women's equality.[25] But although the equitable rules giving 'special treatment' to married women were more acceptable than the common law of coverture, the equitable rights granted to wives were still not the same or even equivalent to the property rights of husbands, were premised on the vulnerability of married women, and were only really available to the wealthy. Second, certain doctrines and remedies have operated to advance women's equality, either by offering them 'special treatment' or by preventing the exploitation of relations of power. Yet by treating women differently from men, these doctrines may entrench gendered assumptions and impede women's equality.[26] In this debate we will consider the claim that certain equitable doctrines and remedies advance women's equality, with reference to the presumption of advancement and rescission.

PRESUMPTION OF ADVANCEMENT

Equity has two presumptions allocating the burden of proof in property disputes which, in the absence of contrary evidence, determine the beneficial ownership of property. First, the presumption of resulting trust presumes that where one transfers property to another, or where property is purchased in the name of another, without the transferor or purchaser receiving payment, that they did not intend to make a gift and that the property is held on trust for the transferor or purchaser.[27] This presumption can be rebutted by evidence of contrary intention or displaced by the presumption of advancement. The presumption of advancement is a presumption, subject to contrary evidence, that the transferor intended to transfer property for the benefit of the recipient. It applies to transfers from a man to his wife, fiancée or child, but not to transfers

---

[24] Otto, n. 3.

[25] See Hudson, n. 16, pp. 236–240; Jonathan Garton (ed.), *Moffat's Trusts Law: Text and Materials* (Cambridge University Press, 6th edn, 2015) pp. 50–56; Auchmuty, n. 17, pp. 13–18.

[26] On the equal/special treatment debate, see Ruth Fletcher, 'Feminist legal theory' in Reza Banakar and Max Travers (eds), *An Introduction to Law and Social Theory* (Hart, 2002).

[27] See *Westdeutsche Landesbank Girozentrale v Islington LBC* [1996] AC 669 and William Swadling, 'Explaining resulting trusts' (2008) 124 *Law Quarterly Review* 72.

from a woman to her husband or fiancé and possibly her child.[28] The upshot is that, in the absence of contrary evidence, a transfer by a man to his wife or children is presumed to be a gift, while a transfer by a woman to her husband (and possibly to her children) is presumed not to be a gift and instead held on trust for her.

The presumption of advancement thus treats men and women differently in respect of their property dealings, while on the face of it the presumption of resulting trust is gender-neutral. There is no single rationale for the presumption of advancement, but it appears to be based on the court's interpretation of probable intentions. This in turn is said to be premised on a husband's and father's 'moral duty' towards his wife and children, which has been explained on basis of 'natural obligation to provide for one's wife'[29] or an obligation to establish the recipient in life or part of a maintenance obligation.[30] The presumption of advancement has been the subject of criticism, particularly for being antiquated and for discriminating between men and women.[31]

In the context of disputes over the family home, the presumption of advancement has been downplayed to the point of irrelevance,[32] leaving the supposedly gender-neutral presumption of resulting trust to apply until finally abandoned in *Stack v Dowden*.[33] As Rosemary Auchmuty has pointed out, the presumption of advancement was largely abandoned because it 'came to be seen as standing in the way of equal justice for *men*' because their financial contributions were presumed to be gifts, while their wives' were not.[34] However, the 'equal justice' of the apparently gender-neutral presumption of resulting trust hid the differential operation of a presumption premised on 'direct financial contributions' in a social and economic context where men's economic resources continued (and continue) to be higher than women's and where so-called 'women's work' does not count as a financial contribution.[35] In *Jones v Kernott*, Baroness Hale and Lord Walker made it unambiguously clear that the presumptions of advancement and resulting trust no longer apply in the family home context:

> In the context of the acquisition of a family home, the presumption of a resulting trust made a great deal more sense when social and economic conditions were different and when it was tempered by the presumption of advancement. The

---

[28] But on the latter consider *Close Invoice Finance Ltd v Abaowa* [2010] EWHC 1920 (QB).

[29] *Murless v Franklin* (1818) 1 Swan 13.

[30] See Jamie Glister, 'The presumption of advancement' in Charles Mitchell (ed.), *Constructive and Resulting Trusts* (Hart, 2009).

[31] See Alysia Blackham, 'The presumption of advancement: A lingering shadow in UK law?' (2015) 21 *Trusts & Trustees* 786.

[32] See *Pettitt v Pettitt* [1970] AC 777 and *Gissing v Gissing* [1971] AC 886.

[33] [2007] UKHL 17; [2007] 2 AC 432; see also *Marr v Collie* [2017] UKPC 17.

[34] Rosemary Auchmuty, 'Unfair shares for women: The rhetoric of equality and the reality of inequality' in Hilary Lim and Anne Bottomley (eds), *Feminist Perspectives on Land Law* (Cavendish, 2007) p. 173.

[35] See Chapter 5, 'Land Law', in this book.

breadwinner husband who provided the money to buy a house in his wife's name, or in their joint names, was presumed to be making her a gift of it, or of a joint interest in it. That simple assumption ... was thought unrealistic in the modern world by three of their Lordships in *Pettitt v Pettitt*. It was also discriminatory as between men and women and married and unmarried couples. That problem might have been solved had equity been able to extend the presumption of advancement to unmarried couples and remove the sex discrimination. Instead, the tool which equity has chosen to develop law is the 'common intention' constructive trust. Abandoning the presumption of advancement while retaining the presumption of resulting trust would place an even greater emphasis upon who paid for what, an emphasis which most commentators now agree to have been too narrow. The presumption of advancement is to receive its quietus when section 199 of the Equality Act 2010 is brought into force.[36]

The basis for the abolition of the presumption of advancement in the Equality Act 2010 was the Labour Government's intention to accede to Article 5 of the Seventh Protocol of European Convention on Human Rights, which provides for equality of rights and responsibilities of a private law character between spouses, and in their relations with their children. The concern was that the presumption of advancement contravened this Article; as Lord Lester observed, it 'discriminates against husbands and is outdated'.[37] However, section 199 is yet to be brought into force, and it seems unlikely it will be any time soon.

Differential treatment of men and women is problematic because it 'serves to reinforce the stereotype of men as breadwinners and heads of families, and women as their dependents'.[38] But introducing a gender-neutral reform is also problematic. First, if the presumption were abolished, then transfers from a man to his wife or child would, in the absence of contrary intention, be held on resulting trust on the basis that they do not intend to make a gift, in the same way as transfers from wives to their husbands. On the other hand, if the presumption were extended to transfers by women to their husbands and children, then such transfers would be presumed to be a gift rather than to be held on trust. Such an approach has developed in Australia as between mothers and children,[39] focusing not on gender but on the relationship (parent and child), an approach that may be emerging in England outside the family home context.[40] But this approach may also be problematic. For Sarmas, the extension of the presumption of advancement may legitimate the presumption 'when in fact, there is no basis for *necessarily* treating a particular class of relationships

---

[36] *Jones v Kernott* [2011] UKSC 53, para. 24.
[37] Quoted in Blackham (n. 31) 790. Also see Jamie Glister, 'Section 199 of the Equality Act 2010: How not to abolish the presumption of advancement' (2010) 73 *Modern Law Review* 807.
[38] Lisa Sarmas, 'A step in the wrong direction: The emergence of gender "neutrality" in the equitable presumption of advancement' (1994) 19 *Melbourne University Law Review* 758, 764.
[39] *Brown v Brown* (1993) 31 NSWLR 582; *Nelson v Nelson* (1995) 184 CLR 538.
[40] See *Lavelle v Lavelle* [2004] EWCA Civ 223, para. 14.

differently from others'.[41] Secondly, neither reform is gender-neutral in its effect, as women have more to lose than men in either change to the law.[42] In this vein Blackham refers to the gender wealth gap – which in 2013 was found to be 17 per cent between women and men – and comments that, 'while it is not desirable to retain the gendered distinctions in the presumption of advancement, it is also not desirable to extend the presumption to transfers by wives or mothers'.[43] Moreover, if reform is concerned with reflecting (presumed) intentions then, Blackham points out, intentions in transferring property and wealth 'are strongly influenced by class and ethnicity'.[44]

RESCISSION

Equity has also developed a number of doctrines and remedies for setting aside – rescinding – gifts and contracts in circumstances falling short of *actual* fraud (subjective intention to deceive) which is required at common law.[45] These principles include undue influence, unconscionable bargain and (in Australia) the 'wife's special equity'. As with the presumptions discussed above, these principles are concerned with intention, but in these cases with procedural fairness in the production of 'authentic' intention and the prevention of exploitation, particularly by those in positions of power. The context in which these principles have come to prominence in the second half of the twentieth century has been liability of sureties to banks for their partner's business debts,[46] but they also apply to exploitative contracts,[47] *inter vivos* gifts,[48] the making of wills,[49] and pre- and post-nuptial agreements.[50] Undue influence has been discussed in Chapter 5 of this book. Here we will consider alternative equitable approaches that appear to provide the basis for a more 'substantive' approach to equality.

The English approach to liability of sureties appears to accord with an 'equal treatment' approach, as banks will have constructive notice of wrongdoing in any case of a non-commercial surety. Lord Browne-Wilkinson explicitly rejected special treatment for women in *O'Brien*. Finding 'no basis in principle for affording special protection to a limited class in relation to one type of transaction only', he decided that undue influence coupled with the extension of constructive notice would provide 'proper protection for the legitimate

---

[41] Sarmas (n. 38) 766.

[42] Ibid. p. 765.

[43] Blackham (n. 31) 796.

[44] Ibid.

[45] *Derry v Peek* (1889) 14 App Cas 337.

[46] See Chapter 5, 'Land Law'.

[47] *Mortgage Express v Lambert* [2016] EWCA Civ 555; [2017] Ch 93.

[48] *Louth v Diprose* (1992) 175 CLR 621 (Aus High Court); *Thompson v Foy* [2009] EWHC 1076 (Ch); *Evans v Lloyd* [2013] EWHC 1725 (Ch).

[49] *Hart v Burbidge* [2013] EWHC 1628 (Ch).

[50] *Thorne v Kennedy* [2017] HCA 49 (Aus High Court).

interests of wives'.[51] This approach has been much criticised as operating to the disadvantage of women.[52] It creates two hurdles for sureties: first, if the bank has followed 'protocol', wives will not succeed in setting aside the transaction notwithstanding any wrongdoing; second, even if the bank did not follow protocol, she will still have to establish equitable wrongdoing.

The position is different in Australia, where the High Court (Australia's highest court) in *Garcia v National Australia Bank*[53] refused to follow *O'Brien* and instead confirmed what has been called the 'wife's special equity'. This principle is that a surety agreement can be set aside when a creditor knows that a wife is standing surety for her husband's debts, without benefit to herself, unless the creditor takes sufficient steps to ensure that the wife understands the transaction. The rationale provided in *Yerkey v Jones*[54] is to prevent abuse that may arise within married relationships and *not* the belief that wives are subservient to their husbands. The key difference from the English approach is that the special equity does not depend on any wrongdoing by the husband, but rather casts the onus on the creditor.

Whether or not we accept this rationale, the principle involves special treatment of women, but is ambiguous in its contribution to women's equality.[55] On the one hand, unlike the presumption of undue influence which requires women to demonstrate they reposed trust and confidence in their husband or partner and may entail adopting certain gendered positions such as appearing weak, vulnerable, unknowledgeable of financial affairs, and generally subservient to their husbands, the principle in *Yerkey* does not require such prostration before the court. The special equity has the potential of moving beyond the *formal* conception of equality preferred in *O'Brien* (one concerned with ensuring that 'consent' has been properly produced)[56] to one which, recognising structural inequality and the possibility of abuse, aims at *substantive* equality.

On the other hand, a 'special equity' for women seems equally capable of perpetuating gendered stereotypes that women are subservient to men, economically inferior, or less likely to act in their own 'self-interest', and thus vulnerable to exploitation and in need of protection. In *Garcia* Kirby J, dissenting, preferred the approach of *O'Brien* and criticised the principle in *Yerkey*

---

[51] *Barclays Bank v O'Brien* [1994] 1 AC 180, 195.

[52] See Chapter 5, 'Land Law'. See also Rosemary Auchmuty, 'Men behaving badly: An analysis of English undue influence cases' (2002) 11 *Social & Legal Studies* 257; Rosemary Auchmuty, 'The rhetoric of equality and the problem of heterosexuality' in Linda Mulcahy and Sally Wheeler (eds), *Feminist Perspectives on Contract Law* (Glasshouse Press, 2005).

[53] [1998] HCA 48; (1998) 194 CLR 395. See Elizabeth Stone, 'Infants, lunatics and married women: Equitable protection in *Garcia v National Australia Bank*' (1999) 62 *Modern Law Review* 604 and Simon Gardner, 'Wives' guarantees of their husbands' debts' (1999) 115 *Law Quarterly Review* 1.

[54] (1939) 63 CLR 649.

[55] Tim Wright, 'The special wives' equity and the struggle for women's equality' (2006) 312 *Alternative Law Journal* 66, 69.

[56] See *Huguenin v Baseley* (1807) 33 ER 526; 14 Ves Jr 273.

for being discriminatory in applying only to a limited class, married women. However, as the majority pointed out in *Garcia,* there is no reason for the principle to be so limited and it could extend to cohabitants and same-sex couples.

An alternative approach to setting aside transactions[57] is provided by the unconscionable bargain. Unlike undue influence, which focuses on the transferor's consent, unconscionable bargain is concerned with the unconscionable behaviour of the transferee in procuring the transaction.[58] It requires a special disadvantage or disability on the part of the transferor, a transactional imbalance, and unconscionable conduct of the transferee in taking advantage of the disadvantage. Once established, the onus is on the transferee to establish that the transaction was 'fair, just and reasonable'.[59] In the context of sureties, the transaction can be set aside directly against the bank itself if it knows of the special disadvantage.[60]

The categories of special disadvantage are not closed, but the 'essence of such weakness is that the party is unable to judge for himself'.[61] Special disadvantages have included poverty, age, level of education, unfamiliarity with the English language and drunkenness. It has been suggested that as some of these disadvantages 'may be characterized as structural, as arising from institutional arrangements of social power', there is potential for structural gender inequality to be remedied through unconscionable bargain.[62] However, this is yet to materialise.[63] Moreover, the way in which some of the cases have been argued suggests that the need for disadvantage and exploitation continue to channel gender stereotypes. A classic example is the Australian High Court's decision in *Louth v Diprose.*[64] Mr Diprose became infatuated with Ms Louth. They had a brief affair, but she was not interested in a relationship. Her living arrangements were not secure and she was at times suicidal. He made many gifts to her, including a house. When he finally realised that there was no possibility of a relationship, and their friendship had also broken down, Mr Diprose sought to set aside the gift on the basis of unconscionable bargain. The Australian High Court accepted this argument. They found that his special disadvantage was his 'emotional dependency' on her and that Ms Louth, knowing this, had deliberately manufactured a personal crisis to take advantage of him. On

---

[57] It was thought to apply only to contracts, but has been extended to gifts: see n. 48, above.

[58] *Commercial Bank of Australia Ltd v Amadio* [1983] HCA 14, (1983) 151 CLR 447.

[59] See *Fry v Lane* (1888) 40 Ch D 312.

[60] *Commercial Bank of Australia Ltd v Amadio*, n. 58.

[61] *Blomley v Ryan* (1956) 99 CLR 363, 405.

[62] Otto (n. 3) 815.

[63] But consider the judgments in *Thorne v Kennedy*, n. 50, regarding both undue influence and unconscionable bargain.

[64] (1992) 175 CLR 621. See Lisa Sarmas, 'Storytelling and the law: A case study of *Louth v Diprose*' (1994) 19 *Melbourne University Law Review* 701, Paula Baron, 'Give and take: Unconscionability and the pervasiveness of gender stereotypes' in Heather Douglas, Francesca Bartlett, Trish Luker and Rosemary Hunter (eds), *Australian Feminist Judgments: Righting and Rewriting Law* (Hart Publishing, 2014) and Otto (n. 3) 816–818.

another reading of the facts, however, it is Ms Louth who is vulnerable and Mr Diprose who is exploitative: he subjected Ms Louth to sexual harassment, sent her pornographic poems he had written and held the balance of power between them because of his financial stability and position as a solicitor.

The case highlights how structural inequality in relationships can be ignored and how the requirement for exploitation of a special disadvantage can reinforce gender stereotypes and require litigants to enact these roles in court proceedings.[65] As Lisa Sarmas has observed, the majority's reasoning follows the narrative of 'damned whore' claiming against 'love-struck knight in shining armour', but the dissenting judgments are equally problematic in their reversal rather than elimination of the stereotypes: '[Ms Louth] turns from undeserving whore into pitiful victim, a status which makes it acceptable for the minority to find that she should keep the house.'[66]

CONCLUSION

Equity has traditionally accorded women, particularly married women, different treatment, often to provide protection from men's exploitation. However, after the passing of the Married Women's Property Acts 1870 and 1882, equity's presumptions and remedies have increasingly been framed as gender-neutral. This may appear to recognise women's formal equality but, as Auchmuty states, '[i]f women continue to suffer structural social and economic disadvantage at the hands of men, then the removal of a gendered basis for intervention can place them at a *legal* disadvantage too'.[67] But special treatment is no panacea: while the special equity may recognise the structural imbalance of power between women and men, 'this very tenderness' may perpetuate 'a far broader and largely hidden tendency to view women as "other" and in need of differential treatment'.[68]

FURTHER READING

Alysia Blackham, 'The presumption of advancement: A lingering shadow in UK law?' (2015) 21 *Trusts & Trustees* 786.

Dianne Otto, 'A barren future? Equity's conscience and women's inequality' (1992) 18 *Melbourne University Law Review* 808.

Lisa Sarmas, 'Storytelling and the law: A case study of *Louth v Diprose*' (1994) 19 *Melbourne University Law Review* 701.

Susan Scott-Hunt and Hilary Lim (eds), *Feminist Perspectives on Equity and Trusts* (Routledge, 2001).

---

[65] Otto (n. 3) 817.

[66] Sarmas (n. 64) 719.

[67] Auchmuty (n. 34) p. 180.

[68] Claire de Than, 'Equitable remedies: Cypher wives, weak women and "equity's special tenderness"' in Scott-Hunt and Lim (n. 1) p. 218.

CHAPTER 7

EU Law

Alina Tryfonidou

What is today the European Union (EU)[1] began life in the 1950s as a supranational organisation comprising three Communities: the ECSC, the EEC, and Euratom. Established as a response to the catastrophe brought by the Second World War, the long-term aim of the Communities was to maintain peace and to prevent another war in Europe; their immediate objective, however, was to achieve economic integration among the participating states by building a common market.[2] Accordingly, gender and sexuality issues were very far from the Treaty drafters' minds back in the 1950s, when the founding Treaties of the Communities were prepared. Hence, it is not surprising that those Treaties did not make any reference to lesbian, gay, bisexual and transgender (LGBT) rights, nor did they include any provisions requiring equality between the sexes, bar an article which required equal pay for equal work between men and women (what is, currently, Article 157 TFEU), the rationale behind which was, at the time, mainly economic.[3] However, equality between the sexes and the protection of LGBT rights now occupy a central position in EU law and, as a result of the introduction of mainstreaming provisions,[4] the EU institutions are required to take these aims into account when taking action in any policy area. Unfortunately these rarely feature in the subject matter of undergraduate modules on EU law. The following debates will demonstrate their importance.

---

[1] When referring to the present, the terms EU/EU law will be used since the Treaty of Lisbon abolished the pillar structure and the Communities (which comprised Pillar 1 of the EU construct) have been subsumed within, and have been replaced by, the EU. However, when describing the situation prior to the coming into force of the Treaty of Lisbon, the terms Community/EC law will be used, unless referring to a situation which does not fall within (what used to be) the first pillar.

[2] For more on the history of the EU see Paul Craig and Gráinne de Búrca, *EU Law: Text, Cases and Materials* (Oxford University Press, 2015), Chapter 1.

[3] Case 43/75 *Defrenne v Sabena II* [1976] ECR 455. See J. Maliszewska-Nienartowicz, 'Pregnancy discrimination in the European Union Law. Its legal character and the scope of pregnant women protection' (2013) 4 *Mediterranean Journal of Social Sciences* 441.

[4] Article 8 TFEU and Article 10 TFEU.

Debate 1

Should discrimination against pregnant women be considered direct discrimination on the ground of sex?

It is generally accepted that women continue to be at a disadvantage in the employment market when competing with male workers, and the EU employment market is no exception to this.[5] Despite the fact that discrimination against pregnant women was widespread, especially in the early years in the Community's existence, none of the original Treaties or directives outlawing sex discrimination explicitly included a prohibition of such discrimination. The first challenges against it arose in the early 1990s, in the 'sister' cases of *Dekker*[6] and *Hertz*.[7]

Dekker concerned the refusal of a training centre to employ the eponymous applicant on the ground that she was pregnant, despite the fact that she had been put forward as the most suitable candidate for the job. The European Court of Justice (ECJ) found that this amounted to direct discrimination on the ground of sex, contrary to the 1976 Equal Treatment Directive.[8] The Court explained that 'only women can be refused employment on grounds of pregnancy and such a refusal therefore constitutes direct discrimination on grounds of sex'.[9] The Court also explained that

> the reply to the question whether the refusal to employ a woman constitutes direct or indirect discrimination depends on the reason for that refusal. If that reason is to be found in the fact that the person concerned is pregnant, then the decision is directly linked to the sex of the candidate. In those circumstances the absence of male candidates cannot affect the answer to the first question.[10]

In this way it demonstrated that in cases involving discrimination on the ground of pregnancy, there is no need to draw a comparison between men and women but, rather, a finding of discrimination on the ground of sex can *automatically* be made.

In its judgment in *Hertz*[11] – delivered on the same day – the Court was concerned again with the issue of discrimination against pregnant women, but

---

[5] Petra Foubert, 'Does EC pregnancy and maternity legislation create equal opportunities for women in the EC labor market? The European Court of Justice's Interpretation of the EC Pregnancy Directive in *Boyle* and *Lewen*' (2002) 8 *Michigan Journal of Gender and Law* 219, 220.

[6] Case C-177/88 *Dekker v Stichting Vormingscentrum voor Jong Volwassenen (VJV-Centrum) Plus* [1990] ECR I-3941.

[7] Case C-179/88 *Handels- og Kontorfunktionaerernes Forbund i Danmark, acting on behalf of Hertz v Dansk Arbejdsgiverforening* [1990] ECR I-3979.

[8] Directive 76/207 on the implementation of the principle of equal treatment for men and women as regards access to employment, vocational training and promotion, and working conditions [1976] OJ L39/40.

[9] *Dekker* (n. 6) para. 12. This was confirmed in a number of subsequent cases, such as Case C-32/93 *Webb* [1994] ECR I-3567 and Case C-207/98 *Mahlburg* [2000] ECR I-549.

[10] *Dekker* (n. 6) para. 17.

[11] n. 7.

in this case the facts involved the dismissal of (as opposed to the refusal to employ) a pregnant woman. Here, the Court provided the further clarification that dismissal because of absence *during the period of maternity leave* is discrimination because of pregnancy and is, thus, direct discrimination on the ground of sex, while dismissal on account of repeated periods of sick leave *which appear after the period of maternity leave has expired* does not constitute direct discrimination on grounds of sex if a man would be dismissed for similar absenteeism.[12] Hence, a disadvantage suffered by a pregnant woman *in the period after her pregnancy and after her maternity leave has expired* does not *automatically* amount to (direct) discrimination on the ground of sex but, rather, a comparison must be drawn with members of the opposite sex in order to establish whether there is, indeed, (indirect) discrimination.[13]

ARGUMENTS AGAINST CONSIDERING PREGNANCY DISCRIMINATION AS DIRECT DISCRIMINATION ON THE GROUND OF SEX

The main argument against considering discrimination against pregnant women as (automatically) amounting to direct discrimination on the ground of sex without needing to draw a comparison with a man, is that this rejects the inherently comparative concept of discrimination. Moreover, some believe that if a comparative approach was taken, a finding of (direct) discrimination would not be made: if

> an absolute comparability approach is adopted, less favourable treatment of a pregnant woman cannot be directly discriminatory. A man is not capable of becoming pregnant and so the pre-requisite of equal treatment, that is, two similarly situated persons, is absent.[14]

Ellis has taken the argument further by considering the dynamics behind decision-making in cases involving pregnancy discrimination. She considers that the Court's approach in the pregnancy cases 'is unfortunate from the point of view of the underlying components of Community anti-discrimination law'[15] because

> an element of comparability is important to the component of adverse impact; if direct discrimination is defined simply as 'nasty treatment' on the ground of sex, enormous discretion is placed in the hands of courts and tribunals, who

---

[12] *Hertz* (n. 7) paras 14 and 16. This was confirmed in subsequent cases such as Case C-400/95 *Handels- og Kontorfunktionærernes Forbund i Danmark, acting on behalf of Helle Elisabeth Larsson v Dansk Handel & Service, acting on behalf of Føtex Supermarked A/S* [1997] ECR I-2757.

[13] For a criticism of *Hertz* see Nicholas Bamforth, 'The treatment of pregnancy under European Community sex discrimination law' (1995) 1 *European Public Law* 59, 61–62.

[14] Leo Flynn, 'Gender blindness in the face of real sex differences' (1993) 15 *Dublin University Law Journal* 1, 12.

[15] Evelyn Ellis, 'The definition of discrimination in European Community sex equality law' (1994) 19 *European Law Review* 563, 571.

remain overwhelmingly male in composition, to decide what is to the detriment or advantage of complainants, the majority of whom are female. For reasons of objectivity, it is preferable if the adversity of the treatment received by the complainant is measured by means of a comparison with the treatment received or receivable by a member of the opposite sex, placed in broadly the same circumstances as the complainant.[16]

Another view is that a finding of discrimination against pregnant women *does* require a comparison to be made (and, thus, rejects the position that such discrimination *automatically* amounts to direct discrimination on the ground of sex), *albeit not with members of the opposite sex*. In particular, it has been suggested that the comparator should not be *another*, male, person but, rather, the *same* person albeit without the pregnancy: under such a view, the correct approach would be 'to compare the situation of the victim with that *that person* would have been in had it not been for the purported discriminatory cause'.[17] This is because pregnancy discrimination may have nothing to do with gender at all but may be 'caused by a desire to hurt the young, the heterosexual or the non-celibate, or caused by the jealousy of those (men or women) who are [not] able to have children'.[18]

Moreover, some argue that discrimination against pregnant women is not *direct* discrimination on the ground of sex as not all women (can/want to) become pregnant,[19] and, thus, the category of those suffering a disadvantage (i.e. pregnant women) does not coincide exactly with the category of persons (that is, women in general) who bear a prohibited characteristic (sex), nor does the category of persons who receive an advantage (i.e. men and women who cannot/do not want to become pregnant) coincide exactly with persons of only one sex and, in particular, with persons of the sex which is normally advantaged (i.e. men).[20] Along these lines, Wintemute has argued that all claims of discrimination require the identification of an appropriate comparator and that, in the case of pregnant women, the comparator should be a non-pregnant (usually male) person with a comparable need for leave with pay (e.g. because of illness). Such a comparison – he points out – will indicate in many cases that there is neutral treatment of pregnant women and ill men which, nonetheless, has a worse impact on women and, thus, amounts to indirect discrimination on the ground of sex.[21]

---

[16] Ibid. 571–572.

[17] Simon Honeyball, 'Pregnancy and sex discrimination' (2000) 29 *Industrial Law Journal* 43, 49.

[18] Ibid. 51.

[19] Sally J. Kenney, 'Pregnancy discrimination: Toward substantive equality' (1995) 10 *Wisconsin Women's Law Journal* 351, 352.

[20] See, however, the different view of Advocate General Sharpston in paras 51–57 of her Opinion in Case C-73/08 *Bressol and Others v Gouvernement de la Communauté française* [2010] ECR I-2735.

[21] Robert Wintemute, 'When is pregnancy discrimination indirect sex discrimination?' (1998) 27 *Industrial Law Journal* 23.

The ECJ's response to all the above arguments has been that because pregnancy is biologically unique to women, it is not necessary to compare pregnant women with a man to prove that there is discrimination; the mere existence of a disadvantage which is based on *biological features unique to women* suffices for an automatic finding that discrimination against pregnant women amounts to *direct* discrimination on the ground of sex.

ARGUMENTS IN FAVOUR OF CONSIDERING PREGNANCY DISCRIMINATION AS DIRECT DISCRIMINATION ON THE GROUND OF SEX

Bamforth has been a proponent of the Court's approach in the pregnancy cases, noting that it 'outflanks the traditional liberal symmetry approach, a result which is surely to be welcomed given the weakness of the symmetry approach in countering sex discrimination and in ensuring substantive equality'.[22] Similarly, Jo Shaw has commented favourably on the Court's approach in this context, pointing out:

> It is now possible to argue that discrimination is not concerned so much with comparing the treatment of women with that of men, that is, setting up men as a norm against which women are to be tested as being the same as men, or different from men, but with examining the treatment of women which occurs *because they are women*. No longer is 'being treated equally' solely a male-defined standard of what constitutes desirable social treatment, but rather an absolute evaluation by society of how women should be treated.[23]

Another argument which supports the ECJ's stance in its pregnancy case law and its departure from an approach which compares pregnant women with ill men is that the latter approach equates pregnancy to illness and, thus, creates the impression that pregnancy is something unwanted and negative whereas in the vast majority of cases pregnancy is a desirable and socially important condition.[24]

It will be evident that for this debate it suffices to use the more traditional, binary, definition of 'gender', whereby gender (as, essentially, gender identity and expression) is taken to coincide with the (biological) sex of an individual. For the next debate, a broader approach to 'gender' needs to be taken whereby a clear distinction between gender and sex is drawn, this meaning that a person's gender identity, expression, and/or life choices (including choice of partner) do not match those which – *stereotypically* – are demonstrated or made by someone belonging to that person's (biological) sex.

---

[22] Bamforth (n. 13) 68.

[23] Jo Shaw, 'Pregnancy discrimination in sex discrimination' (1991) 16 *European Law Review* 313, 319–320.

[24] Sandra Fredman, 'A difference with distinction: Pregnancy and parenthood reassessed' (1994) 110 *Law Quarterly Review* 106, 113.

Debate 2

Is discrimination on the ground of sexual orientation also discrimination on the ground of sex?

The question of whether discrimination on the ground of sexual orientation should be considered to amount to discrimination on the ground of sex is a question which has emerged under EU law in particular but, like the first debate, has been also considered in other legal contexts, both national and international. This debate is not merely of academic interest and this was even more the case when the above question first emerged in the EU context in the mid-1990s. This is because back then, the (then applicable) EC Treaty only prohibited discrimination on the grounds of sex and nationality,[25] and, thus, discrimination on the ground of sexual orientation would only be considered prohibited under EC law if it could be considered as a guise of one of these types of discrimination. Accordingly, until discrimination on the ground of sexual orientation was first prohibited by Directive 2000/78,[26] the only way under EU law to protect gays and lesbians from discrimination based on their sexual orientation was by recognising that such discrimination amounted to discrimination on the ground of sex. Nowadays, however, discrimination on the ground of sexual orientation is prohibited by Directive 2000/78 (in the employment context) and by Article 21 of the EU Charter of Fundamental rights (in all situations falling within the scope of EU law). Yet because discrimination on the ground of sex continues to be prohibited in more instances and in a broader context than discrimination on the ground of sexual orientation,[27] it remains important to establish whether discrimination on sexuality grounds can also be claimed as *sex* discrimination.

The *Grant* case,[28] where the ECJ was firstly faced with the question which is the subject of this debate, was not the first instance that the Court was called on to rule on the rights of LGBT persons under EC law. A couple of years earlier, in *P v S*,[29] the Court had already been invited to rule on the right of a male-to-female transsexual[30] to be protected from discrimination on the

---

[25] Angela D. Byre, 'Equality and non-discrimination' in Kees Waaldijk and Andrew Clapham (eds), *Homosexuality: A European Community Issue* (Martinus Nijhoff, 1993) p. 211.

[26] Directive 2000/78 establishing a general framework for equal treatment in employment and occupation [2000] OJ L303/16.

[27] See, inter alia, Mark Bell and Lisa Waddington, 'Reflecting on inequalities in European equality law' (2003) 28 *European Law Review* 349; Erica Howard, 'The case for a considered hierarchy of discrimination grounds in EU law' (2006) 13 *Maastricht Journal of European and Comparative Law* 445.

[28] Case C-249/96 *Grant v South-West Trains* [1998] ECR I-621.

[29] Case C-13/94 *P v S and Cornwall City Council* [1996] ECR I-2143.

[30] The term 'transsexual' is taken to mean 'someone who is intending to undergo, is undergoing or has undergone gender reassignment treatment'. However, persons 'who do not perceive or present their gender identity as the same as that expected of the group of people who were given the equivalent sex designation at birth' are referred to as 'trans', which is an umbrella term which includes transsexuals. For more on these definitions see Stephen Whittle, *Respect and Equality: Transsexual and Transgender Rights* (Routledge, 2002) pp. xxii f.

ground of having undergone gender reassignment surgery. In fact, it was the Court's pronouncement in this case, according to which discrimination on the ground of gender reassignment *is* a form of discrimination on the ground of sex, that formed the basis for the argument in *Grant* that discrimination on the ground of sexual orientation is, also, a guise of discrimination on the ground of sex. As explained by Lardy and Campbell, one way of reading the *P v S* judgment is to consider that the principle of equal treatment for men and women requires that

> individuals (men and women) should be protected against less favourable treatment being accorded them because they do not share society's current perception of the different social roles and conduct appropriate to men and women.[31]

This approach to equal treatment in fact formed the basis of the argument made by the claimant in *Grant*. In this case, at issue was the refusal of South-West trains to grant to the female partner of one of their *female* employees the same travel concessions as were granted to the female partners of their male employees. The reason for the refusal was, simply, that Ms Grant's partner was female and, thus, of the same sex as her. Ms Grant claimed that although UK law at the time did not prohibit discrimination on the ground of sexual orientation, the contested refusal amounted to discrimination on the ground of sex and, thus, was contrary to Article 119 EC (now, Article 157 TFEU) and the EU and UK sex equality legislation applicable at the time. The issue was referred to the ECJ, which held that a) discrimination on the ground of sexual orientation was not discrimination on the ground of sex and b) discrimination on the ground of sexual orientation was not – at the time – prohibited by EC law. This position was confirmed by the ECJ in *D and Sweden v Council*[32] which reached it on appeal a few years after the *Grant* judgment.

Since the cases which came after *Grant* and *D and Sweden v Council* and which involved discrimination on the ground of sexual orientation could be resolved by recourse to the prohibition of discrimination on the ground of sexual orientation laid down in Directive 2000/78[33] or under the EU Charter of Fundamental Rights,[34] the Court has not – since then – had to deal again

---

[31] Heather Lardy and Angus Campbell, 'Discrimination against transsexuals in employment' (1996) 21 *European Law Review* 412, 416.

[32] Joined Cases C-122 and 125/99 P *D and Sweden v Council* [2001] ECR I-4319.

[33] Case C-267/06 *Maruko v Versorgungsanstalt der deutschen Bühnen* [2008] ECR I-1757; Case C-147/08 *Römer v Freie und Hansestadt Hamburg* [2011] ECR I-3591; Case C-267/12 *Hay v Crédit agricole mutuel de Charente-Maritime et des Deux-Sèvres* ECLI:EU:C:2013:823; Case C-81/12 *Asociaţia Accept v Consiliul Naţional pentru Combaterea Discriminării* ECLI:EU:C:2013:275.

[34] Case C-528/13 *Léger v Ministre des Affaires sociales, de la Santé et des Droits des femmes and Etablissement français du sang* ECLI:EU:C:2015:288.

with the question of whether discrimination on the ground of sexual orientation amounts to discrimination on the ground of sex. However, for the reasons
explained earlier, this question remains important.

ARGUMENTS AGAINST CONSIDERING DISCRIMINATION ON THE GROUND OF SEXUAL ORIENTATION AS DISCRIMINATION ON THE GROUND OF SEX

Proponents of the view that discrimination on the ground of sexual orientation
is *not* discrimination on the ground of sex base their position on the so-called
'equal misery'[35] argument. According to this view, the treatment suffered by
same-sex couples is equally bad irrespective of the sex of the parties comprising them (i.e. whether it is two men or two women), and, thus, discrimination
against same-sex couples cannot amount to discrimination on the ground
of sex. Similarly, homophobic people and organisations tend to discriminate
against *all* lesbians and gays and it is, thus, in very limited circumstances that
there is only discrimination against male gay persons but not, also, against gay
female persons or vice versa.[36] Hence, under this view, gay men and lesbians
are (usually) treated equally badly and, thus, an Aristotelian approach to discrimination which requires that persons similarly situated are treated equally,
*and which takes as its point of reference for judging whether two persons are sim-
ilarly situated their sexual orientation,* leads to a conclusion that there is no
discrimination on the ground of sex in situations involving discrimination
against gay persons.

The ECJ has espoused this view. Hence, in *Grant* the Court noted that

> [t]hat condition, the effect of which is that the worker must live in a stable rela-
> tionship with a person of the opposite sex in order to benefit from the travel
> concessions, is, like the other alternative conditions prescribed in the undertak-
> ing's regulations, applied regardless of the sex of the worker concerned. Thus
> travel concessions are refused to a male worker if he is living with a person of the
> same sex, just as they are to a female worker if she is living with a person of the
> same sex.[37]

---

[35] Christine Denys, 'Homosexuality: A non-issue in community law?' (1999) 24 *European Law Review* 419, 422.
[36] An example of a situation where there is discrimination only against *male* gay persons can be seen in the context of blood donations whereby various countries impose a ban on giving blood on the MSM (i.e. men who have sex with men) population. For a case where there was a challenge of such a ban in the EU context see *Léger* (n. 34). For comments see Alina Tryfonidou, 'The *Léger* ruling as another example of the ECJ's disappointingly reticent approach to the protection of the rights of LGB persons under EU Law' (2016) 41 *European Law Review* 91.
[37] *Grant* (n. 28) para. 27.

Arguments in Favour of Considering Discrimination on the Ground of Sexual Orientation as Discrimination on the Ground of Sex

It is argued that the 'equal misery' approach ignores the fact that an accurate discrimination assessment requires only *one* of the circumstances of the person to be changed – in the case of sex discrimination, this being the sex of the persons compared – and if the sex of the person to whom a person is attracted is *also* taken into account, this leads to a change of two of the circumstances in the assessment.[38]

This, in fact, demonstrates that the 'equal misery' approach seems to be based on a stereotypical reading of 'gender' which conflates sex and sexual orientation by considering that persons of one sex can only be attracted to persons of the *opposite* sex. In other words, according to this approach, women must love men and men must love women, and any women or men who do not fit this model can simply be ignored by the law and can be (legitimately) treated worse. Accordingly, by ruling that discrimination on the ground of sexual orientation is not also a form of discrimination on the ground of sex, the Court does not merely fail to protect lesbian and gay people and same-sex couples but in fact reinforces the discrimination suffered by them by insisting on a stereotypical view of sex and gender. As Ms Grant – the applicant in the *Grant* case – argued, 'differences in treatment based on sexual orientation originate in prejudices regarding the sexual and emotional behaviour of persons of a particular sex, and are in fact based on those persons' sex'.[39]

Academics on both sides of the Atlantic are also of the view that discrimination on the ground of sexual orientation is a form of discrimination on the ground of sex. Andrew Koppelman has argued that discrimination against lesbians and gay men reinforces the hierarchy of males over females and, thus, amounts to discrimination on the ground of sex: '[t]he effort to end discrimination against gays should be understood as a necessary part of the larger effort to end the inequality of the sexes.'[40] The same author explained this by noting that

> if the same conduct is prohibited or stigmatized when engaged in by a person of one sex, while it is tolerated when engaged in by a person of the other sex, then the party imposing the prohibition or stigma is discriminating on the basis of sex …

---

[38] Leo Flynn, 'Annotation of Case C-13/94, *P v S and Cornwall County Council,* Judgment of the Full Court of 30 April 1996, [1996] ECR I-2143' (1997) 34 *Common Market Law Review* 367, 382; Robert Wintemute, 'Recognising new kinds of direct sex discrimination: Transsexualism, sexual orientation and dress codes' (1997) 50 *Modern Law Review* 334, 347.

[39] *Grant* (n. 28) para. 18.

[40] Andrew Koppelman, 'Why discrimination against lesbians and gay men is sex discrimination' (1994) 69 *New York University Law Review* 197, 202.

If a business fires Ricky, or if the state prosecutes him, because of his sexual activities with Fred, while these actions would not be taken against Lucy if she did exactly the same things with Fred, then Ricky is being discriminated against because of his sex. If Lucy is permitted to marry Fred, but Ricky may not marry Fred, then (assuming that Fred would be a desirable spouse for either) Ricky is being discriminated against because of his sex.[41]

In another part of his article, Koppelman noted that '[l]aws that discriminate against gays rest upon a normative stereotype: the bald conviction that certain behavior – for example, sex with women – is appropriate for members of one sex, but not for members of the other sex'.[42] Similarly, Bennett Capers has noted that discrimination based on sexual orientation is essentially discrimination based on sex stereotyping and is, thus, a form of discrimination on the ground of sex; it is a 'subset of heterosexism':[43] '[d]iscrimination against lesbians and gays simultaneously flows from and perpetuates traditional notions of appropriate sex roles'.[44]

In the European context, the most prominent supporter of the view that discrimination on the ground of sexual orientation is also discrimination on the ground of sex has been Robert Wintemute. He explains that in order to establish discrimination on the ground of sexual orientation, the comparator of the gay person is 'a heterosexual individual of the same sex as the gay, lesbian or bisexual individual' or – in the case of same-sex couples – an opposite-sex couple. Wintemute has explained that

> because an individual's sexual orientation can only be defined by reference to the sex of the individual (and a couple's by reference to the sexes of its members), distinctions based on sexual orientation necessarily involve distinctions based on the sexes of the individuals.[45]

In other words '[w]hat makes the sexual orientation of a gay, lesbian or bisexual individual or a same-sex couple objectionable is the sex of the individual or of the members of the couple'.[46] Discrimination against gay persons and same-sex couples is discrimination on the ground of sex 'because it is an example of individuals' choices (whether of employment or of partner) being limited because of their sex'.[47]

---

[41] Ibid. 208.

[42] Ibid. 219.

[43] I. Bennett Capers, 'Sex(ual orientation) and Title VII' (1991) 91 *Columbia Law Review* 1158, 1159.

[44] Ibid. 1159. See, also, John McInnes, 'Annotation of Case C-249/96, *Lisa Jacqueline Grant v. South West Trains Ltd*, Judgment of the Full Court of 17 February 1998 [1998] ECR I-636' 1051.

[45] Robert Wintemute (n. 38) 347. See, also, McInnes (n. 44) 1049.

[46] Robert Wintemute (n. 38) 347.

[47] Ibid.

Despite the strength of the above arguments, the position of the Court appears to be still that discrimination against lesbians and gay men does not amount to discrimination on the ground of sex and, thus, under EU law, such persons can only rely on the prohibition of discrimination on the ground of sexual orientation when they are disadvantaged.

CONCLUSION

This chapter has sought to demonstrate how gender issues have featured in EU law through the analysis of two 'debates' for which valid arguments may be made on both sides of each debate. I would tend to agree with the Court's position as regards pregnancy discrimination since, as pregnancy is a biological condition which is *unique* to women, a comparison with men is unnecessary: differential treatment which disadvantages women *because* they are pregnant should therefore be automatically considered to amount to discrimination on the ground of sex. The argument that discrimination on the ground of pregnancy cannot be considered *direct* discrimination on the ground of sex because not *all* women become pregnant seems to ignore the fact that policies and actors which consider pregnancy as an unwanted state create a structural disadvantage against *all* women, and not just women who actually become pregnant: the *mere potential* that each woman has for becoming pregnant puts her at a disadvantage in relation to men and, thus, it is not only women who are *actually* pregnant who are discriminated against by anti-pregnancy policies.

On the other hand, the ECJ's approach in cases involving discrimination against lesbians and gays appears too superficial and indicates an inability to see that the reason behind such discriminatory treatment is not merely a person's homosexual sexual orientation but also – and more deeply – his or her failure to comply with the social expectations for his or her gender. Accordingly, if the Court wishes to outlaw discrimination on the ground of sex in all instances where this emerges, it should in future hold that discrimination against gays and lesbians is not merely discrimination on the ground of sexual orientation but is, also, a guise of discrimination on the ground of sex.

FURTHER READING

Evelyn Ellis and Philippa Watson, *EU Anti-Discrimination Law* (Oxford University Press, 2013), Chapter 7.

Sandra Fredman, 'A difference with distinction: Pregnancy and parenthood reassessed' (1994) 110 *Law Quarterly Review* 106.

Alina Tryfonidou, 'Discrimination on the grounds of sexual orientation and gender identity' in Stefan Vogenauer and Stephen Weatherill (eds), *General Principles of Law: European and Comparative Perspectives* (Hart, 2017).

Robert Wintemute and Mads Andenas (eds), *Legal Recognition of Same-Sex Partnerships: A Study of National, European and International Law* (Hart, 2001).

CHAPTER 8

International Law and Human Rights

Nora Honkala

The scope of international law has grown significantly and it now covers areas as diverse as the regulation of space, international trade, the environment, laws of war and international human rights. The mainstream view is that international law concerns the rules and obligations of states. Broadly, this means that substantive international law applies to states, which have legal personality and thus legal standing. As such, statehood is fundamental to how one understands and uses international law. This is not to say that the concept of the state is without contention. It is merely to suggest the traditional assumption that is presupposed when speaking of the 'context' of international law. This traditional view is stated within the jurisprudence of the International Court of Justice in a seminal case from 1927 commonly known as the '*Lotus*' case:

> International law governs relations between independent States. The rules of law binding upon States therefore emanate from their own free will as expressed in conventions or by usages generally accepted as expressing principles of law and established in order to regulate the relations between these co-existing independent communities or with a view to the achievement of common aims.[1]

Although states are no longer the exclusive subjects of the international system where other entities such as international organisations and, to a more limited extent, individuals are now recognised as having some measure of legal personality, states remain the primary subjects of international law. In light of this mainstream view, what might be the role and significance of gender?

Feminist interventions into international law have been relatively recent, really only starting with the publication of Charlesworth, Chinkin and Wright's ground-breaking 'Feminist approaches to international law' in 1991.[2] A diverse

---

[1] *S S Lotus* (1927) (Judgement) Series A No.9 Permanent Court of International Justice, p. 18, at n. 11.

[2] Hilary Charlesworth, Christine Chinkin and Shelley Wright, 'Feminist approaches to international law' (1991) 85 *American Journal of International Law* 613.

range of topics has since been debated, and the two debates discussed here are inspired by scholars challenging international law from an appreciation of gender and the international legal order. The first debate concerns the question of whether the traditional structures of international law are themselves gendered. The second focuses on one area of international law that has been said to pose challenges to state sovereignty: human rights. This is an area of international law in which the role of the individual has been significantly strengthened. A number of international treaties enable the individual to bring a claim against a state for their human rights violations, through either international or regional mechanisms. How a state treats people within its jurisdiction may no longer therefore be said to be solely its own business. Given such central concepts as equality and non-discrimination, many have viewed human rights as a conducive space to challenge gendered inequalities, while others maintain scepticism about the usefulness of this arena.

Debate 1

Is international society gendered?

GENDER AND THE INSTITUTIONAL CHARACTER OF INTERNATIONAL SOCIETY

Women remain unrepresented or under-represented in national and global decision-making processes. Very few states have female heads of state, equal representation in parliaments or large numbers of female diplomats. According to the UN, there are currently 10 women serving as heads of states and only 22.8 per cent of all national parliamentarians are women.[3] States, feminists claim, are patriarchal structures as they not only exclude women from elite positions and decision-making roles but also because 'they are based on the concentration of power in, and control by, an elite as well as the domestic legitimation of a monopoly over the use of force to maintain that control'.[4] Radical feminists such as Catharine MacKinnon view the state as male and law as instrumental in institutionalising the power of men over women, as well as institutionalising power in its male form.[5]

Some legal scholars, such as Fernando Tesón, have argued that, although women may be 'statistically underrepresented', this is not necessarily unjust.[6]

---

[3] UN Women, *Facts and Figures: Leadership and Political Participation*, http://www.unwomen.org/en/what-we-do/leadership-and-political-participation/facts-and-figures, accessed 15 February 2017.

[4] Charlesworth, Chinkin and Wright (n. 2) 622.

[5] Catharine A. MacKinnon, *Towards a Feminist Theory of the State* (Harvard University Press, 1989) p. 238.

[6] Fernando Tesón, 'Feminism and international law: A reply' (1993) 33 *Virginia Journal of International Law* 651.

For Tesón, this under-representation is only an injustice in situations where the state is preventing women from exercising their right to political participation.[7] He describes an example of this kind of injustice as when a state discriminates against women in its processes for admission to the diplomatic services.[8] Feminist scholars have pointed out the hollowness of this type of formal equality argument as it fails to engage with the many economic, social and cultural barriers that women continue to face around the world. For example, the nature of foreign service deployment, including long-term posts around the world, may have different implications for men and women. Historically it has been the diplomats' wives who have, with their unpaid work, contributed to the sustaining of an atmosphere conducive to diplomacy.[9] Such an integral part were these 'wifely duties' to the service of his government that it was not until 1972 that American diplomats' wives stopped being assessed in their husbands' efficiency reports.[10] Nor was it until 1972 that British and American married women could serve as diplomats. From a feminist perspective, Tesón's limited formal equality argument is not enough, as it can only offer equality when women and men are in the same position.[11] It does not address the underlying causes of the inequalities because it assumes a world where people are autonomous individuals making free choices starting a 'race' from the same position.[12] As Nicola Lacey points out, the position is inadequate to analyse a world in which the distribution of goods and opportunities are structured along gender lines.[13]

The structures of international organisations continue to reflect those of the states,[14] the United Nations being no exception. Negative correlation between level and representation of women persists, or in other words, the higher the position, the less representation of women.[15] Even in the human rights bodies, women remain largely under-represented. Two practical examples can be used to explore the gender implications of international institutions and their mechanisms: the International Court of Justice (ICJ) and the Security Council. The example of the ICJ is significant as it has a 'special function in creation and

---

[7] Ibid. 652.

[8] Ibid.

[9] Martin Griffiths, *Fifty Key Thinkers in International Relations* (Routledge, 2009) p. 404.

[10] Cynthia H. Enloe, *Bananas, Beaches and Bases: Making Feminist Sense of International Politics* (University of California Press, 2000) p. 107.

[11] Hilary Charlesworth, 'Feminist critiques of international law and their critics' (1994) *Third World Legal Studies* 8.

[12] Nicola Lacey, 'Legislation against sex discrimination: Questions from a feminist perspective' (1987) 14 *Journal of Law and Society* 415.

[13] Ibid. 415.

[14] Charlesworth, Chinkin and Wright (n. 2) 622.

[15] Although the P1 and P2 levels exceeded the goal of equal representation, the representation of women continued to correlate negatively with level of seniority; with every increase in grade, the representation of women decreased. UN General Assembly: 'Improvement in the Status of Women in the United Nations System: Report of the Secretary-General', 69th session, A/69/346, para. 9.

progressive development of international law'.[16] Before the appointments in 2010 of two women judges, there had only been one woman judge in the history of the ICJ.[17] This under-representation is relevant for two reasons. First, there is an inherent problem with women being excluded from decision-making processes that have an influence on their daily lives. Second, the long-term domination of institutions or bodies of political power has resulted in the view that issues traditionally of concern to men are viewed as general human concerns,[18] while those which are considered 'women's concerns' are relegated to a special and limited category at the margins.[19] Before so-called gender mainstreaming in the UN, for instance, 'women's issues' were dealt with in one sector only – namely the United Nations Development Fund for Women (UNIFEM). Nowadays, the UN pursues a 'dual track' approach that includes women inside mainstream institutions, as well as maintaining women-specific institutions and programmes.[20] Whether gender mainstreaming has been successful, however, has been a subject of debate.[21]

What about the institutional character of the international body that is considered to be the most powerful: the Security Council? Because so few women have served throughout the history of the Security Council, feminists have argued that women's voices have been virtually excluded from the major international political and security decisions.[22] This is despite the fact that, as Ann Tickner points out, women have a strong history of organising around issues of war and peace.[23] It was not until 2000 that the Security Council formally acknowledged the necessity of women's participation to achieving and sustaining peace. In 2000, the Security Council in its Resolution 1325 'reaffirmed the important role of women in the resolution and prevention of conflicts' and stressed the importance of equal participation and 'full involvement in all efforts for the maintenance and promotion of peace and security'.[24] It was the first Security Council Resolution to address the disproportionate effect of armed conflict on women. Together with a number of other resolutions, this forms

---

[16] Charlesworth, Chinkin and Wright (n. 2) 623.
[17] There are currently three women judges at the ICJ; Joan Donoghue, Julia Sebutinde and Xue Hanqin, see http://www.icj-cij.org/en/current-members, accessed 16 January 2018.
[18] Charlesworth, Chinkin and Wright (n. 2) 625.
[19] Ibid.
[20] Alice Edwards, *Violence Against Women Under International Human Rights Law* (Cambridge University Press, 2011) p. 49.
[21] See, e.g., Dianne Otto, 'Holding up half the sky, but for whose benefit?: A critical analysis of the Fourth World Conference on Women' (1996) 6 *Australian Feminist Law Journal* 7; Laura Reanda, 'Engendering the United Nations: The changing international agenda' (1999) 6 *European Journal of Women's Studies* 49.
[22] J. Ann Tickner, *Gendering World Politics: Issues and Approaches in the Post-Cold War Era* (Columbia University Press, 2001) p. 111.
[23] Ibid.
[24] United Nations Security Council Resolution 1325, UN Doc. S/RES/1325 (2000), preamble.

part of the Security Council's women, peace and security agenda. Although currently six of the 15 Security Council members are women, according to the UN, out of the 504 agreements signed since the Resolution only 27 per cent included references to women.[25] Of course, merely including references to women in agreements does not equal empowerment of women in the processes. Indeed, between 1992 and 2011, 4 per cent of the signatories of peace agreements and less than 10 per cent of negotiators of peace agreements were women.[26] Beyond merely calling for equal representation in decision-making processes, activists and scholars have emphasised the need for more substantial engagement with feminist critiques. For instance, Gina Heathcote argues that a feminist reappraisal of women's participation needs to integrate recognition and understanding of the intersection between race and gender.[27] She has also stressed the importance of critiquing the ways in which military force has remained embedded in the women, peace and security agenda and has come to be framed as a solution to systematic sexual violence.[28] Feminist scholarship has highlighted the need to examine social and cultural causes of violence against women and to focus on preventative strategies, together with re-imagining the basic norms and values that shape international law.[29] These types of strategies challenge the normative character of international law.

FEMINIST ENGAGEMENTS WITH THE NORMATIVE CHARACTER OF INTERNATIONAL LAW

The institutional image discussed above is a practical one. In contrast, the idea that the international society possesses a normative character is by and large a matter for theory. While it is not possible to do justice to the diversity of feminist engagements with the normative structure of international law in such a short space, a few preliminary points can be made with a view to encouraging further engagement with the scholarship in this area. It is worth remembering that the integration of practice and theory is an important feature of feminist enquiry and that the feminist project in international law is both normative and political.

Feminists critique the assumption that international norms directed at individuals within states are universally applicable and neutral, and argue that such principles affect women and men (and other groups) differently. As a consequence, uncritical acceptance of those principles can silence or discount

---

[25] UN Women, *Facts and Figures: Peace and Security- At the Peace Table*, http://www.unwomen. org/en/what-we-do/peace-and-security/facts-and-figures, accessed 3 February 2017.

[26] Ibid.

[27] Gina Heathcote, 'Feminist perspectives on the law on the use of force' in Mark Weller (ed.), *Oxford Handbook of the Use of Force in International Law (Oxford Public International Law)* (Oxford University Press, 2015), p. 121.

[28] Ibid. p. 128.

[29] Ibid. pp. 127–128.

women's experiences of them. Uncovering the silences within a discipline is a familiar feminist method that questions the objectivity of a discipline, as well as the ways in which law distinguishes certain issues as irrelevant or of little significance.[30] In a symposium on 'Method in International Law', where several approaches to international law were represented by eminent jurists, Charlesworth noted that none of them had displayed any concern with gender, or with the position of women, as an international issue.[31] Feminists have also claimed that not only does the silence of women exist throughout international law, it is an integral part of the structure of the international legal order and a critical element in maintaining its stability.[32] This matter has been recognised by critical legal scholarship more generally. Martti Koskenniemi has argued that the international legal concept of statehood has existed to privilege some voices at the expense of others.[33] In this light, there is much to agree with Charlesworth's suggestion that women form the largest group whose interests remain stifled by the structure of the state and its sovereignty.[34]

Using feminist legal theory to inform the challenging of structures that favour the priorities of a small number of elite men (and women) in positions of power at the expense of addressing pervasive economic, social and political inequalities offers potential for the progressive development of international law. Feminists engaging with international law have sought to deconstruct international law norms to expose their structural biases and to question the value systems that underlie the privileging and prioritising of certain issues over others. Questioning how power operates through the structures and values of the international legal order has therefore been central to feminist enquiry. In line with the political project, feminists have also sought ways in which to reconstruct international law and to transform its practice as well as its normative structures for progressive ends.

Scholars such as Karen Knop see opportunities for women in rejecting the centrality of the state, for instance through non-state groups and networks that make up international civil society in order to influence the development, interpretation and implementation of international law by states.[35] Women's interests and concerns are not defined by state borders, but are rather shaped by gender, sexual orientation, culture and other factors.[36] For many, the most

---

[30] Hilary Charlesworth, 'Feminist methods in international law' (1999) 93 *American Journal of International Law* 381.

[31] Ibid. 392.

[32] Ibid. 381.

[33] Martti Koskenniemi, *From Apology to Utopia: The Structure of International Legal Argument* (Cambridge University Press, 2005) p. 558.

[34] Hilary Charlesworth, 'Alienating Oscar? Feminist analysis of international law' in Dorinda G. Dallmeyer (ed.), *Reconceiving Reality: Women and International Law* (The American Society of International Law, 1993) p. 8.

[35] Karen Knop, 'Re/statements: Feminism and state sovereignty in international law' (1993) 3 *Transnational Law & Contemporary Problems* 308.

[36] Ibid. 309.

successful strategies remain attuned to and grounded in local grassroots feminist activism that reflect the specificity and diversity of women's lived experiences and concerns. Others stress the need to focus on the gendered impact of globalisation and to develop global feminist alliances or, in the words of Chandra Mohanty, to build 'transnational feminist solidarity'.[37] Readers interested to explore how this might look in practice may wish to refer to a collection on 'New Directions in Feminism and Human Rights'.[38]

For those seeking to challenge the patriarchal structures of international law, the dilemma of how to best engage with international law remains a significant one. Feminists have been wary of the consequences of working within the mainstream structures and thereby reproducing unequal power relations as well as the potential risk of remaining in the margins associated with rejecting those structures and working outside their boundaries. Some of these contestations can be viewed through the lens of feminist engagement with human rights law, discussed in the following section.

Debate 2

Can international human rights tackle gender inequality?

CHALLENGES TO RIGHTS

It may seem curious, but some feminists do not view rights as the appropriate strategy to challenge gendered inequalities. A frequent criticism of rights discourse within national contexts has been that formal guarantees of equality through rights do not necessarily bring with them substantive equality.[39] Carol Smart has illustrated this through the example of the right to abortion: 'the law may concede a right but if the State refuses to fund abortions ... it is an empty right'.[40] In the international human rights arena, formally all human rights are declared 'universal, indivisible, interdependent and interrelated'.[41] That being said, this point of view about human rights masks a 'deep and enduring disagreement' over the status of economic, social and cultural rights.[42] In general, traditional civil and political rights have received far greater attention with disproportionate consequences for women, as many of the violations of human rights suffered by women are bound up with inequalities in

[37] Chandra Mohanty, *Feminism without Borders: Decolonizing Theory, Practicing Solidarity* (Duke University Press, 2004).

[38] Dana Collins, Sylvanna Falcon, Sharmila Lodhia and Molly Talcott, *New Directions in Feminism and Human Rights* (Routledge, 2011).

[39] Susan Millns, 'Bringing rights home: Feminism and the Human Rights Act' in Susan Millns and Noel Whitty (eds), *Feminist Perspectives on Public Law* (Cavendish Publishing Limited, 1999) p. 187.

[40] Carol Smart, *Feminism and the Power of Law* (Routledge, 1989) pp. 143–144.

[41] Vienna Declaration and Programme of Action (1993), UN Doc. A/CONF/157/23.

[42] Philip Alston and Ryan Goodman, *International Human Rights* (Oxford University Press, 2012) p. 277.

the economic and social spheres. Normative hierarchies and political decisions inherent in reservations to international treaties are evident when comparing the reservations between the Convention on the Elimination of All Forms of Discrimination Against Women (CEDAW) and the International Convention on the Elimination of All Forms of Racial Discrimination (ICERD).[43] This is also clear from practice and international jurisprudence. For instance, in 1970 in the *Namibia Advisory Opinion*,[44] the ICJ stated explicitly that the South African government's practice of apartheid amounted to a flagrant violation of the purposes and principles of the Charter of the United Nations. No such cases exist with regard to discrimination based on sex/gender.

Another criticism of the usefulness of rights entails concerns over the proliferation of competing rights, such as children's rights and men's rights, which may produce counterclaims to women's rights.[45] There is nothing inherent in the rights analysis to provide guidance on how tensions between different persons' invocation of their competing rights claims can be resolved without resort to a utilitarian calculus.[46] Similarly, rights claims can also be bound up with competing interests. While CEDAW is one of the most ratified human rights conventions,[47] there remain extensive reservations to this treaty. Strong criticism has been voiced with regard to these reservations being contrary to the aim of the treaty: to eradicate discrimination against women in all its forms.[48]

Some states have based their objections to CEDAW provisions on conflicting principles or rules in a religion or a culture,[49] even though the CEDAW Committee has since its inception consistently stressed that using national, traditional, cultural or religious reasons as excuses for violations of women's rights

---

[43] You can explore the current numbers and nature of reservations to treaties by using the United Nations Treaty Collection database, available at https://treaties.un.org/, accessed 8 November 2016.

[44] *Legal Consequences for the States of the Continued Presence of South Africa in Namibia (South West Africa) Notwithstanding Security Council Resolution 276 (1970)*, Advisory Opinion, 21 June 1971, ICJ Reports 1971, at 45.

[45] Elizabeth Kingdom, 'Legal recognition of a woman's right to choose' in Julia Brophy and Carol Smart (eds), *Women in Law: Explorations in Law, Family and Sexuality* (Routledge, 1985) pp. 143–161.

[46] Vanessa Munro, *Law and Politics at the Perimeter: Re-evaluating Key Debates in Feminist Theory* (Bloomsbury, 2017) p. 77.

[47] CEDAW, currently 189 State parties, available at https://treaties.un.org/Pages/ViewDetails.aspx?src=IND&mtdsg_no=IV-8&chapter=4&clang=_en, accessed 8 November 2016.

[48] Article 28(2) provides that 'a reservation incompatible with the object and purpose of the present convention shall not be permitted', CEDAW (1979). For a critique on the number of reservations as well as their derogative nature see, e.g., Marsha Freeman, Christine Chinkin and Beate Rudolf, *The UN Convention on the Elimination of All Forms of Discrimination Against Women: A Commentary* (Oxford University Press, 2012); Belinda Clark, 'The Vienna Convention reservations regime and the convention on discrimination against women' (1991) 85 *American Journal of International Law* 181.

[49] See, e.g., reservations to Article 16 – equality in marriage, UN, 'Reservations to CEDAW' (see n. 43).

is not acceptable.[50] The Committee has insisted that some of these reservations are 'incompatible' with the object and purpose of the Convention and should be reviewed, modified or withdrawn.[51] The Committee, however, has no power to do more than to condemn the reservations and encourage their removal. Yet reservations are said to exemplify some of the major obstacles for effective application of CEDAW as a whole.[52]

While noting that some of the uses of culture can be 'profoundly conservatizing', Dianne Otto has critiqued some of the references to culture as the source of stereotyped gender attitudes and 'custom' as the basis for discrimination.[53] She notes that these are sometimes read by Western feminists to justify efforts to abolish non-Western cultural practices, rather than questioning the specific politics of culture.[54] Otto warns that this contributes to neocolonial narratives of women as powerless victims of their tradition, a central concern raised by postcolonial feminist scholars such as Chandra Mohanty, Ratna Kapur and Sherene Razack.[55] Arati Rao has stressed the importance of asking whose culture is being invoked and who are its primary beneficiaries when evaluating claims based on culture. In this way, she suggests that by placing the very nature of culture in its historical context and investigating the status of the interpreter, we can better understand 'the ease with which women become instrumentalised in larger battles for political, economic, military and discursive competition in the international arena'.[56] All in all, as Deborah Rhode has argued, rights discourse presents a challenge for women because a rights analysis of itself is incapable of resolving complex social issues, which require structural changes in society.[57]

Feminists have also argued that universal human attributes posited in liberal political theory which has shaped human rights discourse are examples of false universalisation from a particular, dominant male standpoint.[58] While many

[50] UN, 'Reservations to CEDAW' (see n. 43).

[51] See, e.g., CEDAW General Recommendations No. 4 and No. 20, available at http://www.un.org/womenwatch/daw/cedaw/recommendations/recomm.htm, accessed 17 January 2018.

[52] Janusz Symonides, *Human Rights: Concepts and Standards* (Ashgate, 2000) p. 238.

[53] Dianne Otto, 'Lost in translation: Re-scripting the sexed subjects of international human rights law' in Anne Orford (ed.), *International Law and Its Others* (Cambridge University Press, 2006) p. 343.

[54] Ibid.

[55] Ibid. See also Chandra Mohanty, 'Under Western eyes: Feminist scholarship and colonial discourse (1988) 30 *Feminist Review* 64; Ratna Kapur, 'The tragedy of victimization rhetoric: Resurrecting the 'native' subject in international/post-colonial feminist legal politics' (2002) 15 *Harvard Human Rights Journal* 1; Sherene Razack, *Casting Out: The Eviction of Muslims from Western Law and Politics* (Toronto University Press, 2008).

[56] Arati Rao, 'The politics of gender and culture in international human rights discourse' in Julie Peters and Andrea Wolper (eds), *Women's Rights Human Rights* (Routledge, 1995) p. 174.

[57] Deborah Rhode, 'Feminist perspectives on legal ideology' in Juliet Mitchell and Ann Oakley (eds), *What is Feminism?* (Blackwell, 1986).

[58] Niamh Reilly, 'Cosmopolitan feminism and human rights' (2007) 22 *Hypatia* 183.

activists, scholars and policy-makers have contested the masculinist under-pinnings of human rights law in order to seek the emancipatory potential of human rights, others have argued that some feminist interventions have played into reproducing other hierarchies.[59] In response to this, Otto suggests build-ing feminist and queer coalitions that would challenge the dichotomy between male and female and its associated asymmetry and adopting an understanding of gender as performative.[60]

There is, of course, an important political dimension added to the question of who is using rights discourse and within which paradigm. Women's rights can be at risk of being co-opted by agendas that do not advance women's rights.[61] The rhetoric of advancement of women's rights employed during the invasion of Afghanistan in 2001 intervention illustrates this risk. Gender was used in this context to invoke images of 'saving the uneducated, corporally punished, burqa-clad women'[62] in connection with and as a justification for the deploy-ment of military force. This echoes Orford's warnings of the difficulties with feminist engagements with international law's 'civilising mission', in which fem-inists could only contribute by seeking to protect the weak through the rule of law.[63] She cautions against international law's understandings of women prin-cipally as victims of conflict, rather than as contributors or active participants.[64]

POSSIBILITIES OF RIGHTS

Although feminist critiques of liberal rights have pointed to the various prob-lems and challenges of rights discourse, many scholars have argued for the potential of human rights discourse for challenging gendered inequalities. Two interconnected arguments can be outlined here.

First, some view rights interpretations as open to feminist theorising due to their potential flexibility. Jennifer Nedelsky points out that, as rights define and structure the relationship of power, the task is to foster interpretations that promote relations of equality.[65] Stephanie Palmer sees the potential in inter-national human rights law as an opportunity to introduce perspectives and

---

[59] Otto (n. 53).

[60] Dianne Otto, 'Queering gender [identity] in international law' (2015) 33 *Nordic Journal of Human Rights* 299.

[61] For a critique of the co-option of LGBTQ rights for Western imperialist and racist projects, see Jasbir Puar, *Terrorist Assemblages: Homonationalism in Queer Times* (Duke University Press, 2007).

[62] Karen Engle, 'Liberal internationalisms, feminism and the suppression of critique: Contemporary approaches to global order in the United States' (2005) 46 *Harvard International Law Journal* 439.

[63] Anne Orford, 'Feminism, imperialism and the mission of international law' (2002) 71 *Nordic Journal of International Law* 278.

[64] Ibid. 282.

[65] Jennifer Nedelsky, 'The practical possibilities of feminist theory' (1993) 87 *Northwestern University Law Review* 1290.

experiences into the courts that have been consistently excluded or marginalised in national contexts.[66] In this view, feminist insights can be brought into law through rights.[67] Similarly, MacKinnon has argued that international law can provide new grounds for theory and action, where national struggles might have failed.[68]

Second, some feminists see the potential in rights to be effective in connecting together the political demands for progressive change.[69] Because women are in a disadvantaged position in societies in a range of ways, rights discourse offers a recognised vocabulary in which to frame political and social wrongs.[70] A traditional approach to human rights views them as a framework of 'basic values' and conceptions of a 'good society'.[71] This is exemplified by Richard Bilder's comment that 'to assert that a particular social claim is a human right is to vest it emotionally and morally with an especially high order of legitimacy'.[72] Some feminist international law scholars recognise this symbolic power inherent in claims based on international law and argue that it can carry considerable political force.[73] Charlesworth and Chinkin argue that the discourse of rights is especially powerful as it is the 'dominant progressive moral philosophy', which presents itself as a persuasive social movement that operates at a global level.[74] Likewise, Palmer contends that political power of a rights-oriented framework cannot be ignored or discarded as irrelevant.[75] However, Charlesworth and Chinkin also stress the importance of engaging with and contesting its parameters in order to employ it usefully for women.[76] Speaking in the US context, Patricia Williams has described the talk of rights as 'the magic wand of visibility and invisibility, of inclusion and exclusion, of power and no power'.[77] For Williams, 'the problem of rights is not that the discourse is itself constricting but that it exists in a constricted referential universe'.[78]

---

[66] Stephanie Palmer, 'Feminism and the promise of human rights: Possibilities and paradoxes' in Susan James and Stephanie Palmer (eds), *Visible Women: Essays on Feminist Legal Theory and Political Philosophy* (Hart, 2002) p. 97.

[67] Ibid. p. 97.

[68] Catharine MacKinnon, 'Disputing male sovereignty: On United States v Morrison' (2002) 114 *Harvard Law Review* 177.

[69] Palmer (n. 66) p. 97.

[70] Hilary Charlesworth, 'What are 'women's international human rights'?' in Rebecca Cook (ed.), *Human Rights of Women* (University of Pennsylvania Press, 1994) p. 61.

[71] Ibid. p. 61.

[72] Richard Bilder, 'Rethinking international human rights law: Some basic questions' (1969) *Wisconsin Law Review* 174.

[73] Charlesworth (n. 30) 393.

[74] Hilary Charlesworth and Christine Chinkin, *The Boundaries of International Law: A Feminist Analysis* (Manchester University Press, 2000) p. 212.

[75] Palmer (n. 66) p. 97.

[76] Charlesworth and Chinkin (n. 74) p. 212.

[77] Patricia Williams, 'Alchemical notes: Reconstructing ideals from deconstructed rights' (1987) 22 *Harvard Civil Rights-Civil Liberties Law Review* 431.

[78] Patricia Williams, *The Alchemy of Race and Rights* (Cambridge University Press, 1991) p. 159.

CONCLUSION

While it can be said that gender issues are now firmly on the international agenda, debate remains about the success of this perceived visibility. For instance, gender mainstreaming, while increasing women's participation in the institutional arena, has been criticised for not fundamentally challenging the structural biases of international institutions or international law. Similarly, international human rights law poses both challenges and possibilities for feminist activists and scholars and contestations between how best to advance feminist goals remain a subject of intense debate. While some feminists do not see rights as the appropriate strategy for tackling gender inequality, others argue for the transformative potential in engaging with rights discourse, alongside other social, economic and political strategies. It is clear that scholarship that engages with gender and international law today is rich and diverse. In a world where women continue to be more deeply affected by such complex issues as poverty and intersectional inequalities, globalisation and climate change, for those committed to gender justice finding ways in which to engage with international law for progressive ends remains a necessary struggle.

FURTHER READING

Hilary Charlesworth and Christine Chinkin, *The Boundaries of International Law: A Feminist Analysis* (Manchester University Press, 2000).

Karen Knop (ed.), *Gender and Human Rights* (Oxford University Press, 2004).

Sari Kouvo and Zoe Pearson (eds), *Feminist Perspectives on Contemporary International Law: Between Resistance and Compliance?* (Hart, 2011).

Dianne Otto, 'Lost in translation: Re-scripting the sexed subjects of international human rights law' in Anne Orford (ed.), *International Law and Its Others* (Cambridge University Press, 2006) pp. 318–356.

CHAPTER 9

Family Law

Alison Diduck and Felicity Kaganas

Family law was one of the first areas of law to be subjected to feminist analysis. This may be because, historically, it did not even pretend to be gender-neutral. In the past, the laws regulating family living and family relationships were created, developed and sustained specifically to treat men and women differently as husbands and wives or as mothers and fathers. Further, because of the family's status as a timeless and private institution, the forms it took and the ways it functioned were simply taken to be 'natural' and were, therefore, largely immune from state interference. The effect, however, of this gender-based difference of treatment, which did indeed seem 'natural' in the nineteenth century, combined with the veil of privacy draped over 'the family', was that women were systematically disadvantaged by family law.

Law reforms were often the result of women's activism. In the nineteenth century, feminists campaigned for the destruction of 'coverture', the legal status of married women which subsumed them into their husband's legal personality,[1] and against the injustices and oppressions that followed from that powerless position – for example, married women's inability to hold property in common law or to separate from a violent husband and the lack of concern paid by the law to domestic violence and wife murder.[2] In the twentieth century, the principle of equality with men became the dominant goal even though feminists differed as to whether they wanted women to have special treatment as wives and mothers or the same treatment so that they could operate on a level playing ground with men.[3] By the 1950s, there was a widespread belief that

[1] Tim Stretton and Krista J. Kesselring (eds), *Married Women and the Law: Coverture in England and the Common Law World* (McGill-Queen's University Press, 2013).
[2] See, for example, Joan Perkin, *Wives and Marriage in Nineteenth-Century England* (Routledge, 1989); Maeve E. Doggett, *Marriage, Wife-Beating and the Law in Victorian England* (Weidenfeld & Nicolson, 1992); Lee Holcombe, *Wives and Property: Reform of the Married Women's Property Law in Nineteenth Century England* (University of Toronto Press, 1983).
[3] See, for example, Ruth Adam, *A Woman's Place 1910–1975* (Chatto & Windus, 1975); Harold L. Smith (ed.), *British Feminism in the Twentieth Century* (Edward Elgar, 1990).

full legal equality between men and women had almost been achieved, though feminists were well aware that this was not so.[4]

Modern family laws speak in gender-neutral terms of spouses, partners and parents, and with the advent of sex discrimination legislation and the Human Rights Act 1998, formal legal equality between men and women seems to have been achieved. The idea of family privacy still persists, but the law now is more prepared to look behind that veil of privacy and try to ensure that fairness, protection and justice prevail. The view of many commentators (and judges) is that the law is now as it should be; but others suggest that, under the guise of equality, the pendulum has swung too far, and that men are now disadvantaged by a family justice system that favours women over them.[5] Finally, still others say that formal equality in family law (as in most spheres) is and always was a flawed goal. They suggest that in a society in which women are materially and socially disadvantaged relative to men, formal legal equality can result in more harm than good.

We wish to explore here the gender implications of family law's engagement with equality. We will focus on the issues of post-separation child contact and money and property distribution on divorce. Both of these issues have engaged equality principles in their discourses; equality combines with fairness in financial issues and with welfare in children's issues. We ask whether family law's uncritical acceptance of the formal equality of men and women in parenting and financial matters has alleviated women's historical disadvantage on family breakdown.

Debate 1

Should formal equality govern money and asset division on divorce?

Post-war law permitted divorcing wives to claim alimony as dependants of their husbands. Judges then, as now, had broad discretion in deciding those claims. Until 1970, there was no power to transfer capital assets like the home (or a share in it) on divorce, and, as homes were then usually held in the husband's name alone, an ex-wife could find herself with maintenance (which may or may not have actually been paid) but few other resources. When the Divorce Reform Act was enacted in 1969, feminist lobbyists held up its implementation until an associated Matrimonial Proceedings and Property 1970 was passed, permitting capital transfers for the first time on divorce. This was not

---

[4] See, for example, Edith Summerskill, *A Woman's World: Her Memoirs* (Heinemann, 1967); Dorothy M. Stetson, *A Woman's Issue: The Politics of Family Law Reform in England* (Greenwood Press, 1982).

[5] This view commonly appears after advances in women's legal situation – for example, in 1950 Lord Denning wrote that the wife had become 'the "spoilt darling" of the law', while the husband was 'the patient pack-horse': Sir Alfred Denning, *The Changing Law* (Stevens and Son, 1953) p. 98.

the measure that the feminists had wanted – they would have preferred a form of Community of Property, a feature of many continental jurisdictions and some American states, whereby marital property is held jointly by the couple and divided equally on divorce. Instead, the provisions, now incorporated into the Matrimonial Causes Act (MCA) 1973, directed judges to a list of statutory factors to determine financial and property distribution on divorce, with the objective of putting the parties as far as possible in the position they would have been in had the divorce not occurred.

Further change came in 1984 to reflect the growing emphasis on principles of sex equality. As Diduck and Kaganas write:

> Interest groups such as Campaign for Justice on Divorce (a divorced men's group) lobbied for change in the law whereby a woman would not be entitled to maintenance from a man simply because she was at one time married to him. Many feminists also thought that entitlement to maintenance based on status simply perpetuated women's dependency.[6]

The 1984 amendments to the MCA 1973 repealed the minimal loss principle and replaced it, not with an alternative objective for financial and property orders but with two new factors for courts to consider: the welfare of children of the family and the appropriateness of imposing a clean break upon the parties. This legislation, with the broad discretion it gives to decision-makers, remains the law today.

Throughout the 1980s and 1990s, courts tended to exercise their discretion by ensuring that the housing needs of the parent with care of the children were met before looking to the non-resident parent's housing needs. They would then try to meet the reasonable needs of the claimant before imposing a clean break if it was anticipated that she could become self-sufficient. Once her reasonable needs were met, it was felt there was no need for any further adjustment by the court. Given that wives are disproportionately more likely than husbands to be financially dependent during marriage, it was assumed that what they were claiming was a share of *his* money or property.

Finally, then, as now, most financial and property orders were made by consent after agreements between the parties. 'Clean break' orders were often agreed after negotiations in which wives would forego long-term support and pension orders in the interests of their and their children's short-term financial welfare and housing needs. Further, the principles developed in those disputes that were litigated, the so-called 'big money' cases, became the shadow of the law in which all claims were resolved. Here, a reasonable requirements ceiling for orders was developed which was said to offer some certainty as to how the court would exercise its broad statutory discretion.

---

[6] Alison Diduck and Felicity Kaganas, *Family Law, Gender and the State* (Hart, 2012) p. 277.

Then, in 1999, the ground shifted again, beginning with the House of Lords decision in *White v White*.[7] It is difficult to overstate the importance of this decision. The court here provided direction for how the MCA discretion ought to be exercised, first by challenging the reasonable requirements ceiling:

> If a husband and wife by their joint efforts over many years, his directly in the business and hers indirectly at home, have built up a valuable business from scratch, why should the claimant wife be confined to the court's assessment of her reasonable requirements and the husband left with a much larger share?[8]

It also identified a new objective of 'fairness' for courts in making financial orders based upon the explicitly stated principles of non-discrimination and equality:

> In seeking to achieve a fair outcome, there is no place for discrimination between husband and wife and their respective roles ... [W]hatever the division of labour chosen by the husband and wife, or forced upon them by the circumstances, fairness requires that this should not prejudice or advantage either party .... There should be no bias in favour of the money-earner and against the home-maker and the child-carer.[9]

And:

> [A] judge would always be well-advised to check his tentative views against the yardstick of equality of division. As a general guide, equality should only be departed from if, and to the extent that, there is good reason for doing so.[10]

Here we see their Lordships attributing value to the previously unvalued work traditionally performed by women in the private sphere and the judgments challenge the idea that only the person who performs work in the public sphere is the rightful owner of its fruits.

The shift continued in *Miller v Miller; McFarlane v McFarlane*[11] in which the House of Lords developed further the principle of fairness by suggesting it comprised three strands: needs, compensation and (equal) sharing. Lord Nicholls went on, however:

> It is not a case of 'taking away' from one party and 'giving' to the other property which 'belongs' to the former. The claimant is not a supplicant. Each party to a marriage is *entitled* to a *fair* share of the available property.[12]

---

[7] [2000] 2 FLR 981 (HL).
[8] Per Lord Nicholls at 992.
[9] Ibid. at 989.
[10] Ibid.
[11] [2006] UKHL 24.
[12] Ibid at para. 9.

The introduction of the principle of 'fairness' offered the promise of a sort of substantive equality to financially vulnerable women. The courts acknowledged that the type of work typically done by women either by choice or force of circumstances has value and that performing that work should not be a source of disadvantage if their marriages end.

But the development of the law did not end there. Beginning in the mid-2000s, the three strands of fairness became increasingly infused with the language of formal equality, autonomy and choice. In 2006, for example, the court saw no reason to compensate a wife for her years of homemaking as a result of her 'choice' not to work: 'I am not persuaded at all that anything has been lost by the 7½ year gap in the applicant's employment, or as a result of the mutual agreement between the parties that she would not work … '.[13] The assumption that spouses were 'similarly situated' and thus to be treated the same regarding their family choices finally received the imprimatur of the Supreme Court in 2010 in the context of upholding a prenuptial agreement:

> The Court should accord respect to the decision of a married couple as to the manner in which their financial affairs should be regulated. It would be paternalistic and patronising to override their agreement simply on the basis that the court knows best.[14]

In a society (and now family) organised around ideas of formal equality, we seem, the cases tell us, to be free to make the wrong choices as well as the correct ones, and in order that we are not 'patronised', we must bear the consequences of those choices ourselves.[15]

Some judges worry, however, that the 'equality' principle has swung too far in favour of women. The court in *H v H*, for example, in ensuring that the 'pendulum does not swing too far from: (i) a discriminatory and unfair award based on "reasonable requirements" …; to (ii) an award that is unfair and discriminates against the party that has made the main direct financial contribution',[16] concluded that, although its award of 'less than half the net income of the marital partnership in recent years' would mean that 'the husband's continued earnings [would] quickly create an economic disparity between him and the wife', this did not warrant a higher award to her because … 'the income taken into account in the assessment generously covers the wife's needs'.[17] In *Charman v Charman* the Court of Appeal expressed anxiety that 'in big money cases the *White* factor has more than doubled the levels of award and it has been said by many that London has now become the divorce capital of the

---

[13] *S v S* [2006] EWHC 2793 (Fam) para. 59.

[14] *Radmacher v Granatino* [2010] UKSC 42 para. 78.

[15] See, for example, Ruth Deech, 'What's a woman worth?' (2009) *Family Law* 1140.

[16] *H v H* [2007] EWHC 459 (Fam) para. 96.

[17] At para. 144.

world for aspiring wives'.[18] Finally, the *Daily Mail* reported the Supreme Court decision in *Sharland v Sharland; Gohil v Gohil*[19] as follows:

> Two designer-clad, middle-aged women posed outside the Supreme Court on Wednesday, both wreathed in triumphant smiles. And little wonder: together they had won an historic victory which means they can go back to court to claim more of *their ex-husbands' money.*[20]

So we are back to the old reasoning.

Some have criticised the turn from a form of substantive equality which seemed to have been heralded by *White*. A formal equality that assumes that all are similarly situated. According to the Equalities and Human Rights Commission (EHRC):

> while many partners do indeed hold 'modern' attitudes toward their family and work responsibilities, the arrangements they put in place for work and child-care are often constrained along traditional lines. Over three quarters of mothers state that in day-to-day life they have the primary responsibility for childcare in the home. There are significant differences between the perceptions of men and women about whether they share responsibility for childcare equally. Whilst a third of men believe that they share equally, only 14 per cent of women agree.[21]

Further:

> Responsibility for housework separate from child care also has not changed in accordance with ideas about 'new' family living: full time working mothers do twice the number of hours of housework per week as their full time working partners.[22]

And, when women do earn, they are faced with a continued gender pay gap, in November 2016 of just over 18 per cent.[23] Indeed,

> The gender pay gap is lowest for the under 30s, rising more than five-fold by the time workers reach 40. It is influenced by a number of factors: lower pay in sectors where women are more likely to choose careers, the effect of career breaks and limited opportunities in part-time work.[24]

---

[18] [2007] EWCA 503 (Civ) para. 116.

[19] [2015] UKSC 60; [2015] UKSC 61.

[20] *Daily Mail Online*, http://www.dailymail.co.uk/news/article-3275160/AMANDA-PLATELL-two-ex-wives-final-nail-coffin-marriage.html, accessed 2 January 2017, emphasis added.

[21] Gavin Ellison, Andy Barker and Tia Kulasuriya, *Work and Care: A Study of Modern Parents* (EHRC, 2009) p. 11.

[22] Jacqueline Scott and Shirley Dex, 'Paid and unpaid work. Can policy improve gender inequalities?' in Joanna Miles and Rebecca Probert (eds), *Sharing Lives, Dividing Assets* (Hart, 2009) p. 48.

[23] Government Equalities Office, 17 November 2016.

[24] Equalities and Human Rights Commission, *How Fair is Britain? Executive Summary* (EHRC, 2010) p. 27.

In this context, it may not be surprising that research shows that men's household income increases by about 23 per cent on divorce once we control for household size, whereas women's household income falls by about 31 per cent. There is partial recovery for women, but this recovery is driven by repartnering.[25]

In the longer term, given the need of carers (usually wives) and their children for housing and some security in income in the years immediately following separation or divorce, there is a trend towards offsetting a claim to future pension entitlement against the home. Lack of pension provision is one of the main causes of poverty for women in later life, and divorced women are hit particularly hard:

> 43% of older divorced women live in poverty and this is directly related to the breadwinner/part time worker norm, which means poor pension accumulation during marriage because of women's reliance on the breadwinner's pension. On divorce, they have too little time to catch up.[26]

Woodward reviewed cases decided in 2009–2010 and found that almost all included an order in respect of the marital home and about half included lump sum (clean break) orders. However, only 13.8 per cent included pension orders and 12.5 per cent included a spousal periodical payments order.[27] This is cause for concern.

Formal equality, then, fails to recognise the constraints affecting family choices, assuming them to be equally and freely made, or the value to society and to the family of the care work that (mostly) women do. As Lady Hale wrote in her strong dissent in *Radmacher*,

> choices are often made for the overall happiness of the family. ... These sorts of things happen all the time in a relationship. The couple will support one another while they are together. And it may generate a continued need for support once they are apart.[28]

Family law's failure to acknowledge this reality too often means women suffer financially on divorce.

---

[25] Hayley Fisher and Hamish Low, 'Who wins, who loses and who recovers from divorce?' in Miles and Probert (n. 22) p. 254.

[26] Diduck and Kaganas (n. 6) p. 307, citing D. Price (2011) 'UK Pension Reform: Implications for Family Law', paper presented at Child and Family Law Quarterly Seminar, Kings College London.

[27] Hilary Woodward, '"Everyday" financial remedy orders: Do the achieve fair pension provision on divorce?' (2015) 27 *Child and Family Law Quarterly* 151.

[28] n. 14, para. 188.

Debate 2

Should childcare be shared equally after separation or divorce?

Research has shown that '[t]he great majority of children live solely or mainly with their mother after separation or divorce'.[29] While some proponents of fathers' rights maintain that this is a reflection of judicial bias and demand equal time, it is in reality a reflection of the fact that it is mothers who tend to be the primary carers of their children[30] and that this arrangement continues after separation or divorce.[31] In fact relatively few fathers seek court orders to have their children live with them, whether exclusively or in a shared care arrangement, and, where courts have been involved, they have tended to confirm parents' agreements or to make orders preserving the existing arrangements for children's residence;[32] courts are reluctant to make orders that will disrupt children's lives. However, while the question of residence is not often in dispute, when it comes to contact between the non-resident parent, usually the father, and his children, conflict is far more common. It is the law that governs these disputes and also the way in which they are resolved that form the focus of this debate.

Fathers' rights groups have claimed that the law is biased in favour of mothers and that fathers are denied equal rights. While the concept of parental responsibility[33] gives mothers and fathers equal decision-making status in law, it is argued that, since fathers are active in raising their children, their involvement in the form of generous contact too should continue after parental separation. Although research findings suggest that 'gender divisions in parenting continue to persist despite idealized notions of equally shared parenting' and that fathers 'occupied helper roles while mothers remained children's primary caregivers even when available parenting time constraints were similar',[34] this is not perceived as undermining the case for contact. This is perhaps in part because the egalitarian argument in favour of contact also gains support from particular understandings of available child welfare knowledge.

---

[29] Liz Trinder, Jo Connollly, Joanne Kellett and Caitlin Notley, *A Profile of Applicants and Respondents in Contact Cases in Essex*, DCA Research Series 1/05 (DCA, 2005) p. 8; Jane Lewis and Elaine Welsh, 'Fathering practices in twenty-six intact families and the implications for child contact' (2005) 1 *International Journal of Law in Context* 81, 94–95.

[30] Ellison, Barker and Kulasuriya (n. 21) p. 11; Lewis and Welsh (n. 29) 94–95.

[31] See, e.g., Julia Brophy, 'Child custody, child care and inequality in Britain' in Carol Smart and Selma Sevenhuijsen (eds), *Child Custody and the Politics of Gender* (Routledge, 1989) p. 220.

[32] See Joan Hunt and Alison Macleod, *Outcomes of Applications to Court for Contact Orders After Parental Separation or Divorce* (Ministry of Justice, 2008) p. 9, Table 2.24; Diduck and Kaganas (n. 6) pp. 434–436.

[33] Section 2 Children Act 1989.

[34] Letitia E. Kotila, Sarah J. Schoppe-Sullivan and Claire M. Kamp Dush, 'Time in parenting activities in dual-earner families at the transition to parenthood' (2013) 62 *Family Relations*, 795. UK findings are comparable. See n. 32 above.

The result of the confluence of welfare and equality has, as Smart[35] has said, made it virtually impossible to resist fathers' claims for generous contact; women, or rather mothers, are often disadvantaged and find it difficult to protect their children.

WELFARE

In all matters affecting a child's upbringing, that child's welfare must be the court's 'paramount consideration'.[36] But the values that should inform the welfare decision are not self-evident.[37] They may reflect policy choices and be influenced by dominant discourses about families and children. Since the 1980s, the law and professional practice have been shaped by an increasingly insistent discourse coupling egalitarian arguments with particular interpretations of child welfare knowledge.[38]

A number of research studies point to the benefits of contact. For example, Wallerstein and Kelly, in an influential book, *Surviving the Breakup*, expressed the view that for children of all ages, 'good ego functioning, adequate or high self-esteem and no depression' were associated with a 'stable, close relationship' with both resident and non-resident parents.[39] However, there is also conflicting research. For instance, Hunt, in a comprehensive review of the research, found that the evidence of the links between contact and children's welfare is contradictory.[40] In particular, the connection between frequency of contact and children's well-being was not established.[41] Other factors, such as the quality of the relationship between the contact parent and the child, might be more important.[42]

In a significant expert report presented to the court in *Re L, V, M and H*, Sturge and Glaser outlined the benefits of contact which included, for example, warmth, approval and feeling special to a parent.[43] However they also listed possible disadvantages, such as the potential for escalating parental conflict, divided loyalties and the undermining of children's stability. King observes that claims about what is good for children gain legitimacy if backed up by the language of science.[44] Yet what is accepted as scientific 'truth' changes over

---

[35] Carol Smart, 'Power and the politics of child custody' in Smart and Sevenhuijsen (n. 31) p. 9.

[36] Section 1(1) Children Act 1989.

[37] Robert H. Mnookin, 'Child-custody adjudication: Judicial functions in the face of indeterminacy' (1975) 39 *Law and Contemporary Problems*, 260.

[38] See Diduck and Kaganas (n. 6). pp. 392–397.

[39] Judith S. Wallerstein and Joan B. Kelly, *Surviving the Breakup; How Children and Parents Cope with Divorce* (Grant McIntyre, 1980) p. 215.

[40] Joan Hunt, *Researching Contact* (One Parent Families, 2003) p. 7.

[41] Ibid. p. 8.

[42] Ibid. pp. 8, 13.

[43] *Re L (Contact: Domestic Violence); Re V (Contact: Domestic Violence); Re M (Contact: Domestic Violence); Re H (Contact: Domestic Violence)* [2000] 2 FLR 334.

[44] See Michael King, 'Welfare and justice' in Michael King (ed.), *Childhood, Welfare and Justice* (Batsford, 1981) pp. 109–113.

time. Moreover, what is accepted as scientific 'truth' at any one time depends on whether any one theory of child development has the support of 'powerful groups within society'.[45] Policy-makers make choices between different theories and research findings and, as King and Piper point out, the law has to choose too. In addition, in order for the law to make sense of complex and nuanced research findings, it has to reconstruct and simplify them so that they can be translated into clear, unambiguous principles that can inform decisions.[46] This is illustrated by the judgment in *Re L, V, M and H*; the court stressed the benefits of contact outlined in the Sturge/Glaser Report while ignoring the disadvantages listed in it. A review of the law suggests that the notion that contact is almost always essential to children's well-being has the backing of government, the legislature, lawyers and child welfare professionals.

THE LAW

The Children Act 1989 was amended to create a statutory presumption which came into force in October 2014 and which entrenches in the law this particular interpretation of welfare. Section 1(2A) of the Act now provides that the court should presume that 'involvement' in the life of the child by the non-resident parent will 'further the child's welfare'. This will be presumed unless it can be shown that involvement will put the child at risk of harm.[47] In addition the terms 'contact' and 'residence' have been replaced by 'child arrangements orders'.[48]

This change was in part a response to the demands of fathers' rights groups. Its significance is debatable, given that for many years the courts, as well as legal and child welfare professionals, were already applying a strong de facto presumption that generous contact with the non-resident parent is best for children.[49] The courts articulated what was in earlier cases referred to as a 'presumption'[50] and later as an 'assumption'[51] that contact between non-resident parents and their children is in the children's best interests. The dominant view is that children 'almost always'[52] need to have a relationship with both parents, even, in many cases, in the face of objections from the primary carer or the children.

It is also assumed that conflict harms children and that it is incumbent upon parents to avoid it. Disputes that return to court are regarded as pathological and parents, usually mothers, who resist contact are branded as implacably

---

[45] Ibid.

[46] Michael King and Christine Piper, *How the Law Thinks About Children* (Arena, 1995) pp. 50–51.

[47] Section 1(6).

[48] Section 8.

[49] Felicity Kaganas, 'A presumption that "involvement" of both parents is best: Deciphering law's messages' (2013) *Child and Family Law Quarterly* 270.

[50] *Re M (Contact: Welfare Test)* [1995] 1 FLR 274, 281.

[51] *Re L* (n. 43) 367.

[52] *Re O (Contact: Imposition of Conditions)* [1995] 2 FLR 124, 128.

hostile and as warranting punishment or therapeutic intervention.[53] Parents who litigate are chastised for damaging their children and are urged to reach a 'sensible' agreement.[54] That agreement must include contact.

Where parents do not agree, courts, mediators, Cafcass[55] officers and lawyers '[bend] over backwards' to make contact happen.[56] Courts have the power to fine or imprison mothers who breach orders for contact. These sanctions have generally been considered measures of last resort.[57] However, there have been some indications of a hardening of attitudes within the judiciary,[58] apparently in response to complaints from fathers' rights groups that courts allow mothers to flout court orders. In the case of *In the Matter of the L-W Children*, the judge suggested that the threat, and if necessary its implementation, of a very short period of imprisonment might be effective.[59]

Mothers who defy orders also face a range of measures introduced into the Children Act 1989 which include attendance at a Separated Parent Information Programme (SPIP), an unpaid work requirement[60] and an order to pay financial compensation for losses caused by the breach of the order.[61] While courts make use of SPIPs, they do not appear to use the other two measures.[62] However there seems to be a greater willingness[63] to transfer residence of the child[64] or to threaten such a transfer by means of a suspended order.[65] Courts also on occasion treat a parent's refusal to allow contact with the other parent as posing a threat of significant harm to the child and so invoke child protection measures.[66]

Neither courts nor professionals are deterred from the push for contact by concerns about issues such as domestic violence. In *Re L*[67] the court stressed that, although domestic violence constituted a failure of parenting, it was not a bar to contact; it 'offset' the assumption in favour of contact but the court retained a discretion to make whatever order it considered to be in the child's best interests.

---

[53] Felicity Kaganas, 'When it comes to contact disputes, what are family courts for?' (2010) 63 *Current Legal Problems* 234.

[54] *Re L (Shared Residence Order)* [2009] EWCA Civ 20 paras 66–70.

[55] Children and Family Court Advisory and Support Service.

[56] Hunt and Macleod (n. 32) p. 190.

[57] Liz Trinder, Joan Hunt, Alison Macleod, Julia Pearce and Hilary Woodward, *Enforcing Contact Orders: Problem-Solving or Punishment?* (University of Exeter, 2013) p. 8.

[58] Ibid.

[59] [2010] EWCA Civ 1253, para. 106.

[60] Section 11 J. This is effectively community service.

[61] Section 11 O.

[62] Trinder et al. (n. 57) p. 10.

[63] Ibid. p. 8.

[64] See, e.g., *V v V* [2004] EWHC Fam 1215; *Re: D (Children)* [2015] EWFC 85, para. 25; *Re S (A Child)* [2010] EWCA Civ 325; *Re C* [2007] EWCA Civ 866.

[65] See, e.g., *Re A (Suspended Residence Order)* [2010] 1 FLR 1679.

[66] See, e.g., *Re K (Children) (Contact: Interim Care Order)* [2014] EWCA Civ 1195.

[67] n. 43.

That courts have been making orders for contact in cases involving violent fathers emerges clearly from research. In Trinder et al.'s sample 'concerns about child or adult safety were raised by one or both parents at some point in 75 per cent of cases' and at both the order and the enforcement stages in 63 per cent.[68] Yet 60 per cent of cases involving serious welfare concerns ended with staying or unsupervised visiting contact. The court took appropriate protective measures in only half the risk cases; 'in others the strength of the contact presumption appears to have diverted the court's attention from effectively assessing and managing risk'.[69]

Similarly, in Hunt and Macleod's study, serious welfare concerns including child abuse, domestic violence and substance abuse were raised in 54 per cent of the cases analysed.[70] Almost half the cases involved allegations of domestic violence and, in most of these, the allegations were admitted, proved or supported by evidence.[71] Nevertheless 70 per cent of completed cases ended with a contact order and, of these, 92 per cent ended with an order for direct, face-to face contact. Half of these were for overnight staying contact. If direct contact was not possible, indirect contact was ordered. In only one case was contact refused.[72] Thiara and Harrison comment: 'In general, non-resident parents applying for contact are likely to get it unless they withdraw, drop out or do not turn up.'[73] Yet, they say, it is unlikely that children benefit from contact with violent men and, indeed, contact may impede recovery from the harm done by experiencing or witnessing violence.[74]

In 2016, the charity Women's Aid produced a report[75] documenting reviews of serious cases in which children had been killed during, or as a result of, unsafe child contact. They found that between 2005 and 2015, 19 children in 12 families were killed and two were seriously harmed through attempted murder by their fathers. Two mothers were also killed. In all these cases the father had contact with the children and, for 12 of the children, the contact had been arranged in court. All the fathers were known to statutory agencies as perpetrators of abuse and 11 were known to the police. Nine were known to have been abusive after the separation.

Since *Re L, V, M and H*, the courts have been expected to ensure the safety of the child and the parent with whom the child lives 'before, during and after … contact'.[76]

---

[68] Trinder et al. (n. 57) p. 27.

[69] Ibid. p. 63.

[70] Hunt and Macleod (n. 32) p. 9.

[71] Ibid. p. 84.

[72] Ibid. pp. 11–12 and 204–205.

[73] Ravi Thiara and Christine Harrison, *Safe not Sorry. Supporting the Campaign for Safer Child Contact* (Women's Aid, 2016) p. 8.

[74] Ibid. pp. 6–7.

[75] Women's Aid, *Nineteen Child Homicides* (Women's Aid, 2016). See also Women's Aid (2017) *Child First*, https://1q7dqy2unor827bqjls0c4rn-wpengine.netdna-ssl.com/wp-content/uploads/2017/01/Child-First-One-Year-On-Final-1.pdf, accessed 9 February 2017.

[76] Practice Direction 12J – Child Arrangements and Contact Order: Domestic Violence and Harm (2017) para. 36. This is the most recent version.

There is a duty on the family courts and Cafcass to ensure,

> where violence or abuse is admitted or proven, that any child arrangements order in place protects the safety and wellbeing of the child and the parent with whom the child is living, and does not expose them to the risk of further harm.[77]

This was revised[78] in the light of the serious failings identified in the Women's Aid report: courts and statutory agencies showed little understanding of domestic violence and, in particular, of the fact that violence often continues or even intensifies after separation. They did not understand the risks posed by domestic violence to children.[79] They did not understand the dynamic of coercive control and did not see incidents as part of a pattern of control. As Thiara and Harrison[80] point out, women's accounts of violence are not believed or are minimised and little attention is paid to anything other than (recent) physical injury.

In addition, there is little acknowledgement or, perhaps, understanding of the legitimacy of mothers' objections to contact, which may be founded on fears of substance abuse, violence, abduction or poor childcare. While such mothers are castigated by courts and professionals, Hunt and Macleod[81] showed that implacable hostility is rare. The frequent accusations of 'parental alienation' made in court, asserting that women alienate their children from their fathers by poisoning their minds, are also rarely borne out. Mothers tend to promote contact even in cases of domestic violence.

RECENT CHANGES

The new statutory presumption is qualified; it does not mandate an equal division of time. Nor does it operate where there is evidence that parental involvement would put the child at risk of harm. However, there is a presumption that involvement will not cause harm unless there is evidence that it would. While there is little in the reported cases that shows this has led to any change as yet in the court's approach, the presumption may well affect mothers' bargaining position detrimentally in the course of mediation or negotiations.

There is a strong emphasis on agreement-seeking and diversion from the court process in the Child Arrangements Programme.[82] It is government policy that separating couples should attend mediation to resolve parenting

---

[77] Ibid. para. 6.
[78] The Hon Mr Justice Cobb, Review of Practice Direction 12J FPR 2010 Child Arrangement and Contact Orders: Domestic Violence and Harm, https://www.judiciary.gov.uk/wp-content/uploads/2017/01/PD12J-child-arrangement-domestic-violence-and-harm-report-and-revision.pdf, accessed 9 February 2017.
[79] n. 75.
[80] n. 73.
[81] n. 32.
[82] Practice Direction 12B, para. 5.

disputes. But mediation carries risks for those who are in a weaker bargaining position and particularly for victims of domestic violence. Mediators are required to screen for domestic violence but Morris's research suggests they do not do so well.[83] So although mediation itself is not compulsory, some mothers may feel coerced into attending if the father wants mediation and they may be pushed into agreeing to unsafe contact. This possibility is made more likely by the fact that, although Legal Aid is available for mediation, it is no longer available for litigation unless the person seeking it has evidence that she is or has been the victim of domestic violence.[84] Although the requirements have been relaxed and the numbers granted Legal Aid have increased,[85] many women are unable to meet the stringent evidential requirements stipulated in the Legal Aid, Sentencing and Punishment of Offenders Act 2012.

The result of this Act and policy promoting out-of-court agreements is that a mother who does not have the means to pay for litigation or lawyer negotiation has to negotiate herself, mediate or become a litigant in person. In all these scenarios, she operates in the shadow of fathers' equality claims and the equation of parental involvement with welfare.

CONCLUSION

In family law, we may now be seeing a curious inversion of the disadvantage experienced by women in the nineteenth century. In the twenty-first century, it seems that it is gender-blind sameness of treatment that is the cause of women's disadvantage as both wives and mothers. Indeed, many feminists are not surprised; they are of the view that formal legal equality without corresponding social and economic equality has rarely served women well. What is needed is gender-based different treatment but in the form of a type of substantive equality that takes account of social and economic realities.

FURTHER READING

Alison Diduck, 'Ancillary relief: Complicating the search for principle' (2011) 38 *Journal of Law and Society* 272.
Joan Hunt and Alison Macleod, *Outcomes of Applications to Court for Contact Orders After Parental Separation or Divorce* (Ministry of Justice, 2008).
Felicity Kaganas, 'A presumption that "involvement" of both parents is best: Deciphering law's messages' (2013) *Child and Family Law Quarterly* 270.

---

[83] Paulette Morris, 'Mediation, the Legal Aid, Sentencing and Punishment of Offenders Act 2012 and the mediation information assessment meeting' (2013) 35 *Journal of Social Welfare and Family Law* 445.
[84] Thiara and Harrison (n. 73) pp. 21ff.
[85] See Ministry of Justice, *Legal Aid Statistics in England and Wales, July–September 2016* (Ministry of Justice, 2016) pp. 24–26.

CHAPTER 10

Employment/Labour Law

Rachel Horton

Evidence suggests that, despite many years of legislative and judicial inter-ventions, inequalities still exist in the UK labour market. In 2016 the average gender pay gap stood at 9.4 per cent for full-time employees and 18.1 per cent for part- and full-time employees combined.[1] 74 per cent of directors and over 90 per cent of executive directors of FTSE (Financial Times Stock Exchange) 100 companies were men.[2] In 2016 the Equality and Human Rights Commission and Department of Business, Innovation and Skills reported a 'shocking' increase in pregnancy and maternity discrimination at work with around half of women experiencing a detrimental effect on their career as a result of having children.[3] Research by the Trades Union Congress and the Everyday Sexism Project found that over half of women experience some form of sexual harassment in the workplace.[4] In addition, a combination of factors including lower pay, higher levels of part-time working[5] and careers interrupted by childbirth and childcare mean that women are more likely to have inadequate pensions savings and to experience poverty in old age.[6]

There is therefore plenty of scope to question the extent to which exist-ing legal provisions – which include the anti-discrimination provisions of the

---

[1] Office for National Statistics (ONS), *Annual Survey of Hours and Earnings* (ONS, October 2016).

[2] Ruth Sealy, Elena Doldor and Susan Vinnicombe, *The Female FTSE Board Report 2016* (Cranfield University School of Management, 2016).

[3] Department of Business, Innovation and Skills/Equality and Human Rights Commission, *Pregnancy and Maternity Related Discrimination and Disadvantage* (2016) (BIS16/145).

[4] Trades Union Congress, *Still Just a Bit of Banter? Sexual Harassment in the Workplace 2016* (Trades Union Congress, 2016).

[5] 42 per cent of women work part-time, compared to 12 per cent of men: ONS *Annual Population Survey* (ONS, November 2015).

[6] Polly Trenow, Jemima Olchawski, Liam Foster and Martin Heneghan, *Closing the Pensions Gap: Understanding Women's Attitudes to Pensions Saving* (Fawcett Society, April 2016); Sandra Fredman, 'Women at work: The broken promise of flexicurity' (2004) 33 *Industrial Law Journal* 299.

Equality Act 2010 and a range of workplace rights aimed at facilitating the reconciliation of paid work and unpaid care – are effective in improving gender equality. What follows will focus on the existing law in the UK but will also consider the wider context of EU law and, where relevant, the law in a number of other jurisdictions.

Debate 1

Are 'gender-neutral' or 'gender-specific' workplace rights, or some combination of the two, the best approach to achieving gender equality in relation to the challenges presented by the competing demands of paid work and unpaid care?

Workplace rights which make it possible for employees to reconcile paid work and unpaid care (whether for children or for dependent adults) are generally seen as being of fundamental importance in improving gender equality at work. Given that unpaid care work is still predominantly undertaken by women,[7] rights which facilitate the reconciliation of paid work and unpaid care (whether through leave or flexible work arrangements) are key to enabling women's participation in paid work and, importantly, in quality paid work.[8] Equally, it is evident that no legal framework governing gender equality in the workplace is likely to succeed while gender inequality persists in the home. The Women and Equalities Committee of the House of Commons, in its enquiry into the gender pay gap in 2016, concluded that

> the evidence is clear that caring responsibilities are a significant barrier to women's pay and progression prospects. As long as women continue to take disproportionate responsibility for the care of children and other family members the gender pay gap will persist.[9]

There is therefore an argument that work-family reconciliation rights have an important part to play in challenging gender stereotypes around work and care and should be structured so as to facilitate or promote a more equal division of labour in both the 'private' space of the home and the 'public' space of paid employment.

Employed parents or parents-to-be in the UK are currently entitled to a mixture of what are often termed 'gender-specific' and 'gender-neutral' rights. By gender-specific rights we normally mean rights where eligibility depends upon the status of the employee as either birth mother of the child or the

---

[7] For recent figures, see ONS, *Women Shoulder the Responsibility of 'Unpaid Work'* (November 2016), http://visual.ons.gov.uk/the-value-of-your-unpaid-work/, accessed January 2018.

[8] Women who work part-time in order to manage caring commitments will often take lower skilled work in order to do so. See, for example, Clare Lyonette, Beate Badauf and Heike Behle, *Quality Part-Time Work: A Review of the Evidence* (GEO, 2010).

[9] Women and Equalities Committee, *Gender Pay Gap* (8 March 2016) HC 584 at 185.

partner of the birth mother. Gender-neutral rights, on the other hand, are those available to employees in their role as a parent or carer, irrespective of biological role or relationship to the birth mother.

GENDER-SPECIFIC RIGHTS

All pregnant employees[10] are entitled to paid time off for antenatal appointments and then to 12 months' maternity leave, at the end of which there is a right to return to the same job. Qualifying mothers (those who have a minimum period of qualifying employment and national insurance contributions) are also entitled to statutory maternity pay which is earnings-related for the first six weeks and then paid at a statutory flat rate. Employed expectant fathers (or partners of expectant mothers – of either sex) are entitled to unpaid time off to accompany the mother to antenatal appointments; those who have a minimum qualifying period of employment are then entitled to two weeks of paternity leave, none of which is earnings-related. The asymmetry between these sets of provisions is immediately striking. The rights available to the birth mother are significantly more generous in relation to eligibility, time and pay.

GENDER-NEUTRAL RIGHTS

Since April 2015 eligible couples have been entitled to shared parental leave (SPL).[11] This provides that, where both parents satisfy the (complex) eligibility requirements, the birth mother and her partner may choose to share between them what would have been the last 50 weeks of her maternity leave entitlement. It is something of a hybrid right in terms of gender neutrality because, while the leave is available equally to both mother and partner in their capacities as 'parents', the father or partner of the mother can only access the leave if the mother herself is both eligible for, *and* willing to convert her maternity leave into, SPL. Fathers and partners have no right to the leave independent of the status of the mother and her decision to elect to take SPL instead of her maternity leave entitlement.[12] In addition to SPL, employees who meet the relevant eligibility requirements are also entitled to 'EU parental leave' – unpaid leave of up to 18 weeks (a maximum of four weeks a year); and all employees with the requisite length of service are now entitled to request to work flexibly, whether or not their reasons for doing so relate to caring responsibilities.

---

[10] It is important to note that most 'family friendly' employment rights in the UK are available to employees only and not to other types of worker or to the self-employed.

[11] SPL has now replaced additional paternity leave, a right introduced by the coalition government in 2010. Additional Paternity Leave Regulations 2010.

[12] See Gemma Mitchell, 'Encouraging fathers to care: The Children and Families Act 2014 and shared parental leave' (2015) 44 *Industrial Law Journal* 123.

ISSUES

A first question is whether, in structuring work-family reconciliation rights, the law should reflect the different experiences of women and men in relation to childbirth and childcare. It is relatively uncontroversial that pregnancy itself, as something unique to women, should attract specific workplace protection for health and safety reasons; and as Alina Tryfonidou discusses in 'EU Law' (Chapter 7), pregnancy discrimination is also recognised as unique to women and subject to special legal protection. A more difficult question, however, is whether the same or different rights should be available once pregnancy and physical recovery from childbirth ends and childcare begins.

Even if 'essentialist' differences between women and men in relation to propensity to care are firmly rejected, the fact remains that, as Busby notes, 'given the organisation of work and care within contemporary society, it is impossible to distinguish between women's roles as the bearers of children and as the providers of care as the two are inextricably linked through corresponding social arrangements'.[13] Should the law therefore reflect these socially constructed differences in the contributions and experiences of women in relation to care by providing different rights for each parent, or should it challenge them by treating men and women no differently in the rights they are afforded? The difficulty, Lewis argues, is that 'if the law does the former then it risks perpetuating particular gender roles; if it does the latter then it risks ignoring the reality of women's needs'.[14] The concern is that, by recognising that women do more care and making explicit and separate provision for this, the law reinforces the perception that caring is 'women's work' and thus makes it more likely that women will continue to do more care; both because structuring leave rights in a way that privileges the mother limits the ability of families to make different choices about how care should be managed, and because employers may be more likely to discriminate against women employees as a result.

This issue is something the courts have struggled with. Initially, the Court of Justice of the EU (CJEU) protected special treatment for mothers in relation to care as well as pregnancy and childbirth. Thus, for example, in *Hofmann* the Court held, controversially, that there was no breach of the Equal Treatment Directive by a national law which entitled mothers but not fathers to state benefits when taking time off to care for infants, noting that the Equal Treatment Directive aimed not only to protect the health and safety of the mother during pregnancy and immediately after childbirth but also to protect 'the special relationship between mother and child'.[15] This, and a number of decisions along similar lines, led to accusations that the Court was promoting a 'dominant

---

[13] Nicole Busby, *A Right to Care? Unpaid Care Work in European Employment Law* (Oxford University Press, 2011) p. 145.

[14] Jane Lewis, *Should We Worry about Family Change?* (Toronto University Press, 2003) p. 90.

[15] Case 184/83 *Hofmann v Barmer Ersatzkasse* [1984] ECR 3047.

ideology of motherhood'[16] and entrenching the disadvantage experienced by women as a result. More recently in *Roca Alvarez* the Court took a different approach, noting that 'the positions of a male and a female worker, father and mother of a young child, are comparable with regard to their possible need to reduce their daily working time in order to look after their child'.[17] This change in approach has been largely welcomed as recognition of the need to encourage a more equal distribution of parental responsibility.[18] On the other hand, the statement of the Court in the case of *Maistrellis* that 'the situation of a male employee parent and that of a female employee parent are comparable as regards the bringing-up of children'[19] has been criticised as being 'on the verge of satire in the gender equality context'[20] because of its failure to acknowledge the cultural and other barriers that make the experiences of working parents of different genders so different.

A closely related issue concerns the role of law in challenging or reinforcing stereotypes. We have already seen that courts have a potentially important part to play in entrenching or shifting attitudes to gender and care. If statutory rights are to be effective in challenging stereotypes, should they be structured as gender-neutral or as gender-specific? On the one hand it may be argued that this is best achieved through gender-neutral rights which appear to make no assumptions as to how care is to be divided. On the other, there is an argument that separate but (more) equal rights may also play a crucial part in changing social and cultural expectations. As James puts it,

[we] should not underestimate the importance of quality father-friendly legislation … as it erodes any assumption that male workers have no caring obligations. By endorsing a father's role as a parent, the legislation outwardly challenges any views that parenting is an instinctively and naturally 'female' task.[21]

A third issue is how best to structure legal rights so as to ensure they do not exacerbate gender inequality and discrimination at work. This is a concern that is raised in relation to rights which treat women and men – or mothers and fathers – differently and in particular those which, as in the UK, reserve the most generous rights for the mother. As Chan notes, '[whatever] its admirable aims, by linking difference-based employment legislation to maternity and

[16] Clare McGlynn, 'Ideologies of motherhood in European Community sex equality law' (2000) 6 *European Law Journal* 29, 29.

[17] Case C-104/09 *Roca Alvarez v Sese Start Espana ETT SA* [2010] ECR I-08661 at para. 24.

[18] See, for example, Eugenia Caracciolo di Torella, 'Brave new fathers for a brave new world? Fathers as caregivers in an evolving European Union' (2014) 20 *European Law Journal* 88.

[19] Case C-222/14 *Maistrellis* at para. 47.

[20] Ulrike Lembke, 'Tackling sex discrimination to achieve *gender* equality? Conceptions of sex and gender in EU non-discrimination law and policies' (2016) 2 *European Equality Law Review* 46, 64.

[21] Grace James, *The Legal Regulation of Pregnancy and Maternity in the Labour Market* (Cavendish, 2009).

childcare, the state risks making things worse.'[22] The concern is that, where rights are structured so as to privilege the mother, employers, in an attempt to avoid the cost of compliance, will be more likely to be tempted to avoid employing – or employing on a permanent basis – women of childbearing age. A number of studies certainly suggest that (unequal) gender-specific rights can indeed have this effect but the picture is far from straightforward.[23] In particular, there is evidence that while gender-specific rights may disadvantage women in highly skilled roles (typically those where significant investment would be required to train a temporary replacement), low-skilled workers are those most likely to benefit from this kind of regulation;[24] and, as Chan argues, '[s]ometimes, raising the floor is more important than smashing the ceiling.'[25] In addition, of course, it is important to remember that exacerbating discrimination need not be a feature of gender-specific rights per se but of *unequal* rights; and, crucially, even where rights are equal or available equally to both parents, the probability of employer discrimination is likely to remain while the likelihood of fathers using the rights to which they are entitled is limited. Until more men *take up* their entitlements, they present less of a 'risk' to employers.[26]

This leads us to a final issue: how best to structure rights so as to ensure they are most likely to be taken up by those eligible to do so. There has not yet been any comprehensive research into the take-up of shared parental leave by fathers and partners in the UK but the government's own estimate was that only somewhere between 2 and 8 per cent of fathers would do so.[27] This contrasts with evidence that over 90 per cent of eligible fathers take some paternity leave,[28] and comparative research from a range of jurisdictions which suggests that fathers are indeed more likely to take leave where it is offered on a non-transferable 'use it or lose it' basis.[29] Sweden, for example, addressed the low take-up of parental leave by fathers by the introduction of a 'daddy month'

---

[22] Winnie Chan, 'Mothers, equality and labour market opportunities' (2013) 42 *Industrial Law Journal* 224, 230. See also Catherine Hakim, 'Is gender equality legislation becoming counterproductive?' (2008) 15 *Public Policy Research* 133.

[23] See discussion in Chan (n. 22).

[24] Hadas Mandel, 'Winners and losers: The consequences of welfare state policies for gender wage inequality' (2012) 28 *European Sociological Review* 241.

[25] Chan (n. 22) 235.

[26] See also discussion in Sandra Fredman, 'Reversing roles: Bringing men into the frame' (2014) 10 *International Journal of Law in Context* 442.

[27] BIS *Modern Workplaces: Shared Parental Leave and Pay Administration Consultation: Impact Assessment* (BIS, February 2013).

[28] Jenny Chanfreau, Sally Gowland, Zoe Lancaster, Eloise Poole, Sarah Tipping and Mari Toomse, *Maternity and Paternity Rights and Women Returners Survey* 2009/10 (Department of Work and Pensions, 2011).

[29] Rebecca Ray, Janet C. Gornick and John Schmitt, 'Who cares? Assessing generosity and gender equality in parental leave policy designs in 21 countries' (2010) 20 *Journal of European Social Policy* 196.

in 1995 – a period of non-transferable leave reserved specifically for fathers. This resulted in a very significant jump in the take-up of parental leave by fathers and the right has subsequently been extended to three months.[30] Such statistics may make a case for a renewed focus on gender-specific rights as a route to encouraging a more equal division of parenting. However, it is crucial to remember that, unsurprisingly, the level of pay during leave is also closely related to the level of take-up by men.[31] In Sweden parental leave is paid (for 13 of the total entitlement of 16 months) at close to 80 per cent of normal pay. If gender-specific or gender-neutral rights are to be attractive to fathers who, because of the equal pay gap, are often the higher earner in the family unit, it is evident that the current low levels of remuneration in the UK will need to be addressed.

The last two decades have seen some significant progress in the development of legal rights, both gender-neutral and gender-specific, aimed both at offering employees more options for reconciling paid work and family responsibilities and, more recently, at encouraging shared/equal parenting. Thus in its consultation on the introduction of shared parental leave the government stated that it wanted 'to encourage more fathers and partners to play a greater caring role [and] enable both parents to retain a strong link with the labour market'.[32] The debate as to how to best achieve these aims, and to improve gender equality across all facets of working life, is ongoing. The ability of law to effect transformation in this area is, inevitably, limited by the wider cultural and social contexts in which it operates but it is clear that the design of legal rights will often be a key factor in the decisions that families are able to make about how best to manage work and care.[33]

Debate 2

Should positive action be permitted or required in the workplace and, if so, to what extent?

The right to take positive action (sometimes called affirmative action) – in this context, understood as the use of gender-based measures to redress disadvantage or under-representation attaching to gender at work – is recognised in a number of international legal instruments. Thus, for example, Article 4 of the Convention on the Elimination of all Forms of Discrimination Against Women provides that 'States are allowed to adopt temporary special measures

---

[30] John Ekberg, Rickard Eriksson and Guido Friebel, 'Parental leave – a policy evaluation of the Swedish "daddy month" reform' (2013) 97 *Journal of Public Economics* 131.

[31] Ibid.

[32] BIS *Consultation on the Administration of Shared Parental Leave and Pay – Government Response* (BIS, November 2013).

[33] James (n. 21) p. 104.

to accelerate de facto equality for women until the objectives of equality of opportunity and treatment have been achieved',[34] and Article 157(4) of the EU Treaty[35] states that,

> [w]ith a view to ensuring full equality in practice between men and women in working life, the principle of equal treatment shall not prevent any Member State from maintaining or adopting measures providing for specific advantages in order to make it easier for the underrepresented sex to pursue a vocational activity or to prevent or compensate for disadvantages in professional careers.

Positive action can take a variety of forms.[36] These may include action to encourage job applications from women in male-dominated roles or sectors (or vice versa); mentoring or training schemes designed to facilitate access for women to promotion or recruitment at higher levels of seniority; selection of a female candidate over an equally well-qualified male candidate for a particular job; or the use of gender quotas to ensure more equal representation of men and women in (usually) senior level roles. These last two forms of positive action (sometimes called 'positive' or 'reverse' discrimination) are particularly controversial. Opponents of measures of this kind are concerned, among other things, that the use of gender criteria to determine access to jobs in this way breaches the principle of equality and/or discriminates against unsuccessful candidates in precisely the same way as does the 'pernicious' gender discrimination which equality legislation is designed to redress.

LAW AND POLICY

In the UK, some limited positive action is permitted in employment under the Equality Act 2010 sections 148 and 149. In relation to recruitment or promotion, employers are permitted (but not required) to use sex as the deciding factor between two equally well-qualified candidates where it is proportionate to do so and where one sex is under-represented or generally disadvantaged in the particular sector or occupation in question. The Act makes clear, however, that it is not permissible for employers to have a policy of automatically or unconditionally promoting or recruiting one sex over another where these conditions apply. This prohibition precludes the use of binding gender quotas which amount to a policy giving automatic preference to a female over a male applicant, or restricting vacancies that arise to women applicants only.[37]

---

[34] Available at http://www.un.org/womenwatch/daw/cedaw/, accessed January 2018.

[35] Consolidated version of the Treaty on European Union C-326/02.

[36] Christopher McCrudden, 'Rethinking positive action' (1986) 15 *Industrial Law Journal* 219.

[37] Other than in relation to roles where being of a particular sex is a genuine requirement of the role. Equality Act 2010 Schedule 9.

UK law acts within the constraints imposed by EU law where the CJEU, while recognising the necessity of positive action for gender equality, has imposed corresponding restrictions on its scope. Noting that 'even where male and female candidates are equally qualified, male candidates tend to be promoted in preference to female candidates particularly because of prejudices and stereotypes concerning the role and capacities of women in working life',[38] the CJEU agreed that the Equal Treatment Directive permits 'measures which, although discriminatory in appearance are in fact intended to eliminate or reduce actual instances of inequality which may exist in the reality of social life.'[39] The court agreed that the scope of permissible action includes 'measures relating to access to employment, including promotion, which give specific advantage to women with a view to improving their ability to compete on the labour market and to pursue a career on equal footing with men.'[40] However, this does not extend to measures which guarantee 'absolute and unconditional priority for women in the event of a promotion'.[41]

ISSUES

The first issue is a concern about effectiveness. On the one hand, it is argued that persistent structural and institutional inequality in the labour market means that laws prohibiting discrimination by employers are, on their own, unlikely to be sufficient to achieve equality. Given the persistence of gender inequality and discrimination over 40 years after the introduction of the Equal Pay Act 1970 and Sex Discrimination Act 1975, this is difficult to contest.[42] Projections as to the length of time it is likely to take to redress gender inequality in the workplace without further action are gloomy. On the other hand, there is a concern that action such as imposition of gender quotas which – temporarily at least – may achieve what looks like gender equality, in fact does nothing to remove the real barriers to long-lasting equality in the workplace because it does nothing to tackle the underlying structural inequalities. Numerical equality, it is argued, does not imply equal opportunities for women and men and, worse, may mask the need to take further action. There is also a worry that the perceptions of 'more favourable treatment' for women in the context of positive action will

---

[38] *Marschall v Land Nordrhein Westfalen* [1998] IRLR 39 at para. 29.

[39] *Commission v France* (1988) ECR 6315 at para. 15; *Kalanke v Freie Hansestadt Bremen* [1995] IRLR 660, para. 18.

[40] *Kalanke* (n. 39) para. 19.

[41] *Kalanke* (n. 39) paras 21 and 22. The debate over the extent to which positive action should be permitted is currently particularly prominent in relation to the question of women on the boards of top companies – see Chapter 12, 'Company Law and Corporate Governance', in this book.

[42] Although see, for example, Hakim who argues that inequality need not be symptomatic of lack of equal opportunities but of preferences, in Catherine Hakim, *Work-Lifestyle Choices in the 21st Century: Preference Theory* (Oxford University Press, 2000).

generate resentment and exacerbate discrimination where the purpose of the action is not well explained and understood.

Second is the objection that preferential treatment because of gender, or other status, is an affront to the principle of equality. Unequal treatment of men and women because of their sex is precisely (it is argued) the wrong that legislation such as the Equality Act sets out to prevent. However, the question of whether positive discrimination is compatible or incompatible with equality of course depends on the conception of equality one appeals to. Unsurprisingly there is considerable disagreement, even (or perhaps especially) among feminist academics, as to what equality means and there is a vast literature devoted to this aspect of the debate.[43] Briefly, 'formal equality' – often aligned with equal treatment – is normally contrasted with 'substantive equality', which may equate to equality of opportunity and equality of results.[44] While positive action may be incompatible with formal equality, it may be compatible with or even required to achieve substantive equality.

Very closely related is a concern that positive action, at least in some of its forms, is just discrimination by another name. Indeed the forms of positive action which include recruitment or promotion based on gender are often termed 'positive discrimination' or 'reverse discrimination'. The worry is that selecting a candidate on the basis of their sex – for any reason – is wrong because it restricts opportunities for individuals for reasons of status rather than merit and thereby fails to respect the dignity of the excluded individuals in exactly the same way as does pernicious discrimination. It treats group membership as a relevant factor in decision-making rather than assessing each individual solely on the basis of their individual merits and needs. It is this type of worry which is evident in the limits imposed on the boundaries of public action by the CJEU, above. The counter argument to this view is to point out that 'positive' and 'pernicious' discrimination are fundamentally different because, unlike much pernicious discrimination, positive action is not based on prejudice or stereotype, nor does it serve to exclude those who belong to a socially or historically disadvantaged group. For these reasons, it is argued, it does not undermine the dignity of the individual(s) who may lose out as a result.[45]

This leads us to a further objection, and perhaps the one most commonly raised in the popular and political debate, which is that strong forms of positive action, such as quotas, disregard individual merit in a way that is both unfair and economically inefficient: unfair because applicants for jobs or promotions

---

[43] For an excellent account of these issues see Sandra Fredman, 'Substantive equality revisited' and reply by Catharine MacKinnon, 'Substantive equality revisited: A reply to Sandra Fredman' both in (2016) 14 *International Journal of Constitutional Law* 712 and 739.

[44] See, for example, Sandra Fredman who identifies four dimensions to substantive equality: redistributive, recognition, transformative, participative, in *Discrimination Law* (Oxford University Press, 2011).

[45] See, for example, Denise G. Reaume, 'Discrimination and dignity' (2003) 63 *Louisiana Law Review* 645.

in the labour market should be judged on their merits; inefficient because what business needs to maximise success is the most highly qualified and able workforce available. Objections of this type were evident in UK debate on board membership where the Davies review, having consulted on the question of legal quotas, rejected this approach 'because we believe that board appointments should be made on the basis of business needs, skills and ability'.[46] A concern not to undermine the use of merit as the key criterion in recruitment and promotions decisions is also evident in the requirement that positive action under the Equality Act only be used as a tiebreak where candidates are equally qualified.

There are a number of different responses to this argument. One is to counter that selection based on merit does not guarantee equal opportunities for women and men because, for reasons of past discrimination or disadvantage, women may be less likely to have had an opportunity to acquire particular skills and experience. A second is that merit is itself a gendered concept because it will normally be defined by the dominant group to reflect the status quo.[47] A third is to argue that gender may itself often comprise an essential component of what is meant by 'merit' in relation to a particular workplace role, in the same way as do other qualifications and attributes. This is because diversity and equal representation are recognised to be important to the success of organisations; and because without female role models it will more difficult to break the barriers to promotion and recruitment in certain roles and sectors.[48] The Davies review itself identified both of these considerations as important reasons to take steps to increase the representation of women on boards, noting that 'the relatively low number of successful female role models often compounds stereotypes and reinforces perceived difficulties in rising up the corporate ladder' and that '[t]here is a body of research which demonstrates how the appointment of female directors can improve a company's performance … [b]etter decision-making is assumed to occur as a result of directors having a range of experiences and backgrounds'.[49]

CONCLUSION

Even when policy-makers agree that something must be done to redress under-representation of women in various sectors and industries and in positions of seniority and influence, the use of positive action remains highly contested. Given that positive action can involve making decisions about

---

[46] Lord Davies of Abersoch, *Women on Boards* (BIS, Feburary 2011) p. 18; and see Chapter 12, 'Company Law and Corporate Governance', in this book.

[47] Fredman (n. 44).

[48] See, for example, Richard Dworkin who makes this argument in support of affirmative action on race in the United States in *A Matter of Principle* (Harvard University Press, 1985).

[49] n. 46 at p. 19 and p. 8. See also Charlotte Villiers, 'Achieving gender balance in the boardroom: Is it time for legislative change?' (2010) 30 *Legal Studies* 556.

individuals on the basis of their gender, something which, in other contexts, we tend to think is deeply wrong, this is perhaps unsurprising. If positive action is to be used it is therefore essential to be able to provide a robust defence of both its theoretical rationale and its strategic necessity.

FURTHER READING

Eugenia Caracciolo di Torella, 'Brave new fathers for a brave new world? Fathers as caregivers in an evolving European Union' (2014) 20 *European Law Journal* 88.

Winnie Chan, 'Mothers, equality and labour market opportunities' (2013) 42 *Industrial Law Journal* 224.

Sandra Fredman, 'Reversing discrimination' (1997) 113 *Law Quarterly Review* 575.

Grace James, *The Legal Regulation of Pregnancy and Maternity in the Labour Market* (Cavendish, 2009).

Christopher McCrudden, 'Rethinking positive action' (1986) 15 *Industrial Law Journal* 219.

Charlotte Villiers, 'Achieving gender balance in the boardroom: Is it time for legislative change?' (2010) 30 *Legal Studies* 556.

CHAPTER 11

Health Law, Medicine and Ethics

Marie Fox and Jaime Lindsey

In common with many relatively new legal disciplines, health or medical law is often cast as a 'mongrel' subject lacking clear parameters or disciplinary boundaries.[1] In part because of its origins in more established subjects, including criminal, tort, contract and public law, underpinning principles have been crucial in shaping health law.[2] Autonomy is widely viewed as the core of these principles,[3] although others such as the protection of bodily integrity and patient dignity have been significant. Autonomy is equally key to the question of gender, since the concept has been interpreted in ways which support a particular exclusionary conception of the human person. In determining who is autonomous, conceptions of disembodied rationality remain the benchmark. In this chapter, therefore, we address two issues which take up various aspects of autonomy and embodiment. Our first debate deals with consent to medical treatment, focusing on informed consent and capacity to consent. The second focuses on abortion regulation, demonstrating how the criminalisation of abortion in the UK is at odds with the construction of patients as autonomous citizens.

Debate 1
Are women more likely to have their healthcare decisions overruled?

UK courts have consistently reaffirmed the importance of autonomy, highlighting that consent to medical treatment can be refused even if it results in death, and that 'concern for the foetus cannot outweigh a competent woman's autonomy'.[4]

---

[1] Margaret Brazier and Nicola Glover, 'Does medical law have a future?' in David Hayton (ed.), *Law's Future(s)* (Hart, 2000).
[2] Imogen Goold and Jonathan Herring, *Great Debates in Medical Law and Ethics* (Palgrave, 2014) pp. 1–10.
[3] Onora O'Neill, *Autonomy and Trust in Bioethics* (Cambridge University Press, 1996).
[4] Samantha Halliday, *Autonomy and Pregnancy: A Comparative Analysis of Compelled Obstetric Intervention* (Routledge, 2016) p. 54.

Autonomy therefore works to protect adults from medical paternalism but can also be used to justify intrusions where a person is deemed not to be competent. Autonomy entails respect for self-determination. Traditional accounts equate autonomy with rationality[5] and generally exclude other factors, such as caring responsibilities, that influence decision-making. Rationalist accounts also sideline bodily constraints on autonomy,[6] instead focusing on abstract reasoning. Consequently, those who do not meet expectations of abstract rationality might not be seen as fully autonomous. As the cases below highlight, this is particularly true for women with mental disabilities, a group often characterised as inherently vulnerable by virtue of their disability.[7] This understanding contrasts with views positing that all adults can be both autonomous and vulnerable to varying degrees at different stages in their lives. Therefore, notwithstanding clear statements that a competent adult has full autonomy to give or withhold consent, the concept of capacity is simultaneously used to undermine particular patients' rights to have their healthcare decisions respected.

THE IMPORTANCE OF CONSENT

Provided that consent is voluntary,[8] informed and capacitous, all patients are able to provide or refuse consent to medical treatment for reasons which are 'rational or irrational, or for no reason'.[9] Invasive medical treatment should not be provided without consent,[10] otherwise healthcare professionals could be guilty of battery in civil[11] and criminal law.[12] Consent is also an important aspect of negligence law: the absence of a patient's informed consent to treatment could constitute a breach of the healthcare professional's duty of care. Yet, as Donnelly explains, for much of medical history a patient's wishes were not relevant and deference to medical opinion prevailed.[13] Therefore consent has played an important role in protecting autonomy and resisting paternalism in healthcare.

---

[5] Immanuel Kant, *Groundwork of the Metaphysics of Morals* (Cambridge University Press, 1998).

[6] Ngaire Naffine and Rosemary Owens (eds), *Sexing the Subject of Law* (LBC Information Services, 1997); Ruth Fletcher, Marie Fox and Julie McCandless, 'Legal embodiment: Analysing the body of healthcare law' (2008) 16 *Medical Law Review* 321.

[7] Jaime Lindsey, 'Developing vulnerability: A situational response to the abuse of women with mental disabilities' (2016) 24 *Feminist Legal Studies* 295.

[8] Voluntariness is not considered in detail as it is a less used aspect of the test. It applies where a patient has given consent under circumstances of coercion or undue influence – see *Re T (Adult: Refusal of Treatment)* [1992] 3 WLR 782 and Ruth Faden, Tom Beauchamp and Nancy King, *A History and Theory of Informed Consent* (Oxford University Press, 1986) p. 339.

[9] *Sidaway v Board of Governors of the Bethlem Royal Hospital* [1985] AC 871, at 904–905.

[10] *Collins v Wilcox* [1984] 1 WLR 1172.

[11] *Freeman v Home Office* [1984] 1 All ER 1036.

[12] *Attorney General's Reference (No. 6 of 1980)* [1981] 1 QB 715.

[13] Mary Donnelly, *Healthcare Decision-Making and the Law: Autonomy, Capacity and the Limits of Liberalism* (Cambridge University Press, 2010) pp. 11–12.

A pregnant woman's right to refuse treatment was affirmed in *St George's Healthcare NHS Trust v S* [1999] Fam 26. It concerned an appeal against a declaration that it would be lawful to carry out a Caesarean section on a 28-year-old pregnant woman, S, without her consent and against her wishes. Pending the appeal, S delivered the baby by Caesarean. The Court of Appeal subsequently held that her detention had been unlawful and that she had capacity to refuse a Caesarean. Therefore, the intervention forced on her without her consent had been unlawful. Those who support a woman's right to make decisions about her own body have welcomed the symbolism of the ruling,[14] which reinforces the right of any *competent* adult to refuse medical treatment. However, this and other rulings turn on the question of competence; an adult who is deemed incompetent can still have her healthcare decisions overruled. As such, the role of capacity is central to the debate over whether women's healthcare decisions are more likely to be overridden.

Capacity to Consent

The Mental Capacity Act 2005 (MCA) offers a clear legislative framework for deciding whether a person lacks capacity. Section 2(1) MCA states:

> a person lacks capacity in relation to a matter if at the material time he is unable to make a decision for himself in relation to the matter because of an impairment of, or disturbance in the functioning of, the mind or brain.

The test for whether someone is unable to make a decision requires that the person (a) understands the information relevant to the decision,[15] (b) can retain that information,[16] and (c) can use or weigh that information as part of the process of making the decision.[17] They must also be able to communicate their decision.[18] Importantly, a person is not to be treated as unable to make a decision because it is an unwise decision.[19] However, the way that capacity assessments are carried out has prompted observations 'that gender stereotyping of "feminine" behaviour may lead to a greater likelihood of women's capacity being questioned and found lacking'.[20]

If capacity assessments *are* more likely to result in women being deemed to lack capacity than men, that is of serious concern. There is limited empirical

---

[14] Kirsty Moreton and Marie Fox, 'Re MB (An Adult: Medical Treatment) [1997] and St George's Healthcare NHS Trust v S [1998]: The dilemma of the 'court ordered' Caesarean', in Jonathan Herring and Jessie Wall (eds), *Landmark Cases in Medical Law* (Hart, 2015).

[15] s. 3(1)(a) MCA.

[16] s. 3(1)(b) MCA.

[17] s. 3(1)(c) MCA.

[18] s. 3(1)(d) MCA.

[19] s. 1(4) MCA.

[20] Donnelly (n. 13) p. 168.

research about capacity assessments[21] and further work is clearly needed to interrogate this hypothesis. However, case law indicates it may be true. For example, in *Re MB* [1997] 2 FLR 426, a pre-MCA case, a pregnant woman was deemed temporarily incompetent to consent to intravenous anaesthetic to enable a Caesarean to be safely carried out and therefore it could be administered against her wishes. As Halliday writes:

> in all of the cases [bar one] that preceded *MB* ... the women refusing treatment were held to be incompetent; it therefore seems a rather hollow victory to say that a competent woman may refuse treatment given the unlikelihood of a woman refusing treatment necessary to save the foetal life being adjudged competent.[22]

This has been reaffirmed in MCA cases. For example, in *A University Hospital NHS Trust v CA* [2016] EWCOP 51 Baker J held a Caesarean could lawfully be performed on a 24-year-old woman with a diagnosis of autism and learning disability as she lacked capacity to make decisions about her medical treatment. Yet CA's reasons for resisting medical treatment were arguably highly rational; it was understood she had undergone episodes of 'tribal' cutting[23] and female genital mutilation[24] as a child and the judge rightly explained that as a result 'the prospect of a Caesarean section may well carry risks of psychological or other trauma'.[25] However, he added, 'On the other hand, for a woman who has undergone FGM (of whatever type) there is an increased risk of tearing, blood loss and infection through the process of natural childbirth',[26] thereby importing irrationality back into her decision. Ultimately all appears to have turned out well as CA underwent a successful Caesarean during which only 'minimal restraint was required to hold her hand to administer intravenous sedation'.[27] However, the case highlights that even where case law sets out a clear right to refuse medical treatment, in reality particular women's decisions are more likely to be overridden on the basis of incompetence, placing that principle on shaky ground.

Once an adult is found to lack capacity, the court determines what treatment can be provided in her best interests.[28] The best interests test is adapted from section 1 Children Act 1989, highlighting the infantilising link often drawn between adults with mental disabilities and children.[29] For example, in *Sheffield City Council v E and another* [2004] EWHC 2808 (Fam), E, a 21-year-old woman, is

---

[21] Ibid., and Anna Murrell and Leona McCalla, 'Assessing Decision-making Capacity: The Interpretation and Implementation of the Mental Capacity Act 2005 Amongst Social Care Professionals' (2016) 28 *Practice* 21.

[22] Halliday (n. 4) p. 55.

[23] *A University Hospital NHS Trust v CA* [2016] EWCOP 51, para. 12.

[24] Ibid. para. 13.

[25] Ibid. para. 14.

[26] Ibid.

[27] Ibid. para. 49.

[28] s. 1(5) MCA.

[29] See further, David Shoemaker, 'Responsibility, agency, and cognitive disability' in Eva Feder Kittay and Licia Carlson (eds), *Cognitive Disability and its Challenge to Moral Philosophy* (Wiley-Blackwell, 2010) pp. 203–204.

described as a 'girl' who 'functioned at the level of a 13 year old'. Furthermore, as Fletcher, Fox and McCandless explain, the best interests approach does not 'fully protect the subjective value of embodiment to those who are self-aware but not autonomous'.[30] Conseqently capacity legislation can diminish the role of an individual's preferences in the name of what clinicians think is best. This is apparent in forced sterilisation cases where it has been ordered that it is in the adult's best interests to be sterilised,[31] despite the availability of effective and less intrusive forms of contraception. This points to a problematic understanding of the interplay between disability, reproduction and gender.[32] Such concerns apply to men and women with disabilities, but the greater physical impact of sterilisation on women and the fact that women's bodies are more likely to be the focus of law highlights the gendered interpretation of best interests.[33]

INFORMED CONSENT

The doctrine of informed consent requires that patients have sufficient information to understand the treatment they are consenting to. The issue was central to *Montgomery v Lanarkshire Health Board (Scotland)* [2015] UKSC 11. It concerned a clinician's alleged negligent failure to inform a pregnant woman that there was a risk of shoulder dystocia for the baby if she proceeded with vaginal delivery and the related failure to discuss the alternative possibility of Caesarean section. The Supreme Court held that the clinician had been negligent in failing to disclose the risks and alternative options for delivery and, but for that negligence, the acute hypoxia suffered by Mrs Montgomery's son during delivery would not have occurred, as she would have opted for a Caesarean.[34] In *Montgomery* the Supreme Court made clear that clinicians are:

> under a duty to take reasonable care to ensure that the patient is aware of any material risks involved in any recommended treatment, and of any reasonable alternative or variant treatments. The test of materiality is whether, in the circumstances of the particular case, a reasonable person in the patient's position would be likely to attach significance to the risk, or the doctor is or should reasonably be aware that the particular patient would be likely to attach significance to it.[35]

---

[30] Fletcher, Fox and McCandless (n. 6) 336.

[31] *An NHS Trust v DE* [2013] EWHC 2562 (Fam), *Mental Health Trust v DD* [2015] EWCOP 4.

[32] Kirsty Keywood, '"I'd rather keep him chaste": Retelling the story of sterilisation, learning disability and (non)sexed embodiment' (2001) 9 *Feminist Legal Studies* 185; Beverley Clough, '"People like that": Realising the social model in mental capacity jurisprudence' (2015) 23 *Medical Law Review* 53.

[33] Marie Fox and Therese Murphy, 'The body, bodies, embodiment: Feminist legal engagement with health' in Vanessa Munro and Margaret Davies (eds), *Ashgate Research Companion to Feminist Legal Theory* (Ashgate, 2013).

[34] The decision was a departure from *Sidaway v Board of Governors of Bethlem Royal Hospital and the Maudsley Hospital* which applied the Bolam test to consent; see Margaret Brazier and Jose Miola, 'Bye bye Bolam: A medical litigation revolution?' (2000) 8 *Medical Law Review* 85.

[35] *Montgomery v Lanarkshire Health Board (Scotland)* [2015] UKSC 11, para. 87.

This formulation better enables adults to make decisions about treatment based on their own values and have those decisions respected. For example, those who have caring responsibilities may place greater weight on a short recovery time when choosing between different treatments, even though a clinician may not think that is in the patient's *medical* best interests. The *Montgomery* decision is an important move away from the paternalistic model of medicine towards an understanding of patient autonomy which values the individual's own ideals.[36] This has long been argued for by feminists who contend that the paternalistic model ignores the experiences of marginalised groups.[37] The development of the law on informed consent might now provide better protection for patients, though it is striking, as Montgomery and Montgomery have observed, that its rhetorical support for patient autonomy was justified by disregarding the actual choices of an 'intelligent, educated, articulate, independent and well-supported woman'.[38]

Debate 2

Should abortion be decriminalised?

The downplaying of choice is still more apparent in our second debate, which considers governance of abortion decision-making. As with assessing capacity, law's approach to regulating abortion demonstrates how the rhetoric and ideals of modern health law are not always translated into particular areas of practice. While male partners may, of course, be involved in abortion decision-making,[39] ultimately the decision to proceed with or terminate a pregnancy directly impacts only on the woman's body. In considering law's approach to abortion it is important to note how commonplace abortion is. In 2015, 185,824 women had abortions in the UK, 98 per cent of which were funded by the National Health Service.[40] As such figures suggest, abortion is now a safe and established medical procedure, especially in the early stages of pregnancy. Therefore, one might expect that a competent woman would be trusted to elect whether or not to have a termination, just as she makes decisions about whether to undergo other medical procedures. After all, the General Medical

---

[36] However, Farrell and Brazier suggest that little may change in practice as a result of *Montgomery* as it simply confirms GMC guidance on consent as well as current professional practice: Anne Maree Farrell and Margaret Brazier, 'Not so new directions in the law of consent? Examining *Montgomery v. Lanarkshire Health Board*' (2016) 42 *Journal of Medical Ethics* 285.

[37] Fletcher, Fox and McCandless (n. 6) 330.

[38] Jonathan Montgomery and Elsa Montgomery, '*Montgomery* on informed consent: An inexpert decision?' (2016) 42 *Journal of Medical Ethics* 89, 89.

[39] Marie Fox, 'Abortion decision-making: Taking men's needs seriously' in Ellie Lee (ed.), *Abortion Law and Politics Today* (Macmillan, 1998); Sally Sheldon, 'Unwilling fathers and abortion: Terminating men's child support obligations' (2003) 66 *Modern Law Review* 175.

[40] https://www.gov.uk/government/statistics/report-on-abortion-statistics-in-england-and-wales-for-2015, accessed 8 February 2017.

Council (GMC) guidance to doctors is clear that their obligation is to work in partnership with patients. It requires them to

> (l)isten to, and respond to, their concerns and preferences. Give patients the information they want or need in a way they can understand. Respect patients' right to reach decisions with you about their treatment and care.[41]

Under the current legal framework, however, abortion is a criminal offence. Our central question, therefore, is whether the time has come to decriminalise it.

The Legal Framework

The bedrock of the current legislative framework is a Victorian statute, the Offences Against the Person Act (OAPA) 1861, which renders 'procuring a miscarriage' illegal in England, Wales and Northern Ireland. It was also a crime at common law in Scotland. The 1861 Act provides that the offence is punishable by life imprisonment. The crime can be committed by the pregnant woman herself as well as abortion providers (s. 58). Those who aid and abet abortion provision are liable to a five-year sentence (s. 59). As Sheldon has observed, this is the oldest extant statute governing a medical procedure.[42] The Law Commission has signalled the need for radical reform of the 1861 Act, although it excluded the provisions governing abortion from its purview. In consequence, Sheldon has argued that

> the refusal of successive governments to update the law governing abortion leaves intact an archaic legal framework that suffers from many of exactly the same problems that the Commission sees as providing a compelling case for general reform of the OAPA.[43]

The 1967 Abortion Act, which applies to England, Wales and Scotland, but not to Northern Ireland, ameliorates the harshness of the 1861 Act by providing doctors with a defence provided termination of pregnancy is carried out on the grounds stipulated by the Act. Effectively it installs doctors as gatekeepers to abortion. If two doctors agree in good faith that a given pregnancy is putting a woman's health or the health of her existing children at risk, then she can lawfully terminate a pregnancy up to 24 weeks.[44] This law gives no rights

---

[41] GMC, *Good Medical Practice*, 2013, para. 31, https://www.gmc-uk.org/guidance/good_medical_practice.asp, accessed 25 January 2018.

[42] Sally Sheldon, 'British abortion law: Speaking from the past to govern the future' (2016) 97 *Modern Law Review* 283, 284.

[43] Sally Sheldon, 'The decriminalisation of abortion: An argument for modernisation' (2016) 36 *Oxford Journal of Legal Studies* 334–335.

[44] Linda Clarke, 'Abortion: A rights issue?' in Robert G. Lee and Derek Morgan (eds), *Birthrights: Law and Ethics at the Beginnings of Life* (Routledge, 1989). s. 1(1)(a) Abortion Act. The Human Fertilisation and Embryology Act 1990 included amendments to the 1967 Act, the most significant of which was the reduction of the upper time limit on most abortions from 28 weeks of gestation to 24 weeks.

to anyone other than doctors, who have rights to terminate when abortion is permissible and rights (under section 4 of the Act) to conscientiously object.[45] After 24 weeks, a pregnancy may be terminated if the woman's life is at risk or if her health is at risk of grave permanent injury, or if the foetus is at risk of suffering serious abnormalities (s. 1(1)(c)–(d)). In an emergency one doctor may give the necessary permission to save the life of the pregnant woman or prevent grave permanent injury to her physical or mental health (s. 1(4)). Additionally, although abortion is a relatively low-tech procedure, it may only legally be performed by a doctor and must be carried out either in a hospital or in a place approved by the Secretary of State for Health (s. 1(4)).[46]

In effect, what took place over the course of the twentieth century in England, Wales and Scotland was a shift in the governance of abortion from criminalisation to medicalisation, with the Abortion Act providing a therapeutic exception[47] to the criminal offences established by the 1861 Act. The medicalisation of abortion undoubtedly has had major benefits in ensuring that the abortion decision is a matter for a woman and her doctor,[48] thereby protecting her decision to terminate from legal challenge by a partner, parents or other third parties. However, simultaneously it has left women vulnerable to medical discretion in a way that appears out of line with contemporary health law. Critics charge that the regulation of abortion reflects the medical paternalism that prevailed when the 1967 statute was enacted and that, given changing understandings of the doctor/patient relationship, it is indefensible that access to abortion remains dependent on the beneficent exercise of medical discretion.[49]

THE CASE FOR DECRIMINALISATION

Modern British abortion law, therefore, reflects a paternalism at odds with the approach underpinning more recent statutes such as the Mental Capacity Act, and fails to vindicate a woman's right to decide. In addition to feminist

---

[45] As McGuinness and Thomson have demonstrated, it was professional interests rather than women's activism that were most powerful influences in shaping the 1967 Act – Sheelagh McGuinness and Michael Thomson, 'Medicine and abortion law: Complicating the reforming profession' (2015) 22 *Medical Law Review* 177.

[46] In 2011 the British Pregnancy Advisory Service (BPAS) sought a judicial review of this interpretation of 'treatment' in the 1967 Act. They argued that the current interpretation is out of step with legislative intention, which was to ensure that abortion was provided safely and that the term 'treatment' covered prescribing and issuing, but not necessarily the administration of the drugs. However, Superstone J rejected this view – *BPAS v the Secretary of State for Health* [2011] EWHC 23; Kate Greasley, 'Medical abortion and the golden rule of statutory interpretation' (2011) *Medical Law Review* 314.

[47] Sheldon (n. 42).

[48] *Paton v BPAS* [1979] QB 276; *Paton v UK* (1980) 3 EHRR 408.

[49] Sally Sheldon, *Beyond Control: Medical Power and Abortion Law* (Pluto, 1997); Sheldon (n. 42 and n. 43); Emily Jackson, 'Abortion, Autonomy and Prenatal Diagnosis' (2000) 9 *Social and Legal Studies* 467.

arguments grounded in choice, equality and bodily integrity,[50] good medical reasons also support law reform. In practice the 'two-doctor' rule has been criticised for delaying access to treatment. Conversely it is claimed that doctors sometimes bypass the requirement by pre-signing the requisite documentation.[51] In 2007 the British Medical Association conference recommended abolition of the two-doctor rule, a recommendation endorsed by the House of Commons Science and Technology Committee later that year.[52] However, the proposed amendment was removed from the debate programme while the Human Fertilisation and Embryology Bill was debated in Parliament in October 2008, together with other liberalising reforms which would have gone some way to updating the legislation.[53] The upshot is that practitioners continue to operate within a legal framework rooted in the 1960s. Thus, notwithstanding the historical significance of the Abortion Act, which has rightly been lauded as an important step towards women's equality, it is no longer fit for purpose. As Sheldon contends, we are left with 'a badly outdated piece of law, with multiple inadequacies rendered ever more apparent in the face of evolutions in clinical practice'.[54] Indeed, 'medical abortions', entailing the sequential administration of the drugs mifepristone (taken orally) and misoprostol (taken vaginally) to induce miscarriage, have become the norm for women who have terminations within the first ten weeks of pregnancy. Early medical abortions now represent over half of all legal abortions performed in the UK, while most remaining procedures are performed by the relatively low-tech vacuum aspiration.[55] The fact that these newer methods of abortion mean that drugs could theoretically be taken at home by the woman herself or be performed by nurses or other health professionals has prompted questions about the continuing subjection of abortion to medical and state control.

Debates about the governance of abortion treatment and care have therefore centred on the outdated nature of the legislation, the medicalisation of a common and safe procedure, and the unjustifiable restrictions on both women and health professionals. This has led Sheldon to argue compellingly for the decriminalisation of abortion law. As she contends, British law generally reflects a widespread consensus that women should be enabled fully to participate in the public sphere on equal terms with men and that control of one's own

---

[50] Catharine MacKinnon, 'Reflections on sex equality under law' (1991) 100 *Yale Law Journal* 1281; Drucilla Cornell, *The Imaginary Domain: Abortion, Pornography and Sexual Harassment* (Routledge, 1997).

[51] For discussion of the controversy regarding whether this practice contravenes the Abortion Act, see Sheldon (n. 42) 297–300.

[52] House of Commons, Science and Technology Committee, *Scientific Developments Relating to the Abortion Act 1967*, Twelfth Report of the 2006–7 Session (TSO, 2007).

[53] Sally Sheldon, 'A missed opportunity to reform an outdated piece of legislation' (2009) 4 *Clinical Ethics* 3.

[54] Sheldon (n. 43) 335.

[55] See Sheldon (n. 42) for further detail on abortion methods.

fertility is a fundamental prerequisite for such full participation.[56] This makes it problematic for the state to criminalise the actions of abortion-seeking women. In Sheldon's view it follows from this consensus, and the reality that criminal law entails the most onerous and draconian of state powers, that criminal sanctions should be invoked only if they offer a necessary and proportionate response to a citizen's actions. Therefore, currently UK abortion regulation is out of line with both clinical practice and prevailing moral values and a radical overhaul of abortion governance is required. As Sheldon argues, the offence of 'procuring a miscarriage' should be repealed since law is failing in its asserted aims of protecting women and preventing intentional destruction of foetal life. For those who believe in women's equality, autonomy and bodily integrity this argument appears unanswerable. Even those who believe that the embryo/ foetus has moral value are hard pressed to defend criminalisation.[57] However, as Margaret Brazier and Emma Cave observe,

> A belief that the embryo must be respected as fully human from fertilisation requires that a woman rejects abortion as an option for herself. As that belief is unprovable, she cannot legitimately enforce it on other women.[58]

— but services almost non-existant ·· (June 2017) and needs updating

legalised Abortion in 2019

THE CASE OF NORTHERN IRELAND

Arguments in favour of decriminalisation apply with greater force in Northern Ireland.[59] The harsh consequences of criminalisation were highlighted by the prosecution of a woman who helped her 15-year-old daughter procure abortion pills online, and other similar cases.[60] Nevertheless, self-administered abortions have become the most accessible solution for women in the jurisdiction, given the limited circumstances in which abortion is lawfully available. As noted above, the 1967 Act never extended to Northern Ireland and any exemptions to the general OAPA prohibition on abortion were left unclear until a series of cases in the mid-1990s confirmed that the 1939 ruling of *R v Bourne*[61] – which was technically not binding in Northern Ireland – applied.[62] In *Bourne*,

---

[56] Sheldon (n. 43) 336.

[57] As confirmed by *Paton* and *Re MB*.

[58] Margaret Brazier and Emma Cave, *Medicine, Patients and the Law* (Manchester University Press, 6th edn, 2016) p. 410; Margaret Brazier, 'Embryos "rights": Abortion and research' in Michael Freeman (ed.), *Medicine, Ethics and Law* (Stevens, 1988).

[59] Marie Fox, 'The consequences of criminalisation: Abortion in Northern Ireland' in Amel Alghrani, Rebecca Bennett and Suzanne Ost (eds), *The Criminal Law and Bioethical Conflict* (Cambridge University Press, 2012).

[60] Amelia Gentleman, 'Woman who bought abortion pills for daughter can challenge prosecution', *The Guardian*, 26 January 2017; e.g. Alan Erwin, 'Man and woman cautioned over "abortion pills" in Northern Ireland', *Belfast Telegraph*, 18 January 2017.

[61] *R v Bourne* [1939] 3 All ER 615.

[62] See, e.g., *Re A.M.N.H.* [1994] N.I.J.B. 1.

McNaghten J held that if the doctor was of the opinion that the pregnancy would render the woman 'a physical or mental wreck' she was justified in performing an abortion, and this vague standard[63] remains the test for lawful abortion in Northern Ireland. In 2015, in a landmark case, the High Court in Belfast ruled that Northern Irish law breached human rights in denying abortions to women who were carrying a foetus with a fatal abnormality or who had become pregnant as a result of rape.[64] A controversial appeal by the Attorney General was allowed by the Northern Ireland Court of Appeal in June 2017.[65] As this volume goes to press a ruling by the Supreme Court is pending. In the meantime, the breach of the human rights of Northern Irish women was at least partially ameliorated by a further development in June 2017. In order to avoid a potentially divisive vote on an amendment to the Queen's Speech proposed by Stella Creasy MP, which would have committed the Westminster Government to funding abortion services for Northern Irish women who travelled to Great Britain,[66] Chancellor Philip Hammond announced that Westminster was prepared to fund procedures for these women.[67] This was followed by similar pronouncements from his counterparts in Scotland and Wales.[68] Yet, and notwithstanding the importance of these developments, women forced to travel from Northern Ireland still face considerable financial and emotional costs in accessing abortion care. Given this, this it is unsurprising that they resort to purchasing abortion pills online, thereby risking criminal prosecution.[69] Such prosecutions exemplify Cornell's contention that denying women access to safe abortion effectively reduces them to their maternal functions and denies women the conditions of self-determination that men enjoy, which is why protection of abortion choices and bodily integrity is a key issue for feminist legal scholars.[70]

---

[63] Michael Thomson, 'Abortion Law and Professional Boundaries' (2013) 22 *Social and Legal Studies* 191; recent Department of Health Guidance for HSC Professionals on Termination of Pregnancy, March 2016 seems to give an unduly restrictive interpretation to *Bourne*. https://www.health-ni.gov.uk/publications/guidance-hsc-professionals-termination-pregnancy-northern-ireland, accessed 28 February 2017.

[64] *In the Matter of an Application for Judicial Review by the Northern Ireland Human Rights Commission; In the matter of the law on termination of pregnancy in Northern Ireland* [2015] NIQB 96.

[65] *In the matter of an Application by the Northern Ireland Human Rights Commission for Judicial Review* [2017] NICA 42.

[66] These developments followed a majority ruling by the UK Supreme Court in *R (on the application of A and B) v Secretary of State for Health* [2017] UKSC 41 that the Secretary of State was not obliged to fund abortion services for women from Northern Ireland who had abortions in England and Wales, even though they were UK taxpayers.

[67] Jessica Elgot and Henry McDonald, 'Northern Irish women win access to free abortion as May averts rebellion', *The Guardian*, 29 June 2017.

[68] Jessica Elgot, 'Wales and Scotland offer free abortions to women from Northern Ireland', *The Guardian*, 4 July 2017.

[69] Tamara Hervey and Sally Sheldon, 'Abortion by telemedicine in Northern Ireland: Patient and professional rights across borders' (2017) 68 *Northern Ireland Legal Quarterly* 1.

[70] Cornell (n. 50).

CONCLUSION

Our selected debates have sought to highlight the importance of autonomy and consent in healthcare law. The general presumption is that any adult should be informed and have their healthcare decisions respected. However, in practice consent often plays out in gendered ways. Thus, despite the apparently clear right to refuse medical treatment, pregnant women are regularly deemed to lack capacity, which can result in medical interventions against their will. In the abortion context, the impact on women's bodies and choices is even starker, harking back to an era when women lacked clear rights. In the future, as new technologies are developed to fragment as well as repair human bodies, new challenges to women's autonomy are likely to be generated. In the face of such challenges it is important not to lose sight of what are arguably more fundamental issues – ensuring that capacity is not defined in ways which mean that women's choices are overruled and that access to abortion is regulated in line with modern health law ethics and practice.

FURTHER READING

Mary Donnelly, *Healthcare Decision-Making and the Law: Autonomy, Capacity and the Limits of Liberalism* (Cambridge University Press, 2010).

Ruth Fletcher, Marie Fox and Julie McCandless, 'Legal embodiment: Analysing the body of healthcare law' (2008) 16 *Medical Law Review* 321.

Imogen Goold and Jonathan Herring, *Great Debates in Medical Law and Ethics* (Palgrave, 2014).

Samantha Halliday, *Autonomy and Pregnancy: A Comparative Analysis of Compelled Obstetric Intervention* (Routledge, 2016).

Catharine MacKinnon, 'Reflections on sex equality under law' (1991) 100 *Yale Law Journal* 1281.

Sally Sheldon, 'The decriminalisation of abortion: An argument for modernisation' (2016) 36 *Oxford Journal of Legal Studies* 334.

CHAPTER 12

Company Law and Corporate Governance

Sally Wheeler

Much about the institution of the company from a legal perspective is indefatigably male and masculine. Many company law textbooks for an academic and practitioner audience are written by men,[1] the protagonists in the traditional canon of cases are almost uniformly male,[2] and very little of the periodical literature (still mostly written by men)[3] that academics and students draw upon in the study of company law and corporate governance offers a feminist perspective.[4] Women legal academics fractionally outnumber male legal academics today but men considerably outnumber women in the more senior grades of employment.[5] This employment pattern does not account for the disparity in authorship in the field of company law and business/commercial law more generally.[6] Anecdotally it seems that male law students are attracted to company and commercial law in greater numbers than female students whose preference is for what they see as subjects more relevant to social justice and social welfare law.[7]

The picture of the company and its executives from popular culture adds to the idea of male control of the written narrative of corporate law. Film

---

[1] See *Gore-Browne on Companies* LexisNexis (Looseleaf). Exceptions are Sarah Worthington who has a part share of *Gower and Davies: Principles of Modern Company Law* (Sweet and Maxwell, 2012) and wrote *Sealy and Worthington's Text, Cases and Materials in Company Law* (Oxford University Press, 2016), and Brenda Hannigan whose contribution is *Company Law* (Oxford University Press, 2015).

[2] See, however, *Clements v Clements Bros Ltd* [1976] 2 All ER 268.

[3] Exceptions would be, for example, Charlotte Villiers, Lorraine Talbot and Peta Spender.

[4] See the review of US literature in Kellye Y. Testy, 'Capitalism and freedom – for whom?: Feminist legal theory and progressive corporate law' (2004) 67 *Law and Contemporary Problems* 87, 95–99.

[5] HESA 2013–14 Tables 7–9, https://www.hesa.ac.uk/data-and-analysis/publications/staff-2013-14. Accessed 1 December 2016.

[6] Barbara Ann White, 'Feminist foundations for the law of business: One law and economics scholar's survey and (re)view' (1999) 10 *UCLA Women's Law Journal* 39, 57–58.

[7] Amy Bradshaw, 'Exploring law students' attitudes, beliefs and experiences about the relationship between business law and public interest law' (2005) 20 *Wisconsin Women's Law Journal* 287.

and television portrayals of corporate power and those who exercise it give us images of companies as soulless money-making vehicles directed and managed by, at best, amoral, entrepreneurial men.[8] A woman vice-president of the energy trading company Enron, acting as a whistle-blower, and a woman journalist, who was the recipient of the information disclosed, triggered the company's collapse as it was revealed to be a fraudulent and bankrupt shell.[9] Their apparent honesty and openness stands in sharp contrast to the altogether darker figures of the male executives in Enron, Jeff Skilling and Ken Lay. A gender dimension has been added to the Global Financial Crisis; the crisis would have not occurred or would have played out differently if women – financially more responsible and conservative in nature – had been in charge instead of men – more dynamic and inventive but also reckless risk-takers.[10]

Male dominance and masculine culture extend into the performativity of the corporation itself. A positive experience of corporate life is often the experience of corporate man rather than corporate woman.[11] Much of what constitutes the lived experience of women does not form part of the discourse of the company: women as care providers, women as employees and pension contributors, women as part of the corporate governance framework. Women are often the unseen burden-carriers of a corporate culture that emphasises 'long hours' and requires 'sales meetings' attendance in remote locations. They provide essential 'support' services that enable males to play the role of model corporate employees.[12] Despite over 40 years of equal pay legislation in developed countries, women are still likely to suffer salary discrimination[13] and be less represented in the highest echelons of corporate management. The most menial and most poorly remunerated jobs in any corporation are likely to be performed by women. Limited liability, the cornerstone of corporate success, might seem to be the very opposite of the model of responsibility that is so central to feminist values and culture.[14]

This first debate focuses on the concept of shareholder value (SV) and, to a lesser extent, the activity that has supported it in recent years, financialisation. SV is at the heart of the Anglo-American model of the company, which

---

[8] Bernard Sarachek, 'Images of corporate executives in recent fiction' (1995) 14 *Journal of Business Ethics* 195.

[9] Jayme Walenta, 'Corporate bodies of desire: An investigation into the "Women of Enron"' (2006) 13 *Gender, Place and Culture* 437.

[10] Elisabeth Prügl, '"What if Lehman Brothers had been Lehman Sisters..." Gender and myth in the aftermath of the financial crisis' (2012) 6 *International Political Sociology* 21.

[11] Kathleen A. Lahey and Sarah W. Salter, 'Corporate law in legal theory and legal scholarship: From classicism to feminism' (1985) 23 *Osgoode Hall Law Journal* 543.

[12] See Sheila Jeffreys, 'Globalization and the male/female divide: An overview' in Ralph Petteman (ed.), *Handbook on International Political Economy* (World Scientific Publishing, 2012) pp. 285–302.

[13] *The Global Gender Gap Report 2015* (World Economic Forum, Davos), http://reports. weforum.org/global-gender-gap-report-2015/, accessed 10 November 2016.

[14] Theresa A. Gabaldon, 'The lemonade stand: Feminist and other reflections on the limited liability of corporate shareholders' (1992) 46 *Vanderbilt Law Review* 1387.

is very different from the more economically democratic models found in most parts of Europe. SV encourages directors to adopt policies that maximise shareholder value, often using opportunities created by deregulated financial markets to construct complex and opaque financial trading vehicles and products.[15] There is a wealth of literature that debates whether SV delivers on its central (and paternalistic) claim of improving the prosperity of all connected with the company and society at large.[16] However, the first debate examined here is whether SV is a gendered approach to the company and its governance based on neoliberal (and masculine) values such as self-interest, autonomy, control and hierarchy.[17]

The second debate looks at a contextual and more micro issue in corporate governance that follows from the macro issue examined in the first debate: the participation of women as corporate board members. Under-representation of women as directors, despite their participation in the workforce in ever-increasing numbers, is a global problem. Individual states and the EU have employed various strategies to encourage more diverse board membership, and women's participation in corporate governance is increasing as a result. These strategies might be seen as affirmative action policies and could be considered in the context of the considerable literature surrounding those.[18] Mandating or encouraging companies to appoint more women might raise questions about the extent to which the listed company is a public or private actor within the neoliberal state. However, the debate focuses on a rather different set of questions around why women in the boardroom are thought to enhance corporate performance or improve governance practice and whether women are simply being slotted into a model that reflects patriarchal ideas of organisation.[19]

Debate 1

Is shareholder value a form of gendered governance?

The cornerstone of shareholder value (SV) was the realisation by Berle and Means in 1932 that companies employed professional managers who were often not shareholders.[20] While patterns of share ownership have changed

---

[15] See Ewald Engelen, Ismail Ertürk, Julie Froud et al., *After the Great Complacence* (Oxford University Press, 2011) pp. 36–65.

[16] Lynn A. Stout, *The Shareholder Value Myth* (Berrett-Koehler, 2012).

[17] Robin West, 'Jurisprudence and gender' (1988) 55 *University of Chicago Law Review* 1 and Kathless P. Iannello, *Feminist Interventions in Organization Theory and Practice* (Routledge, 1992) pp. 46f.

[18] Siri Terjesen and Ruth Sealy, 'Board gender quotas: Exploring ethical tensions from a multi-theoretical perspective' (2016) 26 *Business Ethics Quarterly* 23.

[19] Ronnie Cohen, 'Feminist thought and corporate law: It's time to find our way up from the bottom (line)' (1994) 2 *American University Journal of Gender and the Law* 26f.

[20] Adolf A. Berle and Gardner C. Means, *The Modern Corporation and Private Property* (Transaction, 1991, reprinted from 1932 original).

since 1932,[21] the separation of ownership and control remains a live issue. There is an accountability problem between shareholders and professional managers. Shareholders, in the words of Berle and Means, had traded 'a set of definite rights for a set of indefinite expectations'.[22] That said, shareholders play a central role in the corporate governance matrix when contrasted with other potential governance rights holders (stakeholders such as employees, for example), despite relatively few matters being assigned to their exclusive competence by the Companies legislation or case law. For Bainbridge, control rights for shareholders are the second limb of the shareholder value theory.[23] It is clear from case law that directors are not the agents of shareholders[24] and that shareholders cannot dictate to directors by means of shareholder resolutions on matters outside their competence unless they have reserved that power to themselves by means of the company's constitution.

The Companies Act 2006 requires directors 'to act in a way that promotes the success of the company for the benefits of its members as a whole having regard to a range of interests including employees, the community and the environment';[25] as Talbot powerfully argues, this is a requirement 'to represent the interests of shareholders',[26] as the interests that make up the 'range of interests' do not have a value independent of shareholders. SV is entrenched as the pre-eminent theory that explains how companies behave. We can see the empirical effects of SV on corporate activity in the rise of finance capital as a distinct form of capital. The activity known as financialisation,[27] whereby financial and non-financial companies engage in financial transactions and activities as a profit-making activity in their own right rather than simply as a mechanism for raising capital to support other productive activities, is widespread across listed companies.[28] For example, Enron began its corporate life as a builder of energy generation plants across the world; shortly before its bankruptcy it was trading energy as its principal corporate activity.[29] The driver for

---

[21] In 1963 over 50 per cent of shares in UK listed companies were owned by retail (individual investors), by 2014 12 per cent were owned in this way, see *Ownership of UK Quoted Shares: 2014* (Office for National Statistics, 2 September 2015).

[22] n. 20, p. 244.

[23] Stephen Bainbridge, 'Director primacy: The means and ends of corporate governance' (2003) 97 *Northwestern University Law Review* 547.

[24] *Automatic Self Cleansing Filter Syndicate v Cuninghame* [1906] 2 Chapter 34.

[25] CA 2006 s. 172(1).

[26] Lorraine Talbot, 'Trying to save the world with company law? Some problems' (2016) 36 *Legal Studies* 533.

[27] For a variety of definitions of 'financialisation', see Shaun French, Andrew Leyshon and Thomas Wainwright, 'Financializing space, spacing financialization' (2011) 35 *Progress in Human Geography* 798, 800–804.

[28] William Lazonick, 'In the name of shareholder value: How executive pay and stock buybacks are damaging the US economy' in Thomas Clarke and Douglas Branson (eds), *The Sage Handbook of Corporate Governance* (Sage, 2012) p. 476.

[29] William W. Bratton, 'Enron and the dark side of shareholder value' (2002) 76 *Tulane Law Review* 1275.

this is the acquisition of high value returns[30] assessed over a short time period on capital, which appeals to shareholders more than conventionally generated profits which require more investment and take longer to accrue.[31]

SV in the UK is evidenced by the key role of shareholders in appointing directors and setting their pay[32] and the rise of executive share options. The UK Corporate Governance Code contains numerous references to the need to explain corporate decisions to shareholders and to communicate with them outside formal corporate reporting requirements. Other groups connected with the company, such as employees, are not afforded the same prominence and privilege. From 2002[33] onwards directors have been obliged to disclose executive pay to shareholders on an annual basis and to seek their approval in the form of an advisory vote. In 2013 this was augmented to require, additionally, the presentation to shareholders of a detailed forward-looking remuneration policy on which there has to be a binding shareholder vote every three years.[34]

The answer to the accountability problem has been to use non-executive directors to monitor managers (executive directors) to ensure that managers do not pursue their own interests at the expense of shareholders. In this analysis managers become agents and shareholders become their principals. Within agency theory,[35] shareholders are deemed to be those most at risk from under-performance by the company. In exchange for exposing themselves to this risk they receive the right to be regarded as residual claimants to any surplus corporate assets. Once they have been designated residual claimants they then assume the role of monitor to the performance of managers. The shareholders' interest as residual claimants is different from the interest held by any other group, whose interest will be fixed at the amount the firm owes them as employees or suppliers of components, for example.

Managers conduct the affairs of the company so as to maximise the return on capital to shareholders. Shareholder value is maximised through the adoption of efficient structures that eliminate agency costs by both policing the behaviour of potentially errant managers – errant in the sense that they might

---

[30] Lynne Dallas, 'Short-termism, the financial crisis and corporate governance' (2012) 37 *Journal of Corporation Law* 265.

[31] The Kay Review identified quarterly reporting as something that should be discontinued as it encouraged short-term share-holding which itself prevented investment for long-term growth, see *The Kay Review of UK Equity Markets and Long-Term Decision Making*, https://www.gov. uk/government/uploads/system/uploads/attachment_data/file/253454/bis-12-917-kay-review-of-equity-markets-final-report.pdf, accessed 1 December 2016.

[32] Randall S. Thomas and Chrisoph Van der Elst, 'Say on pay around the world' (2015) 92 *Washington University Law Review* 655.

[33] Directors' Remuneration Report Regulations 2002.

[34] The Large and Medium-sized Companies and Groups (Accounts and Reports) (Amendment) Regulations, Statutory Instrument 2013 No. 1981, Part 4.

[35] See, for example, Eugene F. Fama and Michael C. Jensen, 'Separation of ownership and control' (1983) 26 *Journal of Law and Economics* 301.

indulge in 'opportunistic behaviour' at the expense of shareholders[36] – and ensuring that accurate and sufficient information is relayed to shareholders. These efficient structures include taking steps to align the interests of shareholders and managers through the use of devices such as share options and executive bonuses to reward management performance. Regulatory structures within company law enable this efficient monitoring to take place, and judgement on managerial performance is exercised by the market through what is known as the market for corporate control; poorly performing managers will find the equity in the corporation acquired by others through a takeover bid and they will be ousted by the new owners.[37]

The agency relationship proposition that is used to support shareholder primacy is often explained by recourse to the idea that the company is not a separate legal person but rather a 'nexus' for a set of contracts between the participants in the company: shareholders, employees, customers, managers, suppliers etc.[38] Here the term 'contract' is not being used to denote a legally binding arrangement but, more broadly, to describe any mechanism that creates, modifies or transfers assets.[39] Company law offers a series of default rules (a contract) which participants can bargain to change if they wish. Shareholders in this analysis are making a high-risk firm-specific investment as the company, through its managers, holds and controls their entire investment. It is not possible for shareholders to enter into a complete *ex ante* contract with the firm to protect their position and consequently they are given the extra privilege of certain safeguards internal to the firm, for example the right to appoint and dismiss directors. Employees and other participants in the corporate endeavour can protect themselves either by *ab initio* bargaining which leads to contracts that specify all rights and all obligations (complete contracts) or are protected by employment laws or insolvency laws.

THE ROLE OF GENDER IN SHAREHOLDER VALUE

SV is both by design and effect a gendered discourse. It is reductionist in its reasoning and excludes values that might be considered more feminine such as connectivity, care and relational responsibility. At its base lies an interest in protecting a particular form of abstract capital founded on property rights to the exclusion of other practical and identifiable interests. Shareholder capital is facially neutral[40] but it is without doubt a patriarchal concept, as most

---

[36] Oliver E. Williamson, *The Economic Institutions of Capitalism* (Free Press, 1985).

[37] Fama and Jensen (n. 35).

[38] Frank H. Easterbrook and Daniel R. Fischel, 'The corporate contract' (1976) 89 *Columbia Law Review* 1416.

[39] William Bratton, 'The "nexus of contracts" corporation: A critical approach' (1989) 74 *Cornell Law Review* 407.

[40] Elizabeth Warren, 'What is a women's issue? Bankruptcy, commercial law, and other gender-neutral topics' (2002) 25 *Harvard Women's Law Journal* 19; women have gained most traction in law and policy arenas to argue for an improved, but still far from perfect, position where the subject matter is obviously female or clearly affects women more.

property-based ideas are. Historically the capital that now finds expression as equity capital will have mostly belonged to men as land-based capital supporting agricultural production and later becoming the equity capital in listed companies.[41] At the very least it will have been controlled by generations of male heirs and married men through inheritance and marriage settlements.[42] To the extent that women have an interest in the performance of equity capital generally it is as contributors to defined contribution pension schemes. The rise of these schemes[43] does mean that the clear lines between investment capital and labour capital are becoming blurred. Women usually earn less than men and are more likely to suffer pension detriment through taking career breaks for childbearing and child raising. Their stake will consequently be lower than that of male employees.

The activities that underpin SV reflect ideas of self-interest and self-absorption. Activities that companies pursue under the umbrella of corporate social responsibility are only undertaken if they can be shown not to have a negative effect on SV. The responsibility for others that this might demonstrate is entirely subordinated to profit maximisation.[44] Corporate social responsibility is a poor substitute for a wider consideration of other interests and issues that might be affected by the pursuit of SV. Alleviation of poor working conditions for those in the supply chain and avoidance of environmental degradation are examples of what might be considered in a company charged with a broader notion of care and citizenship[45] rather than one that sees these as costs that can be externalised as long as minimum regulatory standards (which the corporate sector bargains down as low as possible to protect SV) are observed.[46]

Aggressive pursuit of SV in tandem with the prevailing economic conditions of low inflation, high liquidity and low interest rates led to financialisation.[47] One of the consequences of financialisation was the pulling into the credit market of large numbers of individuals and households who previously would not have satisfied lending conditions. Much of this lending took place at high interest rates and high fees. Companies were able to take advantage of

[41] Daniel Verdier, 'Capital mobility and the origins of stock markets' (2001) 55 *International Organization* 327.

[42] Unmarried women and widows had the opportunity to hold and invest capital, see David R. Green and Alistair Owens, 'Gentlewomanly capitalism: Widows and wealth holding in England and Wales, c. 1800–1860' (2003) 56 *Economic History Review* 510.

[43] Defined benefit pension schemes are in numerical decline. Defined contribution schemes place an employee's pension contribution in an investment fund with retirement income dependent on the performance of the invested fund.

[44] Peter Fleming and Marc T. Jones, *The End of Corporate Social Responsibility* (Sage, 2012).

[45] Janis Sarra, 'The gender implications of corporate governance change' (2002) 1 *Seattle Journal for Social Justice* 457.

[46] Ronald Daniels, 'Stakeholders and takeovers: Can contractarianism be compassionate?' (1993) 43 *University of Toronto Law Journal* 315.

[47] Thomas Clarke, 'The impact of financialisation on international corporate governance: The role of agency theory and maximizing shareholder value' (2014) 8 *Law and Financial Markets Review* 39.

state rhetoric (consider the UK and the US) around the importance of market citizenship[48] – home ownership was a status to be aspired to in an era when public housing stock was being sold off and not replaced. Mis-selling of financial products was rife and in the Global Financial Crisis many of these loans unravelled, leading to widespread repossessions and considerable financial discomfort.[49] Not only did lower-income households, and disproportionately female and ethnic and racial minority householders,[50] suffer more as a result of this particular manifestation of SV, what income they had was diverted to corporate investors, thus deepening existing inequalities.

The SV model of the company has at its heart a very particular idea of efficiency: one that maximises return to shareholders and does not include any other goals such as the partial redistribution of wealth or the attainment of social justice. This does not give efficiency a neutral value. There is no place for engagement with other interested groups on the basis of cooperative social relations. There is no conception that corporations exist and operate within the domain of the collective known as society, which may have expectations of certain kinds of behaviour from its constituent members. There is no formal role given to the participation of other interest groups such as employees in governance. Power is centred hierarchically in one group (shareholders) that takes the rewards of corporate success.

The idea of shareholders, presented as an undifferentiated and depersonalised block with no individual interests or distinguishing features,[51] occupying the role of residual claimants, presumably comes from an analogy with insolvency law where they rank last in the distribution of corporate assets,[52] meaning that they will only receive a return of their capital if and when other creditors have been paid in full. They rank below employees who are preferential creditors for the purposes of any unpaid wages and outstanding holiday pay, hence the idea that employees are fixed claimants for their contracted financial entitlement. If the company cannot satisfy their contract then insolvency law protects their position. However, there is no obvious rationale for why the insolvency distribution rules should influence the running of a solvent company. Many things change on insolvency, not least the position of directors who, at that point, but not before, owe a duty to creditors, but that does not mean the insolvency position should be adopted before insolvency. Shareholders of substance can diversify their investment interests through portfolio management. They can sell their shares on the open market and in some circumstances can

[48] Adrienne Roberts, 'Financing social reproduction: The gendered relations of debt and mortgage finance in twenty-first-century America' (2013) 18 *New Political Economy* 21.

[49] See Saskia Sassen, *Expulsions* (Harvard University Press, 2014) p. 138.

[50] Gary Dymski, Jesus Hernandez and Lisa Mohanty, 'Race, gender, power, and the US subprime mortgage and foreclosure crisis: A meso analysis' (2013) 19 *Feminist Economics* 124.

[51] William Lazonick, 'Controlling the market for corporate control: The historical significance of managerial capitalism' (1992) 1 *Industrial and Corporate Change* 445.

[52] Insolvency Act 1986 s. 175, s. 328 and Sch. 6.

pass a resolution changing the constitution of the corporation.[53] In this way they have more mobility than employees, who have made a firm-specific investment of their human capital and personal skills and may well have no other claims outside the company that employees them.

Employees whose defined contribution pension funds are exposed to the market have a residual interest in the firm, as do suppliers of plant and goods. Once the labels 'fixed claimant' and 'residual claimant' are elided, these interests would seem to share the same monitoring problem as shareholders; all contribute value (human capital, equity capital and debt capital) to the firm and all are reliant on managers to maximise this value and produce the ability to pay a dividend, wages[54] and invoices. Employees have at least a duality of interests in the company: what might benefit them as defined contribution plan savers (high profit levels) might hurt them as employees (for example, corporate relocation to pursue even higher profit levels, changed shift patterns to generate more profit). However, the SV approach assumes all employees have a unitary identity and a single interest. While shareholders have been in charge of monitoring managers, their solution of aligning executive interests with their own shareholder interests through executive salary rises and stock options has led to executive pay soaring in relation not only to average earnings[55] but to the levels of remuneration enjoyed by executives in systems where there is greater participation by other interests.[56] Recent evidence suggests that paying executives more in the SV system does not result in improved management performance.[57]

In its reliance on agency theory, SV employs a classic conception of contract to make up its nexus of contracts; these contracts are for the most part rigid and fixed, made by autonomous individuals. They are self-contained arrangements planning for all contingencies except, vitally, when shareholders are involved. These are adjectives that Mary Joe Frug would use to describe a masculine approach to contract.[58] Contracts in the nexus of contracts are not necessarily legal enforceable contracts – company law is clear that there is no contractual relationship between director and shareholder, for example. However, the arrangements that are most significant to a gender-based reading are legally enforceable contracts: employment contracts, contracts with customers and

---

[53] Andrew R. Keay, 'Shareholder primacy in corporate law: Can it survive? Should it survive?' (2010) 7 *European Company and Financial Law Review* 369.

[54] Kent Greenfield, 'The place of workers in corporate law' (1998) 39 *Boston College Law Review* 299.

[55] In 1998 the average CEO compensation at a large listed company was in a ratio of 47.1 to the average employee wage. In 2015 the ratio was 128.1, see Department for Business, Energy and Industrial Strategy, *Corporate Governance Reform Green Paper*, November 2016.

[56] Andrew Hill, 'UK Chief executives earn much more than European peers' (2016) *Financial Times*, 21 December.

[57] https://www.cfauk.org/media-centre/cfa-uk-executive-remuneration-report-2016, accessed 1 December 2016.

[58] Mary Joe Frug, *Postmodern Legal Feminism* (Routledge, 1992) pp. 111–124.

contracts with suppliers. Everything we know about the real world of contracting would seem to say that contracts are not experienced like this.[59] There is no more reason for an employment contract (or a supply contract) to be complete than there is for a shareholder's contract to be incomplete.[60] An employment contract can never define the social relationships at play during the employment relationship. It cannot speak to the human interactions which will see the contract evolve and change over time: the care that is required of the employee, the discretion that is retained by managers and the initiative that both need to display for the relationship to work.[61]

There is an assumption that shareholders exclusively take the risk of corporate success and failure. Other interest groups can apparently use contract as a way of bargaining to ensure continued employment and continued use as a corporate supplier. But freedom of contract is often illusory. Parties do not always have equal bargaining strength. Some contract terms would be very expensive indeed even if they could be negotiated. The lionising of freedom of contract based around *ex ante* bargaining instead of more personalised concepts founded in experience can be seen as an embodiment of masculine values.[62] Contracts that begin as the simplest of standard form relationships need the cooperation and best endeavours of both parties if they are to be anything more than the most discrete of contract transactions. Shareholders are aided in their non-legally enforceable *contract* with directors in having the power to dismiss directors, change the corporate constitution and ultimately sell their shares and recover their stake and potentially more.

The design of corporate governance could be fundamentally altered by introducing a variety of measures that would take it away from its current shareholder focus; for example, requiring worker, customer and supplier participation on boards or creating advisory boards from these groups, setting out an avowed focus, underpinned by legislation, on advancing the interests of the corporate enterprise in a genuinely holistic sense or capping earnings ratios between the chief executive and the average employee wage.[63] These design changes would make corporate governance appear less gendered; however, there are caveats on whether the experience of company life would be less gendered. Requiring particular pay ratios does not necessarily raise the wages of the lowest paid. Extended participation in the governance structure of the

[59] There are obvious links between Ian Macneil's idea of relational contract and the type of relational feminism that is advanced by Gilligan and her inheritors, see Debora A. Threedy, 'Feminists and contract doctrine' (1999) 32 *Indiana Law Review* 1257.

[60] See Andrew Keay and Hao Zhang, 'Incomplete contracts, contingent fiduciaries and a Director's Duty to Creditors' (2008) 32 *Melbourne University Law Review* 141, 153–155.

[61] Richard E. Speidel, 'Characteristics and challenges of relational contracts' (2000) 94 *Northwestern University Law Review* 823.

[62] Patricia A. Tidwell and Peter Linzer, 'The flesh-colored band aid – contracts, feminism, dialogue, and norms' (1991) 28 *Houston Law Review* 791.

[63] See *Corporate Governance Reform Green Paper* (n. 55) pp. 38–41.

company is not something that will be attractive to those juggling employment with care responsibilities and family life. It is likely to be more a more exclusionary experience than it is an inclusionary one.[64]

Debate 2

Boardroom participation – good for business, bad for equality?

A recent communication (2016) from the European Commission tells us that just over 23 per cent of board members of the EU's largest listed companies are women.[65] This figure is just under double the female board membership of 2010 with increases in female membership occurring in 24 of the 28 member states. These figures mask some serious disparities at member state level; in France 33 per cent of board members are women, while in Portugal 11 per cent are women. The rate of change in the period from 2010 to 2015 varies hugely between member states: Italy recorded a 21 per cent increase (the largest in the EU) while 20 states had increases below 12.4 per cent. There are only eight member states in which women number more than a quarter of board members. More women than men are emerging as graduates from universities across the EU[66] and US,[67] with this gap set to widen. Maintaining the current rate of progress for women in board membership will not keep pace with the increase of educated women.[68]

The EU has adopted a twin strategy for increasing board membership. It has used its recommendations on corporate governance[69] and its equality strategy to press for increased female participation.[70] It followed this up with a proposal in 2012 for boards of directors across the EU to include 40 per cent of the unrepresented gender; this will almost invariably be women.[71] While some EU states

[64] Theresa A. Gabaldon, 'Corporate conscience and the white man's burden' (2002) 70 *George Washington Law Review* 944.

[65] See http://ec.europa.eu/justice/gender-equality/files/gender_balance_decision_making/1607_factsheet_final_wob_data_en.pdf, accessed 20 January 2018.

[66] See http://ec.europa.eu/eurostat/statistics-explained/index.php/Tertiary_education_statistics#Gender_distribution_of_participation, accessed 1 December 2016.

[67] Daniel Borzelleca, 'The male to female ratio in college', *Forbes*, 6 February 2012.

[68] *Gender Balance on Corporate Boards – Europe is Cracking the Glass Ceiling* EU Commission Fact Sheet (October 2015), http://ec.europa.eu/justice/gender- equality/files/womenon-boards/factsheet_women_on_boards_web_2015-10_en.pdf, accessed 1 December 2016.

[69] European Commission, Green Paper: The EU Corporate Governance Framework COM (2011) 164, http://ec.europa.eu/internal_market/company/docs/modern/com2011-164_en.pdf, accessed 1 December 2016.

[70] *Strategy for Equality between Women and Men 2010–2015*, COM (2010) 491 final, http://ec.europa.eu/justice/genderequality/files/documents/strategy_equality_women_men_en.pdf, accessed 1 December 2016.

[71] Proposal for a Directive of the European Parliament and of the Council on improving the gender balance among non-executive directors of companies listed on stock exchanges and related measures COM (2012) 614 final, http://eur-lex.europa.eu/legal-content/EN/TXT/?uri=CELEX%3A52012PC0614, accessed 1 December 2016.

such as Norway and Spain had already legislated in 2003[72] and 2007[73] respectively to introduce quota mechanisms to promote gender diversity in the boardroom, others acted on the threat of a potential quota imposition from the EU with their own arrangements to support diversity-based appointments, some through legislative intervention requiring inclusion, for example France and Italy, others, such as the UK, through amended Codes of Corporate Governance and *comply or explain* mechanisms to support voluntary initiatives.[74] The picture outside the EU's member states is similar in that there are some jurisdictions where rapid progress has been made and others where progress is appears glacial; Canada has almost doubled the number of board seats held by women in the period 2010 to 2016 from 11 per cent to 21.5 per cent,[75] with a similar picture in Australia,[76] while Japan[77] has progressed over the same time period from 1 per cent to 3.5 per cent. The US reports a lower overall percentage of board seats held by women (20 per cent) than the top-performing European states.[78]

The structure of the corporate sector in each jurisdiction is different, as is the approach of each state to gender equality. These contexts affect how pressure for change is exerted and how successful it is likely to be. Using soft strategies of voluntary compliance can be seen as aiming at equality of access whereas adopting hard strategies around quotas can be seen as focusing on achieving equality of outcome.[79] The use of quotas is more likely to occur in jurisdictions where quotas have already been employed to achieve balance in other areas, for example political representation.[80] Some states have a large number of family-controlled companies where boardroom continuity and the practices of inheritance are important.[81] Other states have companies with concentrated

---

[72] Lov om allmennaksjeselskaper des 2003 nr. 120, § 6-ll a, translated as Norwegian Public Limited Liability Companies Act 1997, amended in 2003.

[73] Effective Equality Act 2007.

[74] Siri A. Terjesen, Ruth V. Aguilera and Ruth Lorenz, 'Legislating a woman's seat on the board: Institutional factors driving gender quotas for boards of directors' (2015) *Journal of Business Ethics* 233.

[75] Canadian Board Diversity Council, *2016 Annual Report Card*, https://www.boarddiversity. ca/sites/default/files/CBDC-Annual-Report-Card-2016.pdf, accessed 1 December 2016.

[76] http://www.companydirectors.com.au/~/media/resources/director-resource-centre/ governance-and-director-issues/board-diversity/board-diversity-pdf/gender-diversity- quarterly-report-june-august-final.ashx, accessed 1 December 2016.

[77] Credit Suisse, *The CS Gender 3000: The Reward for Change* (2016), https://www.credit-suisse. com/microsites/next/en/entrepreneurism/articles/the-cs-gender-3000-the-reward-for-change. html, accessed 20 November 2016.

[78] Renuka Hodigere and Diana Bilimoria, 'Human capital and professional network effects on women's odds of corporate board directorships' (2015) 30 *Gender in Management* 523.

[79] Cathrine Seierstad and Tore Opsahl, 'For the few not the many? The effects of affirmative action on presence, prominence, and social capital of women directors in Norway' (2011) 27 *Scandinavian Journal of Management* 44.

[80] Darren Rosenblum 'Feminizing capital: A corporate imperative' (2009) 6 *Berkeley Business Law Journal* 61.

[81] For example, in Italy two-thirds of companies are family owned; see Magda Bianco, Angela Ciavarella and Roella Signoretti, 'Women on corporate boards in Italy: The role of family connections' (2015) 23 *Corporate Governance* 129.

or block ownership of shares where those shareholders expect to exert more influence over boardroom appointments, and for others the presence of overseas registered companies where less diversity pressure exists in their domestic exchanges[82] makes pushing for female appointments more difficult. In each state a different constellation of actors and political processes have combined to pressure companies to appoint more women to boardroom positions.[83]

THE DIVERSITY ARGUMENT FOR FEMALE PARTICIPATION

The case for driving up the number of female directorial appointments in every jurisdiction is made through the discourse of *diversity*, that is by focusing on the potential for improved business outcomes from employing a workforce that captures all the talent available. The idea is that a culturally diverse work environment fosters creativity and innovation because in that environment individuals work to their full potential.[84] Diversity management began to replace the discourse around *equality* in the US in the 1990s and migrated to other jurisdictions thereafter.[85] This focus on diversity means that the arguments of equality and social justice for women in the corporate sector and society more generally have been sidelined.

There is now a large academic literature that examines whether the boardroom presence of women does improve a company's financial performance in terms of increased profits or an increased share price. There is no definitive answer.[86] Results are recorded across a spectrum from positive effect to negative effect. Mapping share price movement against boardroom diversity could be taken as a proxy for whether the market values female directors or not. However, while it is possible to track share price movement on the announcement of a particular directorial appointment, it is not possible to know whether that movement is a reflection of a judgment on gender, skill or another variable. A similar lack of clarity exists for whether the presence of female directors improves a company's corporate social responsibility (CSR) performance, not least because there is no definitive benchmark of CSR performance from which to determine an improvement; CSR is an entirely voluntary activity for a company. Conflicting evidence in these studies can be explained by the difficulties of comparing time periods and aligning variables across different methodologies.[87]

---

[82] Susan Vinnicombe, Val Singh, Ronald J. Burke, Diana Bilimoria and Morten Huse, *Women on Corporate Boards of Directors: International Research and Practice* (Edward Elgar, 2008).
[83] See Cathrine Seierstad, Gillian Warner-Søderholm, Mariateresa Torchia and Morten Huse, 'Increasing the number of women on boards: The role of actors and processes' (2017) 141 *Journal of Business Ethics* 289.
[84] John Wrench, 'Diversity Management can be bad for you' (2005) 46 *Race and Class* 73.
[85] The Higgs Report, *Review of the Role and Effectiveness of Non-Executive Directors* (2003), http://www.ecgi.org/codes/documents/higgsreport.pdf, accessed 29 November 2016.
[86] See Corinne Post and Kris Byron, 'Women on boards and firm financial performance: A meta-analysis' (2015) 58 *Academy of Management* 1546.
[87] Renee B. Adams, Jakob de Haan, Siri Terjesen and Hans van Ees, 'Board diversity: Moving the field forward' (2015) 23 *Corporate Governance* 77.

The years since the Global Financial Crisis have seen inquiries at the level of the EU, the state and industry into corporate governance failures. A unifying theme in these inquiries' conclusions and subsequent recommendations was that more diverse board membership would have been better at controlling risks and challenging senior managers. Diversity means, in this context, greater female membership. These women would broaden the board's skill set and would be able to move beyond the perceived 'psychological limitations' of the group dynamic of boardroom deliberations[88] and their inherent biases.[89] Despite claims to the contrary, however, there is no evidence from either the psychology literature or the studies on boardroom behaviours that the mere introduction of women can achieve the desired change of increased challenge and objectivity.[90] This is not surprising. Women are being appointed into organisations that are inherently male by design (e.g. limited liability) and that are being run to achieve masculine goals (SV).

While the business case justification for female participation in board-rooms is not supported by any evidence, it has been successful at increasing the number of women directors in listed companies. There is huge symbolic value in this. Women are becoming visible leaders in the private sector and, given the totemic status of some companies, they are becoming role models in the public sphere. As Spender puts, it this visibility does lay down a chal-lenge to 'traditional conceptions of authority'.[91] These traditional conceptions are of men in leadership positions. Women as high-profile corporate directors are offering a different picture of leadership and ambition in that the social construction of women is as caring and listening. They are not very likely, the evidence suggests, to change individual company strategy or to improve the labour market outcomes for women,[92] but they will change the image of lead-ership, and potentially the shape of wider society.

SOCIAL JUSTICE ARGUMENTS FOR FEMALE PARTICIPATION

Despite the success of the diversity/business case justification, it does not promote the most positive picture of women. It offers a non-threatening way of encouraging female appointments by asserting that business will benefit

[88] Marleen A. O'Connor, 'The Enron board: The perils of groupthink' (2003) 71 *University of Cincinnati Law Review* 1233.

[89] Nicola Faith Sharpe, 'The cosmetic independence of corporate boards' *Seattle University Law Review* 1435.

[90] Sally Wheeler, 'Independent directors and corporate governance' (2012) 27 *Australian Journal of Corporate Law* 168.

[91] Peta Spender, 'Gender quotas: Is it time for Australia to lean in?' (2015) 20 *Deakin Law Review* 95.

[92] Marianne Bertrand, Sandra E. Black, Sissel Jensen and Adriana Lleras-Muney, 'Breaking the glass ceiling? The effect of board quotas on female labor market outcomes in Norway' (National Bureau of Economic Research Working Paper 20256, 2014).

from them. It is an argument that implicitly rejects female participation as a right based on social justice principles; women have a right to participate in the governance of powerful economic actors. The unrealistic idea that the operating culture of companies could be changed by the appointment of a group of individual women is evidence of an idea called the *romance of leadership* where organisational success depends on charismatic individuals rather than external and contextual factors.[93] It is also a disappointing essentialising of women into a closed category. Women appointed to board positions may well introduce new ideas and independent thinking but they do so as talented individuals, not as a uniform group with a fixed identity and socially constructed behaviours. Setting up female directors as a stereotypical business tonic is demeaning and depersonalising.

The social justice case for participation is an argument about extending a role within the economically powerful to those who traditionally have been outside it. It sees women's appointments as needing no justification other than those made in pursuit of the values of equality and non-discrimination. Appointment to a directorship should be an expectation, not something which has to be justified by appealing to the possibility of enhancing the economic value of the business in question. The social justice case presents a moral and political argument about the place of women in society and the role of the corporate sector in recognising and supporting female ambition. It can achieve rapid, but perhaps contested, change if supported by quota requirements. To succeed, quotas need to be nestled into a basket of measures around childcare strategies, caring responsibilities more generally and effective mentoring to ensure that there are sufficient numbers of women who feel able to accept an appointment.[94]

CONCLUSION

Whether you prefer the business case argument or the social justice argument depends on how you see the company in society. If you see it as a vehicle that should have a role in delivering economic and social justice and in democratising society then the social justice argument has more traction. If you view the company as a private actor that allows individual achievement and ambition to be achieved then the business case has more traction. If we pull the two debates together then appointing more women to the boardroom on the basis of the business case will not alter the dynamics of the SV model. It will perpetuate the company in its current form. The social justice case has much more disruptive potential.

---

[93] Peta Spender, 'Gender diversity on boards in Australia – waiting for the great leap forward' (2012) 27 *Australian Journal of Corporate Law* 28.
[94] Charlotte Villiers, 'Achieving gender balance in the boardroom: Is it time for legislative action in the UK?' (2010) 30 *Legal Studies* 553.

FURTHER READING

Joel Bakan, *The Corporation: The Pathological Pursuit of Power and Profit* (Free Press, 2004).

Janis Sarra, 'The gender implications of corporate governance change' (2002) 1 *Seattle Journal for Social Justice* 457.

Lorraine Talbot, *Great Debates in Company Law* (Palgrave, 2014).

CHAPTER 13

Intellectual Property Law

Catherine Easton

Intellectual property (IP) law is an umbrella term that encompasses a range of protections for the intangible property emanating from human creativity and innovation. Early approaches saw a distinction between principles relating to literary and artistic works, such as copyright, and approaches to what was termed 'industrial property', including patents and trademarks.[1] This distinction has been diluted and the law has evolved to the point at which a product such as mobile phone can be covered by numerous patents, trademarks and copyright protections. This complexity is exacerbated by this area of law's international reach, originating in early bilateral instruments and continued through to the Paris and Berne Conventions and to the Agreement on Trade-Related Aspects of Intellectual Property Rights (the TRIPS agreement), an international agreement between all the member states of the World Trade Organization.

The ownership of intangible property is of global economic importance; pharmaceutical, manufacturing and chemical industries' business plans, for example, rely strongly on the ability to protect their intangible assets. The film and music industries centre on the protection of artistic works, although the ability to enforce this has been severely diminished by the impact of the internet. State-based regulatory policy often emphasises the use of the intellectual property law to encourage innovation and creativity and, in turn, increase gross domestic product. Wider enforcement and protection mechanisms can, however, perpetuate power imbalances, for example because of registration fees and the need to pay legal professionals to police IP protections. Furthermore, many key rights are transferable and can become centralised in powerful institutions such as music companies, far removed from the initial creative impulse. Overly strong legal protections can impede the ability of new inventors to develop new products or hinder artists' potential to create new artistic works.

---

[1] John Iselin, 'The protection of industrial property' (1898) 46 *Journal of the Society of the Arts* 293.

While IP laws may be written in a formally neutral way, their substantive application can exacerbate economic and societal divisions. Such imbalances can have wider impacts on how society develops and the monetary and social value placed on certain types of creativity and innovation. With its intrinsic link to new technologies and creative expression, IP law is fundamentally linked to the future, human development and progress.

Traditionally, IP law is not an area in which gender-focused research and scholarship has been active. As Halbert notes:

> Feminist scholars rarely, if ever, mention the words copyright, patent, or intellectual property; intellectual property scholars rarely, if ever, appeal to feminist interpretations to better understand the law.[2]

However, a growing body of scholarship and policy initiatives has developed to highlight and critique the interaction of IP law and gender, shedding light on stark disparities on the position of women when assigning protection to creativity and innovation. A key theme is that the wider framework surrounding the substantively neutral law has developed to exacerbate existing socio-economic divisions and to increase marginalisation of certain groups. To examine this within the framework of gender, two key issues have been chosen: the need for more flexibility in patenting, and the extent to which copyright law protects women's creativity.

Debate 1

Do we need more flexible patents?

Patents provide the highest form of IP protection, giving their owner a monopoly over the relevant invention. This needs to be inventive, not obvious, and capable of being put to industrial, practical use. Harmonised by Article 33 of the TRIPS agreement, their term of protection is usually fixed at 20 years. These strong rights are awarded as incentives to innovate and come with strict registration and disclosure requirements.

The global economy is becoming increasingly focused on invention and innovation, with 2.9 million patents filed in 2016, a 7.8 per cent increase on 2015.[3] The number of patent registrations in a country is considered to be an indicator of development and economic progress and provides quantifiable indications of participation in science and technology research and development. The holding of a patent not only provides economic opportunities in its development and licensing but is also an important tool in gaining future investment and funding. Furthermore, for the individual rightsholder, patents

---

[2] Deborah Halbert, 'Feminist interpretations of intellectual property' (2006) 14 *Journal of Gender, Social Policy and the Law* 434.

[3] World Intellectual Property Organisation Global Patent Applications 23 November 2016, http://www.wipo.int/pressroom/en/articles/2016/article_0017.html, accessed 2 April 2017.

held can increase stature and promotions within commercial environments,[4] a factor that also applies to the increasingly commercialised academic sector. Strikingly, however, the number of female patent holders is woefully low with, in 2010 in the USA, around 7.7 per cent of primary inventors being female[5] and in 2008 8.3 per cent of the patents awarded by the European Patent Office being made to women as a primary applicant.[6] Social and economic trends relating to female participation and innovation are intrinsically linked to this clear-cut gendered distinction in access to this legal protection.

A simple answer to this issue could be women's historic lack of access to money, resources and, more specifically, participation in scientific development. However, more nuanced conclusions can be drawn through an examination of both historic and contemporary data. Due to the strict registration requirement, records can be accessed to determine trends in female patenting. However, problems are created in analysing this area due to most patent registration procedures not requiring an express indication of the gender of the applicant. Researchers often employ name-matching techniques, with the development of in-depth methodologies for determination of gender.[7]

The first British patent granted to a woman was recorded as early as 1637, 76 years after the first ever British patent.[8] It was granted to Amye Everard Ball for a tincture of saffron and roses. In America, the first registered patent for a resident of the British Colonies was granted in 1715 to the husband of a woman who had invented a corn-cleaning machine. It then took until 1809 for the first recorded patent issued to a US woman to be awarded to Mary Kies for an invention relating to straw weaving with silk or thread.[9] Charlotte Smith, President of the Woman's National Industrial League of America, provided an impassioned foreword to the 1890 pamphlet 'The Woman Inventor' in which she criticised the contemporary legal situation whereby a husband could patent and exploit a wife's invention with no legal remedy. This situation persisted across many of the States despite an 1845 New York State provision that 'secured to every married woman who shall receive a patent for her own invention, the right to hold and enjoy the same, and all the proceeds, benefits and profits as her separate property … as if unmarried'.[10]

---

[4] Robert P. Merges, 'The law and economics of employee inventions' (1999) 13 *Harvard Journal of Law and Technology* 1.

[5] Jessica Mili, Barbara Gault, Emma Williams-Baron, and Mika Berlan, 'The gender patenting gap' (Institute for Women's Policy Research, 2016), http://iwpr.org/publications/pubs/the-gender-patenting-gap/, accessed 16 January 2017.

[6] European Commission Evaluation on Policy: Promotion of Women Innovators and Entrepreneurship DG Enterprise and Industry Final Report (GHK, Technopolis, 2008).

[7] Fulvia Naldi and Ibarrio Vannini Parenti, *Scientific and Technological Performance by Gender Vol. II* (Methodological Report EUR 20309, 2002).

[8] PATGB104.

[9] Fred Amran, 'The innovative woman' (1984) *New Scientist*, 24 May.

[10] Bibi Zorina Khan, *The Democratization of Invention: Patents and Copyrights in American Economic Development, 1790–1920* (Cambridge University Press, 2009) p. 166.

The stated aims of 'The Woman Inventor' included the need to foster women's innovation and to press for fairer laws to enable women to gain their just rewards and protection. In its first volume, published in 1890, Smith looked to the future with the call:

> Let us hope with the dawn of a new century, that unjust wrongs will be righted, and that man will broaden the boundaries that have heretofore separated the barriers of women's inventive genius from man's.[11]

This needs to be placed within the context of research spearheaded by Smith[12] herself that estimated that from 1790 to 1895 one in every 100 patents granted were to women. Sarada et al.'s work[13] in the USA analyses the Annual Report of the Commissioner of Patents from 1870 to 1940 as against the corresponding ten-year US population data. Over this 70-year time frame the percentage of female patent holders, which starts at 2 per cent of 50 per cent of the population, grows slowly over the first 50 years until a slightly greater rise in 1920. This, holds the authors, corresponds with the impact of the women's rights movement in the USA but predates the increased female workforce participation brought about by the Second World War. More recently, in the USA the share of patents with any women inventors has risen more than fivefold from 3.4 per cent in 1977 to 18.8 per cent in 2010.[14] Research carried out by the UK Intellectual Property Office shows an increase in female patenting globally of 60 per cent in the last 15 years from 7.1 per cent in 2001 to 11.5 per cent in 2015.[15] While this indicates some improvements it is far from Smith's predicted revolutionary dawn at the start of the twentieth century.

In the context of the low levels of female patenting, the actual activities can be examined to determine the nature of those engaging with this form of legal protection. Classes need to be assigned when registering utility patents for new inventions. In the late 1800s in the USA the categories with most female patent holders were 'Culinary Utensils' and 'Wearing Apparel', followed by 'Furniture and Furnishings' and 'Washing and Cleaning'.[16] While this may demonstrate that women's activities are confined the realm of the home, women's clothing and fashion, Khan's nineteenth-century-focused work highlights that while

[11] Charlotte Smith (ed.), *The Woman Inventor* (1890) April and June, Vol. 1, p. 2.

[12] Government Printing Office, *Women Inventors to Whom Patents Have Been Granted By the United States Government, 1790 to July 1, 1888*, Vol 1 (Washington, DC).

[13] Sarada, Mike Andrews and Nicolas Ziebarth, *The Demographics of Inventors in the Historical United States* (Northwestern University, 2016), http://www.law.northwestern.edu/research-faculty/searlecenter/events/innovation/documents/Sarada_patent_grantees_Dec_2015.pdf, accessed 16 January 2017.

[14] n. 5.

[15] UK Intellectual Property Office, 'Gender Profiles in Worldwide Patenting: An analysis of female inventorship', 2016.

[16] US Department of Commerce, 'Buttons to Biotech U.S. Patenting By Women, 1977 to 1996' (Patent and Trademark Office, 1999).

female patenting may mainly relate to the sphere in which they had most influence and experience, many of these inventions were made commercially available and were profitable. They improved the lives of men and women alike and had influence outside the domestic sphere, leading to industrial progress. In an ongoing reflection of the early categorisations, a 2016 UK Intellectual Property Office survey[17] found the highest number of female patent holders for inventions relating to 'brassieres, clothing, footwear, cosmetics, furniture and food'. Conversely the lowest numbers related to patents for 'combustion engines, tools and weapons'.

Given the high level of patents that emanate from the science and engineering sectors, the lack of female patent holders could be seen as a direct result of historically low participation in these sectors. However, research carried out by Hunt et al.[18] found that women with degrees in these areas patent only at a slightly higher level than other women. On further detailed analysis they did find a correlation between the specific under-representation of women in the patent-intensive fields of mechanical and electrical engineering. Furthermore, within this, the actual position occupied by women had an impact, with under-representation in design and development leading to a low relative level of patenting. This raises wider societal questions relating to the impact of female input in the process of innovation. Kahler[19] highlights the dangers of a lack of 'cognitive diversity', in which strategies and views are overlooked due to women's different perspective on problem-solving. This can be placed within research that has found that the more diverse a team is, the more successful it will be.[20]

Examining the issue in more specific fields, Ding et al.'s work[21] presents a longitudinal study of gender and patenting in academic life sciences. While adjusting their parameters for 'productivity, social network, scientific field, and employer characteristics'[22] it was found that women patent at 0.40 times the rate of their male counterparts. The authors examined whether women were carrying out research of differing quality to men and chose to test this by examining the number of citations and journal impact factor. They found that in their sample the women actually achieved higher in relation to the impact factor and concluded that in general women do not do work that is less significant by

[17] n. 15.

[18] Jennifer Hunt, Jean-Philippe Garant, Hannah Herman and David J. Munroe, 'Why are women underrepresented amongst patentees?' (2013) 42 *Research Policy* 831.

[19] Annette Kahler, 'Examining exclusion in woman-inventor patenting: A comparison of educational trends and patent data in the era of Computer Engineer Barbie' (2011) 19 *Journal of Gender, Social Policy and the Law* 773.

[20] Scott E. Page, *The Difference: How the Power of Diversity Creates Better Groups, Firms, Schools, and Societies* (Princeton University Press, 2008).

[21] Waverly W. Ding, Fiona Murray and Toby E. Stuart, *Gender Differences in Patenting in the Academic Life Sciences*, 2006, https://ssrn.com/abstract=1260388, accessed 17 January 2016.

[22] Ibid. p. 4.

these measures. Interviews probed these issues further and suggested that the differing levels of patenting could be linked to women having a lower number of vital commercial connections and finding it difficult to balance commercial pursuits with academic and educational work. The research outlined here shows that there is a need for further examination of why, when women are increasing their education and participation in the fields of science and engineering, the levels of female patenting remains so low. Kahler indicates the lack of 'comprehensive and longitudinal empirical studies of woman-inventor patenting across technologies, organizations, and geography'.[23] Hunt et al. see the need for mentoring schemes to match those working in development and design roles with young female engineers.[24]

The statistics on female patenting are stark and they link strongly to the role of and attitudes towards women in society. Intellectual property law protects the development of knowledge, which in itself is constructed by society. Firestone's *The Dialectic of Sex* (1970) argues that culture is developed and experienced indirectly by women, with men dictating both its value and its nature, stating: 'cultural dicta are set by men, presenting only the male view'.[25]

A distinction has been highlighted that identifies the cultural with the masculine and the natural with the feminine.[26] This sees men as moving human knowledge and production forward with the role of women being to nurture and support. Women's labour in this way could be seen to have been separated from the 'industrialised', male forms of productivity. The locations and networks of this industrial production and creativity have, through history, denied women equal access.[27] The terms of creativity are, in this way, constructed from a non-neutral, masculine perspective. This, in its turn, pervades intellectual property law, the outward substance of which may be expressed neutrally, but whose premise can be seen to be based on the male creation of knowledge. Specifically, in relation to patent law and the monopoly it produces, by its very nature it gives preference to one social form of activity over another. While it may not be overtly recognisable, Halbert[28] holds that the masculine forms of production, labour and knowledge enjoy a position of privilege within the protective legal framework. As Barwa and Rai state:

> One can hardly be surprised that there are so few women inventors patenting their inventions. It is still more surprising that inventions made by women exist at all and that they are not only patented but also commercially developed.[29]

---

[23] Kahler (n. 19) 777.

[24] n. 18.

[25] Shulamith Firestone, *The Dialectic of Sex: The Case for Feminist Revolution* (William Morrow and Company, 1970) p. 178.

[26] Sherry B. Ortner, 'Is female to male as nature is to culture?' (1972) 1 *Feminist Studies* 5.

[27] Sandra Harding, *The Science Question in Feminism* (Cornell University Press, 1986) p. 143.

[28] Halbert (n. 2).

[29] Sharmishta Barwa and Shirin Rai, 'Knowledge and/as power: A feminist critique of trade related intellectual property rights' (2003) 7 *Gender, Technology and Development* 91.

They[30] tell the stories of the female inventors whose contributions were exploited and often overlooked; they see this as a continuing product of societal and institutional prejudices that impede women's participation in public life. Used as an example is herbal medicines, which were often developed, honed and used in the home by women but, when their commercial potential was realised, moved into the realm of predominantly male patent holders. This is then drawn back into the TRIPS agreement which, with its market-based focus on centralised, exclusive protections, gives legal validity to those who can prove a claim based on a patriarchal definition of knowledge. This, in turn, increasingly marginalises, among others, women and exacerbates existing social and economic divisions.

While recognising that the TRIPS agreement, with its global protectionist stance, can perpetuate market-based inequalities, Shiva[31] suggests the development of 'social patenting', a shared legal protection that would recognise the ongoing work of the communities that leads to the end result, the invention. This would address the disparities that are seen to arise in the individualistic, winner-takes-all current patent law framework. However, support for such a fundamental change is lacking.

Debate 2
Does copyright law protect women's creativity equally?

While the low number of female patent holders is a statistically verifiable indication of gender disparities in IP law, other areas show more nuanced patterns. Unlike patents that require strict registration standards to be met, copyright, following the principles laid down in the Berne Convention, does not require registration to be afforded protection. Copyright protection is, in most jurisdictions, automatic on fixation, with countries of the Union created by the Convention protecting 'production in the literary, scientific and artistic domain'[32] being open to create specific rules relating to categories that do not attract protection unless they are 'fixed in some material form'.[33]

The Berne Convention was the culmination of a series of conferences beginning in 1858 with the Congress of Authors and Artists;[34] its main driving force was the Association Littéraire et Artistique Internationale (ALAI) and its founder, the author Victor Hugo. Its key aims included securing international copyright standards and ensuring ease of protection. With prominent novelists as key proponents of the legal harmonisation, the approaches taken were

---

[30] Ibid.

[31] Vandana Shiva, 'Poverty and globalisation' in Natalie Goldstein, *Globalization and Free Trade* (Checkmark Books, 2008) pp. 226–238.

[32] Art. 2(1).

[33] Art. 2(2).

[34] Stephen P. Ladas, *The International Protection of Literary and Artistic Property* (Macmillan, 1938) pp. 71–72.

based on the individualised protection of the artistic, literary work. As with the debate above on patent law, this leads to collective production of knowledge, often carried out by women, struggling to fit within existing frameworks.

Halbert[35] analyses the position of knitting, a predominantly female craft-based activity in which patterns were traditionally handed down by relatives and shared and transformed through communal interaction. Increasingly, however, knitting patterns are published in commercial publications with copyright asserted that, for example, prohibits the knitter from sharing the pattern or a modified version of it with others, or selling the finished article for profit. Knitters are increasingly aware[36] of this profit-focused use of copyright that hampers organic creative development. This is supported by copyright law provisions, developed within a framework that prioritises ownership and market relations. As Halbert states:

> A feminine way of producing knowledge within the realm of craft has been replaced with a way of producing knowledge that emphasizes abstract originality and authorship in the production of knowledge, instead of the relations built into culture and custom.[37]

Similarly, the practice of quilting as a predominantly female craft that strengthened intergenerational ties and depicted complex narratives[38] revolves around collective production which, while original and artistic, does not fit with the individualised legal concept of for-profit IP protection.

Wider movements to address global inequalities in IP protection could have some impact on shaping future legal developments. In 2003 UNESCO adopted the Convention for the Safeguarding of the Intangible Cultural Heritage (ICH Convention), an international instrument developed in order to protect traditional culture across the globe, particularly in the face of increasing globalisation. Its creation rests on two key aims: to regulate the interaction of copyright protection and ownership of cultural heritage, and, secondly, to protect activities deemed important to cultural patrimony.[39] It lists, among others, knowledge and practices concerning nature and the universe, and traditional craftsmanship as domains that comprise 'intangible cultural property'.[40] States parties are tasked with creating and updating inventories in order to protect the activities identified as cultural heritage. The effectiveness of the measures relies upon clarifying the nature of the Convention rights and finding methods of translating these rights into tangible legal protections. Brown

---

[35] Halbert (n. 2).

[36] Copyright for Crafters (2008), http://girlfromauntie.com/copyright/, accessed 19 October 2017.

[37] Halbert (n. 2) 442.

[38] Pat Ferrero, Elaine Hedges and Julie Silber, *Hearts and Hands: The Influence of Women and Quilts on American Society* (Quilt Digest Press, 1987).

[39] Richard Kurin, 'UNESCO's adoption of the convention for the safeguarding of the intangible cultural heritage' (2004) 56 *Museum International* 66.

[40] Art. 2(2).

highlights the potential for 'sweeping claims of cultural ownership that have little basis in fact' and holds that a balanced approach to protecting valid cultural heritage needs also to facilitate open creative development.[41] Cominelli and Greffe[42] examine the interaction of the culturally developed creativity with traditional IP rights, highlighting problematic issues such as collective authorship, duration of protection, and the fixation of traditional knowledge which by its very nature is usually created through flexible, evolutionary interaction.

While the ICH Convention runs alongside the individualistic, market-driven IP framework, its operation can, argues Lixinski,[43] empower communities to have some control over collective heritage. Furthermore, there is potential for this recognition of collaborative creation, often the realm of women, to draw new values into the concept of artistic creativity and production. Tellingly, however, the UK and the USA have not, as yet, ratified the ICH Convention, following an identified trend of Western states undervaluing protections for cultural heritage. Blakely[44] outlines the position of the tartan as intangible cultural heritage, with the majority not covered by copyright due to difficulties relating to determining authorship or expiration of a potential term of protection. She sees the protection of intangible cultural heritage as providing 'the opportunity for community groups to leverage the existing knowledge of that heritage for further social and cultural protection'[45] and calls for measures to protect tartans in the light of increasing commercialisation, including the UK's ratification of the ICH Convention. The discussion follows the theme of collaborative, community-driven creative production not conforming to the male-designed notion of authorship.

Underscoring this approach, Bartow[46] notes how female creative production is, on the whole, given less attention and deemed to be less valuable than male. She highlights how, for example, male writers, directors, composers and visual artists are dominant across the cultural sphere. In copyright law, the wider framework of licensing and distribution has a fundamental impact on the prominence given to production emanating from certain sectors of society. These factors lead to the financial benefits of a framework that commodifies creativity being enjoyed more by males than females. She states: 'Copyright laws were written by men to embody a male vision of the ways in which creativity and commerce should intersect.'[47] Negotiating complex distribution and

---

[41] Michael Brown, 'Heritage Trouble: Recent work on the protection of intangible cultural property' (2005) 12 *International Journal of Cultural Property* 40, at 53.

[42] Francesca Cominelli and Xavier Greffe, 'Intangible cultural heritage: Safeguarding for creativity' (2012) 3 *City, Culture and Society* 245.

[43] Lucas Lixinski, 'Selecting heritage: The interplay of art, politics and identity' (2011) 22 *European Journal of International Law* 81.

[44] Megan Blakely, 'Pattern recognition: Governmental regulation of tartan and commodification of culture' (2015) 22(4) *International Journal of Cultural Property* 487.

[45] Ibid. 500

[46] Ann Bartow, 'Fair use and the fairer sex: Gender, feminism, and copyright law' (2006) 14 *American University Journal of Gender, Social Policy and the Law* 551.

[47] Ibid. 557.

licensing arrangements and access to the law requires resources and access to male-dominated structures and frameworks. At a basic level, the lack of formalities and low minimum threshold to attract copyright protection could, following the resource argument, be held to act in favour of women. However, this very lack of formalities, it is argued,[48] leads to a lack of clarity in relation to what is due copyright protection, which, in turn, disadvantages those creators who do not have equal access to legal advice and frameworks.

Writing in relation to fan fiction, Katyal[49] emphasises how the traditional construction of IP laws needs to evolve to address new issues of production in the online sphere. Fan fiction, at a basic level, involves building upon elements of existing works, such as characters, to develop storylines and situations. It covers a diverse range of creative activities in which, for example, new narratives are developed in existing worlds or characters in the original works move on different trajectories.[50] The Harry Potter and Twilight books and films are examples of works that have spawned extensive fan fiction communities, strengthening end-user connections to the works and creating new, dynamic, interactive worlds. The internet provides a space, free from fixed structures and identities, that has facilitated collaborative production, mainly carried out by women, in a reflection of the discussion on craft protection above. In the UK, under the Copyright, Designs and Patents Act 1988 the rights of an original author can be infringed if a substantial aspect of that original work is used. A core premise of copyright law is that the protection extends to the expression relating to a work, for example, dialogue, characters and situations, rather than its core central idea, for example the idea of a boy wizard at school. Depending upon the nature of the fan fiction, it often involves infringing activities due to unauthorised use of protected works.

In the USA, the doctrine of fair use can be applied to fan fiction, with its assessment of the purpose and character of the use, the nature of the copyrighted work in question, the proportionate amount of the copyright work that is used, and the effect on the market relating to the copyright work. A recent US case relating to the publication of a book emanating from the online community site, the Harry Potter Lexicon, focused on the 'transformative' nature of the use of the original work.[51] In the UK, following recommendations in the influential Hargreaves report,[52] which stated that 'Government should firmly resist over-regulation of activities which do not prejudice the central objective

---

[48] Christopher Sprigman, 'Reform(aliz)ing copyright' (2004) 57 *Stanford Law Review* 485.

[49] Sonia Katyal, 'Performance, property, and the slashing of gender in fan fiction' (2005) 14 *Journal of Gender, Social Policy and the Law* 463.

[50] Henry Jenkins, *Textual Poachers: Television Fans and Participatory Culture* (Routledge, 1992) pp. 24–27.

[51] *Warner Bros v RDR Books* (2008) 575 F Supp.2d 513 (Southern District, New York).

[52] Ian Hargreaves, *Digital Opportunity: A Review of Intellectual Property and Growth* (Department for Business, Innovation and Skills, 2011).

of copyright, namely the provision of incentives to creators', an exception has been introduced into the statutory framework to allow fair dealing with a work for the purposes of parody, caricature or pastiche.[53] This is a move that is expressly permitted by the European Union's Copyright Directive.[54] Within the UK framework it provides protection for those extending original works in this manner, based on fair dealing principles which require an assessment of the scale of the copyrighted work used, the actual use made of the work, and the potential for the works to be in direct commercial competition. This reform is to be commended as it allows for more flexibility in relation to user-generated works but it is unclear the extent to which fan fiction will be protected as, it has been identified, it does not always specifically parody or criticise the original but adds to and extends it.[55]

CONCLUSION

With a lack of clarity in the legal framework, fan fiction is an example of another area of IP law in which predominantly female creativity has been marginalised through the framework of legal protection. Coombe[56] evaluates how this framework can either support or damage the interests of creators and the wider availability of certain kinds of works. She argues that the commodification of these rights of ownership has served to benefit those operating in the accepted mainstream while so-called outsider groups, including women, have been increasingly marginalised. Collective, collaborative, responsive, community-based forms of creation are not protected on the same basis as the mainstream in, what Craig identifies as

> a copyright regime which propertizes and over-protects the works of some authors while dismissing others as copiers and trespassers; which encourages some kinds of creativity while condemning others as unlawful appropriation; which values so-called original contributions but silences responses in the cultural conversation.[57]

While copyright law may operate under a substantive guise of neutrality it is its wider application, particularly in relation to its commercialisation, that leads to an unequal enjoyment of the wealth created by the legal framework.

[53] S30A Copyright, Designs and Patents Act 1988.

[54] Directive 2001/29/EC on the harmonisation of certain aspects of copyright law in the information society. Article 5(3)(k).

[55] Meredith McCardle, 'Note, fan fiction, fandom, and fanfare: What's all the fuss?' (2003) 9 *Boston University Journal of Science and Technology Law* 434, 441.

[56] Rosemary J. Coombe, 'Objects of property and subjects of politics: Intellectual property laws and democratic dialogue' (1991) 69 *Texas Law Review* 1853.

[57] Carys J. Craig, 'Reconstructing the author-self: Some feminist lessons for copyright law' (2007) 15 *American University Journal of Gender, Society, Policy and Law* 207.

FURTHER READING

Dan L. Burk, 'Do patents have gender?' (2011) 19 *Journal of Gender, Social Policy and the Law* 881.

Deborah Halbert, 'Feminist interpretations of intellectual property' (2006) 14 *Journal of Gender, Social Policy and the Law* 431.

Kara W. Swanson, 'Intellectual property and gender: Reflections on accomplishments and methodology' (2015) 24 *Journal of Gender, Social Policy and the Law* 175.

UK Intellectual Property Office, *Gender Profiles in UK Patenting, An Analysis of Female Inventorship* (2016).

CHAPTER 14

Jurisprudence/Legal Theory

Joanne Conaghan

A jurisprudence is a theory of the relation between life and law.[1]

Few courses elicit such mixed student responses as jurisprudence and/or legal theory. For some, it is a welcome relief from the doctrinal emphasis of the core curriculum; for others, an irritant to be endured, or, even better, avoided, assuming one follows a programme in which jurisprudence is not required. It is true that in recent decades the subject has undergone considerable transformation. The traditional emphasis on general jurisprudence, cast as a seemingly irresolvable tension between certain schools of jurisprudential thought (usually legal positivism and natural law), has given way to a more diverse, eclectic selection of themes, encompassing both the traditional syllabus and a proliferation of new legal theories somewhat different in orientation and approach. Whereas legal positivism and natural law are preoccupied in various ways with the question of what law *is*, new approaches – feminism, critical legal studies and critical race theory – appear more concerned with what law *does*, with the effects of law on lived experience and the potential of law to transform that experience in positive ways. Too often, though, the jurisprudence curriculum unfolds as a succession of discrete debates within self-referential bodies of literature with little or nothing to say to one another. For example, feminism is deeply interested in how law is implicated in the production and maintenance of gender norms but struggles to get excited about whether the rule of recognition is a convention, fiction or social fact. Similarly, legal positivism, while enthusiastically engaging with questions pertaining to the relationship between law and morality, has no discernible interest in probing the relationship between law and gender.

In this chapter, I consider two debates which occupy a central place in the jurisprudence curriculum to show how attention to gender can throw useful

---

[1] Catharine MacKinnon, *Towards a Feminist Theory of the State* (Harvard University Press, 1989) p. 237.

light on mainstream jurisprudential debate. The first is the 'what is law?' question, on which I bestow a gendered twist by probing feminist assertions that (the concept of) law is gendered. The second is an equally familiar focus of jurisprudential angst, namely the question of whether there is a right answer to legal disputes.

Debate 1
Is (the concept of) law gendered?

What does it mean to say that law is gendered? No one would deny that certain laws reflect, or contribute to the production of, gendered social arrangements. Indeed, much feminist scholarship has been devoted to exposing and critiquing the role law has played, historically and contemporaneously, in promoting and maintaining gender inequalities in the family, workplace, and intimate sexual relations. But to claim that law – as opposed to particular legal regimes – is gendered is to assert that gender is implicated in a general sense, that it is part of what we apprehend as law and/or is relevant to understanding how and what law does. This larger claim more readily corresponds with the ethos and spirit of general jurisprudence and, unsurprisingly, features centrally in feminist engagements with legal theory. As Nicola Lacey, one of the few female scholars successfully to penetrate the bastion of the jurisprudential mainstream, remarks, 'the idea of feminist legal theory ... suggests there is something not merely about particular laws or sets of laws, but rather and more generally, about the very structure or method of modern law which is hierarchically gendered'.[2] Similarly, Ngaire Naffine speculates that 'a problem of sex [is] bias built into the very forms of law'.[3] Both scholars intimate that gender relates not only to the content of law but also to how law is conceived, structured and practised.

    Pioneering feminist legal scholar Catharine MacKinnon goes further. She asserts that law is *male*, expressing and enacting men's power over women. How does law do this? Surely law is, or aspires to be, neutral, rational and objective, if not in content, certainly in application. According to MacKinnon, it is anything but: 'Law sees and treats women the way men see and treat women.'[4] The perspective or standpoint of law is male. Critically, however, law does not present itself as such but uses notions of neutrality, rationality and objectivity to mask the partiality of its position, law's investment in sustaining male power. The adoption of a gender-neutral stance in relation to the application of legal norms places gender-differential outcomes outside the formal scope of law's operations. The recasting of messy social problems as abstract dilemmas of rationality filters out of legal consideration 'extraneities' such as

---

[2] Nicola Lacey, *Unspeakable Subjects* (Hart, 1998) p. 2.
[3] Ngaire Naffine, *Law and the Sexes* (Allen & Unwin, 1990) p. x.
[4] MacKinnon (n. 1) p. 162.

gendered asymmetries of power and privilege. And, of course, the stubborn adherence to a stance of dispassionate indifference to the consequences of its own operations cements law's position as 'a neutral arbiter among conflicting interests',[5] neither responsible for existing distributions of power and resources nor charged with redressing them. Hence, 'what counts as [legal] reason corresponds with the way things are'.[6]

Within feminist theory, MacKinnon's stance is often criticised as presenting an uncompromising picture of law as enacting male power.[7] The operations of power are more complex, it is argued, and not so relentlessly one-way. While it is true that, broadly speaking, legal and social arrangements do still tend to work to men's benefit and women's disadvantage, the gendered effects of regulatory regimes may vary, making it wrong to assert that law, always and inevitably, assumes a male point of view. To reject the claim that law is *male*, however, is not to conclude that law is not *gendered* in just the ways MacKinnon suggests. This is because the power of her critique lies not in exposing law's perspective as male but in excavating the modalities that law deploys to promote the appearance of not having a perspective at all: 'Male dominance', she declares, 'is perhaps the most pervasive and tenacious system of power in history … Its point of view is the standard for point-of-viewlessness, its particularity the meaning of universality.'[8] It is important to clarify the scope and limits of what MacKinnon is propounding here. It is sometimes suggested that the feminist critique of law is misplaced; law, it is argued, makes no claim to neutrality as between different interests as legal operations almost always produce outcomes which benefit some and disadvantage others. That the content of law may be tilted in ways which reinforce male (or other group) interests, critics submit, constitutes no great theoretical insight. However, this is to misunderstand MacKinnon's claim. Her critique, and that of feminist legal scholarship more broadly, goes further, implicating not just law's substance but also law's form in gendered operations and effects. The engagement is not only with *what* law does but *how* law does it. Law's modus operandi, the conventions and techniques which govern it as a discursive practice – the primacy of logic, impetus to abstraction, deference to coherence, valorisation of a priori reasoning – these are the target of feminist critique.

This is more than an assertion that because law is blind to power, it allows power to operate unchecked. In fact, law is not blind to power though such a conception of the law–power relation is enabled by a modality in which the legal and the social are invariably placed at an appropriately safe distance from one another. This is precisely the point. To think of law in its own terms, that is, to apprehend it as a distinct corpus of norms subject to specific techniques of derivation, navigation and application, is to plot the terrain of law's operations

[5] Ibid. p. 159.
[6] Ibid. p. 162.
[7] See, e.g., Carol Smart, *Feminism and the Power of Law* (Routledge, 1989) Chapter 4.
[8] MacKinnon (n. 1) p. 116.

with the coordinates already fixed and in place. Within this mapping, law is formally positioned in relation to its 'others' (morality, politics, society), reflecting a conceptual schema so familiar to legal thought as rarely to provoke challenge, a schema in which power is seen to be exercised by and through law but is not *of* law.[9] Law is always located at a conceptual and normative remove from the objects, implications and effects of its operations.

What is at issue here is no less than the relation between law and life, between legal and social being. Granted, mainstream jurisprudence accepts the social and legal are related. Within this framing, the legal is generally posited as a derivation of the social: Les Green, for example, regards law as 'a social construction … made by people thinking and acting'.[10] But, Green continues, 'law exists in a physical universe that is not socially constructed and it is created by and for people who are not socially constructed either'.[11] What does Green mean when he says that people are not socially constructed? Is he referring to the materiality of their bodies, the cognitive operations of their minds or what? What about people's gender? Is that socially constructed? Elsewhere Green agrees that gender is 'as socially constructed as it gets',[12] though sex he regards as a brute biological fact. Green draws here on a distinction common in social theory between sex as nature and gender as social construction.[13] This distinction has been the focus of repeated challenge in feminist theory for positing too sharp a division between nature and culture.[14] In particular, our perception of sex, understood as biological difference, is arguably already overlaid by cultural assumptions about what corporeal divergences signify.[15] Nevertheless, returning to the notion that 'people' are not socially constructed but that gender is, are people then genderless (but presumably sexed)? When we say that 'people thinking and acting' produce law, do they think and act without reference to gender (because gender is socially constructed and people are not)?

This ambiguity is not accidental and reflects a deeper problem with the way in which the legal and the social are configured in mainstream jurisprudence. Focusing on the nature of law, jurisprudence pays scant attention to the nature of social being; this is merely part of the background to the main enquiry into legal phenomena. Whether or not gender is natural or social is irrelevant for jurisprudential purposes because nature and society are irrelevant

---

[9] See, e.g., Les Green arguing that laws 'express and channel social power' in 'Introduction' to H.L.A. Hart, *The Concept of Law* (Clarendon Press, 1994) p. xxxiii.

[10] Ibid. p. xvi.

[11] Ibid.

[12] Les Green, 'Sex-neutral marriage' (2011) 64 *Current Legal Problems* 1, 4.

[13] See, e.g., Robert Stoller, *Sex and Gender* (Hogarth Press, 1968).

[14] For further discussion, see Joanne Conaghan, *Law and Gender* (Clarendon Press, 2013) pp. 17–25.

[15] Until the eighteenth century, women were commonly viewed not as anatomically different from men but as anatomically deficient: there was only *one* sex and it was male. Thomas Laqueur, *Making Sex: Body and Gender from the Greeks to Freud* (Harvard University Press, 1990).

except insofar as they provide the context for law's operations. But how do we know we can explore what law is with limited reference to or exploration of the relation between law and its 'context'? And how do we know people are not socially or even legally constructed? The assumption that 'people' are in some unspecified sense beyond law and society is precisely that, an assumption about the nature of social being, taking the form of a truth, which is then cemented in the architecture of legal thought.

At this point, feminism converges with other critical theories in taking a different view of people and their relation to law. Let's begin with the distinction between what is real and how we perceive and/or represent what is real, the troubling dichotomy between matter and meaning. One approach, broadly associated with modernity, is to assume that reality can be accurately represented. The object of knowledge becomes the correct depiction of the real. Objective knowledge of the world, the product of detached, unsituated contemplation, is therefore both possible and desirable. Another approach, generally attributed to postmodernism, asserts that because what we perceive to be real is always mediated through language, reality cannot exist outside our social/linguistic constructions: knowledge is socially situated and subjective. On the one hand then, we have matter, stuff, the physical world to which Green alludes. On the other, we have meaning, the ideas, concepts and beliefs which inform how we apprehend, interpret and experience the material world, including corporeality. Putting the dilemma in the crudest possible terms, modernist thinking tends to assume that matter determines meaning while postmodernists veer towards the notion that meaning determines matter.[16]

Let's bring this back to how we conceive the relation between law and life: it seems that modernism views life as producing law while postmodernism sees law as producing life. Framed in this way, one or other position would appear to be wrong, but let us suppose that neither is. Suppose instead that law and life are just so hopelessly intertwined that depicting their relation in some total or unconditional sense is simply not possible. The precise nature of the relation between law and life is arguably as complex as that between meaning and matter. Surely what is critical is to acknowledge that complexity, not assume it away. Theoretical physicist and feminist theorist Karen Barad describes the relation between matter and meaning as *entangled*. Barad rejects accounts of the world in which the natural and social are conceived as distinct and separate realms, problematising ideas of human agency and causation and challenging simplistic conceptions of natural realism versus social constructivism.[17] Perhaps this is a good way to view the relation between life and law: both the social and the legal act upon, within and through one another so that while it may be true that law comes into being through people thinking and acting, it is equally

---

[16] For a good introduction to these issues, see Susan Hekman, *The Material of Knowledge: Feminist Disclosures* (Indiana University Press, 2010), especially Chapter 1.

[17] Karen Barad, *Meeting the Universe Halfway: Quantum Physics and the Entanglement of Matter and Meaning* (Duke University Press, 2007).

true that people come into being through law thinking and acting. People *are* socially constructed but they are also embodied and materially situated: the challenge is surely to articulate a jurisprudence which encompasses the entanglement of matter and meaning in social and legal being.

This is where the form law takes in the mainstream jurisprudential imagination becomes a problem. MacKinnon calls attention to the liberal view of law as 'the mind of society',[18] that is, as rational, disembodied, immaterial. She argues that this conception of law actively enables and empowers gender and other hierarchies. Law is conceived as 'other' than matter, formally distinct from, though acting upon, the material world.[19] The Cartesian metaphor helps to support an idea of law as discrete, bounded, autonomous, reinforcing the conceptual and normative distance of law from life, and of the legal subject from his/her embodiment. The concepts which underpin this realisation of law, for example the unitary legal subject, formal equality, dualistic configurations of legal space (public/private, self/other, reason/affect) also presuppose the expulsion of matter from law. Even the distinction between form and substance, between how and what law does, is intelligible only within a frame in which the intra-constitution of being and doing (the way in which what we are and what we do shape and inform each other) is disregarded. In other words, the conditions for the existence of the concept of law which is the predominant focus of mainstream jurisprudence include a set of assumptions about the relation of matter and meaning, reality and representation, which are at the very least contestable.[20] It may be, too, that the highly prized jurisprudential quest to formulate a unified concept of law, separate from and independent of the contexts in which law operates, is quixotically misplaced. Increasingly this seems to be recognised by jurisprudential scholars. Brian Tamanaha, for example, calls for a 'non-essentialist' conception of law, attentive, first and foremost, to the relation of law and society in any given context.[21] Lacey, too, insists on contextualising the conceptual structures of law within broader social practices, not least to ensure that changes in those structures over time and place can be tracked and analysed.[22]

Let's return now to our original question: is (the concept of) law gendered? Gender is clearly not a category of formal significance in conventional jurisprudence. It is that very absence which occasions pause for thought: how can law, which all agree is a social construct, be without gender (which is 'as socially constructed as it gets') and a primary feature of social ordering? Scratching the

---

[18] MacKinnon (n. 1) p. 159.

[19] See also Margaret Davies, *Law Unlimited, Materialism, Pluralism and Legal Theory* (Routledge, 2017) p. 44.

[20] Ibid.

[21] Brian Tamanaha, *A General Jurisprudence of Law and Society* (Oxford University Press, 2001).

[22] Nicola Lacey, *In Search of Criminal Responsibility* (Oxford University Press, 2016).

surface of legal theory, we find that law is not only without gender but without sex: matter, including corporeality, is formally expunged from law's contours which are purely intellectual, disembodied, immaterial, rationally derived. As Margaret Davies observes: 'The assumption seems to be that law is separate from and indeed precedes the acts through which it is made manifest.'[23] To put it another way, what counts for purposes of jurisprudential reflection is an *idea* of law, already conceived as separate and distinct from its multiple and power-inflected instantiations in everyday life.

Suppose for a moment we resist the impulse so ingrained in legal thought to disconnect law from everything else. Suppose instead we seek out the connectedness of law, including the connection between law and material life. Why *should* materiality be expunged from law? If we accept instead that matter and meaning are deeply entangled, then to posit a notion of law unmarked by materiality seems highly questionable. From there, it is no small step to speculate that the materiality of law (bearing in mind the conditions in which law, as we currently understand it, has come into being) *is* male or at the very least gendered. In other words, recognising the entanglement of matter and meaning brings gender (as well as race and other features of identity which may be corporeally mediated) to the foreground of legal thinking and theorising. Correspondingly, probing the absence of gender flushes out the suppressed materiality in conventional legal thought, allowing it to emerge.

In a recent feminist analysis of H.L.A. Hart's *Concept of Law*, Emma Cunliffe tracks the various ways in which gendered, specifically masculine traits creep into Hart's construction of the 'ordinary citizen', from whose perspective Hart explores the idea of legal obligation.[24] Cunliffe shows how Hart's general non-empirical legal subject is underpinned by assumptions about individual autonomy and human rationality which are historically and contextually contingent as well as symbolically, culturally or socially aligned with masculinity. Her critique illustrates how a stance which purports to be genderless may nevertheless incorporate gendered assumptions into reasoning about how people experience and apprehend law or how they are positioned in relation to law's operations which in due course transmute into apparently unassailable assertions about the nature of legal obligation. Ultimately, the important question here is not whether law is gendered but how that gendering process may be understood within the framework of a broader enquiry into the relation between life and law, underpinned by a theoretical orientation which is unrestricted and acknowledges the significance of materiality in jurisprudential endeavours.

---

[23] Davies (n. 19) p. 44.

[24] Emma Cunliffe, 'Ambiguities: Law, Morality, and Legal Subjectivity in HLA Hart's Concept of Law' in Maria Drakopoulou (ed.), *Feminist Encounters with Legal Philosophy* (Routledge, 2013) p. 185.

Debate 2

Is there (always) a right answer to legal disputes?

No one is more in pursuit of a right answer to a legal dispute than the first-year law student. Correspondingly, it is a matter of regret to most graduates that the cumulative effect of their legal education is to disabuse them of the notion that any right answer exists. In only one element of their legal studies does the holy grail of legal correctness still tantalise. No self-respecting course in jurisprudence fails to give sustained attention to the question of whether, and to what extent, legal norms *actually determine* legal outcomes. From the rigidity of legal formalism to the indeterminacy of rule-scepticism,[25] the degree of constraint which law imposes on judicial decision-making continues to excite scholarly debate.

What bearing does the dilemma of legal in/determinacy have on gender and feminist theory? An obvious concern is that if legal norms *do* deliver right answers, how do we account for past decisions plainly imbued with dubious assumptions about gender roles and relations? Did the common law *really* require that Miss Bebb be denied entry into the legal profession because of her sex?[26] One can of course dismiss such objectionable decisions as erroneous: there was/is a right answer but in this instance the court failed to reach it. The notion that judges sometimes get things wrong is plausible but, from the perspective of Miss Bebb and feminist theory, hardly satisfying. Judges seem to have got things wrong *a lot* in times gone by, especially when it came to women. The more likely explanation is that judges were/are influenced by social and cultural norms when interpreting and applying the law, including gender norms. What is the status of these norms – many of which were contestable even within the historical contexts in which they arose – in legal decision-making? If judges *acting properly* can rely on values and beliefs which in retrospect are plainly objectionable, how is it possible to say there is a right answer to legal disputes?

Why does the notion that law delivers right answers hold such appeal, notwithstanding its patent fallibility? Moreover, what consequences flow from organising our expectations of, and aspirations for, law around this idea(l)? Clearly the belief that law delivers right answers buttresses law's authority and therefore its effectiveness as a mode of governance. Judges, too, are more comfortable with the idea that they expound rather than create law and are loath to abandon the view that their capacity to determine legal outcomes *is* appropriately constrained by the doctrinal framework. Duncan Kennedy argues that judges are in denial about the fact that they bring into play their own ideological

---

[25] Hart, *The Concept of Law* (n. 9) ch. VII. Hart argues against the idea that law always delivers a right answer, acknowledging that in 'hard cases' judges must exercise 'discretion' and make new law.
[26] *Bebb v the Law Society* [1914] 1 Ch 286.

preferences in legal decision-making.[27] That judges experience themselves as constrained is not in question, Kennedy contends: it is this experience of constraint which enables them to engage in what are effectively political acts while wilfully blind to the fact that they are doing so. For Kennedy law is a form of political practice, but a distinct form in which the ideological preferences of judges find expression within techniques of legal reasoning.

Dworkin, too, agrees that law is political. However, unlike Kennedy, who sees judges as bad faith political actors, Dworkin views recourse to political (and moral) arguments as part of what doing law entails. Far from acting in bad faith, legal fidelity requires judges to interpret and apply law so that it fits with what has gone before, drawing on the political and institutional history of the relevant legal materials. In this process, there may well be room for judicial disagreement about what is the right outcome but there *is* a right outcome nevertheless (although it can require Herculean judicial superpowers to reach it).[28]

Kennedy and Dworkin are much preoccupied with the political dimensions of law, reflecting the concerns and anxieties of North American legal scholars. By contrast, Hart has little to say about politics and even less about adjudication. Moreover, notwithstanding that he characterises law as a union of primary and secondary rules, Hart does not deny that judges make law at least in hard cases when the limits of a rule-based system are confronted. Building on this framework, Scottish jurist Neil MacCormick elaborates a theory of legal reasoning within Hart's positivist vision, stressing the syllogistic character of legal rules and, therefore, the role of logic in legal reasoning processes.[29] MacCormick's invocation of logic powerfully reaffirms the idea that law delivers right answers. At the same time, MacCormick agrees there are occasions when deductive reasoning, that is, the syllogistic application of rules, fails to determine outcomes.[30] What if the rule is ambiguous and requires interpretation or what if the claim raises a novel question of law? What then does the judge do? In the absence of a determining rule, says MacCormick, the judge must choose between competing *arguments*, the process no longer one of deductive reasoning but evaluation. This dimension of legal reasoning entails identifying and/ or deploying those arguments likely to carry the greatest legal weight.

Where do legal arguments come from and how might they be characterised? According to MacCormick they derive from principles and values, not just any principles and values, but those which have penetrated legal terrain and gained approval. 'New' values or principles may be introduced but they will struggle for recognition unless and until they find full acceptance in the courts.[31] Consent is a value so deeply embedded in the fabric of law that it carries huge

[27] Duncan Kennedy, *A Critique of Adjudication* (Harvard University Press, 1997).

[28] Ronald Dworkin, *Law's Empire* (Harvard University Press, 1986), especially Chapters 2 and 3.

[29] Neil MacCormick, *Legal Reasoning and Legal Theory* (Oxford University Press, revised edn 1994) Chapters I–III.

[30] Ibid. pp. 66–72.

[31] Ibid. p. 238.

weight when invoked. By contrast, the principle of sex equality is relatively new to law and has taken centuries to secure a sufficient grip on legal argument to displace the presumption of irrevocable consent once justifying the marital rape exemption.[32] The legal contortion of consent to secure a husband's dominion over his wife's body evidences law's historical investment in male power, the accumulation of shared values and beliefs held by generations of (male) law-makers. If values and principles garner weight in legal argument according to the extent to which they are accepted as legally relevant, the result will almost inevitably be a normative regime which reflects the viewpoints of those who get to participate in legal practice.

What happens if the legal community becomes more diverse, bringing into legal contention a wider range of values and principles? One hopes that historically entrenched power relations will be dislodged as new voices find expression within the conventions of legal argument. Does legal reasoning aid normative inclusion here or are there features of the reasoning process which inhibit the alignment of law with the interests and concerns of historically marginalised groups? Two features of MacCormick's analysis bear further attention in this context. The first is his emphasis on the logical structure of law as a rule-based system. It is true that legal outcomes are not always (or even often) the product of pure logic but the normative regime is underpinned by logic: logical operations structure and inform legal argumentation. Because legal recourse to values and principles occurs within a discursive framework which is founded on logic, it is easy to assume that when judges are engaged in weighing and balancing arguments (as opposed to the syllogistic application of rules) they are still, in a sense, engaged in logic. Notions of rightness thus infuse the whole adjudicative process, obscuring the role played by evaluative operations in the determination of legal outcomes.

A second aspect of MacCormick's analysis of legal reasoning more directly troubles the notion that diversity provides an easy solution to the historical problem of law's positionality. MacCormick argues that the functioning needs of law as a system for regulating human conduct impose certain constraints on the development and application of values and principles in law, constraints which also serve as justificatory devices in legal argument. Specifically, for law to do its job, decision-making should be *consistent,* that is like cases should be treated alike and they should be *coherent* in the sense of fitting seamlessly within the broader fabric of law (echoing Dworkin's notion of law as integrity). A further constraint identified by MacCormick is that the *consequences* of decisions must be considered, requiring judges to gauge the likely impact of decisions beyond the immediate circumstances of the case. Together these constraints place significant limits on how values and principles grow and develop in legal argument. Normative contestation takes place but subject to necessary strictures to ensure the functioning of the legal whole.

---

[32] *R v R* [1992] I AC 599 (discussed in Conaghan (n. 14) pp. 48–69).

This means that any attempt to change the normative tilt of law through the creative deployment of legal argument (as opposed to legislative reform) is similarly restricted. Efforts to purge legal doctrine of its patriarchal past must confront the requirement that new decisions cohere with the existing legal fabric, imbuing problematic principles with authority independent of their merits (consider again the remarkable durability of the marital rape exemption) and promoting the continuation of intellectual structures, conventions and canons of authority in which deep cognitive biases inhere.[33] Meanwhile, regard for consistency enshrines into legal form an aesthetic of sameness and difference, privileging conformity to unarticulated normative preconceptions, which, inter alia, affords a standpoint through which gender (and gender difference) is legally conceived and situated. Finally, attention to consequences leads judges into making speculative pronouncements about the future, often based on very partial knowledge and limited experience. Of course, the extent to which consequences can be correctly predicted essentially depends on what one knows; however, what one knows is invariably related to what one values. When a judge concludes that imposing a duty of care on the police will impede effective policing, he is approaching the issue from the perspective of one who *knows* the police need no threat of liability to encourage them to do their job.[34] On the other hand, someone who *knows* there is a serious problem with domestic violence and is concerned that the police appear repeatedly to fail domestic violence victims may well view the imposition of duty of care more positively.[35] In other words, consequential reasoning is only as good as the knowledge which underpins it and is an inescapably value-laden exercise.

This suggests that greater judicial and practitioner diversity, by expanding the knowledge base of legal actors, should enhance law's potency as a channel for progressive argumentation. However, while few would deny that diversity is a goal to which to aspire, there remain real difficulties with integrating diverse perspectives into a discursive form which relies for its authority and legitimation on a claim to univocality. How are we to know what constitutes a good legal argument in the absence of some consensus, some shared ethical and/ or political orientation with regard to the values and principles which legal reasoning activates? Diversity poses a critical challenge to legal reasoning as it has been understood and practised for centuries. The very notion of a single correct answer to a legal dispute is at odds with the idea that diverse views on how to act may properly – legally – co-exist. Although we see such diversity in play every day in the differing conclusions reached by judges, we still rely upon the principle that only one prevails. This is more than simply the pragmatic acknowledgement that some definitive conclusion must be reached if law is to

---

[33] See, e.g., Martha Chamallas and Jennifer Wriggins' powerful critique of the cognitive structures of tort law, *The Measure of Injury: Race, Gender and Law* (New York University Press, 2010).

[34] *Hill v Chief Constable of West Yorkshire* [1988] 1 AC 53 per Lord Keith at 63.

[35] *Michael v Chief Constable of South Wales* [2015] UKSC 2, per Lady Hale at para. 198.

perform the functions assigned to it. The unity of law, its integrity and impenetrability, is critical to the authority it asserts in our political culture. It is not that law always and everywhere *has* to take this singular form, but that once taken it becomes difficult to conceive otherwise. Take the principle of equality before law which we value and respect without question: yet this very same principle makes it challenging for law to recognise diverse subjects. The legal impulse is to suppress difference (including gender difference), rendering the notion of diverse, fragmented legal subjects unintelligible within the contours of legal rationality.

To return then to our question, is there (always) a right answer to legal disputes or can diverse legal answers co-exist? I have argued that a commitment to the belief that right answers exist remains deeply embedded in the practices of legal reasoning and the justifications which support those practices. At the same time, adherence to the idea of a right answer (with its associated suppositions) poses difficulties in the context of efforts to deploy legal argument progressively to equality-enhancing ends. This is not to suggest that the tools of legal argument are not worth utilising but rather to acknowledge that utilising them effectively in the interests of diversity is demanding and requires a deep and sophisticated grasp of the techniques of legal reasoning and the limitations of the legal form.

Further Reading

Joanne Conaghan, *Law and Gender* (Clarendon Press, 2013), especially Chapters 5 and 6.

Margaret Davies, *Law Unlimited: Materialism, Pluralism and Legal Theory* (Routledge, 2017), especially Chapters 1–4.

Nicola Lacey, *Unspeakable Subjects* (Hart, 1998), especially pp. 2–14 and Chapter 5.

Catharine MacKinnon, *Towards a Feminist Theory of the State* (Harvard University Press, 1989), especially Chapters 8 and 13.

CHAPTER 15

Legal History

Rosemary Auchmuty

Legal history, both as taught in UK universities and generally, is largely the history of men. Students rarely encounter any discussion of women's place in law, let alone a consideration of gender. The debates chosen for this chapter will illustrate each of these gaps.

The first asks 'Are women persons?' – an extraordinary question to modern eyes, but one which occupied courts and legislature for a good century until it was finally conceded that, for some purposes at least, they were. The second debate moves from the specific to the general to ask 'What is legal history?' This debate considers the *content* of legal history and whether legal history should confine itself to the formal development of the law, the law-making institutions and the law-makers, or whether it should also consider informal legal processes, the impact of law on both men and women, women's efforts to work with and change it, and men's responses to these efforts. The first debate shows how the men in charge of law-making used law to maintain their monopoly, while the second shows how legal history has been used to create a myth of steady progress by male law-makers towards a myth of gender equality today.

Debate 1

Are women persons?

The starting point for the 'persons cases' is a statute of 1850, an Act for Shortening the Language Used in Acts of Parliament or 'Lord Brougham's Act', section 4 of which states that 'words importing the masculine gender shall be deemed and taken to include females, unless the contrary is provided'. The limits of this apparently clear instruction were tested in 1868 when, following the Representation of the People Act 1867 (which extended the parliamentary franchise to every 'man' who fulfilled the property qualification and was not subject to any legal incapacity), feminists mounted a campaign to place the names of suitably qualified women on the electoral register.

173

In this chapter we only have space to discuss two of the 'persons cases' that ensued, but here is a list of the main reported decisions, which you can read if you are interested in this topic:

> *Chorlton v Lings* (1868–69) LR4 CP 374 (women's right to vote in parliamentary elections)
>
> *Jex-Blake v Senatus* (1873) 11 McPherson 784 (women's right to attend medical school at the University of Edinburgh)
>
> *Beresford-Hope v Lady Sandhurst* [1889] 23 QBD 79; *De Souza v Cobden* [1891] 1 QB 687 (women's right to be elected to local councils)
>
> *Hall v Incorporated Society of Law Agents in Scotland* [1901] Cases Decided in the Court of Sessions Vol III, 1059 (women's right to become law agents in Scotland)
>
> *Nairn v Scottish Universities* (1909) AC 147 (the right for Scottish women graduates to elect the MP for their university)
>
> *Bebb v Law Society* [1914] 1 Ch 286 (women's right to become solicitors in England and Wales)
>
> *Committee for Privileges. Viscountess Rhondda's Claim* [1923] 2 AC 339 (the right for peeresses to sit in the House of Lords)
>
> *Edwards v the Attorney-General for Canada* [1930] AC 124 (the right for women to sit in the Canadian Senate)

CHORLTON V LINGS (1868)

Historically, the right to vote in parliamentary elections (the parliamentary *franchise*) was linked to property ownership. Until the Representation of the People Act 1832, this meant it was confined to wealthy landowners; after 1832, middle-class men who had made their fortunes in the Industrial Revolution were added to the electoral roll, and by the 1860s both political parties (Liberals and Conservatives) were vying to extend the franchise in the hope of capturing more electoral support. A group of feminists seized this moment to press for women's inclusion on the same terms as men. They formed a Women's Suffrage Committee and collected a petition of 1,500 signatures for the newly elected MP for Westminster, John Stuart Mill, to present to Parliament. Mill proposed an amendment to replace the word 'man' with 'person' in the current Representation of the People Bill. The amendment was defeated and the word 'man' remained in the statute finally enacted by the Conservatives in 1867. Feminist campaigners nevertheless encouraged women to register to vote on the basis that Lord Brougham's Act stated that masculine words in legislation included females.[1]

---

[1] Marian Ramelson, *The Petticoat Rebellion: A Century of Struggle for Women's Rights* (Lawrence & Wishart, 1972) pp. 82–83; Albie Sachs and Joan Hoff Wilson, *Sexism and the Law* (Martin Robertson, 1978) pp. 23–24.

There was a huge response: in Manchester alone, 5,000 women with the necessary property qualifications presented themselves to the returning officers. When their applications were refused, the women exercised the right of appeal available to any persons aggrieved by a returning officer's decision. Several cases were heard in the lower courts before a test case went before the Queen's Bench and then on appeal to the Court of Appeal. This was *Chorlton v Lings*, in which the Lord Chief Justice and three other judges held that women were subject to a 'legal incapacity' simply by being women and were thus ineligible to vote under the Representation of the People Act 1867. Moreover, they held, the word 'man' did not include women, even though there was no express denial in the statute; rather, if Parliament had intended to include women it should expressly have said so in the statute.

The report of *Chorlton v Lings* is worth reading for the carefully researched arguments of Counsel for the appellant, Coleridge QC, who, assisted by Richard Pankhurst (whose wife and daughter were later to lead the suffragettes), pointed out that there was clear evidence that women had voted in elections in the distant past and that the 1832 Act had used the word 'person' (not 'man'), suggesting that women did potentially have the vote at that time even if it had fallen into disuse. They noted that 'man' did include 'woman' in many areas of the law, for example criminal law, and argued that, since the right to vote was dependent on payment of taxes, there was no justification for excluding those thousands of women who paid property taxes. Mellish QC for the respondent conceded that the 1867 Act was ambiguous but concluded that, in such circumstances, the court should simply look to 'modern usage'; women had not voted for 300 years, so they should not vote now. You will see this reasoning employed in every 'persons case' from then on; for example, Miss Bebb's claim to be admitted to the solicitor's profession (*Bebb v Law Society*, 1914) was denied because women had never been lawyers or, at any rate, not for hundreds of years, so they could not be lawyers now.[2]

What the judgments in *Chorlton v Lings* demonstrated was that the merits of the women's claims and even the precedents cited in support were not going to be considered: the cases would be decided entirely on the basis of statutory interpretation. Dismissing the women's reliance on Lord Brougham's Act, Willes J said:

It is not easy to conceive that the framer of that Act, when he used the word 'expressly,' meant to suggest [that] what is necessarily or properly implied by language is not expressed by such language. It is quite clear that what the language used necessarily or even naturally implies is expressed thereby. Still less did the framers of the Act intend to exclude the rule alike of good sense and grammar and law, that general words are to be restrained to the subject-matter with which the speaker or writer is dealing.[3]

---

[2] Rosemary Auchmuty, 'Whatever happened to Miss Bebb? *Bebb v The Law Society* and women's legal history' (2011) 31 *Legal Studies* 199.
[3] *Chorlton v Lings* (1868–69) LR4 CP 374, p. 387.

Read carefully – and these remarks must be read carefully to make any sense – this passage suggests that an express provision excluding women is not required under the 1850 Act when the context makes it clear that the word 'man' should carry its 'necessary' or 'natural' meaning and that it is 'good sense' to confine it to the context. Of course, there is nothing necessary or natural about a decision to exclude women when the statute says they should be included in the absence of an express exclusion. But to these male judges, the women's interpretation was not just contrary to 'good sense', it was unimaginable.

It is true that Lord Brougham's Act was not intended to enfranchise women, but whether they had ever been formally excluded from the vote (since it was indisputable that some women had once voted) remained an open question. The century after the Industrial Revolution in Britain was an era in which women's rights and lives became more restricted and their exclusion from public life more entrenched. The judges in *Chorlton v Lings* could not have been unaware of the burgeoning women's movement that was already challenging these restrictions in education and employment, as well as claiming the right to vote.[4] So much is clear from Willes J's defensive justification of women's legal incapacity:

> What was the cause of it, it is not necessary to go into; but … I must protest against its being supposed to arise in this country from any underrating of the sex either in point of intellect or worth. That would be quite inconsistent with one of the glories of our civilization, – the respect and honour in which women are held.[5]

The debate that arises from the 'persons cases', then, is how to interpret the courts' decisions. A traditional legal history will simply explain them on the basis of statutory interpretation. A history which asks the gender question will ask why these male law-makers (legislators and judges) refused to countenance reasoned arguments based on precedent and justice. It is not enough to say (or to take for granted) that *things were like that then* – with the additional assumption that *they are not like that now*. We need a better explanation, if only in order to protect ourselves against the possibility that this situation may happen again.

VISCOUNTESS RHONDDA'S CLAIM (1923)

From the earliest 'persons case' we leap to one of the last – the right for women to sit in the House of Lords. Although women were able to stand for Parliament from 1918, the House of Lords remained solidly male. Life peers did not exist

---

[4] See, e.g., Ramelson (n. 1); Ray Strachey, *The Cause: A Short History of the Women's Movement in Great Britain* (Virago, 1978; first published 1928); Josephine Kamm, *Rapiers and Battleaxes: The Women's Movement and its Aftermath* (George Allen and Unwin, 1966); Philippa Levine, *Victorian Feminism 1850–1900* (Hutchinson, 1987).
[5] *Chorlton v Lings* (n. 3) p. 388.

at that time; when a government wished to ennoble a good citizen, a hereditary peerage was created which, like the ancient English titles, passed down the male line. Those bishops, too, who sat in the House of Lords were always men, since the Church of England did not allow women priests. In 1916, however, the government rewarded David Thomas, the Welsh 'coal king' and politician, with the title Viscount Rhondda, giving him a special dispensation that his title would pass, in default of male heirs, to his daughter (he had no sons) and thence to her male heirs; but with the right to sit in the House of Lords expressly restricted to male heirs. Viscount Rhondda died in 1918 and his daughter Margaret assumed the title Viscountess Rhondda. With substantial wealth at her disposal, she became one of the most prominent feminists of the interwar period. She founded the Six Point Group, which campaigned for equal rights for women, and edited and financed the feminist journal *Time and Tide*, whose contributors included many of the most famous writers of the period.[6]

When the Sex Disqualification (Removal) Act was passed in 1919, permitting women to become lawyers and magistrates and to sit on juries, Lady Rhondda claimed the right to sit in the House of Lords on the basis of section 1, which stated: 'A person shall not be disqualified by sex or marriage from the exercise of any public function.' Her claim was considered by the House of Lords' Committee for Privileges, a body made up of peers both lay and legal. When first considered, the claim was accepted without opposition; but when the Lord Chancellor, Lord Birkenhead, no friend of women, took note of what had happened, he called for the question to be reconsidered. In the ensuing process, Lady Rhondda's claim was turned down by a majority of the 26 Lords present.

Lady Rhondda's argument was simple. The only thing that had disqualified women peers from sitting in the House of Lords before 1919 was their sex, and that impediment had been removed by the Sex Disqualification (Removal) Act. But after an exhaustive trawl through the precedents from *Chorlton v Lings* to *Bebb v Law Society*, the Lord Chancellor concluded that, if Parliament had wanted to allow women peers to sit in the House of Lords, it would have so provided expressly.[7] Most of the Lords present were laymen, who understood none of the legal points in the debate and simply wanted to keep women out of their masculine domain. Of the Law Lords, however, two spoke in favour of Lady Rhondda's claim. Both Lord Haldane and Lord Wrenbury criticised the Lord Chancellor for suggesting that what Parliament had in mind when legislating could ever be relevant to statutory interpretation: 'Decisions of the highest authority show that the interpretation of an Act of Parliament must be collected from the words in which the Sovereign made into law the

[6] Angela V. John, *Turning the Tide: The Life of Lady Rhondda* (Parthian Books, 2014); Dale Spender, *Time and Tide Wait for No Man* (Pandora Press, 1984); Sachs and Wilson (n. 1) pp. 33–34.

[7] *Viscountess Rhondda's Claim* [1923] 2 AC 339, p. 367.

words agreed upon by both Houses'.[8] This was an inflexible rule of statutory interpretation at the time. Even if extraneous material were considered, the draftsman of the 1919 Act had (to Lord Haldane's certain knowledge) chosen the wording of section 1 expressly to repeal the court's view in preceding 'persons cases'.[9] Thus to revert back to that earlier view was in fact to disregard Parliament's wishes.

Following the rejection of Lady Rhondda's claim, her supporters, including Lord Astor (husband of the first woman MP, Nancy Astor), introduced bills into Parliament calling for reform from 1924 until 1931. It was not until 1958, however, with the passing of the Life Peerages Act, that women were able to sit in the House of Lords, and hereditary peers like Lady Rhondda were not admitted until 1963. Sadly, she had died in 1958 so never got to take her seat.

What the 'persons cases' demonstrate is that a majority of the senior men of law were prepared to use all legal tools at their disposal to block women's claims to entry into political life; and that, moreover, their most powerful tool was a narrow form of statutory interpretation under which women could not be considered persons. The 'Are women persons?' debate has been consigned to history; the debate for legal historians today is no longer whether they are or they are not but *why* they were not considered to be persons in the first place and *why* it took so long for them to be granted full personhood. Gender was the central issue in a significant body of litigation and legislation in the nineteenth and twentieth centuries, and that is why legal historians cannot ignore it.

Debate 2
What is legal history?

On the face of it, the answer to the question 'What is legal history?' is obvious: legal history is the history of the development of the law and legal institutions. Given that women were excluded from law-making until the twentieth century, one would not expect to find much mention of women in traditional legal histories – the women just weren't involved in law or the legal institutions. Once the focus is *gender*, however, the obvious question arises: why weren't they there? What was keeping women out of law-making? And when and how were they allowed in?

There are three approaches to this question in legal history writing. The first is silence. The 'persons cases', the debates and campaigns about women's rights, go completely unmentioned, as if this matter, of the highest significance for half the population, is of no relevance to legal history. The second mentions women when women must be mentioned, for example when they were admitted to the vote or the legal profession, but presents the reform as evidence

---

[8] Ibid. p. 380.
[9] Ibid. p. 386.

of a gradual evolution towards today's gender equality – a tale of steady progress, initiated by enlightened courts and legislators. Of the feminist campaigns that forced the issue onto the law-makers' attention either nothing is said, or else the feminists are presented as extremists who damaged rather than furthered their cause. The third approach foregrounds gender and the relationship between the women trying to work under and with the law and the men fighting to keep them out.

The great majority of legal histories adopt the first approach. Women just don't come into the story apart from the odd incidental mention. There is no consistent account of *their* place in law; women's exclusion from the political and legal sphere in the nineteenth century is simply assumed and their inclusion in the twentieth equally assumed – but it is often unclear how and when they got there. This is the approach of most undergraduate textbooks which, though they tend to skip over history in favour of a presentation of the modern principles, do sometimes include a few paragraphs or pages on the development of that jurisdiction or principle. But older judgments in these accounts will be treated simply as statements of evolving law rather than historical documents requiring contextual analysis.

The second approach is most evident in published work that deals with topics where women simply can't be ignored – the emergence of equity, changing matrimonial provisions or sexual offences – or in general institutional histories. This approach has its roots in late-nineteenth-century self-satisfaction with the state of the nation and the Empire after a period of great social change. When in 1896 A.R. Cleveland (quite correctly) noted the enormous advances in women's legal position in the second half of the nineteenth century,[10] he ascribed them to 'the progress of civilization' rather than to the vigorous feminist campaigns of the period; and in absolving men of any responsibility for past brutalities, he managed to avoid any reference to those that still existed:

> That the laws were cruel and harsh to women during many centuries, was not because they were made by men, but because they were made by a majority of ignorant and often semi-civilized and brutal men, compared with whom the women of the period were only a little, if at all, more civilized or less brutal.[11]

These two features – excusing men for keeping women out, and ignoring women's campaigns to get in – continued to characterise this approach to gender issues in legal history well into the twentieth century. Consider the following explanations for the delayed admission of women to the legal profession in Britain in 1919, long after other Western countries had admitted them and only after a 50-year campaign by women seeking to become lawyers, a series of unsuccessful Bills in Parliament and the court case mentioned earlier in this

---

[10] Arthur Rackham Cleveland, *Woman Under the English Law* (Hurst and Blackett, 1896) p. 255.
[11] Ibid. pp. 299–300.

chapter, *Bebb v Law Society* (1914). First, Michael Birks in his history of the Bar, aptly titled *Gentlemen of the Law*:

> In opposing the admission of women to their ranks, solicitors were doing little more than following current ideas on the inequality of the sexes. This episode has left no mark on the profession and merely serves to illustrate the solicitors' cautious and sometimes hostile attitude to change.[12]

On the contrary, as Lisa Webley's chapter on the legal profession (Chapter 18) in this book reveals, the legal profession remains an inhospitable place for women in many respects.

Twenty years later, in his general text *Modern Legal History* (1980), A.H. Manchester offered a modern version of the 'progress of civilisation' theory:

> After the First World War, and the dramatically changed role which women played during the course of that conflict, society began to take a radically different view of women's proper role in society. In 1919 the Law Society itself resolved that women might be admitted to the profession.[13]

Note the use of phrases like 'changed social attitudes' to account for legal change. They tell us nothing, since no explanation is offered for *why* attitudes changed. In particular, no mention is made of the decades of feminist organising. Unfortunately it is still possible to read legal histories of this type, in which the rhetoric of progress towards civilisation is replaced by one of ever-increasing access to rights and the perfection of gender (and other) equality.

The third approach to the writing of legal history emerged in the 1970s. The very title of Albie Sachs and Joan Hoff Wilson's *Sexism and the Law* revealed its feminist origins: 'sexism' was a new word coined by feminists to describe the manifestations of male supremacy that, because there was no word to describe them, had long gone unacknowledged in law and social life. The date is significant, too, for the book was a response and a contribution to the second wave of feminism that took off in this decade.[14]

To understand the features of feminist legal history, we need look no further than the treatment of the 'persons cases' in *Sexism and the Law*. First, there is the subject matter, which clearly relates to gender; no one had seriously analysed these cases before. Second, there is the recognition that the legislature and courts were 'not merely bodies from which women happen historically to be absent' but institutions from which they were deliberately excluded.[15] Third, there is the conclusion that the focus on statutory interpretation in these cases, which enabled successive courts to ignore the women's substantive arguments

---

[12] Michael Birks, *Gentlemen of the Law* (Stevens, 1960) p. 278.

[13] A.H. Manchester, *Modern Legal History* (Butterworths, 1980) p. 71.

[14] See, for example, 'Sisterhood and after: An oral history'. British Library, https://www.bl.uk/sisterhood, accessed 21 March 2017.

[15] Sachs and Wilson (n. 1) p. 12.

as well as relevant precedents, was really a means by which the judges could impose their own view of women's place on society, and called into question the cherished notion of judicial impartiality.

Sachs posits three answers to the question of *why* the judges behaved this way. The first is simply 'habitual and unconscious male arrogance'[16] (and Sachs well recognises that, as a man, he can make this claim where women would feel the need to be more tentative or polite). Those in power become accustomed to exercising it; it seems right and natural to them, and they do not welcome interference in their comfortable male preserves. Second, the judges had a social and *financial* stake in keeping control of the highest paid, most respected professions, for money is power and the best way to control women is to keep them poor and dependent. Third, they sustained their position with a vision of womanhood that was clearly at odds with what the feminists wanted and, indeed, what they represented. Faced with educated litigants who could, and did, formulate rational arguments and command large-scale political movements, and who very often earned their own living, the judges nevertheless persisted in their conviction that women were delicate creatures requiring men's protection from the rough and tumble of public life. The image of womanhood they presented was not simply the result of romantic wishful thinking or failing to move with the times; rather, it was born of self-interest:

> These men had a direct, material stake in keeping their wives at home, running their households, attending to their comforts and providing the ambience necessary for the furtherance of their careers.[17]

What we see in a feminist analysis like this is not just a focus on explicitly gendered subject matter but an account of the development of law that goes beyond – indeed, is critical of – the standard tools of legal analysis (statutory interpretation, the doctrine of precedent) and exposes how these can be, and have been, used to perpetuate a relationship of male power over women. It treats the law as a set of historical documents requiring analysis in context, and law-makers not as neutral actors applying clear and wise rules but as men engaged in a power struggle with women.

The feminist approach to the writing of legal history drew on developments that had occurred in the discipline of history in preceding decades. It is no accident that *Sexism and the Law* united the insights of Joan Hoff Wilson, an American historian, with the legal scholarship of Albie Sachs, then a university lecturer, later a distinguished South African judge. Until the 1960s the study of history, like law, was largely concerned with public life, great events, major institutions and famous men. Social history, insofar as it existed, consisted of descriptions of 'the way we lived then' and was not taken very seriously by academic scholars. From the 1960s, however, this view came to be challenged by

---

[16] Ibid. p. 6.
[17] Ibid. p. 62.

a new concern for 'history from below': the history of those left out of, and subject to, ruling-class power: working-class people, black people, women. The first phase of this new history was devoted to finding our roots, the lost history of ignored and oppressed groups. Class came first, then race, inspired by the civil rights movement in the United States in the 1960s. Following them, feminists from the women's movement of the 1970s set themselves the task of recovering women's hidden history.[18]

In the 1980s the focus shifted to gender in recognition of the fact that the relationship between men and women, like those of class and race, was one of power by one group over another. The goal of feminist historians was not simply to add a new area of study but to transform historical scholarship generally, to 'engender' it, so that it would no longer be possible to study history without considering the gender angle, and without confronting the fact that history has always been written from the point of view of men and as if men were the only actors in history. As Joan Wallach Scott put it, the study of gender would not simply produce 'a new history of women, but also a new history'.[19]

CONCLUSION

I end this chapter by drawing your attention to a recent example of legal history writing that, in placing the question 'What is legal history?' at the forefront of its ambition, provides an excellent example of 'engendered' legal history. Felice Batlan is a distinguished American legal historian who, in full awareness of the 'all-too-separate fields of women's history and legal history', published a new history of Legal Aid in the United States in 2015.[20] It's a subject that has been covered before, but where, in previous work, the story starts with the creation of the first formal law centres by qualified (male) lawyers, Batlan locates the roots of the movement in associations set up by (unqualified, because the law schools were closed to them) women to assist poorer women with employment and domestic problems requiring legal solutions. These enterprises were to be dismissed as mere philanthropy or social work by later professionals yet, as Batlan shows, they did legal work; they were first; they were directed at women, who were the most vulnerable and suffered the worst abuses; and they were motivated by a more expansive ideal of social justice than the later, formal Legal Aid societies.

By writing women's contribution back into history, Batlan extends our definition of what constitutes appropriate subject matter for legal history, as well as definitions of what a lawyer is and even what law is. It is clear that these

---

[18] See, for example, Sheila Rowbotham, *Hidden from History: 300 Years of Women's Oppression and the Fight Against It* (Pluto, 1973).

[19] Joan W. Scott, 'Gender: A useful category of historical analysis?' (1986) 91 *American Historical Review*, 1053, 1054.

[20] Felice Batlan, *Women and Justice for the Poor: A History of Legal Aid, 1863–1945* (Cambridge University Press, 2015) p. 4.

untrained women, working with sympathetic professional lawyers, were well able to learn the law and provide the necessary advice. Wherein, therefore, did what they do differ from 'lawyering' and in what ways was it not 'law'? By insisting that only 'real' lawyers could provide legal advice, men were able to take control of a sphere that had once been women's, and in the process to change it to suit their own interests. (The same thing happened in medicine, where the women who had traditionally provided healthcare were edged out by university-trained doctors who just happened to be men because the medical schools barred women from studying – see *Jex-Blake v Senatus*, one of the 'persons cases'.) In both law and medicine the takeover by men led to reduced understanding of and attention given to women's issues – less sympathy for domestic violence in law, less concern for women's health in medicine. As Batlan observes, 'The history of legal aid fits into a much larger pattern of men professionalizing women's work and then using that professionalism to exclude women.'[21]

Batlan's book is testimony to the ways in which the writing of legal history has itself been used as a tool to marginalise and exclude women and thus assert (or re-assert) men's power. In recovering a history that had been lost, she exposes 'the "real" history of legal aid, a story that the predominantly male leaders in the field of legal aid intentionally masked'.[22] Though Legal Aid was actually started by women, in the published histories which start from the creation of formal law centres it is men who get the credit, thus feeding the myth that men are the only actors in history worth mentioning. It followed that, once law was professionalised, women who wanted to practise law had to seek to join a masculine preserve entirely on men's terms – which brings us right back to the 'persons cases', and the reason why gender is of central importance in legal history.

FURTHER READING

Rosemary Auchmuty, 'Whatever happened to Miss Bebb? *Bebb v The Law Society* and women's legal history' (2011) 31 *Legal Studies* 199.

Rosemary Auchmuty and Erika Rackley, 'The Women's Legal Landmarks project: Celebrating 100 years of women in the law in the UK and Ireland' (2016) 16 *Legal Information Management* 30.

Felice Batlan, *Women and Justice for the Poor: A History of Legal Aid, 1863–1945* (Cambridge University Press, 2015).

Albie Sachs and Joan Hoff Wilson, *Sexism and the Law: A Study of Male Beliefs and Judicial Bias* (Martin Robertson, 1978).

Joan W. Scott, 'Gender: A useful category of historical analysis?' (1986) 91 *American Historical Review* 1053.

---

[21] Ibid. p. 5.
[22] Ibid. p. 3.

CHAPTER 16

Law and Literature/Literary Jurisprudence

Melanie L. Williams

Why turn to literature – fiction – to learn about law in the lives of people, when textbooks, journal articles and, above all, cases themselves can tell you about the actual, 'real' relationship between law and its subjects? There are a number of points to make[1] but perhaps the most important is that literature may provide a powerful challenge to the orthodoxies of law in understanding the moral and legal status to be attached to the acts and omissions of persons. This chapter will consider two examples of phenomena concerning gender and law: violence against women, and the problems for female personhood, referencing some literary sources in order to demonstrate how these may extend the insights developed in law.

First, some general observations. The field 'law and literature' is often explained as dividing into 'law as literature' and 'law in literature'.[2] It may also be helpful to remember that literary works are products of vision and experience and may therefore reflect upon matters relevant to law in a range of ways not so readily reducible to these categories. In literature and art, gender issues may be revealed or represented in ways novel to the orthodoxies of law and society, often problematising or nuancing conventional understandings.

Ideological – including religious – and cultural systems tend to institute and perpetuate certain beliefs, which they may call 'principles' or 'tenets', concerning the personal characteristics and behaviours of individual persons. Such systems evolve to provide frameworks or controls for communities and often set out to regulate sexual behaviours as well as regularise gender identities. They may also function to entrench power and prejudice, sometimes with the assistance of claims made by 'scientific fact' or by 'morality', yet both these modes of guidance may derive from flawed evidential sources, tainted by their

---

[1] For example, that fiction provides an opportunity to depart from the received orthodoxies of the dominant culture and media; the understanding fiction provides is best described as an extended 'practical ethics' hypothesis, such as offered in philosophy and jurisprudence.

[2] Richard A. Posner, 'Law and literature: A relation reargued' (1986) 72 *Virginia Law Review* 1351.

origin in time or ideology. Literary works may provide an opportunity to think beyond such constraints, the work of fiction providing, for example, a means to create a 'practical ethics' laboratory, elaborating and testing the feasibility of an entire life scenario. There are clear parallels here with courtroom interrogations – of credible human actions and reactions.

Our world centres upon binary arrangements and oppositions, not least that distinguishing between male and female; many belief systems, religious and secular, make use of such arrangements to support their assertions of a 'natural order' or a Divine hand. For decades, science has endorsed such binarism, though more recent enquiries suggest a spectrum rather than binary model.[3] Nevertheless, religions and societies the world over tend to organise themselves in terms of sexual identity, with power and hierarchical position almost inevitably placed in the hands of the male. Levi-Strauss hypothesises the use of females as an early form of currency and source of tribal power,[4] women serving not merely as a commodity for immediate sexual consumption but also as a means, through reproduction, of asserting and establishing male blood lines. We may believe such abuse only survived beyond law, in the crime of rape or as a weapon of war, until we recall that most legal systems up until modern times entrenched such power relations through the regularisation of marriage and property ownership, prioritising male power and conjugal rights and recognising – and effacing – certain offspring through legitimation.[5]

These structures can be charted through the study of legal history, marking the reign of coverture, of 'marital rape',[6] of gender as a legal 'disability' affecting the ability to assert legal personhood, the capacity to contract,[7] maintain physical integrity,[8] undertake work and so on a wholesale denial of equal rights for women with their male counterparts. Less traceable through legal frameworks, however, are the subtle social and cultural norms endorsing such values, yet these subtle influences assist in maintaining the discriminatory practices; we may recognise 'legal' personhood,[9] for example, while still undermining

---

[3] https://www.theguardian.com/science/the-h-word/2015/feb/19/nature-sex-redefined-we-have-never-been-binary, accessed 16 January 2018.

[4] Claude Levi-Strauss, *The Elementary Structures of Kinship* (Beacon Press, 1971).

[5] Not only are the institutions of marriage, property and legitimation sources of perpetuating male power, they frequently involve the erasure of the matrinymic, especially ironic given the fact that, until the recent use of DNA to establish paternity, maternity was the only certain fact of biological parenthood.

[6] See *R v R* [1991] UKHL 12.

[7] For example, it was only in 1976 that women in Ireland were permitted to own their homes outright, while only from 1982 were women given the right to spend their money in English pubs without being refused service – https://www.theguardian.com/money/us-money-blog/2014/aug/11/women-rights-money-timeline-history, accessed 20 January 2018.

[8] Physical integrity springs from legal and social support for a range of rights, from the requirement of consent to sexual contact to control of one's own reproductive process (see *Re MB (Caesarean Section)* [1997] EWCA Civ 1361).

[9] See *Viscountess Rhondda's Claim* (1922) 2 AC 339, and Chapter 15, 'Legal History', in this book.

psychological or cultural 'personhood' – fulfilling a rounded and empowered identity and autonomy as far as practically possible. Statute or judicial pronouncement may reflect the prejudices of the time – the doubt as to physical or mental strength, the resort to quasi-science or mythology – and such phenomena provide instructive materials in themselves. Such norms – and their deeply permeating effects on the male and female psyche – may be explored through the prism of literature, reflective exploration then permitting reconsideration of understandings in law.

Perceptive authors may advance wisdom and insight concerning the 'truths' of gender relations and their ramifications for society and law. Though not setting out to write a particularly 'feminist' or 'gender-aware' or law-centred account or perspective, an author can depict scene and character, action and interaction, in a way that engages and challenges orthodoxies; thus the nuanced picture may emerge, though at first blush a text may not be an 'obvious' source of jurisprudential insight. Writers may set out to make direct assaults and provide a richly instructive tapestry wherein the gender and legal facets invite substantial re-examination or, conversely, may create such a totalising reproof as to succeed in communicating the heart of an issue but arrest further exploration. Famously expository and apposite texts may be named[10] which, demonstrating the ability of gender-discriminatory cultural norms to degrade human rights, dignity, capacity, being, are a necessary extension to purely factual or evidential accounts.

Debate 1

How is sexual violence failed by culture and law?

The world is suffused with all kinds of information sources of varying degrees of reliability making claims about the characteristics of gender identities and of the relationship between the sexes. Scientific studies may seek to establish facts in relation to the physical or psychological phenomena attaching to the sexes while, at the same time, popular media sources, social media and cultural beliefs circulate additional claims, prejudices or beliefs. All such sources, even scientific ones, risk promoting misleading, harmful or untrue ideas about gendered persons, and such untruths may in their turn promote behaviours.[11] In addition, the state – and its law – must be 'alive' to issues of fact concerning

---

[10] Alice Walker, *The Color Purple* (Harcourt, Brace, Jovanovich, 1982); Jean Rhys, *Wide Sargasso Sea* (Andre Deutsch, 1966); Charlotte Perkins Gilman, *The Yellow Wallpaper* (The New England Magazine, 1892); Doris Lessing, *The Golden Notebook* (Michael Joseph, 1962); E.M. Forster, *Maurice* (Hodder Arnold, 1971); Leslie Feinberg, *Stone Butch Blues* (Firebrand Press, 1993); Mark Merlis, *American Studies* (Createspace, 1994).

[11] A Google search of 'facts – women' throws up some bizarre claims. More disturbing, however, is the history and currency of science concerning 'scientific' facts about women – see, for example, the ongoing debate concerning the 'function' of female orgasm and attempts to tie this in to differing political assertions concerning women – http://www.isciencemag. co.uk/blog/on-the-origins-of-the-female-orgasm/, accessed 16 January 2018.

gender but should resist reinforcing prejudicial claims.[12] For example, for many years it was simply unthinkable to suggest that men might be victims of intimate or sexual violence or of domestic violence.[13] Rightly, the fact that men too may be victims, and there is no shame attached to this, is becoming accepted by the most important category in this regard: men themselves.[14] Groups and charities supporting men have also emerged, making the issue more visible, more sayable.[15] In addition, it is important to note that our understanding of the harms produced in the domestic setting has been expanded to include 'coercive and controlling behaviour' and that such harms too may be perpetrated by either sex.[16] Home Office statistics reflect the fact of domestic violence perpetrated against men – whether the significant other perpetrating the violence is female or male.

Yet statistics can be misleading. The support group Mankind states that '[f]or every three victims of domestic abuse, two will be female, one will be male'[17] and this kind of 2:1 ratio is echoed in the Office for National Statistics (ONS) reports, leading to a perception that men have a surprisingly high incidence of being victims of domestic violence with, it is claimed, an indication that women may be perpetrators in higher numbers to a previously unrecognised degree.[18] Disaggregation of the statistics on domestic violence allows a more nuanced understanding of the bare numbers and of the proportion of incidents which result in serious injury or death. Home Office figures reveal that on average, 100 women a year[19] and around 30 men a year are killed within a domestic

---

[12] For example, Jessica Pishko, 'A History of Women's Prisons', JstorDaily, 4 March 2015, https://daily.jstor.org/history-of-womens-prisons/, accessed 16 January 2018.

[13] Traditional gender cultures – and official documentation – representing men as the inevitably dominant 'heads of household' have obstructed the ability of men to admit victimhood, or to be taken seriously by outside agencies and this remains an issue. Statistically, men are more likely to be victims of violence in public places at the hands of other men, women more likely to be victims of domestic violence at the hands of male partners or ex-partners – http://webarchive.nationalarchives.gov.uk/20160105160709/; http://www.ons.gov.uk/ons/dcp171778_298904.pdf, accessed 16 January 2018.

[14] For example, the revelations concerning sexual abuse of men and boys within the football profession – https://www.theguardian.com/football/2016/dec/05/football-sexual-abuse, accessed 16 January 2018.

[15] See support groups such as Mankind – http://new.mankind.org.uk/, accessed 16 January 2018; mainstream abuse charities also increasingly offer specialist support for men – http://www.refuge.org.uk/get-help-now/help-for-men/, accessed 16 January 2018.

[16] S. 76 Serious Crime Act 2015, which created a new offence of controlling or coercive behaviour in an intimate or family relationship.

[17] 'Key facts' represented by Mankind – http://new.mankind.org.uk/statistics/, accessed 20 January 2018; see https://www.ons.gov.uk/peoplepopulationandcommunity/crimeandjustice/compendium/focusonviolentcrimeandsexualoffences/yearendingmarch2015/chapter2homicide, accessed 20 January 2018.

[18] https://www.theguardian.com/society/2010/sep/05/men-victims-domestic-violence, accessed 20 January 2018.

[19] The numbers now seem to be well in excess of 100 – see https://kareningalasmith.com/counting-dead-women/; https://www.theguardian.com/society/2016/dec/07/men-killed-900-women-six-years-england-wales-figures-show, accessed 20 January 2018.

abuse context. Women are almost exclusively killed by men whereas, in contrast, approximately one-third of the men are killed by other men and a little under a third are killed by women against whom they have a documented history of abuse ('victims turned perpetrators').[20] Thus while in excess of 100 women a year are killed in the domestic setting, almost exclusively by men, approximately 10 men are killed by women; but of these 10 women killers, many will have been victims of domestic abuse at the hands of the man they eventually kill – a rather different picture from the 2:1 ratio indicated by bare records. To put the matter crudely, violence against women in the domestic sphere is more widespread, serious and often fatal, yet there is a risk that, due to entrenched stereotypes about male and female behaviour, the rare occasions when women commit such crimes have more impact than the scores committed by men.

The incidence of violence perpetrated against women on the 'domestic' front ('domestic' in terms of the home *or* within 'the state') becomes expanded overwhelmingly when one considers the international scale; see, for example, the World Health Organization statistics, or those gathered by the United Nations. It is estimated that of all women who were the victims of homicide globally in 2012, almost half were killed by intimate partners or family members, compared to less than 6 per cent of men killed in the same year. Around 120 million girls worldwide (slightly more than one in 10) have experienced forced intercourse or other forced sexual acts at some point in their lives. By far the most common perpetrators of sexual violence against girls are current or former husbands, partners or boyfriends. At least 200 million women and girls alive today have undergone female genital mutilation/cutting (FGM) in 30 countries, according to estimates published on the United Nations' International Day of Zero Tolerance for Female Genital Mutilation in 2016. In most of these countries, the majority of girls were cut before the age of five.[21]

Whether inflicted by intimate partners, relatives or community members, such violent acts emerge not just as manifestations of impulsive violence but also because of cultural beliefs concerning women: that women who are raped or murdered in some way 'brought it upon themselves', that they should not risk public freedoms, bring 'shame' upon their families by making autonomous choices,[22] that their sexuality must be controlled through the use of FGM[23] – and so on.

---

[20] Susan S.M. Edwards, 'From victim to defendant: The life sentence of British women' (1994) 26 *Case Western Reserve Journal of International Law* 261. Available at: http://scholarly-commons.law.case.edu/jil/vol26/iss2/2.

[21] http://www.unwomen.org/en/what-we-do/ending-violence-against-women/facts-and-figures, accessed 20 January 2018.

[22] 'More than a quarter of Europeans believe that rape is sometimes justified study finds: 27 per cent of people living in Europe believe rape is acceptable under some circumstances, most commonly citing drug or alcohol intake, "revealing" clothes or going home alone with an attacker', http://www.independent.co.uk/news/world/europe/one-in-four-europeans-be-lieve-rape-is-sometimes-justified-study-finds-a7445721.html, accessed 20 January 2018.

[23] See http://www.bbc.co.uk/newsbeat/article/36838870/the-first-ever-fgm-figures-show-nearly-6000-new-cases-in-england, accessed 20 January 2018.

Why turn to literature when these issues are so 'live'? Legal systems around the world have attempted, to greater or lesser degrees, to address the problems associated with prejudice and violence against women; nevertheless, conviction rates for rape of women remain poor,[24] the incidence of violence and murder of women victims seems untouched[25] by the efforts of the civil and criminal justice systems, and the jurisprudence concerning women victims-turned-perpetrators makes little progress.[26] Legal systems make use of rules and precedents which tap into stereotypes concerning expectations of male and female behaviour and, despite attempts to break the power of such stereotypes, justice remains tenuous. Furthermore, since law relies upon the 'story' told by legal cases in respect of particular words, actions and circumstances 'visible' to the law obtaining between the legal subjects concerned, it cannot reflect the cultural – and sometimes material – but 'invisible' factors underpinning those scenes. These 'invisible' factors, of social and cultural beliefs concerning 'types' of victim and perpetrator, of narrative credibility and evidence, of jurisprudential stasis in relation to cultural influences, of factors inhibiting victim choices and liberating perpetrator actions, may be reflected in literary constructions of similar fact scenarios.

Considering the crime of rape, there are innate social prejudices, sometimes extending to the judiciary, about 'deserving' and 'undeserving' victims.[27] In addition, cultural attitudes to sexuality and consent are reflected not only in received 'norms' of behaviour but in fantasy too, and, paradoxically, some of the most avid consumers of such fantasies are women themselves, adding to a confusion and conflation of concepts concerning sex and consent.[28] Indeed there is a history in law as well as literature of 'conflation' of the notions of 'rape' and 'seduction', with underlying notions that a woman's 'no' 'really means' 'yes', and that a woman once 'conquered' will 'succumb'.[29] Reading

---

[24] http://thejusticegap.com/2015/11/women-experience-disbelief-as-only-12-of-reported-rapes-result-in-charges/, accessed 20 January 2018.

[25] http://www.genevadeclaration.org/fileadmin/docs/Co-publications/Femicide_A%20Gobal%20Issue%20that%20demands%20Action.pdf, accessed 20 January 2018.

[26] See https://www.penalreform.org/wp-content/uploads/2016/04/Women_who_kill_in_response_to_domestic_violence_Full_report.pdf, accessed 20 January 2018.

[27] https://www.criminallawandjustice.co.uk/features/Crime-Rape-and-Justice-Victims, accessed 16 January 2018. Sexual history evidence has been a particular issue of contention – https://www.theguardian.com/law/2016/oct/27/law-concerning-use-of-sexual-history-in-trials-could-be-reformed, accessed 16 January 2018.

[28] There are, for example, lists of 'good reads' of 'romances' cataloguing 'forced seduction or rape by the hero' – https://www.goodreads.com/list/show/27204.Romances_with_forced_seduction_or_rape_by_the_hero with sales of *Fifty Shades of Grey* – and its sequel, *Grey* – recorded as the best-selling books 'of all time' https://www.theguardian.com/books/2015/jun/23/fifty-shades-of-grey-sequel-breaks-sales-records, accessed 16 January 2018.

[29] Nick Cohen, 'In Rape Cases "no" means "no" to everyone except the British public' – https://www.theguardian.com/commentisfree/2009/dec/20/nick-cohen-rape-jury-law, accessed 16 January 2018 – a problem highlighted also in American universities – http://urbanette.com/campus-rape-epidemic/, accessed 16 January 2018.

some of these 'romances' together in class is likely to stimulate lively debate and also force you to question the assumptions made by one another, by juries and by legal argumentation, concerning the realities of sexual assault.

RAPE, FACT AND FICTION

Of course, sexual exploitation and abuse are primarily a matter of power, as sex trafficking and associated sex industries attest.[30] A number of books and films in modern times have explored the power nexus facilitating exploitative sexual relationships, from the semi-autobiographical *The Color Purple* to the dystopic vision of *The Handmaid's Tale*.[31] For a truly intellectually and culturally insightful text concerning social norms, sexual identity and victimhood, however, I would recommend *Tess of the d'Urbervilles*.[32] The book reflects a vision of social norms as perceived by the author, Thomas Hardy. Born into the English peasant class and rising to become a foremost man of letters, Hardy conveyed in his writing his deep consciousness of the injustices experienced by individuals disadvantaged by their social class, gender or both; phenomena no doubt observed by Hardy himself in his journey from poverty but also gathered from stories told at his grandmother's knee, news reports and his work as a magistrate. Though published in 1895, the book offers a still-relevant critique of modern social and legal controversies, including the conflation of rape and seduction, but also how social norms can render victims, and the crimes against them, invisible, feeding through into the law – 'Once victim, always victim – that's the Law!' as Tess herself reports.[33]

Hardy also understood that subtly coercive and controlling behaviour could be visited upon the socially and sexually powerless and that such coercion feeds upon imbalances of power not only between individuals but within a wider social and cultural context. One might note the modern manifestations of this, such as the victims of child sex exploitation scandals in Rotherham and elsewhere,[34] where victims were selected because of their youth and vulnerability, 'groomed' with gifts and attention, sexually exploited and then ridiculed and bullied by their rapists. Supremely confident, the rapists carried out their offences over a period of many years with impunity, in large part because they knew that their victims had no 'voice' in society. Local councillors, social services and the police all either ignored evidence of the crimes or

---

[30] See http://www.soroptimist.org/trafficking/faq.html, accessed 20 January 2018.

[31] *The Color Purple* (n. 10); Margaret Atwood, *The Handmaid's Tale* (McLelland and Stewart, 1985).

[32] Thomas Hardy, *Tess of the d'Urbervilles* (Osgoode, McIlvaine & Co, 1895) (reprinted Wordsworth Editions, 1992). For a discussion of the rape/seduction 'debate', see Melanie L. Williams 'Rape or seduction, fact or fictions?', in *Secrets and Laws* (Routledge-Cavendish, 2005).

[33] *Tess* (n. 32) p. 291.

[34] http://www.bbc.co.uk/news/uk-england-south-yorkshire-28939089, accessed 20 January 2018.

actively obstructed investigation of them. When girls plucked up the courage to approach the police about their plight, they were disbelieved, ridiculed or rebuffed as unreliable, insignificant – effectively, invisible.[35]

All of these factors are reflected in the story of Tess, written over 100 years before the Rotherham case. When the book was published in the 1890s, some critics reviled the text as 'immoral',[36] implying that Tess was to blame for her misfortunes: as with many cultures around the world, educated and privileged commentators failed to challenge, sometimes even endorsed notions of victims as architects of their own destruction. Most dramatically, Hardy understood that Tess, as one whose prized virginity had been lost, became thereby a social outcast. That this marked her as tainted, regardless of whether the loss had been voluntary, is demonstrated by Hardy in his characterisation, not just of her initial exploiter, Alec d'Urberville – who is not concerned with the damage to her identity – but of Angel Clare her husband, a man deliberately crafted for his educated and enlightened rationality, his 'clarity' of mind, yet still ultimately bound by conventions which judged the sexually tainted Tess as 'untouchable'. Then, as now, deep cultural prejudices dominate our seemingly objective and 'rational' world; the law both a symptom and a cause in perpetuating such prejudices.

Lastly, the text of *Tess* may be studied for the contribution it offers to the jurisprudence concerned with victims-turned-perpetrators who kill their abusers, especially where the law struggles with the notions of provocation, self-defence, diminished responsibility and the potential connections between these concepts.[37] After the passage of years and events, Tess kills her abuser, and the text leaves no doubt as to the outcome of the murder trial – Tess is hanged as a murderer.[38] Even today, the case would present significant problems for a criminal defence team – Tess's tormentor has assured access to her sexually not just by force of character but by steady harassment, combined with provision of material benefits to her impoverished family. Tess is clothed in finery and, to all outward appearances, lives a comfortable bourgeois life as the mistress of Alec; nor is there any suggestion that he beats her or abuses her physically, *other than claiming ownership of her and her body*. Outwardly, then, Tess is 'well treated', yet her will has been so thoroughly overborne, her autonomy so destroyed, her choices so curtailed that she has lost all sense of identity – as the text tells us, 'his original Tess had spiritually ceased to recognise the body before him

---

[35] http://www.independent.co.uk/news/uk/crime/rotherham-child-abuse-scandal-threats-and-collusion-kept-justice-at-bay-9692578.html, accessed 20 January 2018.

[36] See http://www.theparisreview.org/blog/2015/06/29/immoral-situations-and-other-news/, accessed 20 January 2018.

[37] Melanie Williams, 'Tess of the D'Urbervilles and the law of provocation' *Law and Literature* (1999) 2 *Current Legal Issues* 167.

[38] The tale of Tess and her subsequent hanging is believed to have been inspired by the real-life case of Martha Brown, whose execution was witnessed by the young Hardy, see https://www.theguardian.com/books/2016/feb/19/thomas-hardy-tess-of-the-durbervilles-bones-found-at-prison, accessed 20 January 2018.

as hers, allowing it to drift, like a corpse upon the current, dissociated from her living will'.[39] It would take almost exactly 100 years before 'dissociation' was recognised as a diagnostic feature of 'slow burn' or 'battered woman syndrome'; Hardy's use of the word was prophetic.[40] Yet even in modern times, a case such as the case of Tess would be unlikely to receive understanding in criminal law, due to the subtle and invisible nature of her spiritual destruction, supported as it is by social norms. Such spiritual destruction is possible even in the absence of sexual or physical violence.[41]

Debate 2
Who are law's persons?

As we have seen, it is possible to identify texts providing a journey into the various aspects of discriminatory experience. Such fictions may assist in considering some particular aspect of discrimination, or reveal just how some experiences amount not just to discrimination but to a wholesale denial of personhood. To be made to feel invisible, a non-entity in human and civic terms, is the ultimate impotence. Advanced society suggests that all citizens have equal rights, opportunities and recognition; and laws may suggest that structures are in place to support such recognition. Yet girls and women throughout the world receive constant signs and subliminal – and not so subliminal – indications of their devaluation or invisibility in the eyes of society.[42] A world which boasts legal protections that prove ineffective for some is a world of 'weirdness' best mirrored by the weird imaginings of science fiction.

Many films and fictions 'normalise' such placing even while depicting it. Postmodern and science fiction are particularly suited to conveying the totality of trauma created by social annihilation of the individual on grounds of gender, the nightmare that is the wholesale denial of personhood. These genres allow the 'practical ethics' experiment provided by fiction to be carried forward and engage the political or psychological realms of life. The modernist writings of Virginia Woolf – *To the Lighthouse* (1927) and *A Room of One's Own* (1929) – identify the bizarreness of being female in a male world.

---

[39] *Tess* (n. 32) p. 333.

[40] See http://www.independent.co.uk/news/people/law-report-battered-woman-syndrome-relevant-to-defence-1526492.html, accessed 20 January 2018. The Coroners and Justice Act 2009 represented an attempt to make the law more responsive to the plight of women driven to kill their abusers, but this statutory change may not herald great reform because, as Vera Baird points out, 'the bar is set very high for the defence' – http://verabaird.info/speeches/homicide-partial-defences-and-gender-equality-university-of-hertfordshire/, accessed 20 January 2018.

[41] Although 'coercive and controlling behaviour' is given recognition in the Serious Crime Act 2015, without physical violence it seems officials may still fail to respond – see https://www.theguardian.com/society/2016/aug/31/police-failing-to-use-new-law-against-coercive-domestic-abuse, accessed 20 January 2018.

[42] See the Everyday Sexism Project – https://everydaysexism.com/, accessed 20 January 2018.

J.M. Coetzee's postmodern novel *Foe* (1986) continues this critique with more political reflexivity, recognising that the woman absent from the particular story *Robinson Crusoe* is symbolic of her exclusion from the more general story that is the social contract and indeed from history itself. Marge Piercy's *Woman on the Edge of Time* (1976) continues a theme begun by the revolutionary tale by Charlotte Perkins Gilman in *The Yellow Wallpaper* (1892), suggesting that perhaps the logic of madness is an inevitable consequence of the lived dystopia, while for Piercy the interplay between madness and the notion of a just world held by futuristic fantasy provides only the distant prospect of resolution to the woman living in a present of prejudice.

In examining the progress made over the years around the world in relation to recognition of women's rights, with treaties and legislation created in support of these aims, it could be argued that any such progress is slow and frequently stalled, or even reversed, by social objection or apathy.[43] The problems of inequality and misogyny, apparently entrenched throughout the majority of cultures and through the ages (and frequently reappearing in new forms as soon as existing forms are challenged)[44] can give rise to a sense of hopelessness, especially when one realises that, to succeed, such attitudes must depend upon the – at least tacit – cooperation of women themselves.[45]

FEMINIST SCIENCE FICTION AND THE FLIGHT FROM HEGEMONY

The failure of society – the hegemony – to eliminate discrimination implicates the worlds of politics and law, the alleged guardians of progress and social change. With some justification, women may feel that they are constantly treated as 'Other'.[46] True recognition that they are persons first, gendered second, may never be realised in our lifetimes, despite all evidence of their capabilities, scientific and otherwise, and women themselves often fail to 'see' the part they play in this inertia. Let us consider two feminist science fiction short stories for their ability to allow us to reflect upon the complex interaction between science, culture, chauvinistic values and women's collusion.

---

[43] CEDAW (The Convention on the Elimination of all Forms of Discrimination Against Women) is a prominent example – see Chapter 8, 'International Law and Human Rights', in this book.

[44] New manifestations of misogyny appear constantly in social media platforms – see https://www.theguardian.com/technology/2016/may/25/yvette-cooper-leads-cross-party-campaign-against-online-abuse, accessed 20 January 2018 – though perhaps 50 per cent of these are generated by women – https://www.theguardian.com/technology/2016/may/26/half-of-misogynistic-tweets-sent-by-women-study-finds, accessed 20 January 2018.

[45] http://www.nbcnews.com/storyline/isis-uncovered/how-all-female-isis-morality-police-khansaa-brigade-terrorized-mosul-n685926, accessed 20 January 2018; https://www.theguardian.com/society/2014/feb/07/female-genital-mutilation-kenya-daughters-fgm, accessed 20 January 2018.

[46] For the origins of identifying woman as 'Other', see Simone de Beauvoir – https://www.marxists.org/reference/subject/ethics/de-beauvoir/2nd-sex/introduction.htm, accessed 20 January 2018.

The first tale, *The Women Men Don't See* (1973), by the popular science fiction writer James Tiptree Junior,[47] imagines two intelligent female characters, Ruth Parsons and her daughter Althea, so certain that they will never be treated fully as persons that they feel only one prospect remains open to them: to leave the planet. Living on Earth requires that women merely 'live in the chinks of Man's world-machine'[48] – a potent description of wholesale displacement. The 'flight' from Earth is a flight from the blind hegemony. The plot demonstrates the embedded nature of chauvinist norms through the deployment of a male protagonist narrator, Don Fenton. Holidaying in Mexico, Fenton is permitted to share a plane chartered by Ruth and her daughter. The plane crashes and Fenton is perplexed when Ruth does not exhibit the behaviours he would expect – hysteria or dependence. While Fenton tries to 'save' her from extra-terrestrials arriving on the island, Ruth, along with her daughter, regards the aliens not as interlopers but as rescuers. The aliens depart with the Parsons women and Fenton remains bewildered, questioning why the two women would rather leave with aliens than stay on Earth. 'Going away' is precisely the reason for the journey of the Parsons – they are liaising with the aliens in order to make good their escape from a world so blighted by misogyny and chauvinism:

'For Christ's sake Ruth, they're aliens!'[49]

'We survive by ones and twos in the chinks of your world-machine … I'm used to aliens'. She'd meant every word. Insane.[50]

Written almost 30 years later, the story 'What I Didn't See' (2002) by Karen Joy Fowler[51] is a recognised 'homage' to *The Women Men Don't See*, this time setting the story of the male/female tensions and the encounter with 'aliens' within the context of a jungle expedition researching gorillas, with gorillas substituted in the story as a kind of 'alien species'. This alteration or 'updating' of the story may be significant for a number of reasons; predominant features include the juxtaposition with 'real' near-aliens and their significance to current debates in feminist theory concerning the 'science' of essentialist and anti-essentialist perspectives,[52] as well as a recognition of the role, however unwitting,

---

[47] James Tiptree Jr, *The Women Men Don't See* (1973) republished in James Tiptree Jr, *Her Smoke Rose Up Forever* (Tachyon Publications, 2004). James Tiptree Jr was the pen name of Alice Bradley Sheldon, the male identity helpful in the – then especially – chauvinistic field of science fiction.

[48] *The Women Men Don't See* (2004) (n. 47) pp. 115–143, at p. 134.

[49] Ibid. p. 140.

[50] Ibid. p. 142.

[51] Karen Joy Fowler, 'What I Didn't See' in *What I Didn't See and Other Stories* (Small Beer Press, 2002).

[52] Jamilla Musser, 'On the orgasm of the species: Female sexuality, science and sexual difference' (2012) 102 *Feminist Review* 1.

of other women in the subjugation or abuse of other women: 'internalised sexism' or 'gender collusion'.[53]

The predominantly male expedition group is accompanied by two women as well as some native male 'bearers'. The story signals a number of beliefs regarding the nature of animal and of human behaviour and links between them: the alien world that is our own and the 'alienation' of women as Other. Unlike Tiptree's story, of women driven, literally, to leaving Earth, the expedition story reflects upon the surreal actuality of women living on the planet. One stimulus for Fowler's new plot was hearing of the 'actual' incident on such an expedition: Fowler came across Donna Haraway's essay[54] which references an expedition carried out in 1920 by the curator of the New York National Museum of History. According to the account of this venture, one male member of the expedition proposed a novel means by which gorillas could be protected. He suggested that circumstances should be orchestrated to enable a woman to be witnessed in the act of killing a gorilla, thus removing the usual association between hunting and masculinity and thereby the 'thrill' of the kill. The fiction takes this core incident and expands upon the complex mythologising which supports the 'othering' of women, including the objectifying speculations of culture and of science. The inevitable absorption of women themselves by the dominant discourse is portrayed. Their subsequent ambivalence or suspicion of other women who contribute to this 'othering' is subtle, often obscured yet inevitable.

CONCLUSION

Conflation of the concepts of rape and of seduction, as the 'romance' literature mentioned earlier attests, remains a problem in society and law.[55] *Tess* provides a fascinating example of how cultural beliefs play into the gathering and assessing facts. As with most 'real'-life cases, the circumstances of the sexual encounter are private between two people and there is no witness – not even Hardy as 'omniscient narrator' – to detail the sexual act moment by moment. Yet, unlike most 'real'-life cases, the narrative provides ample clues as to how the encounter should be understood: Tess is manipulated, pressured and then tricked, ultimately lost, literally as well as figuratively, in a dark wood with Alec. The scene closes with clear references to her will being overborne, of the primal nature and ancient historical incidence of sexual assault upon women by men,

---

[53] Steve Bearman et al., 'The fabric of internalised sexism' (2009) 1 *Journal of Integrated Social Sciences* 10.

[54] Donna Haraway, *Primate Visions: Gender Race and Nature in the World of Modern Science* (Routledge, 1989).

[55] For a discussion and examples of case law concerning seduction, see Williams, *Secrets and Laws* (n. 32).

of the resultant damage to Tess's identity for ever after.[56] Yet despite the clues – one might say 'evidences' provided in the text, it can still give rise to heated debate and disagreement[57] as to the nature of the encounter – as to whether the scene is one of rape or seduction, sought or unsought, showing us how 'facts' are coloured by our 'opinion' or 'beliefs' even in clear disregard of the evidence.

The significance of such encroachments upon autonomy and identity and the role played by social or cultural norms connects to the second topic, of the role played by gender prejudice in the slow haemorrhage of personal identity, of the very sense of selfhood, of personhood. For the feminist writers of science fiction, evidence of the speculative and prejudicial aspects of the 'scientific' accounts of gender demonstrate the infiltration of 'facts' with fiction. Both authors of these science fiction tales are tapping into the notion of the 'alien' being and its relevance to treatment of womankind. The law – like politics – somehow fails to 'see' women as fully entitled 'persons'. From the seemingly delicate hints of old-world Victorian literature to the eccentric interplanetary visions of modern feminist science fiction, the 'other-worldly' insights offered by narrative fiction rebuke our world of failed justice.

FURTHER READING

Maria Aristodemou, *Law and Literature, Journeys from Her to Eternity* (Oxford University Press, 2001).

Justine Larbelestier (ed.), *Daughters of Earth: Feminist Science Fiction in the 20th Century* (Wesleyan University Press, 2006).

Wendy Larcombe, *Compelling Engagements: Feminism, Rape Law and Romance Fiction* (Federation Press, 2005).

Ian Ward, *Sex, Crime and Literature in Victorian England* (Hart Publishing, 2015).

Melanie Williams, *Empty Justice: One Hundred Years of Law, Literature and Philosophy* (Cavendish, 2002).

---

[56] It also gives voice to peasant commentators who observe that a sobbing had been heard in the woods and that 'it might have gone hard with a certain person had there been people nearby' (*Tess,* Wordsworth Editions (n. 32) p. 80) – all clear indications that the sexual encounter was by force, unwanted and unjust.

[57] See the challenge to John Sutherland in Williams, *Secrets and Laws* (n. 32).

CHAPTER 17

Sexuality

Rosemary Auchmuty

The significance of gender to sexuality studies is not immediately apparent. As Alina Tryfonidou shows in her chapter on EU law (Chapter 7), the original attempt to frame sexuality as an aspect of 'sex discrimination' failed to offer adequate protection to lesbians and gay men, and sexuality is now accorded a separate protected status. Gender *is* relevant to sexuality studies, however, for the obvious reason that men and women are different, both biologically and, more importantly, in the way we are socially constructed. Although our current laws treat lesbians and gay men as normal people just like everyone else, in fact, by choosing to relate emotionally and sexually to people of their own sex, they have always challenged the very basis of a patriarchal society premised on men having power over women, as a group in the public sphere and as individuals in the private. Gay men have often seemed to challenge other social constructions of appropriate masculinity by, for instance, adopting what were seen as 'effeminate' mannerisms, or cross-dressing ('drag'), or by hyper-masculine promiscuity, while lesbians challenged notions of ideal womanhood by, for example, cropping their hair and wearing trousers when long hair and skirts were the norm, or by remaining childless – or, worse still, having children without a male head of the family.[1]

Before we consider our two debates, it is worth noting that the law has been very active in the sexuality arena over the past 20 years. After sex between consenting male adults in private was partially decriminalised in 1967[2] – there has never been a specific law targeting lesbian sex, although lesbians have been prosecuted under other laws – a gradual liberalisation of social attitudes in the 1970s and 1980s was followed by a backlash in section 28 of the Local Government Act 1988, which forbade the 'promotion' of homosexuality

---

[1] Children were commonly removed from lesbian parents in custody disputes up to the 1990s. See Susan B. Boyd, 'What is a 'normal' family? *C v C (A Minor)* (Custody Appeal)' (1992) 55 *Modern Law Review* 269.

[2] Sexual Offences Act 1967. 'Partially' because the age of consent was set higher for homosexual men than for heterosexuals and 'private' was narrowly defined.

in schools and other public bodies. This measure created a social climate of repression but no local authority was ever prosecuted under it.[3] During the first decade of the twenty-first century, sexuality became a freestanding ground for anti-discrimination actions, and a series of equalising measures (age of consent, protection from dismissal from the armed services, prohibition of discrimination in the provision of goods and services) culminated in the Equality Act 2010 which brought together 40 years of anti-discrimination legislation, with 'sexual orientation' a fully protected category.

In 2004, the Civil Partnership Act introduced a form of civil registration of same-sex relationships with legal rights and responsibilities very similar to those of marriage. In 2013, the Marriage (Same Sex Couples) Act enabled same-sex couples in England and Wales to marry, albeit on legal terms that resembled civil partnerships rather than conventional marriage.[4] Still, it was called 'marriage' and enjoyed the same status and recognition as traditional marriage. By mid-2015, more than 7,300 same-sex couples had married and another 7,600 had converted their civil partnerships into marriages.[5]

If these last 20 years have been transformative for lesbians and gay men in the UK, a similar process can be observed in some other jurisdictions around the world but by no means all. Same-sex couples could marry throughout Canada by 2005 but still cannot do so in Northern Ireland. And it must not be forgotten that homosexuality remains illegal in 82 countries, almost half of them former British colonies. Much more needs to change before we can speak of real justice for sexual minorities.[6]

Debate 1

Is same-sex marriage a good thing?

Marriage has many meanings. Historically, it was mainly about ensuring that property passed to blood relatives and remained within the family; it was important that a man's children were 'legitimate'. Marriage was also about the financial support of women who (in the higher classes at least) were taken out of (or never permitted to enter) the employment market in order to carry out their pre-ordained function of bearing and rearing children and managing households. For large parts of British history, and still in some communities, women who did not marry were regarded as failures. Men, too, at different times and in different cultures have been pressured to marry. Marriage was seen

---

[3] Section 28 was repealed in Scotland in 2000 and in England and Wales in 2003.
[4] Scotland has separate provisions for same-sex marriage, and Northern Ireland does not yet permit it.
[5] Office for National Statistics, The latest provisional statistics for England and Wales, up to 30 June 2015, athttp://webarchive.nationalarchives.gov.uk/20160105160709/; http://www.ons.gov.uk/ons/rel/vsob1/marriages-in-england-and-wales--provisional-/for-same-sex-couples--2014/sty-for-same-sex-couples-2014.html, accessed 24 February 2017.
[6] Zoe Williams, 'Rights and wrongs', The Guardian G2, 14 September 2011, pp. 5–7.

as a means of domesticating men by curbing their 'natural' tendency to scatter their sexual attentions far and wide. Some people married for religious reasons, some for love and/or sexual attraction. More recently, marriage has been about weddings, religious and civil ceremonies and the recognition of one's relationship by society and one's family. Theoretically, then, marriage remains the inevitable goal of 'normal' people, a privileged and sought-after state. In reality, it has been declining in popularity for over 40 years.[7]

So important are these social meanings that we tend to forget that marriage is also a legal institution, defined by the laws of each country, which means it varies in form from jurisdiction to jurisdiction, as do its associated rights and benefits. When couples aspire to the legal status and protections of marriage, they may well be motivated in part by the accessory advantages offered in their jurisdiction (tax concessions in the UK, for example, or access to healthcare in the US), but they must also accept its rules, including some less positive aspects – for instance, assuming financial responsibility for one's partner both during and after the marriage.

ARGUMENTS IN FAVOUR OF SAME-SEX MARRIAGE

The arguments used by advocates of same-sex marriage in the 1990s and 2000s were mostly framed in terms of equality and rights. There were three obvious reasons for this. First, campaigners who wish to change the law must present their claims within the existing legal framework of the jurisdiction in which they live, which in the UK meant the Human Rights Act 1998, which incorporated the European Convention on Human Rights (to which the UK had been a signatory since 1950) into national law. When Celia Kitzinger and Sue Wilkinson went to court to have their Canadian marriage recognised as marriage in England, they relied on Article 12 of the Convention which guarantees individuals 'the right to marry and found a family'.[8]

Second, by the end of the twentieth century the rights discourse had become the dominant one in UK law reform and the one best understood by the general public. UK campaigns were strongly influenced by jurisdictions with a longer history of framing legal reform in terms of rights, such as the United States and Canada. Equality and rights are, moreover, liberal notions that suited the dominant political ideology of the turn of the century and were attractive to politicians and law-makers because they sidestepped the bitter history of what was not simply 'inequality' and 'absence of rights' but

---

[7] Office for National Statistics, Statistical Bulletin: Marriages in England and Wales 2013, at https://www.ons.gov.uk/peoplepopulationandcommunity/birthsdeathsandmarriages/marriagecohabitationandcivilpartnerships/bulletins/marriagesinenglandandwalesprovisional/2013, accessed 24 February 2017.

[8] *Wilkinson v Kitzinger* [2006] EWHC 2022. They lost the case, Potter J ruling that marriage was defined in English law as between a man and a woman; the couple's relationship was recognised as a civil partnership which had the same status in law. (This was before the Marriage (Same Sex Couples) Act 2013.)

the legal and social oppression of homosexuals. What notions of equality and rights also sidestepped, of course, was whether access to marriage really was an unmitigated privilege or whether, as some commentators suggested, it simply swapped one form of legal regulation of relationships for another.

The third justification for the equality and rights approach is that it is correct in principle that similarly situated people should be treated similarly in law. Advocates of same-sex marriage emphasised the ordinariness of same-sex couples, whose lives were just like any other couple's – they lived with, loved, cared for and wished to provide for each other and their families. While doubtless a true representation of most same-sex couples who sought marriage, this was also reassuring to a nervous state and public who recalled the challenging behaviour of many gay men in the past and the outrageous appearance and statements of lesbian feminists, who appeared at times the very opposite of normal spouses.

The gendered nature of the campaign for same-sex marriage, in which men's voices were dominant, was revealed by two other, in the end probably more successful, arguments. The first, almost solely used by men, was that homosexuality was innate ('We were born this way') and therefore it was unfair to deprive individuals of rights for something they could not help. An analogy was drawn with race. The notion that homosexuality is innate and immutable has long been disputed by lesbian feminists,[9] many of whom had previously been heterosexual. We hear this argument less often today when greater fluidity of sexuality is assumed, but it was powerfully contended at the time.

The second gendered argument concerned access to the legal privileges attaching to marriage. In the UK, as it happens, there *are* very few such privileges, but one is the exemption from inheritance tax of transfers between spouses. If you leave property to your husband or wife, it incurs no inheritance tax; if you leave it to anyone else, there is potential tax liability. Campaigners for recognition of same-sex relationships drew attention to the injustice of forcing the surviving partner of a long-term same-sex relationship to pay tax while a widow or widower did not, and the media featured stories of elderly gay men forced to sell the home they had shared with a deceased partner simply in order to pay the tax.

The reason this argument is gendered is that inheritance tax is charged on only about 5 per cent of estates; most people are not rich enough to exceed the 'nil-rate' band.[10] Men own more property than women and earn more,[11] so gay male couples (especially childless ones) are much more likely to have assets exceeding the inheritance tax threshold than lesbian couples who, as well

---

[9] See, for example, Adrienne Rich, 'Compulsory heterosexuality and lesbian existence', in *Blood, Bread and Poetry* (Virago, 1981) pp. 23–75.

[10] This is the value of estate assets that can pass tax-free, as of 2018, is £325,000.

[11] In 2016 there was a 9.4 per cent pay gap between men and women for full-time work, rising to 18.1 per cent when part-time work was included. http://www.equalpayportal.co.uk/statistics/, accessed 10 March 2017. See also Chapter 10 of this book.

as earning less because they are women, are more likely to have children. So the inheritance tax argument really only applied to better-off gay men, but was presented as universal so successfully that even today many couples wrongly believe they will have to pay the tax unless they marry.

Feminists in favour of same-sex marriage were happy to adopt the rhetoric of equality and rights, if only because 200 years of campaigning for women's rights indicate that formal equality is usually a prerequisite for advancement. As Maria Bevacqua put it:

> for any kind of gay and lesbian social movement to make significant gains on our behalf, it must make the removal of all formal inequalities a priority. The exclusion of a portion of the population from a major social institution creates a second-class citizenship for that group.[12]

But some feminists defended marriage on more ambitious grounds. They argued that by being allowed to marry they could *transform the institution from inside* by showing the world how (and how much better) same-sex couples conducted their relationships. Before we go on to examine why they believed that marriage needed to be transformed and why they thought same-sex relationships set a better example, we need to consider the feminist arguments *against* same-sex marriage.

ARGUMENTS AGAINST SAME-SEX MARRIAGE

How can one argue against same-sex marriage? Don't all couples who love each other deserve recognition by the state and the acceptance and rights that the institution confers? Not everyone thinks so, even today. Many religions, including the Church of England, Roman Catholicism and Islam, as well as branches of particular faiths, do not accept same-sex marriage. For them, and for many other people, marriage should be confined to the union of one man and one woman. This view derives not just from scriptural sources but from a conception of family based on a biological link between parents and children, and often from a conviction that marriage is the best (or the only) forum in which to raise children – indeed that the very purpose of marriage is to bear children.[13]

In the United States, where the movement for same-sex marriage was more fiercely fought than in the United Kingdom, other arguments against same-sex marriage were raised. One that will be familiar to law students was the 'slippery slope' threat: if we let same-sex couples marry, soon people will be wanting to marry their sister or mother, or even their dog. Where will it end? Same-sex

---

[12] Maria Bevacqua, 'Feminist Theory and the Question of Lesbian and Gay Marriage' (2004) 14 *Feminism and Psychology* 36, 37.
[13] As the service for the 'Solemnization of Matrimony' in the Church of England puts it, 'It was ordained for the procreation of children'.

marriage was perceived by these opponents as unnatural (in part because it could not of itself lead to children), in the same way as inter-racial marriage was deemed unnatural and banned in some US states until the ban was struck down by the US Supreme Court in 1967.[14]

The arguments against same-sex marriage summarised above – and it must be emphasised that these were widely held and still are in many places – were arguments against the extension of marriage to couples in same-sex relationships. But there was another set of arguments which focused not on the 'same-sex' aspect but on *marriage*. While the first approach can be characterised as 'homophobic' (anti-gay and lesbian) or at the very least 'heterosexist' (favouring the privileging of heterosexuals), the second was neither: indeed, its advocates included both lesbians and gay men and heterosexuals, who raised two objections to marriage in principle.

First, they pointed out that simply extending the right to marry to one group did nothing to help those who could not marry and enjoy the legal and financial privileges of marriage – brothers and sisters, for instance[15] – and single people. Single-parent families are among the poorest people in the community: shouldn't *they* be given special legal protection?[16] But it was clear that the group to be benefited was one which, save for the sex of the chosen partner, offered no challenge to conventional notions of marriage. Same-sex marriage had nothing to offer the 'families of choice' that lesbians and gays had gathered round them to replace the real families who had rejected them,[17] or the people with multiple sexual partners, or those who 'pursue their most emotionally significant ties with platonic friends', as Lisa Diamond puts it.[18]

A second objection to same-sex marriage focused on the institution itself and drew on a longstanding feminist critique. Marriage, it was argued, was premised on a set of gendered expectations in which women were 'wives' (with all that that implied in terms of status and duties) and men were heads of households (with all that that implied in terms of rights and expectations of servicing, including sexual). As Michele Barrett and Mary McIntosh observed,

> Marriage ... carries with it the whole historical baggage of male power and patriarchal authority. One has only to think of the traditional wedding ceremony, with its symbolic 'giving away' of the bride by her father to her husband ...[19]

---

[14] *Loving v Virginia* (1967) 388 US 1.

[15] *Burden and Burden v The United Kingdom* ECHR 29 April 2008.

[16] American legal scholar Martha Fineman has suggested that the relationship that should be recognised in law is that between mother and child. See *The Neutered Mother, the Sexual Family, and Other Twentieth Century Tragedies* (Routledge, 1995).

[17] Jeffrey Weeks, Brian Heaphy and Catherine Donovan, *Same-Sex Intimacies: Families of Choice and Other Life Experiments* (Routledge, 2001).

[18] Lisa Diamond, 'Three critical questions for future research on lesbian relationships' (2017) 21 *Contemporary Lesbian Relationships* 12.

[19] Michele Barrett and Mary McIntosh, *The Anti-Social Family* (Verso, 1982) p. 55.

This male power is not just symbolic. Legal privileges and social status attach to marriage precisely because the state wishes to regular citizens' behaviour. This includes making men take financial responsibility for their families (so that the state does not have to maintain them) and making wives take on the actual caring (so that the state does not have to provide social child- or elder-care). For this, women may be expected to curtail or give up their career; men never are. Women may find themselves treated in law and economic policy as dependants of their husband; it will be assumed that they (and their children) will take his surname. If they are financially dependent, their freedom will be limited; without alternative means they will find it almost impossible to leave a violent relationship.

Katherine O'Donovan declared that gender equality was impossible within marriage because marriage is wholly defined by gender difference, and operates to privilege men. 'In marriage the rules, both constitutive and behavioural, are based on gender and their sum constitutes the role of husband and wife.' You can try as hard as you like to challenge this idea of marriage in your own relationship, she argued, but society will always revert to the normative assumptions, and 'legal rules cannot be changed by personal redefinition'.[20] Thus, when the idea of same-sex marriage was mooted, feminists and others who had long viewed marriage as intrinsically patriarchal, indeed toxic, reacted with incredulity. Why would anyone choose to marry, given its ignominious history and associations?[21]

CAN MARRIAGE BE TRANSFORMED?

It was in response to the feminist critique of marriage that feminist advocates of same-sex marriage framed their transformational goal. For them, the problem with traditional marriage was simply that it was heterosexual; indeed, heterosexuality, rather than marriage itself, was seen as the real problem.[22] Pro-marriage feminists argued that a same-sex couple could avoid traditional marriage's relationship of dominance and subordination because gender roles could not automatically be mapped on to biological sex. Coming from a position of equal bargaining power (in terms of gender, if not always in terms of other factors), same-sex couples could negotiate roles within the relationship and thereby confound expectations of their sex.[23]

---

[20] Katherine O'Donovan, 'The Male Appendage: Legal Definitions of Women' in Sandra Burman (ed.), *Fit Work for Women* (Croom Helm, 1979) pp. 135–136.

[21] The same reasoning underpins recent attempts by heterosexual couples to be allowed to register civil partnerships, at present confined to same-sex couples. Owen Bowcott, 'Court rules against heterosexual couple who wanted civil partnership', *The Guardian*, 21 February 2017, https://www.theguardian.com/society/2017/feb/21/heterosexual-couples-should-not-be-allowed-civil-partnerships-court-rules?CMP=Share_iOSApp_Other, accessed 24 February 2017.

[22] For example Scarlet Friedman and Elizabeth Sarah (eds), *On the Problem of Men* (The Women's Press, 1982).

[23] See, for example, Nan D. Hunter, 'Marriage, law and gender: A feminist inquiry' in Lisa Duggan and Nan D. Hunter (eds), *Sex Wars: Sexual Dissent and Political Culture* (Routledge, 1995).

There is plenty of evidence to show that many same-sex couples do live more egalitarian lives, with financial responsibilities and domestic tasks more evenly spread and negotiated than in opposite-sex families. This is particularly true of lesbian feminists, for whom equality in relationships was always a political goal.[24] Once children enter the family, however, it becomes much more difficult to avoid gendered roles; public childcare is limited and private expensive, very often obliging one partner to take on the homemaker role, or at least work part-time, while the other takes over as breadwinner. The fact that only one of these roles will accord with gendered expectations goes some way towards challenging ideas of what is appropriate for men and women but does not really alter the hetero-sexual and patriarchal nature of marriage: there will still be inequalities of power within the relationship and they will still be associated with gendered roles. Anti-marriage feminists warn that many younger people and gay men do not approach marriage with the critical perspective and experience of second-wave feminists and increasingly seek to create 'nuclear' families of parents and children as the only model they know. Their high expectations that same-sex couples will work things out better than heterosexuals may well fail in the face of insurmountable institutional barriers to non-gendered egalitarian ways of relating.

The irony is that those who oppose same-sex marriage because they don't like homosexuality and those who oppose same-sex marriage because they don't like marriage are actually talking about the same thing. The anti-gay con-servatives and religious groups perceive marriage as the union of a male head of household and a female homemaker and childrearer. The anti-marriage fem-inists do too, and this is why they reject it, unconvinced that gender equality in marriage is possible in a society ill-designed to facilitate shared earning, home-making and childcare. That said, same-sex couples have spoken movingly of the difference that being able to marry has made to their lives. They feel legit-imised, accepted by both family and society. Formal equality may well be the necessary first step to substantive equality within relationships, but at this stage of history we do not know what the future holds: whether marriage will indeed be transformed into something more egalitarian, partly (though by no means solely) thanks to the example of same-sex couples, or whether, as the marriage rate continues to decline, it will simply cease to matter.

Debate 2
Can we speak of LGBT rights and an LGBT community?

Whether we should or should not speak of LGBT rights and the LGBT commu-nity, the fact is that people *do*; it's a common acronym applied to issues affecting lesbians, gay men, bisexuals and trans people, used in policy statements, research and campaigning (and often with the addition of other initials, for example I for

---

[24] Gillian Dunne, *Lesbian Lifestyles: Women's Work and the Politics of Sexuality* (Macmillan, 1997).

intersex and Q for queer). Yet it is a curious expression, because it links people with quite different interests, not all of them concerned with alternative sexualities; many trans people, for instance, live and identify as heterosexual.

In Support of 'LGBT'

It can be argued that minority groups are strongest and most effective when they work together in the pursuit of common goals. Certainly there have been many occasions when lesbians and gay men have united to secure rights for sexual minorities. During the AIDS crisis in the 1980s, which devastated gay male communities since the disease spread through penetrative sex, lesbians remained largely unaffected but rallied round to help. In the protests against section 28,[25] heterosexuals lent their support to gays and lesbians. Alliances with bisexuals and trans people are more recent, partly because these groups called for inclusion later, but also, no doubt, because policy-makers found it convenient to lump all the 'sexual minorities' together. For LGBT people there are obvious common goals in achieving equality and justice in a tolerant and diverse society, or even in the more ambitious goal of dismantling patriarchy by challenging gender norms and behaviour.

A second argument for viewing LGBT as a homogeneous category is that it groups together people who claim non-traditional *identities*. 'Identities' means the labels people choose for reasons of solidarity and political struggle. It is as a consequence of lobbying by these groups that those who claim these identities are now protected under anti-discrimination law.

Against 'LGBT'

But there, one might argue, the similarities end. The identities of lesbian, gay and bisexual people relate to their *sexual orientation*; a trans identity, on the other hand, relates to *gender*. Sexual orientation is in principle irrelevant to trans people – there are heterosexual trans and gay and lesbian ones – except for individuals who seek to change their gender because their sexual preference is for people of their own sex but who cannot countenance a gay or lesbian identity. These people may hope that by changing gender they will achieve an appropriate and acceptable heterosexuality. Young people in particular may feel pressure to transition because they lack knowledge of the alternatives or support to be different.

Gender, however, *is* central to trans identity but there are two contrasting approaches:

(a) Reinforcing gender norms

A common way of describing the experience of trans people is that they feel 'trapped in the wrong body'. The solution they adopt is to bring the

---

[25] Local Government Act 1988.

body into line with the psychological gender. This may involve hormone treatment, surgery, and/or change of name, hairstyle and clothing. This explanation of trans underpins the terms of the Gender Recognition Act (GRA) which, when first enacted in 2004, required a person to undergo surgical modification of their body before being recognised in their new gender. Following representations by trans people, the surgical requirement was removed, but the legislation continues to reinforce gender norms by insisting that applicants for gender reassignment must live in their acquired gender for two years and 'intend[ ] to continue to live in the acquired gender until death' (s. 2). Indeed, in constructing trans people as suffering from a medical condition, 'gender dysphoria', the GRA formalises in law an *essential* difference between men and women and pathologises those who feel a discord between their biological sex and society's expectations for that gender. Applicants for gender reassignment are forced to adopt obvious gender markers such as name and clothing because appearance is everything: they must pass as a member of the other sex. This is reinforced by the Equality Act 2010 which makes it unlawful to discriminate against, harass or victimise a person in connexion with 'gender re-assignment' (ss. 4, 7). It does not matter whether you have had surgery or not; indeed, the law applies if you are discriminated against because you *appear* to be transgender, even if you are not.

(b) Subverting gender norms

Many trans people, however, reject the binary approach of the law to gender. For them, trans offers an opportunity not to change to the 'other' gender but to *transcend* gender roles. Drawing on queer theory,[26] they argue that gender and sexuality are more complex and fluid than simply male/female and gay/straight; one may mix and match from a range of genders and sexualities or adopt none.[27] These people reject gendered markers in their appearance or incorporate both male and female characteristics in a deliberate effort to subvert gender norms.[28] In so doing, they have much in common with those LGB people who aim to challenge gender norms by making it acceptable for women to look 'masculine' and take on 'masculine' roles, for men to look 'feminine' and take on 'feminine' roles, and for everyone to love and have sex with partners of any sex.

While this book was in preparation, the government opened a consultation on a planned Gender Recognition Bill, under which people would be able to choose their own gender without a doctor's diagnosis, while those claiming a non-binary identity would be able to record their

---

[26] For an explanation of queer theory, see Sharon Marcus, 'Queer Theory for Everyone: A Review Essay' (2005) 31 *Signs* 191.

[27] The 'prefer not to say' option on progressive forms.

[28] With, for example, breasts and a beard, or alternative versions of their name: Carlos/Carla.

gender on official documentation as 'X'. While the latter provision could help to abolish the binary gender division (having to declare oneself male or female), people may be deterred from choosing to be 'X' for fear of being dismissed as bizarre or sick; while the possibility of men deciding to call themselves women simply to have closer access to women has caused anxiety among 'cis' (biological) women: 'We'll now have men-who-say-they're-women in female hospital wards, leisure centre changing rooms, domestic violence refuges, female sport.'[29]

PRACTICAL OBJECTIONS TO 'LGBT'

This leads us to the other objection to treating LGBT as a homogeneous group: our social roles, as well as our biology, have led men and women to behave differently. Lesbians are first and foremost women, who share women's experience of subordination and discrimination. This is also the learned experience of female-to-male trans people. Gay men are still men, accustomed to being dominant and having access to the perks of gendered power. This is also the learned experience of male-to-female trans people. When you hear of discord in women's groups between 'cis' women and trans women, it is almost always because the former see the latter as exhibiting some of the characteristics of the sex they were born into, such as dominant or abusive behaviour.

This has led to two consequences. First, because identity is important to groups who have been discriminated against, 'cis' women are often dismayed when trans women adopt extreme forms of feminine glamour that are not only miles away from the way ordinary women present themselves but represent a damaging return to the idea, from which feminists have long sought to escape, that it is women's duty to make themselves attractive to men. Many noted that the image of Caitlyn Jenner that appeared on the cover of *Vanity Fair* was that of a woman created by and for men.[30]

Second, it is observable that the loudest voices in any mixed group are the ones that get heard. When the words 'homosexual' and 'gay' served to encompass men *and* women, it was men's interests that caught the public's attention. In law, literature and history writing, lesbians were an afterthought if mentioned at all,[31] just as women tend to be overlooked in general discussions of 'mankind' or 'humanity'.[32] The addition of transgender groups to the alliance

---

[29] http://www.independent.co.uk/news/uk/politics/transgender-rules-reform-gender-dysphoria-changes-2004-gender-recognition-self-identify-a7855381.html, accessed 19 October 2017.

[30] Jenni Murray, 'Be trans, be proud – but don't call yourself a "real woman"' (2017), *Sunday Times*, 5 March 2017, http://www.thetimes.co.uk/article/be-trans-be-proud-but-dont-call-yourself-a-real-woman-frtld7q5c, accessed 10 March 2017.

[31] For example, H. Montgomery Hyde, *The Other Love: An Historical and Contemporary Survey of Homosexuality in Britain* (Heinemann, 1970).

[32] Rosemary Auchmuty, Sheila Jeffreys and Elaine Hutton, 'Lesbian history and gay studies: Keeping a feminist perspective' (1992) 1 *Women's History Review* 89.

has done little to alter the balance; very often the inclusive expression 'LGBT' simply masks the fact that the discussion is about men, and women are still absent from consideration.

Many feminists, while wholly supportive of trans people, argue that someone who has been raised as a male cannot become a woman: because 'woman' is a social construction, not just a label and look. As the headline to an article by Jenni Murray put it, 'Be trans, be proud – but don't call yourself a "real woman"'.[33] In response, Gaby Hinsliff objected:

> It ... seems cruel to endure the gruelling process of physical transition only to be hauled up for the one thing no surgeon can remove, namely one's past. For if womanhood is defined as the sum of everything that has ever happened to a woman because of her gender, then logically nobody born with male organs can ever quite attain it.[34]

CONCLUSION

It is clear that the law continues to reinforce gender and sexuality norms both explicitly, as in its approach to trans, or implicitly, as in its approach to marriage. It is equally clear that lesbians, gay men, bisexuals and trans people can all play a role in challenging these norms, but in different and sometimes contradictory ways. Any gesture that disturbs society's ideas of what men and women should be like, whether it be deliberately outrageous behaviour by lesbians and gay men or the not quite 'real' appearance of a trans woman, is one more attack on the straitjacket of gender. Only when there is no longer any 'real' woman or 'real' man will one's gender, along with one's race or sexuality, cease to matter.

FURTHER READING

Rosemary Auchmuty, 'Same-sex marriage revived: Feminist critique and legal strategy' (2004) 14 *Feminism and Psychology* 101.

Rosemary Auchmuty, 'Feminist approaches to sexuality and law scholarship' (2015) 15 *Legal Information Management* 4.

Nicola Barker, *Not the Marrying Kind: A Feminist Critique of Same-Sex Marriage* (Palgrave Macmillan, 2012).

Rosie Harding (ed.), *Law and Sexuality* (Routledge, 2016).

Sheila Jeffreys, *Gender Hurts: A Feminist Analysis of the Politics of Transgenderism* (Routledge, 2014).

Vanessa Munro and Carl Stychin (eds), *Sexuality and the Law: Feminist Engagements* (Glasshouse Press, 2007).

---

[33] Murray (n. 30).

[34] Gaby Hinsliff, 'Scrap the rules. Let women be what they want to be', *The Guardian*, 10 March 2017, p. 21.

CHAPTER 18

Legal Professions

Lisa Webley

Although the diversity of the legal professions in England and Wales (legal executives, solicitors, barristers and judges) has increased substantially since the 1980s, serious challenges remain in relation to access to, and promotion and retention within, the professions for women and minorities, as illustrated by the 2013 figures in the table.[1]

Stage	% Women solicitor route	% Women barrister route
Graduated with UG law degree	65% (n circa 17,000)	65% (n circa 17,000)
Graduated with vocational diploma (LPC/BPTC)	65% (n 6,067)	52% (n 1,793)
Newly admitted to the Bar this year		53% (n 1,852)
Undertaking training contract/ pupillage this year	Training contract 64% (n 5,441)	1st and 2nd six pupillage 40% (n 955)
Newly admitted to the Solicitors' Roll this year	59% (n 8,480)	
Total proportion of practising profession of those who have achieved senior status	Law firm partner 27% (n 37,331)	Queen's Counsel 11% (n 1,318) (27% of those appointed in 2013)
Total in the practising profession	47% (n 136,081)	35% (n 15,270)

The legal profession's historically white male and socially privileged roots are very well established.[2] But unlike many of the other old professions, this has

---

[1] More recent figures are available for both professions, but not in a way that allows a proper comparison. Legal executives are not included here. For judicial diversity statistics, including judges who were previously solicitors or barristers, see n. 23 below.

[2] Hilary Sommerlad, Lisa Webley, Liz Duff, Daniel Muzio and Jennifer Tomlinson, *Diversity in the Legal Profession in England and Wales: A Qualitative Study of Barriers and Individual Choices* (University of Westminster Press, 2013).

been exacerbated by the fact that access to full professional recognition within the practising legal professions is, in most instances, via an apprenticeship controlled by private practice lawyers rather than simply by successful completion of the necessary qualifications followed by registration with the professional body (as in, say, the USA).[3] Consequently, to the extent that there are systemic problems that impede access and promotion within the professions, meaningful change is only likely to occur if the legal professional branches take the lead; individuals alone cannot force change.

During the 1980s, the debate and vocabulary of inequality were replaced by the discourse of equality, diversity and inclusion. This stemmed, in part, from a shift away from concerns that direct discrimination was the main reason why women and minorities were failing to thrive within the legal profession. The gender bar had been removed in 1919 when the Sex Disqualification (Removal) Act was passed.[4] Half of all law graduates were women by the late 1980s. Consequently, there was a developing recognition that indirect forms of discrimination were the most likely explanations for women's continued under-representation.[5] By the 1990s the 'trickle up' theory – the idea that given enough time women would naturally reach senior levels within the professions in keeping with the proportions of women graduating from law school – had been largely discredited. Several initiatives were introduced in an attempt to correct a lack of proportionate female representation. The first debate here considers the effectiveness of these initiatives, while the second considers whether having more women lawyers and judges actually makes a difference.

Debate 1

How effective are the strategies adopted to counter gender inequality in the professions?

Women's lack of progress within the legal professions has been attributed to a range of factors: individual choices and career strategies;[6] structural barriers

---

[3] Lisa Webley, 'Legal professional de(re)regulation, equality, and inclusion, and the contested space of professionalism within the legal market in England and Wales' (2015) 83 *Fordham Law Review* 2349. See, further, Lizzie Barmes and Kate Malleson, 'The legal profession as gatekeeper to the judiciary: Design faults in measures to enhance diversity' (2011) 74 *Modern Law Review* 245.

[4] For a discussion in the context of the Bar, see: 'Gender inequality in the legal profession – distant past or a current concern?', 15 April 2016, http://dangerouswomenproject. org/2016/04/15/gender-inequality-legal-profession/, accessed 27 February 2017.

[5] Louise Ashley and Laura Empson, 'Differentiation and discrimination: Understanding social class and social exclusion in leading law firms' (2013) 66 *Human Relations* 219.

[6] Catherine Hakim, *Work-lifestyle Choices in the 21st Century: Preference Theory* (Oxford University Press, 2000) and Hilary Sommerlad, 'The gendering of the professional subject: Commitment, choice and social closure in the legal profession', in Clare McGlynn (ed.), *Legal Feminisms – Theory and Practice* (Dartmouth, 1998).

within the professions that prevent equal access to opportunities;[7] and the culture within society, the professions and individual organisations that limits female power and status.[8] Equality and diversity initiatives have attempted to address these choices, structures and cultures in different ways. There were three waves: first, measures to remove indirect discrimination within the legal professions; second, measures to encourage women and other low-participation groups to enter and progress effectively within the legal professions; and, third, positive steps to promote an inclusive workplace culture by highlighting and then seeking to eliminate the harmful influence of unconscious bias in decision-making.

FIRST-WAVE INITIATIVES

The first wave of diversity and inclusion initiatives was introduced in the 1990s, following academic research and recommendations, much of it sponsored by legal professional associations and interest groups such as the Association for Women Solicitors.[9] These measures included formal policies and procedures to reduce structural indirect discrimination, primarily to address some forms of gender stereotyping (for example 'women lawyers are good at family law, but can't cope in corporate law environments') and the acknowledged structural inequalities of needing to work full-time though those hours precluded primary caring responsibilities such as school drop-off and pick-up times. Having identified that women were three times more likely to leave preretirement than men, they focused on trying to retain women within the legal professions.[10] They later moved on to consider how to get more women

---

[7] Clare McGlynn, 'The status of women lawyers in the United Kingdom' in Ulrike Schultz and Gisela Shaw (eds), *Women in the World's Legal Professions* (Hart, 2003) and Hilary Sommerlad, 'The myth of feminisation: Women and cultural change in the legal profession' (1994) 1 *International Journal of the Legal Profession* 31; Hilary Sommerlad, 'Women solicitors in a fractured profession: Intersections of gender and professionalism in England and Wales' (2002) 9 *International Journal of the Legal Profession* 213.

[8] Pierre Bourdieu, 'Cultural reproduction and social reproduction' in Richard Brown (ed.), *Knowledge, Education and Cultural Change* (Tavistock, 1973) and Pierre Bourdieu, 'The forms of capital' in John Richardson (ed.), *Handbook of Theory and Research for the Sociology of Education* (Greenwood, 1986) pp. 241–258; Edgar H. Schein, *Organizational Culture and Leadership* (Jossey-Bass, 3rd edn, 2004) Part One.

[9] For example: the Law Society sponsored research by A. Bradshaw and Phil A. Thomas, *'Leaving the Profession': A Survey of Solicitors Not Renewing their Practising Certificates* (Cardiff Law School, 1995); Hilary Sommerlad and Pete Sanderson, 'The legal labour market and the training needs of women returners in the United Kingdom' (1997) 29 *Journal of Vocational Education and Training* 45; Hilary Sommerlad and Pete Sanderson, *Gender Choice and Commitment: Women Solicitors in England and Wales and the Struggle for Equal Status* (Ashgate, 1998); Jo Siems, *Equality and Diversity; Women Solicitors Research Study 48, Volume 1, Quantitative Findings* (The Law Society, 2004); Liz Duff and Lisa Webley, *Equality and Diversity: Women Solicitors Research Study 48, Volume 2, Qualitative Findings and Literature Review* (The Law Society, 2004).

[10] Siems (n. 9).

promoted to senior levels, as the lack of promotion opportunities was seen as one of the main reasons for female attrition from the legal professions. Strategies included the introduction of maternity leave and return-to-work post-maternity policies (still a contentious issue in some chambers at the self-employed Bar) and formal flexible and part-time working schemes which had up until then been considered impossible in most law firms and chambers.

In doing this, law firms and even the judiciary, latterly the Judicial Appointments Commission (the JAC was established in 2006), started the process of reconsidering the ways in which lawyers were recruited and how they were evaluated for promotion. It became apparent to some, such as the JAC, that there was no such thing as a neutral hiring or promotion tool, and that the factors used as proxies or measures for excellent potential and performance could give rise to unintended discriminatory practices and outcomes.[11] For example, a focus on whether someone had achieved Queen's Counsel (QC) status for promotion to the bench disproportionately disadvantaged women, who were much less likely to be promoted to QC level. Instead the JAC started to hire on the basis of competency frameworks (how competent one was at each of a set of key knowledge and skills attributes) and this led to an increase in women entering some sections of the judiciary.

SECOND-WAVE INITIATIVES

Second-wave initiatives have primarily focused on encouraging women and those from low-participation groups to join and rise through the legal professional ranks and on training those faced with decisions about who to choose for a role. These measures have been targeted at individuals rather than structural impediments. Gender remains a key issue, but the intersectionality of other characteristics has led to the recognition of race, sexual orientation, disability and class/socio-economic status as potential hurdles too. These strategies include widening participation initiatives to raise the aspirations of young people from non-traditional law backgrounds, for example the Prime initiative.[12] Aspirational targets, for example for the proportion of women partners in law firms, have been set by some legal organisations to encourage women to apply for promotion and to indicate that their applications will be taken seriously, although quotas remain illegal in most instances in England

---

[11] A proxy, in this context, is an indicator used to help judge whether someone has the 'quality' we have identified as important, in the absence of a way for us to be able to assess the thing itself. Proxies often get confused for the thing itself and so they are applied without discretion in attempt to be fair even though they may lead to unintended discrimination.

[12] For more information about Prime, refer to: http://www.primecommitment.org/, accessed 30 January 2018.

and Wales.[13] At a profession-wide level, 'equal merit' tie principles have been introduced by the JAC so that if there are two candidates equally well qualified for a role then the one from the lower participation group should be appointed as she is equally qualified and her appointment assists in counterbalancing the under-representation of that group. The JAC has also identified diversity champions within the judiciary to encourage women and those from low-participation groups to apply for judicial roles and has run a range of diversity events to promote these campaigns. Some law firms and chambers have done the same. Diversity league table schemes have played a key role in promoting good practice within organisations by placing importance on things such as mentoring and sponsorship schemes and networking groups for women and others with protected characteristics, and this in turn has led to pressure for change within organisations. Diversity monitoring and self-assessment within participating organisations have also increased. All the legal professional regulators now require diversity data to be collected by all legal entities (including law firms and chambers) so that progress over time may be measured.

THIRD-WAVE INITIATIVES

Third-wave initiatives are still in their infancy. They focus on the fact that decision-makers see the world through their own experience and that our unconscious biases play a role in our decision to choose to work with people 'like us':

> The truth is we all have biases and, unless we are able to discuss this, we will continually be thwarted in our desire to achieve diversity and inclusion in our workplaces. Despite the fact that we are all biased, it is a subject that is very difficult to raise in an open blame-free way in organisations today. We are so conscious of the need to appear fair that we hide our prejudices, sometimes even from ourselves.[14]

---

[13] Targets are aspirational statements of the proportion of a particular minority group that one would hope to hire or promote in each year or cycle. Quotas are places reserved exclusively for a class of people and are not open to others. Targets have had some (modest) success but change is still slow and attention is being turned to the potential for quotas, see for example: 'Proof that women in boardroom quotas work', *The Telegraph*, 13 January 2015, http://www. telegraph.co.uk/finance/newsbysector/banksandfinance/11341816/Proof-that-women-in-boardrooms-quotas-work.html, accessed 30 January 2018. For a discussion of why quotas may be necessary in the upper levels of the judiciary see Kate Malleson, 'The case for gender quotas for appointments to the Supreme Court', 23 May 2014, http://ukscblog.com/case-gender-quotas-appointments-supreme-court/, accessed 30 January 2018.

[14] One of Kandola's surveys revealed that 60 per cent of managers said they had unconscious bias, 40 per cent did not believe that they did, and these were the people most in need of the training opportunities: 'Sub-conscious bias: Prof. Binna Kandola', *Diverse Ethics*, 8 July 2010, http://www.diverseethics.com/article/interviews/binna, accessed 30 November 2015.

Unconscious bias is associated with something referred to as 'System 1'[15] thinking or the use of proxies or heuristics. This type of thinking permits us to make quick decisions based on our experiences, but those experiences are rarely evidence-led; rather, they are informed by our own ways of thinking, our biases. System 1 thinking is useful in situations where a snap decision is needed but is less than reliable and likely to be discriminatory in situations where many factors need to be weighed. System 1 thinking is likely to disadvantage women and minorities who have not hitherto frequently been seen as leaders (because there have been relatively few of them to date) or archetypal lawyers. This has led some firms and chambers to rethink their appointment processes and redact information from applications that may provoke system 1 decision-making, for example people's names, A-level grades and the university they attended (but university grades remain). It is an approach that the Law Society of England and Wales has been actively promoting.[16] The equal merit tiebreak principle is also viewed as a way to counter-balance unconscious bias given that, if two candidates are considered equally qualified, it is likely that the non-standard candidate may have been under-marked compared to the standard candidate. These initiatives are still relatively new, and in a pilot phase, but the evidence so far is that they appear to be leading to a more diverse trainee solicitor and judicial pool.[17] They have certainly yielded success in other professional fields.[18]

DISCUSSION

The first-wave measures, although contentious when first introduced, have subsequently become accepted good practice and there are now relatively few robust and evidenced-based criticisms of them, although you will find negative comment under equality news stories in the *Law Society Gazette*, for example, often from men who feel marginalised. The numbers of women rising through the professions increased substantially during the 1990s and early 2000s when these initiatives were first introduced. But the figures in the table at the start of this chapter indicate that women still appear to face a glass ceiling impeding their progress to the more senior levels of the professions. Women seem to be

---

[15] System 1 thinking is defined by Daniel Kahneman as a way of thinking that 'operates automatically and quickly, with little or no effort and no sense of voluntary control' as compared to System 2 thinking that 'allocate[s] attention to the effortful mental activities that demand it, including complex computations. The operations of System 2 are often associated with the subjective experience of agency, choice and concentration': Daniel Kahneman, *Thinking, Fast and Slow* (Penguin Books, 2011), p. 20.

[16] This approach is now being used by a number of firms and has extended beyond the UK, see: Richard Garner, 'Exclusive: Law firm Clifford Chance adopts "CV blind" policy to break Oxbridge recruitment bias', *The Independent,* 9 January 2014, http://www.independent. co.uk/student/news/exclusive-law-firm-clifford-chance-adopts-cv-blind-policy-to-break- oxbridge-recruitment-bias-9050227.html, accessed 30 November 2015.

[17] Lisa Webley and Liz Duff, 'Diversity and inclusion as the key to innovation in innovating talent management in law firms' in T. Mortensen (ed.), *Innovating Talent Management in Law Firms* (NALP, 2016).

[18] For examples see Kahneman, *Thinking, Fast and Slow*, n. 15.

penalised more than men who take up flexible and/or part-time working[19] and women still leave law in much greater numbers than men.[20] Second-wave initiatives have attracted greater controversy, with the more vocal criticisms being that they offer potential for a backlash against women and minority lawyers[21] and that organisations may stereotype them or treat them as tokenistic. There are concerns that the measures designed to counter-balance female inequality, such as mentoring, are being used even more effectively by dominant groups.[22] There is evidence that women and minorities are still to be found in greater proportions in the lower status sectors of the professions, such as the tribunal rather than court judiciary, and in less lucrative areas of practice.[23] But second-wave initiatives have allowed the debate to move forward, paving the way for a more grown-up discussion about the role unconscious bias may play in our thinking. Third-wave initiatives are the most controversial; those who have benefited from the previous system can feel undermined and challenged. Many of us struggle to acknowledge that we have unconscious biases that may lead to unfair outcomes for people who are not like us.[24] In the next debate we shall consider why it may be important to have more women lawyers so you may judge whether the controversy attached to the initiatives above is a price worth paying to ensure greater female representation in the professions.

Debate 2

Does having more women lawyers make a difference?

The need for more equal representation of women within all levels of the legal professions has been justified on a number of fronts, not least that it is the economically rational thing to do (the business case for diversity), given that profit-making legal entities will want the most talented people working for them to maximise their financial standing. But there are other justifications that operate on a principled and pragmatic basis, two of the main ones being the 'rule of law' case – that the legal profession is uniquely charged with the responsibility

---

[19] See Interlaw (www.interlaw.org), *The Gender Report* (Interlaw, 2017).

[20] See *Trends in the Solicitors' Profession Law Society Annual Statistical Report 2014* (The Law Society, 2015): http://www.lawsociety.org.uk/policy-campaigns/research-trends/annual-statistical-reports/, accessed 30 January 2018.

[21] Hilary Sommerlad, 'The commercialisation of law and the enterprising legal practitioner: Continuity and change' (2011) 18 *International Journal of The Legal Profession* 73; Sharon C. Bolton and Daniel Muzio, 'Can't live with 'em; Can't live without 'em: Gendered segmentation in the legal profession' (2007) 41 *Sociology* 147.

[22] Kahneman, *Thinking, Fast and Slow*, n. 15.

[23] See the latest judicial diversity statistics (2016) as an example; you may wish to contrast Figure 2 (courts) with Figure 10 (tribunals), demonstrating greater female representation in the lower courts and in the tribunal sectors: https://www.judiciary.gov.uk/wp-content/uploads/2016/07/judicial-diversity-statistics-2december.pdf, accessed 30 January 2018.

[24] Kandola, n. 14. For insight into this in context see Richard Collier, 'Naming men as men in corporate legal practice: Gender and the idea of "virtually 24/7 commitment" in law' (2015) 83 *Fordham Law Review* 2387.

to maintain the pre-eminence of the law and this includes that unlawful discrimination must be challenged – and the gender, lawyering and judging case that posits that having people from a wide range of backgrounds limits the potential for one set of unconscious biases to favour dominant groups to the prejudice of subordinated ones. We shall consider each of these in turn.

THREE DIFFERENT CASES FOR WHY WOMEN LAWYERS MAKE A DIFFERENCE

The business case for the promotion and retention of women lawyers is by far the most popular within the practising profession, not least as it points to the economic rationality of harnessing rather than wasting female talent with the goal of improving profit.[25] Research by organisations such as McKinsey, Catalyst and Reibey Institute provides some data in support of the first- and second-wave initiatives above.[26] Many people would argue that it is logical that hiring the most talented people, male or female, and retaining them and supporting them (and thus promoting them) makes good business sense. Thus, anything that gets in the way of that – discriminatory structures or practices, lack of encouragement, lack of mentoring or sponsorship to apply for promotion, or unconscious bias in decision-making – should be rooted out.

However, the business case is not without criticism, first because it is hard to find concrete proof that a diverse workforce is a more profitable one because of its diversity rather than other factors such as good management. Perhaps the most important criticism is that it places equality at the mercy of the market: in other words, if it makes business sense not to discriminate then discrimination is wrong, but if discrimination is profitable then it can not only be justified but is the right thing to do.[27] This stands in direct contradiction with the next case for equality, the rule of law case, which argues that unlawful discrimination as a matter of principle and practice is always wrong.

---

[25] Joanne Braithwaite, 'The strategic use of demand-side diversity pressure in the solicitors' profession' (2010) 37 *Journal of Law and Society* 442.

[26] McKinsey and Company, *Women Matter,* 2007 and McKinsey and Company, *Women Matter 2,* 2008. For more information and full references see: *Women Matter 2: Female leadership, a competitive edge for the future,* https://www.mckinsey.com/%7E;/media/McKinsey/Business%20 Functions/Organization/Our%20Insights/Women%20matter/Women_matter_oct2008_ english.ashx, accessed 30 January 2018, and for an alternative viewpoint, including comments, see Mike Buchanan, 'The gender diversity delusion', The Institute of Economic Affairs, 24 April 2012, http://www.iea.org.uk/blog/the-gender-diversity-delusion, accessed 30 November 2015.

[27] Clare McGynn, 'The business of equality in the solicitors' profession' (2000) 63 *Modern Law Review* 42; Lisa Webley and Liz Duff, 'Women solicitors as a barometer for problems within the legal profession – time to put values before profits?' (2007) 34 *Journal of Law and Society* 374; Ashley and Empson (n. 5); Stephen Ackroyd and Daniel Muzio, 'The reconstructed professional firm: Explaining the change in English legal practice' (2007) 48 *Organization Studies* 1; David Wilkins, 'From "separate is inherently unequal" to "diversity is good for business". The rise of market-based diversity arguments and the fate of the black corporate bar' (2004) 117 *Harvard Law Review* 1548.

The augmented or substantive rule of law case for equality is that the law is pre-eminent: law must accord with some basic standards such as equality, not just before the law but through the law.[28] Further, it holds that lawyers are only professionals by virtue of the pre-eminence of the rule of law (our role depends on the law being valued and respected by and within society) and that, as its guardians, we must uphold equality through the law if we are to retain our role as lawyers. All branches of the legal profession have an ethical responsibility within their codes of conduct to practise law free from discrimination against all protected characteristics, which include gender as well as race, sexual orientation and disability.[29] It makes little sense, therefore, to require professionals to practise in a non-discriminatory manner vis-à-vis clients and then permit them to discriminate vis-à-vis colleagues. The rule of law case is championed more by the salaried sections of the legal professions (academia, the judiciary, and some quarters of the self-employed Bar), although 'merit' remains a loaded term.[30] There may be agreement that discrimination is wrong, but there is less agreement about how to spot 'merit' or 'talent' and thus about the extent to which there is evidence that discrimination persists.

The third main argument for greater representation in the professions is that women may practise law or judge cases differently from men, and diversity is important to reflect this. This presupposes that that there are 'male' and 'female' ways of thinking and doing that are distinctive,[31] a proposition that is contested.[32] An alternative argument could be that, although men and women may not practise or judge differently purely by virtue of their gender,

---

[28] For a discussion of the different conceptions of the rule of law, see Tom Bingham, *The Rule of Law* (Penguin Books, 2011) Part II and in particular Chapters 5 and 7.

[29] See, for legal executives: Core Principle 6 Treat Everyone Fairly and Without Prejudice, http://www.cilex.org.uk/pdf/CodeofConduct2015.pdf, accessed 30 January 2018; for solicitors: Chapter 2 Equality and Diversity SRA Code of Conduct 2011, http://www.sra.org.uk/solicitors/handbook/code/part2/content.page, accessed 30 January 2018, covering not everyone and not just clients; for barristers: Core Duty 8: https://www.barstandardsboard.org.uk/media/1813606/bsb_handbook_13_december_2016.pdf, accessed 30 January 2018; and for the judicial oath: https://www.judiciary.gov.uk/about-the-judiciary/the-judiciary-the-government-and-the-constitution/oaths/, accessed 30 January 2018.

[30] See Webley and Duff (n. 17) and further Hilary Sommerlad, 'Minorities, merit, and misrecognition in the globalized profession' (2012) 80 *Fordham Law Review* 2481 and 'The 'social magic' of merit: Diversity, equity and inclusion in the English and Welsh Legal Profession' (2015) 83 *Fordham Law Review* 2325; and Kate Malleson, 'Rethinking the merit principle in the judicial appointments process' (2006) 33 *Journal of Law and Society* 126.

[31] Sue Davis, 'Do women judges speak "in a different voice?": Carol Gilligan, 'Feminist legal theory and the ninth circuit' (1993) 8 *Wisconsin Women's Law Journal* 143; Carrie Menkel-Meadow, 'The comparative sociology of women lawyers: The "feminization" of the legal profession' (1986) 24 *Osgoode Hall Law Journal* 897.

[32] See Rosemary Hunter, 'More than just a different face? Judicial diversity and decision-making' (2015) 68 *Current Legal Problems* 119 for a discussion of the evidence and Judith Resnik, 'On the bias: Reconsideration of the aspirations for our judges' (1988) 61 *Southern California Law Review* 1877; Rosemary Hunter, 'Deconstructing the subjects of feminism: The essentialism debate in feminist theory and practice' (1996) 6 *Australian Feminist Law Journal* 135.

it is important that all are seen to be represented in the law. This approach has more support.[33] It may increase the democratic legitimacy of the judiciary (if not the other branches of the legal profession), signal that the processes of judicial appointment and professional promotion operate fairly, and provide role models for women and girls.[34] It may be the case that women lawyers, including judges, are able to empathise better with women clients and victims because they share some of their experiences, or that women lawyers are able to challenge sexism privately within the profession, educating their colleagues in the process.[35] It is also suggested that men and women by virtue of their different experiences may have different unconscious biases and that a range of biases is better than only one set which goes unchallenged with all erroneously believing it to be neutral in substance and effect.

For those of you wondering at this point whether greater representation by women really matters, this brief thought experiment may be useful: would you care if there were 10 women Supreme Court Justices in the UK and only one man? If not, then you were probably not concerned that the ratio up to recently (2017) was exactly the reverse of that, one woman to 10 men (there was a vacancy on the Supreme Court). If, on the other hand, it feels wrong to you to have such an unequal gender balance in our most senior court, then it is worth considering why so many people do not see a difficulty with our current gender composition.

DISCUSSION

The business case has appeal within the practising profession and has led to many of the initiatives in Debate 1 being introduced and with some benefits for women. However, the positive messages about equality may be reduced to a profit-and-loss calculation if the business case is the only foundation for these measures. The rule of law case has greater appeal, but is at the mercy of the quality of the discussion about 'merit' and 'talent' and the people who make assessments about who is allowed to enter and be promoted. 'Merit' and 'talent' are slippery concepts that we can only really get at via proxies, and proxies are blunt and can be applied with limited discretion, giving rise to discriminatory outcomes. The gender effect on substantive decision-making – whether women decide cases or practise law differently to men – is unproved but, given the evidence on unconscious bias, it is likely that people with different experiences may have different unconscious biases. Biases tend to have

---

[33] Kate Malleson, 'Diversity in the judiciary: The case for positive action' (2009) 36 *Journal of Law and Society* 376.

[34] Hunter, 'More than just a different face?' (n. 32) 123.

[35] In the context of judges see: Brenda Hale, 'A minority opinion?' (2008) 154 *Proceedings of the British Academy* 319; Brenda Hale and Rosemary Hunter, 'A conversation with Baroness Hale' (2008) 16 *Feminist Legal Studies* 237.

less traction when they are uncovered and challenged, so having a diverse leadership or decision-making team will probably lead to better, more evidenced and thoughtful decision-making. This makes for uncomfortable management discussions, but may be the key to making real strides in equality. It may, as a side-effect, lead to higher profits, it should bolster the rule of law, and it may also change the way we practise law, preside over courts and reach judgments.

CONCLUSION

These two debates illustrate some of the tensions associated with gender and the legal profession. As the figures make clear, there is a disjunction between the number of women graduating from law school and those who make it into some branches of the legal profession, and between the numbers who enter the professions and those who rise to the more senior status and leadership positions. This does not happen by chance; it is a product of choices by decision-makers (over other people's careers and their own), structural barriers and cultures. Over the past 30 years the legal professions have developed sophisticated statements and policies to create fairer practices and to some positive effect, but there remains much to do if we are to meet our commitment to the rule of law and work in professions that acknowledge the role that unconscious bias plays and actively manage that to the benefit of all.

FURTHER READING

Rosemary Hunter, 'More than just a different face? Judicial diversity and decision-making' (2015) 68 *Current Legal Problems* 119.

Clare McGlynn, 'The status of women lawyers in the United Kingdom' in Ulrike Schultz and Gisela Shaw (eds), *Women in the World's Legal Professions* (Hart, 2003).

Hilary Sommerlad, 'The gendering of the professional subject: Commitment, choice and social closure in the legal profession' in Clare McGlynn (ed.), *Legal Feminisms – Theory and Practice* (Dartmouth, 1998).

Lisa Webley and Liz Duff, 'Women solicitors as a barometer for problems within the legal profession – time to put values before profits?' (2007) 34 *Journal of Law and Society* 374.

Lisa Webley, Jennifer Tomlinson, Daniel Muzio, Hilary Sommerlad and Liz Duff, 'Access to a career in the legal profession in England and Wales: Race, class and the role of educational background' in Robert Nelson, Spencer Headworth, Ronit Dinovitzer and David Wilkins (eds), *Diversity in Practice: Rhetoric or Reality* (Cambridge University Press, 2016).

INDEX

A

ab initio bargaining, 138

ABK v *KDT & FGH*, 17

abortion, decriminalisation issues
Abortion Act 1967, legal framework, 127–8
arguments for, 128–30
decision-making, gender and, 126–7
medicalisation of, 128
methods of, 129
Northern Ireland and, 130–1
Offences Against the Person Act (OAPA) 1861, law against, 127–8
self-administered, 130–1

Abortion Act 1967, legal framework, 127–9

accountability, corporate governance and, 137–8

Act for Shortening the Language Used in Acts of Parliament, 173

administrative law
judicial review, gender and, 32–3
public interest litigation and, 31

affirmative action (positive action) workplace rights and, 115–6

agency theory, shareholder value and, 137, 141–2

agreement by choice, 39–40

Agreement on Trade-Related Aspects of Intellectual Property Rights (TRIPS agreement), 149, 150, 155

alimony, 96–7

all-black shortlists, 30

all-women shortlists (AWS)
arguments against, 29–31
political parties and, 27–8

ambiguity, in law, 169

AMP v *Persons Unknown*, 17

Anglo-American corporate model, 134–5

Anitha, Sundari, 46

anonymity, in tort law, 18

anti-discrimination law, 73–4

Anti-Social Behaviour, Crime and Policing Act 2014, forced marriage offence, 43

apartheid, 90

Aristotle, 60

Ashworth, Andrew, 40

Asian and minority ethnic (BAME) community, under-representation, 30

asset division, formal equality divorce and, 96–101

Association Littéraire et Artistique International (ALAI), 155

Astor, Nancy, 178

Astor (Lord), 178

Atkinson (Lord), 32

Auchmuty, Rosemary, 55–7, 63, 65, 173–183, 198–210

Australian High Court, 68, 69–70

authentic intention, 67

autonomy
bodily, abortion and, 129–30
contract law and, 8
healthcare, gender and, 121–2.
See also healthcare, gender and

AWS. *See* all-women shortlists

B
Bainbridge, Stephen, 136
Baird v *M&S*, 11
Baker J, 124
BAME. *See* Asian and minority ethnic
    (BAME) communities
Bamforth, Nicholas, 75
Barad, Karen, 165
Bartow, Ann, 157
Barwa, Sharmishta, 154
Batlan, Felice, 182–3
'battered women's syndrome', 193
Bebb v *Law Society*, 168, 174, 175,
    177, 180
bedroom tax, 34
benefit cap cases, 34–5
Beresford-Hope v *Lady Sandhurst*, 174
Berlant, Lauren, 1, 8
Berle, Ann, 135–6
Berne Convention, 149, 155
best interests test, medical
    decision-making, 124–5, 126
Bevacqua, Maria, 203
biases, legal profession third wave
    initiatives, 215–16
Bilkhu, Rani, 46
binarism, 186
binary gender division, 208–9
Birkenhead (Lord), 177
Birks, Michael, 180
Blackham, Alysia, 67
Blair, Tony, 29
Blair's Babes, 29
Blakely, Megan, 157
Bleak House (Dickens), 62
board room participation, gender and
    diversity argument for female, 145–6
    social justice arguments for, 146–7
    See also corporate governance
bodily autonomy, healthcare and, 121–2.
    See also healthcare, gender and
boilerplate, 7–8
'born this way' same-sex marriage
    and, 202
Brazier, Margaret, 130
breaches of contracts, 11–12
Bree [2007], 39–41
British Medical Association, 129
Browne-Wilkinson (Lord), 67–8

Busby, Nicole, 112
business debts, 67

C
Campaign for Justice on Divorce, 97
Campbell, Angus, 77
capacity
    best interests test, 124–5
    criticisms, 48–40
    drunken consent and, 39–40
    Medical Capacity Act, 123–5
    medical consent and, 123.
        See also healthcare, gender and
capacity assessments, gender and, 123–4
Capers, Bennett, 80
capital, shareholder, 138–9
capitalism
    contracts and, 2, 8
    risk-taking in, 6
capital transfers, divorce and, 96–7
carers, unpaid, 110
caring, as women's work, 112
Cartesian metaphor, law, 166
Cases, 55
    Bebb v *Law Society*, 168, 174, 175,
        177, 180
    Beresford-Hope v *Lady Sandhurst*, 174
    Bree [2007], 39–40, 40–1
    Charman v *Charman*, 99
    child welfare, 103–4, 106
    Chorlton v *Lings*, 174–6, 177
    *Committee for Privileges. Viscountess
        Rhondda's Claim*, 174, 176–8
    D an Sweden v *Council*, 77
    Dekker, 72–3
    Earl of Oxford's case (1615), 60, 63
    Edwards v *the Attorney-General for
        Canada*, 174
    Eves v *Eves*, 61
    Garcia v *National Australian Bank*,
        68
    Gobil v *Gobil*, 100
    Grant, 77, 78, 79
    Hall v *Incorporated Society of Law
        Agents in Scotland*, 174
    Hertz, 72–3
    H v *H.* [EWHC], 99
    Jex-Blake v *Senatus*, 174, 183

Jones v *Kernott*, 53–4
Kamki, 44
Lloyds Bank v *Rosset*, 53
Louth v *Diprose*, 69–70
Maistrellis, 113
In the Matter of the L-W Children, 105
McFarlane v *McFarlane*, 98
Miller v *Miller*, 98
Montgomery v *Lanarkshire Health Board (Scotland)* [2015], 125–6
Nairn v *Scottish Universities*, 174
O'Brien, 67–8
Olugboja (1982), 38–9, 40–1
Pettitt v *Pettitt*, 66
P v *S*, 76–7
Radmacher, 101
Re L, 106
Re MB [1997], 124
Roberts v *Hopwood*, 31–2
Roca Alverez, 113
Royal Bank of Scotland v *Etridge*, 55
R v *A (no. 2)*, 33–4
R v *Bourne*, 130–1
R v *Secretary of State for Work and Pensions*, 34
Sharland v *Sharland*, 100
Sheffield City Council v *E and another* [2004], 124–5
Short v *Poole Corporation*, 32
St. George's Healthcare NHS Trust v *S* [1999], 123
Stack v *Dowden*, 53–4, 65
University Hospital NHS Trust v *CA* [2016], 124
White v *White*, 98
women as persons, legal history, 173–8
Yerkey v *Jones*, 68
Cave, Emma, 130
Chan, Winnie, 113–4
change, lobbying, litigation and, 31
Charlesworth, Hilary, 83–4, 88, 93
Charman v *Charman*, 99
child abuse, custody and, 106
Child Arrangements Programme, 107–8
child contact
   agreement-seeking arrangement programme, 107–8
   parental gender and, 102
Children Act 1989, 104, 124
Children and Family Court Advisory and Support Service (Cafcass) officers, lawyers, 105, 107
Childs, Sarah, 29
child welfare, divorce and, 97
   domestic violence, child abuse and, 105–7
   legal considerations, 104–7
   legal protections, changes in, 107–8
   parental contact, importance, 103–4
Chinkin, Christine, 83–4, 93
choice, freedom and capacity and, 39–40
   criticisms, 40–2
   definitions, 37–8
choice, working/homemaking *v.* divorce and, 99
Chorlton v *Lings*, 174–7
Church of England, 177
Citron, Danielle Keats, 15
civilisation theory, law, 179–80
civil liability, Human Rights Act filling gaps, 22–23
Civil Partnership Act, 200
civil remedies, forced marriage and, 44
'clean break' orders, divorce and, 97
Cleveland, Arthur Rackham, 179
Codes of Corporate Governance, UK, 144
Coetzee, J. M., 194
cohabitation, property and, 52–4
   equity, gender and, 61
   equity doctrine of undue influence and, 54–6
   financial contributions, gender and, 53–4
Coleridge QC, 175
colonialism, 8
Color Purple, The (Walker), 191
Cominelli, Francesca, 157
Commissioner of Police of the Metropolis v *DSD and another*, 19
Committee for Privileges. Viscountess Rhondda's Claim, 174, 176–8
common intention, property co-ownership and, 52–4
community-based forms of creation, 159
Community anti-discrimination law, 73–4

Community of property, 97
Companies Act 2006, 136
company law
    regulatory structures, 138
    contractual relationships, 141–2
    See also shareholder value (SV),
        corporate governance
competency, medical consent and, 123.
    See also healthcare, gender and
Conaghan, Joanne, 60, 161–172
Concept of Law (Hart), 167
conflict, child harm and, 104–5
Congress of Authors and Artists, 155
consent
    autonomy, healthcare and, 122–3
    definitions of, 40–2
    drunken, 38–40
    forced marriage and, 42. *See also* forced
        marriage *entries*
    freedom and capacity, choice and,
        37–8
    informed, medical decision-making,
        125–6
    law and, 169–70
    reluctant acquiescence, 38–9
    tort law and, 18
    See also healthcare, gender and
consequential reasoning, judges and,
    170–1
Conservative party, gender quotas, 27
Conservative Women's Organisation, 28
constructive trust, 53
context
    contracts, 3, 8
    language, gender and, 176
    workplace rights, gender equality and,
        113
Contostavlos v *Mendahun*, 16
contract law, 1
    autonomy in, 8
    contracts *v.*, 10–11
    equity in, 6
    intentions and, 2, 3
    privity in, 8
    regulation and, 2
    sovereignty in, 8
contracts, 1
    Baird v *M&S*, 11
    boilerplate, 7–8

breaches of, 11–12
capitalism and, 2, 8
company law and, 138, 141–2.
    See also shareholder value (SV),
        corporate governance
context, 3, 8
contract law *v.*, 10–11
court's role in, 5
expectations of foresight and, 7
family relationships in, 9–10
freedom of, 1–12, 142
gender inequality in, 3–4
as node in relationships, 9–10
power in, 3–6, 11–12
reclaiming market behaviour, 10
relational theory of, 8–12
social relationships and, 142
structural inequalities in, 4–6
uncertainty in, 6–8
contrary intention, 64, 66
control
    ownership, shareholder value an,
        135–8
    tort, reclaiming through, 15, 23
    See also power
Convention for the Safeguarding of the
    Intangible Cultural Heritage (ICH),
    156–7
Convention on the Elimination of All
    Forms of Discrimination Against
    Women (CEDAW), 90–1, 115–6
Coombe, Rosemary J., 159
co-ownership, legal title and
    cohabitation, 52–4
copyright law
    community-based forms of creation
        and, 159
    culturally developed creativity and,
        156–7
    EU, 159
    fair use doctrine (US), 158
    fan fiction and, 158
    infringement, 16n13
    intangible cultural and, 156–7
    knitting pattern protection by, 156
    by men for men, 157–8
    profit-focused, 156
    quilting and, 156
    women and, 155–9

Copyright, Designs and Patents Act 1988
    (UK), 158
Cornell, Drucilla, 131
corporate governance
    altering shareholder focus, 142–3
    Anglo-American model of, 134–5
    board room participation, gender
        and, 143–5. *See also* board room
        participation, gender and
    EU board room participation, gender
        and, 144–5
    male domination of, 133–4
    shareholder value, gendered
        ownership/control and, 135–8
    share price movement, board room
        diversity and, 145
    social responsibility, 139, 145
    See also shareholder value (SV),
        corporate governance
corporate social responsibility (CSR),
    139, 145
Court of Justice of the EU
    quotas, binding gender, 117
    workplace rights, gender and, 112–3
courts
    contract law and, 5, 7
    contracts, duties, 11
    duties of care in domestic abuse, 21–4
    gender composition of, 220
coverture, reign of, 186
Cowan, David, 49
Cox, Jo, 30
craft-based activities, 156
Craig, Carys J., 159
Creasy, Stella, 131
creativity
    culturally developed, 156–7
    industrial production and, 154–5
Criminal Justice and Public Order Act
    1994, 38
criminal law, tort law and, 13, 15
criminal offence, forced marriage as.
        See forced marriage *entries*
cross-dressing, 199
cultural issue, forced marriage as, 45–6
culturally developed creativity, 156–7
cultural norms, gender-discriminatory,
    187
cultural ownership, 157

cultural patrimony, 156
culture
    belief systems and, 185–6
    discrimination and, 91
    sexual violence failed by, 187–91
Cunliffe, Emma, 167
custody, child. *See* child contact

D
Daily Mail (news), 100
data protection, 16n13
D and Sweden v *Council*, 77
Davies, Margaret, 167
Davies review, 119
decision-making
    consequential reasoning and, 170–1
    gender and, 62–3, 220–1
    legal reasoning and, 170
    medical capacity, gender and, 123–4
    unconscious biases and, 215–16
declarations of trust, property ownership
    and, 54
Dekker, 72–3
Denning (Lord), 53, 61
Department of Business, Innovation, and
    Skills, 109
Derry, Caroline, 37–47
Dialectic of Sex, The (Firestone), 154
Diamond, Lisa, 203
Dicey, A. V., 25
Dickens, Charles, 62
Diduck, Alison, 95–108
difference-based employment legislation,
    113–4
Ding, Waverly W., 153
direct financial contributions, resulting
    trust and, 65–6
director primacy, shareholder value and,
    136
disability, gender as legal, 186
discretion, 63
discrimination
    apartheid, 90
    custom/culture, as basis for, 91
    divorce, financial orders and, 98–9
    'due regard' and, 33
    European Convention on Human
        Rights and, 33

discrimination (*Continued*)
  feminist science fiction, hegemony
    and, 194–6
  Gender Recognition Act, 208
  legal profession and, 212–13, 219.
    See also legal profession
  pernicious, 118
  positive, reverse, 29, 116, 118
  pregnancy discrimination as sex, 72–5
  salary, 134
  sexual orientation and, 76–81
  special equity for women and, 68–9
diversity
  argument for female boardroom,
    145–6
  legal profession and. *See* legal
    profession
  legal reasoning and, 171–2
divorce
  child contact, gender and, 102
  child welfare and, 97, 103–8. *See also*
    child welfare, divorce and
  financial orders, fairness and, 98–9
  gender pay gap, settlements and,
    100–1
  money, asset division and, 96–101
  poverty, older women and, 101
  shareholder capital settlements and,
    139
  substantive equality *v.*, 100
    See also marriage *entries*
Divorce Reform Act 1969, 96–7
doctors, as abortion gatekeepers, 127–8
doctrine of precedent, 181
domestic abuse
  gender and, 20
  government response to, 20–1, 20n35
  tort as redress for, 13, 21–4
domestic violence
  child welfare and, 105–7
  mediation and, 108
  reporting, 32
  statistics, 188–9
Donnelly, Mary, 122
Douglas, Gillian, 52
drunken consent, 38–41
drunken intention, 41
'due regard', 33

Dunn LJ, 38–9
duress, in contract law, 5–6
duties, imposing on contracts, 11
duty of care, domestic abuse and, 21–4
Dworkin, Ronald, 169, 170

E
Earl of Oxford's case (1615), 60, 63
Easton, Catherine, 149–160
'economic atomism' of markets, 9–10
Edwards v *the Attorney-General for
  Canada*, 174
Ellesmere (Lord Chancellor), 60
Ellis, Evelyn, 73–4
emotional dependency, 69–70
employees, pension funds, 141
employment contract, 142
employment legislation, difference base,
  113–4
England, abortion in, 127–8
Enright, Máiréad, 1–12
Enron, 13, 136–7
Equalities and Human Rights
  Commission (EHRC), 100
equality
  between contractual subjects, 3–4
  gender, marriage and, 205
  LGBT persons and, 207
  numerical, workplace rights and,
    117–8
Equality Act 2010, 33, 66, 110, 116,
  119, 200, 208
Equality and Human Rights
  Commission, 109
equality of outcome, 144
equality through rights, 89
equal justice, presumption of
  advancement and, 65
equal merit, 215
equal misery argument, 78, 79
equal pay, 31–2, 117
Equal Pay Act 1970, 117
Equal Treatment Directive, 72, 112–3
equitable doctrines, special treatment,
  women, 64
equitable interest, property
  and, 52–4

equity
  in contract law, 6
  ethic of care and, 62–4
  as female, 60–2
  law *v.*, 63–4
  presumption of advancement and, 64–7
  rescission and, 67–70
  workplace, 32
equity capital, 139
Equity Stirring (Watt), 61
ethic of care, equity and, 62–4
ethic of rights, male legal reasoning, 62
EU. *See* European Union
European Commission, 143
European Convention on Human Rights, 16, 33, 66
European Court of Human Rights, Article 14 and, 33–4
European Court of Justice (ECJ), 72–5, 76–8
European Union (EU)
  board room participation, gender and, 143–4
  Charter of Fundamental Rights, 76–7
  Copyright Directive, 159
  sex discrimination, pregnancy discrimination as, 72–5
  sexual orientation discrimination, as sexual discrimination, 76–81
  Treaty on European Union, 116, 116n35
Everard, Amye, 151
Evershed, Raymond (Lord), 61
Everyday Sexism Project, 109
Eves v *Eves*, 61
exploitative contracts, 67
express trust, property ownership and, 53

F
fairness principle, divorce and, 98–9
'families of choice', same-sex marriage, 203
family-controlled companies, 144
family law
  child arrangement orders, divorce and, 104–7
  child welfare, maintenance an, 97

female activism, reform and, 95–6
  poverty in older women, divorce and, 101
  privacy an, 96
Family Law Act 1996, forced marriage and, 42–3
family life, women in politics and, 29
family relations, contracts and, 9–10
fan fiction, copyright law and, 158
fatherhood, workplace rights and, 112–3
father's rights groups, child custody and, 102, 104
female, equity as, 60–2
female activism, legal reform and, 95–6
Female Equity, stereotype, 61
female genital mutilation, 124, 189
feminine jurisprudence, 59, 62–3
feminism, 3–4, 165, 168, 194–6, 206
  human rights, gender inequality and, 92–3
  international legal norms and, 87–9
  law as gendered theory, 162–3
  same-sex marriage rhetoric and, 203
  writing legal history and, 181
'Feminist approaches to international law' (Charlesworth, Chinkin & Wright), 83–4
feminist legal theory, 88
fertility, equity as female and, 61–2
fiction, rape and, 191–3
financial contributions, property ownership and, 53–4
financialisation, shareholder value and, 136–7, 139–40
Financial Times Stock Market (FTSE), 109
Firestone, Shulamith, 154
'fixed claimant', 141
Fletcher, Ruth, 125
flexibility, 63
forced marriage
  Anti-Social Behaviour, Crime and Policing Act 2014 and, 43
  debate, 42–3
  opposition to, 45–7
  prosecution of, 46–7
  why created, necessary, 44
Forced Marriage Unit (FMU), 42

For (Coetzee), 194
formal equality
    asset division divorce and, 96–101
    equal treatment and, 118
    marriage and, 206
Fowler, Karen Joy, 195–6
Fox, Marie, 121–132
Franks, Mary Anne, 15
freedom and capacity, Sexual Offences
        Act 2003
    criticisms, 40–2
    definitions, 37–40
freedom of contract, 1–8
    relational contract theory and, 8–12
    shareholder value and, 142
Frug, Mary Joe, 141

G
Gan, Orit, 5
Garcia v *National Australian Bank*, 68
gay men, 199. *See also* LGBT persons;
        sexuality, gender and
Gelpern, Anna, 7
gender
    board room participation and, 143–4.
        See also board room participation,
        gender and
    capacity assessments and, 123–4
    definitions, xiii–xv, 199
    domestic abuse and, 20
    equitable doctrine of undue influence
        and, 55–6
    female lawyers, importance, 218–20
    financial contributions, property
        ownership and, 53–4
    force marriage and, 43
    healthcare and. *See* healthcare, gender
        and
    intellectual property and, 150
    international society, leadership and,
        84–7
    justice, divorce and, 97
    leadership, underrepresentation of
        women, 84–7
    legal academics and, 133–4. *See also*
        corporate governance
    Legal Aid and, 32
    legal disability, 186

    legislative quotas, in politics, 26–7
    murder and, 189
    other, women as, 194–6
    Parliament composition and, 25–31
    political party, quotas and, 27
    preferential treatment, workplace, 118
    presumption of trust, relationship *v.*,
        66–7
    public interest litigation and, 31–5
    quotas, politics and. *See* quotas
    sexuality and. *See* sexuality, gender and
    sexual offense definitions and, 38
    sexual orientation discrimination and,
        78
    sexual violence victimhood and, 188
    social ordering and, 166–7
    social structure of, 164
    tort law and, 13–24
    trans persons and, 208–9
    voting rights, parliamentary, 174–6
    vulnerability in bargaining, 7–8
    women as persons, legal history, 173–8
gender balance, arguments for improving
        political, 29
gender-based violence, 33–4.
        See also consent; domestic violence
'gender collusion', 196
gender discrimination, maternity leave as,
        72–81. *See also* sex discrimination,
        pregnancy discrimination as
gender-discriminatory cultural norms, 187
gender dysphoria, 208
gendered jurisprudence, equity as female,
        60–2
gendered law, 161–7. *See also* law, as
        gendered
gender identity, 208–9
gender inequality
    contracts and, 3–4, 9
    difference-based employment
        legislation, 113–4
    human rights, international society
        and, 89–93
gender justice, 33
gender-neutral workplace rights, 110,
        111. *See also* workplace rights
        gender-neutral/gender-specific
gender norms, 161, 208–9
gender pay gap, 100–1

gender quotas, 116
gender reassignment surgery, 76–7, 208
Gender Recognition Act, 208–9
gender-specific workplace rights, 110, 111. *See also* workplace rights gender-neutral/gender-specific
general jurisprudence, 161
General Medical Council (GMC), 126–7
Gentlemen of the Law (Birks), 180
Gibson-Graham, J. K., 9–10
gifts, rescission and, 67–70
Gill, Aisha K., 46
Gilligan, Carol, 62, 63
Gilman, Charlotte Perkins, 194
Global Financial Crisis, 13, 140, 146
Gobil v *Gobil*, 100
government regulation, 2
Grant v *South-West Trains*, 76n28, 77, 78, 79
Green, Les, 164
Greffe, Xavier, 157
Guardian (news), 47
Gulati, Mitu, 7

H
Halbert, Deborah, 150, 154, 156
Haldane (Lord), 177
Hale (Lady), 34–5, 54, 65–6, 101
Halliday, Samantha, 124
Hall v *Incorporated Society of Law Agents in Scotland*, 174
Hammon, Philip, 131
Handmaid's Tale, The, 191
harassment
    image-based sexual abuse and, 17
    tort law and, 17
Haraway, Donna, 196
Hardy, Thomas, 191–3, 196
Hargreaves report, 158
Harrison, Christine, 106, 107
Harry Potter Lexicon (fan fiction), 158
Hart, H. L. A., 167, 169
healthcare, gender and
    abortion, decriminalisation of. *See* abortion, decriminalisation issues
    autonomy and, 121–2
    best interests test, 124–5
    consent and, 122–3

informed consent and, 125–6
    Medical Capacity Act, 123–5
Heathcote, Gina, 87
hegemony, feminist science fiction and, 194–6
herbal medicines, 155
Hertz, 72
Hinsliff, Gaby, 210
home ownership, 140
homosexuality, legal issues, 199–200.
    See also sexuality, gender and
Honkala, Nora, 83–94
Horsey, Kirsty, 13–24
Horton, Rachel, 109–120
House of Commons
    gender composition, 26
    Science and Technology Committee, 129
    Women and Equalities Committee, 28
    See also Parliament
House of Lords
    Committee for Privileges, 177
    gender composition, 26
    Life Peerages Act, 178
    Poplar Borough Council and, 31–2
    women's right to stand for, 176–8
    See also Parliament
Hudson, Alistair, 62–3
Hugo, Victor, 155
Human Fertilisation and Embryology Bill, 129
human rights
    abortion availability and, 131
    feminists, equality and, 92–3
    gender inequality and, 89–93
Human Rights Act 1998 (HRA), 22, 33, 96
Hunt, Jennifer, 153–4
Hunt, Joan, 106, 107
H v *H.* [EWHC], 99

I
'identities', non-traditional (LGBT), 207
image-based sexual abuse
    bespoke tort for, 14–19
    defined, 14, 18
    harassment remedy, 17
    privacy remedy, 16–17
    tort as redress, 13, 15

In a Different Voice (Gilligan), 62
incapacity, women's legal, 176
Independent Office for Police Conduct
    (IOPC), 21
industrial production, creativity and,
    154–5
Industrial Revolution, 174, 176
inequality
    gender, international human rights
        and, 89.
    workplace, gender and, 54
    See also human rights, gender
        inequality and
informed consent
    medical decision-making, 125–6
    test of materiality, 125
    See also healthcare, gender and
inheritance
    board room continuity and, 144
    shareholder capital and, 139
inheritance tax, same-sex marriage and,
    202–3
intangible cultural property, 156–7
intangible property, 149. *See also*
    intellectual property (IP)
intellectual property (IP)
    Annual Report of the Commissioner
        of Patents from 1870–1940 (USA),
        152, 155
    copyright law and, 155–9. *See also*
        copyright law
    gender an, 150
    global economic importance, 149
    industrial production, creativity and,
        154–5
    intangible cultural, 156–7
    knitting pattern protection, 156
    legal definitions, 149–50
    patents, first female holders of, 151
intention
    drunken, 41
    rescission and, 67–70
'internalised sexism', 196
International Convention on the
    Elimination on All Forms of Racial
    Discrimination (ICERD), 90–1
International Court of Justice (ICJ)
    gender, racial inequalities and, 90
    leadership, women and, 85–6

International Day of Zero Tolerance for
    Female Genital Mutilation 2016, 189
international law norms, feminists and,
    87–9
international society
    gender inequality, human rights and,
        89–93
    leadership, underrepresentation of
        women and, 84–7
    legal norms, feminists and, 87–9
Internet
    fan fiction, copyright law and, 158
    social media, sexist abuse on, 30
intersectionality
    gender, property relations and, 56–7
    legal profession, gender, race, sexual
        orientation, 214
inter vivos gifts, 67
In the Matter of the L-W Children, 105
intoxicated complainant, 41
intoxicated defendant, 41
intoxication
    consent and, 38–40
    involuntary, rape and, 40
invention, innovation, patents and,
    150–1
inventors, female patent holders and, 151
involuntary intoxication, 40
IP. *See* intellectual property (IP)
irrationality, consent and, 124
irrebuttable presumptions, 38

J
James, Grace, 113
Jana International, 46
Jenner, Caitlyn, 209
Jex-Blake v *Senatus*, 174, 183
Johns, Fleur, 6
joint ownership, ensuring, 54
Jones v *Kernott*, 53–4
judges
    consequential reasoning and, 170–1
    fallibility/infallibility of, 168–9
    women, views on and, 31–2
Judicature Act 1973, 61
Judicial Appointments Commission
    (JAC), 214
judicial review, gender and, 32–3

Junior, James Tiptree, 195
jurisdiction
    boardroom diversity and, 145–6
    board room quotas and, 144
    homosexuality legalities and, 200
jurisprudence
    defined, 161
    law, as gendered, 161–7. *See also* law,
        as gendered
    women victims, turned perpetrators,
        190
jurisprudence of equity, gender and
    ethic of care and, 62–4
    female, equity as, 60–2
    stereotype, femininity and, 61–2

K
Kaganas, Felicity, 95–108, 105
Kahler, Annette, 153–4
Kamiki, 41
Kapur, Ratna, 91
Katyal, Sonia, 158
Kelly, Joan B., 103
Kennedy, Duncan, 168–9, 169
Khan, Bibi Zorina, 152–3
Kies, Mary, 151
King, Michael, 104–5
Kirby J, 68–9
knitting patterns as IP, 156
Knop, Karen, 88–9
Koppelman, Andrew, 79–80
Koskenniemi, Martti, 88

L
Labour Party, gender quotas, 27
Lacey, Nicola, 41, 85, 162
land-based capital, 139
language
    Lord Brougham's Act, parliament and,
        174–6
    reality and, 165
Lardy, Heather, 77
law
    ambiguity in, 169
    civilisation theory of, 179–80
    conceptual structures of, 166
    context of, 165

females, in legal profession and, 219
    infallibility of, 168–9
    modernism/postmodernism and, 165
    morality and, 161
    political as, 168–9
    reform, female activism and, 95–6
    same-sex marriage and, 201
    sexual orientation and, 199–200.
        See also sexuality, gender and
    sexual violence failed by, 187–91
    tort. *See* tort law
law, as gendered
    Cartesian metaphor of, 166
    concept of, scholarship on, 162–3
    connectedness of, material life and, 167
    judges, fallibility/infallibility of, 168–9
    legal reasoning, 170
    objective knowledge, 165
    power and, 163–4
    social construction, 164
    social ordering, gender, 166–7
law, literature and
    defining concepts in, 185–7
    feminist science fiction, hegemony and,
        194–6
    personhood, denial of, 193–4
    rape, fact/fiction and, 191–3
    sexual violence, failed by culture and,
        187–91
Law Commission, 127
law-power relationship, 163–4
Law Society Gazette, 216
Lay, Ken, 13
leadership
    international underrepresentation of
        women in, 84–7
    romance of, 147
    social justice argument, female board
        room, 146–7
    women in corporate, 146
Legal Aid, Sentencing and Punishment of
    Offenders Act (LASPO), 32, 108
Legal Aid societies, 182–3
legal arguments, origins of, 169–70
legal disputes
    diversity, legal reasoning and, 171–2
    judges, consequential reasoning and,
        170–1
    law, infallibility of and, 168–9

legal history
  defining, 178–82
  marital rape, 186
  parliament, women's right to stand for,
    176–8
  women as persons, court cases, 173–8
legal incapacity, women and, 176
legal obligation, 167
legal personhood, 186–7
legal positivism, 161
legal profession
  alternative judgment, gender and,
    219–20
  biases, third-wave initiatives, 215–16,
    217
  diversity/inclusion initiatives first wave,
    213–14, 216–17
  equality/diversity initiatives, 212–13
  participation, second wave initiatives,
    214–15, 217
  traditional gender composition,
    211–12
  women lawyers make a difference,
    218–20
legal reasoning
  diversity and, 171–2
  gender and, 62–3, 170
legal systems, violence against women
    and, 190
legal title, property, cohabitation and,
    51–4
legislation, gender difference
    employment, 113–4
lenders
  co-ownership and, 53
  financial crisis responsibility of,
    139–40
lesbian women, 199. See also LGBT
    persons; sexuality, gender and; sexual
    orientation
Lester (Lord), 66
Levi-Strauss hypothesis, 186
Lewis, Jane, 112
LGBT persons, 76–7
  Gender Recognition Bill, 208–9
  identity, 209–10
  policy statements and, 206–7
  support alliances with, equality/justice
    and, 207

See also gay men; lesbian women;
    sexual orientation discrimination, as
    sexual discrimination
liability of sureties, 67–8
Liberal Democrats, AWS and, 28
liberal political theory, human rights and,
    91–2
Life Peerages Act, 178
life peers, 176–8
limited formal equity, women in
    leadership and, 85
Lindsey, Jaime, 121–132
Linzer, Peter, 9
literature, law and, 185–7. See also law,
    literature and
Lixinski, Lucas, 157
Lloyds Bank v Rosset, 53
Local Government Act, 199–200
Lord Brougham's Act, gender and legal
    language, 173, 174–6
Louth v Diprose, 69–70

M
Macaulay, Stewart, 10
MacCormick, Neil, 169, 170
MacKinnon, Catharine, 41–2, 84, 93,
    162–3, 166
Macleod, Alison, 106, 107
Macneil, Ian, 10
maintenance, divorce and, 96–7
Maistrellis, 113
male, law as, 161–7. See also law, as
    gendered
Manchester, A. H., 180
Manji, Ambreena, 49–57
Mankind support group, 188
market citizenship, 140
markets
  contracts managing risk, 6–7
  'economic atomism' of, 9–10
  reclaiming relationality, 9–10, 12
  transactions, contracts as, 2
marriage
  equitable doctrines, remedies and,
    64–70. See also equitable doctrines
    gender and
  female patent holders and, 151
  forced. See forced marriage entries

gendered expectations, 203–4
gender equality and, 205
historical definitions, 200–1
legal privileges, inheritance tax, 202–3
legal protection of, 203
prenuptial agreements, 99
rape, law and, 170–1
same-sex, 200–6. *See also* same-sex
   marriage
See also divorce *entries*
Marriage (Same Sex Couples) Act, 200
Married Women's Property Acts 1870
   and 1882, 70
Marx, Karl, 1–2
maternity leave
   gender discrimination, 72–5
   gender-specific right, 111
   See also sex discrimination, pregnancy
   discrimination as
Matrimonial Causes Act (MCA) 1973,
   42–3, 97, 98
Matrimonial Proceedings and Property
   1970, 96–7
MCA. *See* Matrimonial Causes Act
   (MCA) 1973
McCandless, Julie, 125
McFarlane v *McFarlane*, 98
McGlynn, Clare, 14, 18
McKinsey, Catalyst and Reiby Institute,
   218
McNaghten J., 131
Means, Gardner C., 135–6
mediation, domestic violence and, 108
medical abortions, 129
Medical Capacity Act 2005 (MCA),
   123–5
medical decision-making
   abortion, gender and, 126–7
   capacity to consent and, 123–5
   informed consent and, 125–6
medicalization of abortion, 128
medical paternalism, 122, 128
medical treatment, consent and, 122–3.
   See also healthcare, gender and
Mellish QC, 175
mental capacity, healthcare decisions and,
   124–5. *See also* healthcare, gender
   and
Mental Capacity Act (MCA), 128

mental disabilities, autonomy and, 122
mental health, gender dysphoria and,
   208
mentoring, 116
Merchant of Venice (Shakespeare), 60
merit-based hiring
   equal merit, 215
   as unfair, 118–9
'Method in International Law', 88
Michael v *Chief Constable of South Wales
   Police*, 21–22, 24
military force, women and, 87
Mill, John Stuart, 174
Miller v *Miller*, 98
minority communities
   forced marriage and, 45–6
   sexual, 200. *See also* sexuality, gender
   and
   under-representation of, 30
Mitropoulos, Angela, 6
modernism, law and, 165
Modern Legal History (Manchester), 180
Mohanty, Chandra, 89, 91
money, asset division formal equality and,
   96–101
Montgomery v *Lanarkshire Health Board
   (Scotland)* [2015], 125–6
morality, law and, 161
moral value, abortion and, 130
mortgage lending, undue influence and,
   55–6
motherhood, workplace rights and,
   112–3
'motive moderation', 62
Mulcahy, Linda, 6
murder
   gender and, 189
   tort law and, 19–20
Murray, Jenni, 210
Murray, Rainbow, 30
myths, rape, 41–2

N
Naffine, Ngaire, 162
Nairn v *Scottish Universities*, 174
Namibia Advisory Opinion, 90
National Health Service (NHS), 126
natural law, 161

natural realism, social constructivism *v.*, 165
Nedelsky, Jennifer, 92
negligence, domestic abuse and, 19–23
'New Directions in Feminism and Human Rights', 89
Nicholls (Lord), 98
Nirvana, Karma, 44
non-binary gender identity, 208–9
non-essentialist conception, law, 166
Northern Ireland
    abortion in, 127–8, 130–1
    same-sex marriage in, 200
Northern Ireland Assembly, gender composition, 26
Northern Ireland Court of Appeal, 131
numerical equality, workplace rights and, 117–8

O
objective knowledge, 165
O'Brien, 67–8
O'Donovan, Katherine, 205
Offences Against the Person Act (OAPA), abortion legality and, 127–8, 130–1
Office for National Statistics (ONS), 188
Olugboja (1982), 38–9, 40–1
'ordinary citizen', 167
'other', women as, 194–6
Otto, Dianne, 91, 92
ownership
    cultural, 157
    property, parliamentary voting rights and, 174

P
Palmer, Stephanie, 92–3, 93
Pankhurst, Richard, 175
parental contact, divorce, child welfare and, 103–4
parental issues
    child contact, shared/equal, 115
    work leave, fathers and, 114–5, 115
    See also workplace rights, gender-neutral/gender-specific
Paris Convention, 149

Parliament
    composition of, gender and, 25–31
    improving gender balance, arguments for, 28–9
    women's right to stand for, 176–8
    women's right to vote for, 174–6
parliamentary elections, right to vote in, 174–6
passivity, in contracts, 2
Pateman, Carole, 3
patents
    Annual Report of the Commissioner of Patents from 1870–1940 (USA), 152
    first female holders of, 151
    intellectual property, 151
    lack of female diversity in, 153–4
    social patenting, 155
    utility categories of, women and, 152–3
    See also intellectual property (IP)
paternalistic model of medicin6, 124
pension funds, 141
pensions, poverty in older women and, 101
pernicious discrimination, 118
personhood
    denial of, 193–4
    hegemony, flight from and, 195
    legal, 186–7
persons, women as
    court case, voting rights and, 174–6
    legal history, 173, 178–82
    parliament, right to stand for, 176–8
Pettitt v *Pettitt*, 66
Phillips, Anne, 28
Piercy, Marge, 194
Piper, Christine, 104
Piška. Nick, 59–70
police
    duties of care, 21–4
    failure to protect, 13
    response to domestic abuse, 20–1
political participation, women and, 85
political parties
    all-women shortlists and, 27–8
    gender quotas for, 26–7
politics
    gender quotas for, 26–7

international human rights, gender
    inequality and, 92
law as, 168–9
Poplar Borough Council, 31–2
portfolio diversification, 140–1
positive action (affirmative action)
    quotas, binding gender, 116–7
    workplace rights and, 115–6, 118
positive discrimination, 29, 116, 118
Posner, Richard, 62
postmodernism, law and, 165
poverty, divorce, older women and, 101
power
    contracts and, 3–4, 11–12
    hierarchical, shareholders and, 140
    law and, 163–4
    male over women, 181, 205
    relationality and, 11–12
    See also control
preferential treatment, workplace, 118
pregnancy, discrimination sex
        discrimination against women, 72–5,
        112
    incidences of, 109
    medical decision-making, capacity and,
        124
    See also healthcare, gender and
prejudice, women in politics and, 30.
    See also discrimination entries
prenuptial agreements, 99
presumption of advancement, 59
    abolition of, Equality Act and, 66
    equitable doctrine and, 64–7
    relationship, gender v., 66–7
    resulting trust, gender-neutral
        presumption of, 65–6
presumptions, irrebuttable, 38
principle of equal treatment, 116
privacy
    family and, 96
    image-based sexual abuse and, 16–17
    tort law and, 16–17
privity, contract law and, 8
property
    intangible cultural, 156–7
    intangible/intellectual, 149–50
    shareholder capital as, 138–9
    voting rights and ownership, 174
    See also intellectual property (IP)

property, cohabitating couples and, 52–4
    disputes, 52–3
    doctrine of constructive trust, 53
    equitable doctrine of undue influence,
        mortgages and, 55–6
    express trust, 52
    gender, financial contributions and,
        53–4
    joint ownership, ensuring, 54
    mandatory declarations of trust, 54
    tyranny of the transaction and, 56
property-based capital, 138–9
property disputes, 52–3
property distribution, divorce and, 96–7.
    See also divorce entries
property transfers, presumption of
    advancement and, 64–7
protected categories, 33, 200
Protection from Harassment Act 1997,
    17
prudent man of business, 59
public interest litigation, gender and,
    31–5
public law theory, public interest
    litigation and, 31
P v S, 76–7

Q
Queen's Council, 214
Queen's Speech, 131
queer theory, 208. See also LBGT
        persons; sexuality, gender and
quilting patterns, as IP, 156
quotas
    binding gender, workplace and, 116–7
    board room participation, gender and,
        144–5
    discrimination, positive/reverse, 29
    gender in politics and, 26–7
    merit, gender and, 214–15
    objections to, 29–30
    'quota woman', 30

R
Rackley, Erika, 13–24
Radin, Margaret Jane, 2
Radmacher, 101

Rai, Shirin, 154
Rao, Arati, 91
rape
    abortion and, 131
    consent, intoxication and, 39–40
    defining, consent and, 38
    European Court of Human Rights
        and, 33
    fact, fiction and, 191–3
    involuntary intoxication, 40
    marital, law and, 170–, 186
    myths, impact of, 41
    no means no, seduction and, 190–1
    social norms, literature and, 191–3
    tort law for, 19–20
    victims-turned perpetrators, 38, 192–3
Razack, Sherene, 91
reality, language and, 165
rescission, equity and, 67–70
    special equity, women and, 68–9
    structural inequalities, 69–70
    unconscionable bargain, 69
regulation types, 2
Re L, 105
relational contract theory, 8–12
relationality markets, 11–12
relationships
    contracts as node, 9–10
    equality in roles, same-sex marriage
        and, 205–6
    male power over women, 181, 205
    presumption of trust, gender v., 66–7
    social, contracts and, 142
    structural inequality and, 69–70
religion, same-sex marriage and, 203
reluctant acquiescence, 38–9
Re MB [1997], 124
Representation of the People Act 1867,
    173, 175
'residual claimant', 141
resulting trust, gender-neutral
    presumption of, 65–6
revenge porn. See image-based sexual
    abuse
reverse discrimination, 29, 116, 118
Rhetoric (Aristotle), 60
Rhode, Deborah, 91
rights, equality through, 89. See also
    human rights, gender inequality and

rights-based litigation, 33
Rights of Women, 45
Roberts v Hopwood, 31–2
Robinson Crusoe, 194
Roca Alverez, 113
romance of leadership, 147
Room of One's Own, A (Woolfe), 193
Rotherham sexual exploitation, grooming
    scandal, 191–2
Royal Bank of Scotland v Etridge, 55
R v A (no. 2), 33–4
R v Bourne, 130–1
R v Secretary of State for Work and
    Pensions, 34

S
Sachs, Albie, 180–1
salary discrimination, 134
same-sex marriage
    arguments against, 203–5
    'born this way' argument, 202
    equality in relationship roles and, 205–6
    expectations, gendered of, 203–4
    gendered arguments in favor, 201–3
    historical marriage, 200–1
    inheritance tax and, 202–3
    religion and, 203
Samuels, Harriet, 25–35
Sanghera, Jasvinder, 44
Sarmas, Lisa, 66, 70
Scotland, abortion in, 127–8
Scott, Joan Wallach, 182
Scottish Nationalist Party (SNP), AWS
    and, 28
Scottish Parliament, gender composition,
    26
seduction, rape and, 190–1, 197
self-administered abortion, 130–1
self-regulation, 2
Separated Parent Information
    Programme (SPIP), 105
sex, as biological fact, 164
sex discrimination, pregnancy
    discrimination as
    arguments against, 73–5
    arguments in favour, 75
    biological feature unique to women, 75
    court cases, 72–5

Sex Discrimination Act 1975, 117
Sex Discrimination (Election Candidates) Act, 27
Sex Disqualification (Removal) Act 1919, 177, 212
sex equality, law and, 170
sexism, 180, 196
Sexism and the Law (Sachs & Wilson), 180–1
sexual abuse
   tort as redress, 13
   See also image-based sexual abuse; rape; sexual violence
sexual discrimination
   pregnancy and, 72–5
   sexual orientation and, 76–81
sexual harassment, 30
sexuality, gender and
   binary gender division, 208–9
   legal issues, 199–200
   LGBT community and, 206–10
   orientation as protected category, 200
   same-sex marriage, 200–6. *See also* same-sex marriage
   trans persons. *See* trans persons *entries*
Sexual Offences Act
   criticisms of, 40–2
   freedom and capacity, choice and, 37–40
sexual offences, victims-turned perpetrators, 38, 192–3
sexual orientation
   legal issues and, 199–200
   LGBT community, 206–10
   trans-identity and, 208–9
   See also LGBT persons; sexuality, gender and; trans persons
sexual orientation discrimination, as sexual discrimination
   arguments against, 78
   arguments for, 78–81
   EU and, 76–8
sexual violence
   dissociation and, 193
   failed by culture, law, 187–91
   men as victim of, 188
   social norms, rape and, 191–3
   victims-turned perpetrator, 38, 192–3
Shakespeare, William, 60

shared parental leave (SPL), 111
shareholder capital, 138–9
shareholder value (SV), corporate governance
   accountability and, 137–8
   agency theory and, 137, 141–2
   altering focus on, 142–3
   board room appointees and, 145
   company law, regulatory structures, 138
   contractual relationships, 141–2
   financialisation and, 136–7
   freedom of contract and, 142
   gender and, 138–43
   hierarchical power structure, 140
   ownership, control and, 135–8
   pension funds *v.*, 141
   portfolio diversification, 140–1
   UK Corporate Governance Code and, 137
   See also corporate governance
share price movement, board room diversity and, 145
Sharland v *Sharland*, 100
Sheffield City Council v *E and another* [2004], 124–5
Sheldon, Sally, 127, 129, 130
Shiva, Vandana, 155
Short v *Poole Corporation*, 32
Six Point Group, 177
Sjölin, Catarina, 39, 40
Skilling, Jeff, 13
slavery, as contract, 4n26
Smart, Carol, 89, 103
Smith, Charlotte, 151–2
Smith, Lionel, 63
social attitudes, legal change and, 180
social construction, law and, 164
social constructivism, natural realism *v.*, 165
social justice, female corporate leadership, 146–7
social media, sexist abuse on, 30
social norms
   marriage and, 200–1
   rape and, 191–3
social patenting, 155
social relationships, contracts and, 142
sovereignty, in contract law, 8

special disadvantages, 69
special equity, women, 68–9
special protection, rescission and, 67–8
Spender, Peta, 146
split responsibility, in contracts, 9
St. George's Healthcare NHS Trust v. S
    [1999], 123
Stack v *Dowden*, 53–4, 65
stereotypes
    behavior, male/female, 190
    custom, culture, discrimination
        and, 91
    gender, work-family reconciliation,
        110
    jurisprudence of equity and, 61–2
    sexual orientation, gender
        discrimination and, 79–80
structural inequalities
    contracts and, 4, 5–6
    relationships, rescission and, 69–70
student loan contracts, 5–6
Sturge/Glaser report, 104
submission, consent and, 38–9
substantive equality, formal *v.*, 100, 118,
    206
substantive equity, 68
supply contract, 142
Surviving the Breakup (Wallerstein &
    Kelly), 103
SV. *See* shareholder value (SV)
Sweden, parental leave in, 115

T
Talbot, Lorraine, 136
Tamanaha, Brian, 166
Temkin, Jennifer, 40
terms, contract, 2
Tesón, Fernado, 84–5
Tess of the d' Urbervilles (Hardy), 191–3
test of materiality, informed consent,
    125
theoretical physics, matter/meaning and,
    165
Thiara, Ravi, 106, 107
Thomas, David, 177
Tidwell, Patricia A., 9
Time and Tide (journal), 177

tort law
    bespoke necessity, 18–19
    criminal law and, 13, 15
    domestic abuse and, 19–24
    failures of, 23
    gender and, 13–24
    harassment, 17
    privacy, 16–17
    victim-survivor role, 15
To the Lighthouse (Woolfe), 193
Trades Union Congress, 109
'transnational feminist soliarity', 89
trans persons
    gender dysphoria, 208
    gender norms, reinforcing, 208–9
    womanhood and, 209–10
Trinder, Liz, 106
TRIPS. *See* Annual Report of the
    Commissioner of Patents from
    1870-1940 (USA)
Tryfoniadou, Alina, 71–81, 112, 198
two-doctor rule, abortion and, 129
tyranny of the transaction, 51, 56

U
UK Corporate Governance Code, 137
UK Intellectual Property Office, 152, 153
uncertainty, in contracts, 6–8
unconscionable bargain, 67, 69
unconscious bias, 215–16, 218
undue influence, mortgage lending and,
    55–6
undue influence, rescission and, 67
UNESCO, 156
United Nations, 85, 90, 189
United Nations Security Council,
    leadership, women and, 85–6
United States
    fair use doctrine in, 158
    female patent holders in, 151–2
    legal history in, 182–3
    same-sex arguments in, 203–4
Universal Declaration of Human Rights,
    marriage and, 42
University Hospital NHS Trust v *CA*
    [2016], 124
unpaid care work, 110

V

Vanity Fair (magazine), 209
victims-turned perpetrators, violence, 38, 192–3
victim-survivors
  duties of care for, 22–4
  human rights arguments for, 22–4
  tort as redress for, 13
  use of term, 13n2
violence, gender-based, 33–4. *See also* domestic violence; rape *entries*
voting rights, women in parliamentary elections, 174–6

W

wages, equal, 31–2
Wales, abortion in, 127–8
Walker (Lord), 65–6
Walker, Alice, 191
Wallerstein, Judith S., 103
Wallerstein, Shlomit, 41
Watt, Gary, 61–2
Webley, Lisa, 180, 211–221
Welsh Assembly, gender composition, 26
'What I Didn't See' (Fowler), 195–6
Wheeler, Sally, 133–148
White v *White*, 98
wife's special equity, 68
Wilkinson v Downton, 16n13
Willes J, 176
Williams, Melanie L., 185–197
Williams, Patricia J., 5, 11, 93
Wilson, Joan Hoff, 180–1
Wintemute, Robert, 74, 80
womanhood, defining, cis/trans *v.*, 209–10
'Woman Inventor, The' (Smith), 151–2
Woman on the Edge of Time (Piercy), 194
Woman's Suffrage Committee (UK), 174–5
Women and Equalities Committee of the House of Commons, 110

women as persons legal history
  defining legal history, 178–82
  Lord Brougham's Act, gender and legal language, 173
  voting rights, court case, 174–6
Women Men Don't See, The (Junior), 195
Women's Aid, 106–7
Women's National Industrial League of America, 151
Women 2 Win, 28
Woolf, Virginia, 193
work and life balance, 29–30
work-family reconciliation rights, 110, 112–3
workplace, gender inequality in, 54
workplace rights gender-neutral/ gender-specific
  difference-based employment legislation an, 113–4
  fathers, parental leave encouraging to use, 114–5
  gender-neutral, defined, 111
  gender-specific, defined, 111
  merit-based hiring, unfair, 118–9
  numerical equality, 117–8
  paid, unpaid work/care and, 110–111
  policy, laws and, 116–7
  positive action (affirmative action), 115–6
  preferential treatment and, 118
  quotas, binding gender, 116–7
  stereotyped roles, carers, 113
  work-family reconciliation rights, 112–3
World Health Organization, 189
World Trade Organization, 149
Wrenbury (Lord), 177
Wright, Shelley, 83–4

Y

Yellow Wallpaper, The (Gilman), 194
Yerkey v *Jones*, 68

Printed in Great Britain
by Amazon